The Wilderness
PROFOUND

DATE DUE

The Wilderness
PROFOUND

VICTORIAN LIFE ON
THE GULF OF GEORGIA

Richard Somerset Mackie

VICTORIA, BRITISH COLUMBIA

Sono
Nis
Press

National Library of Canada Cataloguing in Publication Data

Richard Mackie, 1957-
  The wilderness profound

  Includes bibliographical references and index.
  ISBN 1-55039-126-7

  1. Drabble, George, 1833-1901. 2. Vancouver Island
(B.C.)—Biography. 3. Georgia, Strait of, Region (B.C. and Wash,)—
Biography. 4. Comox (B.C.)—Biography. 5. Surveyors—
British Columbia—Biography. I. Title
FC3844.3.D72M32 2002   971.1'203'092   C2001-911744-2
F1089.V3M33 2002

FIRST PRINTING 1995
SECOND PRINTING 2002

Sono Nis Press most gratefully acknowledges the support for our
publishing program provided by the Government of Canada through
the Book Publishing Industry Development Program (BPIDP), the
Canada Council for the Arts, and the British Columbia Arts Council.

Maps drawn by CLINTON WEBB

Published by
Sono Nis Press
PO Box 5550, Stn. B
Victoria, BC V8R 6S4
1-800-370-5228

sononis@islandnet.com
www.islandnet.com/sononis/

Printed and bound in Canada by
Morriss Printing Company Ltd.
Victoria, British Columbia

This book is dedicated to
GORDON WAGNER (1914-1994)
of Comox
Surveyor, Writer,
and Patron of the Arts

Contents

Acknowledgements

My greatest debt is to Gordon Wagner, who hired me in 1993 to write this biography. Gordon saw an early draft of the manuscript before he died, and he was delighted that it had been accepted by Sono Nis. He had a keen sense of George Drabble's importance to the Comox Valley. I wish he could be here to see the book in print. I am also grateful to Ivy Wagner.

In the year and a half that it took to research and write this book I got married and had a child. Cathy Richardson has helped me every minute of the way. Our daughter, Juliet, was born between chapters 5 and 6, and she is now a year old and adept at pulling books from the lower shelves of our bookcases.

A number of people and institutions have been most helpful. Ann West and Angela Addison of Sono Nis Press offered their encouragement and exerted their editorial weight when necessary, and the result is a better product. Antonia Kemball also read the manuscript carefully and made many valuable suggestions. Jim Bennett designed the book. Donna Halbert typeset the manuscript. Maps 1 through 6 and 8 through 10 are the brilliant work of Clinton Webb; maps 7, 11, and the careful tracings from Drabble's field notes are the work of Clinton Coates and Reah Theobald. Ron Egan of Courtenay drew the sketch of Drabble's mill from information supplied by Stan Rennison. Tom Marshall of Cobble Hill kindly lent C. P. Newcombe's surveying instruments for the photograph on the front cover.

George and Gillian Mackie gave generous support in the latter stages. For accomodation in Victoria I thank them as well as Al and Kjerstin Mackie and Elizabeth Loughran and Jim Rutkowski.

Allan and Betty Brooks placed their knowledge — and their house — at our disposal when we were in the Comox Valley. The staff of the Courtenay and District Museum and Archives gave me the use of the corner of a desk and allowed me to ransack their collection of letters and photographs. Deb Griffiths, Catherine Siba, Pat Trask, Wendy Fried, and Joe Ruttle were particularly helpful. The staff of the Parksville branch of the Vancouver Island Regional Library cheerfully traced books and answered questions.

It helps to talk in public about a big writing project like this. In October 1994 I spoke on Drabble to my enthusiastic Canadian History class at North Island College, Campbell River. Judy Hagen interviewed me on the Courtenay cable station, and I also addressed the fall lecture series at The Museum at Campbell River and the Alaska Historical Society's annual conference in Kodiak.

This book also owes much to my contact with the historical geographers at the University of British Columbia.

I am thankful to all those who allowed me to interview them. Barbara Marriott, Audrey Menzies, Stan and Betty Rennison, Ruth and Tom Barnett, Rene and Bob Harding, Phyllis Currie, Muriel Dann, Bruce and Bob McPhee, Ruth Masters, Pat and Jack Talbot, and Isabelle Stubbs were gracious and helpful.

I am indebted to the many people who looked after the Drabble field books on their circuitous journey to the Campbell River Museum and Archives. Gordon Wagner orchestrated this, but at different times Mary and Chuck Slemin, Fran Gundry of the Provincial Archives, Deb Griffiths of the Courtenay Museum and Archives, Jeanette Taylor and the rest of the staff of The Museum at Campbell River, and others, ensured the preservation of the papers.

I was thrilled to locate and correspond with Drabble's descendents and relations on Vancouver Island and in England: Thomas Drabble King, John King, Christine Bowbrick, Margaret Taylor, Sybil Carr, John Bemrose, Beryl MacNeill, and Doris White.

The staff at the Provincial Archives were as always helpful, especially David Mattison, Kathy Bridge, Brian Young, Brent McBride, and Kim Alspach.

I am especially grateful to Clare McMillan for her genealogical expertise and to Brad Morrison for sharing his research on the *Silistria* passengers and voyage. I also received valuable research assistance from Joan Measham, Allan Pritchard, Alex Christie, Fred Hobson, and Jim Rutkowski. Academics who assisted me included Bob Galois, Louis Knafla, Tina Loo, Douglas Cole, and Ruth Sandwell. Peter Murray offered valuable support and suggestions. For their sleuthing I am grateful to Godfrey Archbold, Al Lompart, Louise Childs, Ken Piotrowicz, and David White at the Surveyor General Branch, and to Diane Turner of the Criminal Justice Branch of the Provincial Government. Others who contibuted, in England and Canada, were Jim and Elizabeth Curtis, Alan Stewart, Michelle Morton, W. Ralph Lewis, John Creasey, K. C. Walton, Mirabelle Jackson, Terry Ashbourne, Paul Rutledge, Dorothy Flanders, Wedlidi Speck, and Sophia Popham.

Preface

We'll write these histories
they are your histories
the histories of people
clam diggers to the sand bar.

FROM *Clam Diggers to the Sand Bar*, by Tim Lander[1]

*T*HE British Columbian past is full of forgotten worthies. Biographies have been written about most of the really well-known individuals—governor James Douglas, "Hanging Judge" Matthew Begbie, magnate Robert Dunsmuir, and artist Emily Carr come to mind—but the memory even of well-known people rarely lasts longer than those who knew them. George Fawcett Drabble (1833-1901) was an early settler with a coastal rather than provincial reputation. His activities changed the landscape of the Comox Valley and northern Gulf of Georgia. He spent a long career working for settlers, business, and government. In his native England he was surveyor, engineer, farmer, and maltster, but in the Comox region he became a Jack-of-all-Trades: farmer, miller, merchant, surveyor, bridge and road builder, school and church trustee, auctioneer, postmaster, Indian Trader, Justice of the Peace, Government Agent, real estate agent, Lands and Works commissioner, and tax collector. Drabble's birth and death dates virtually match the beginning and end of Queen Victoria's reign.

Despite the multitude and respectability of his professions, Drabble's private life was shadowy and enigmatic in the best Victorian sense. He came directly to Vancouver Island in 1862 on a clipper ship from Liverpool. He had children in England and Canada, but he was not a good father; indeed his great grandchildren—who live in bourgeois England and rural Vancouver Island—have never heard of him. He left England in circumstances so irregular that his family there practically disowned him, and later he ignored his son born to a Native woman known as "Drabble's Mary." In the 1890s his reputation was clouded by a

---

[1] Tim Lander, ed., *To an Inland Sea: Poems for the Gulf of Georgia* (Nanaimo: Nanaimo Publishers' Co-operative, 1992), pp. 35-6.

land scandal from which he never recovered, and when he died in 1901 his entire wealth amounted to less than $50.

His children in England barely knew him. His eldest daughter Lylie married and had five children. Sophie, his other daughter, never married; she died in 1956 aged ninety-five. His son Tom Drabble became a pharmacist in Great Yarmouth, Norfolk, dying in 1951 at the age of ninety, and he never married. His Native son Johnny Drabble (Tlagoglas) became one of the leading men at Alert Bay, and his descendents live in the Native and settler communities around the Gulf of Georgia on the coast of British Columbia.

Drabble forsook England for the sparsely settled coast of a newly-formed British colony. The Gulf, where Drabble spent his entire Canadian career, was named after King George III in 1792 by Captain George Vancouver. Vancouver called it "A solemn inland sea, studded with beautiful forest clad islands, covered with towering trees whose branches at high tides are lapped by clear water teeming with fish."[2] Vancouver was mistaken; a gulf is an inland sea with a single access to the ocean, while this vast body of water had both a northern and a southern access. Naval hydrographer George Richards renamed it the Strait of Georgia in 1865, but the old name has persisted. Despite the alteration, Captain Walbran wrote in 1909, "it is to-day always locally spoken of as 'The Gulf.' "[3] The old name still survives in local usage and in the "Gulf Islands."

For the whole of the nineteenth century, a dense forested wilderness covered the islands and shorelines of the Gulf, offering Drabble an outlet for his surveying talents and an escape from the long shadows of his English past. Drabble reduced that wilderness, drew straight survey lines across it, and made it available for colonial settlers, business, and government.

The Gulf of Georgia was famed for its intertidal abundance of clams, mussels, and other shellfish, which attracted settlers and gave rise to local expressions like "when the tide is out the table is set." The natural abundance continued on land, where settlers found copious supplies of wildfowl and deer. The typical settler lived on a pocket of good, clear, watered land on the coastline, or on one of the many islands in the Gulf.

Early settlers tried to be self-suffient in their small waterfront clearings, drawing their food from the sea or from their own gardens and buying staples like flour, sugar, and molasses from passing ships or local

---

[2] George Vancouver, *A Voyage of Discovery to the North Pacific Ocean, and Round the World* (London: G. G. and J. Robinson, 1798).

[3] John T. Walbran, *British Columbia Coast Names 1592-1906* (Vancouver: J. J. Douglas, 1977, first printed Ottawa, 1909), p. 205.

traders. They cleared small patches of land and built their own log houses at remote homesteads and harbours.[4]

From Cape Mudge or Cape Lazo, near Comox, the Gulf stretches away to the south, buttressed by the Coast Range and the Vancouver Island Mountains. The Gulf fades from view from the confines of the cosmopolitan southern cities. Victoria faces the Pacific Ocean and Juan de Fuca Strait, and Vancouver, while bordering on the Gulf, seems vaguely unfamiliar with its coastal location. Few from the south coast have explored the inland sea at their doorstep. One who started was Malcolm Lowry, who described his journey in *October Ferry to Gabriola*.[5]

Drabble always called it "the Gulf." When he arrived it was home to thousands of Native people and a few hundred colonists, most of them living at the coal town of Nanaimo. The Native population, once large and vigorous, had been devastated in the great smallpox epidemic of 1862, and the survivors retreated to their main villages, leaving settlements deserted along much of the shore in the very year of Drabble's arrival. To this day coastal residents and developers uncover skeletons dating from this or previous epidemics.

Vancouver Island's land laws made it illegal to claim land that was actually inhabited by Indians, but the 1862 epidemic decimated whole populations and left the survivors in a shattered state. The depopulation of the Gulf made hundreds of miles of coastline available for colonial settlement. Over the next few decades a massive influx of settlers and capital moved into the empty space. Drabble, implicated in this extension of commerce and settlement, surveyed hundreds of the first pre-emptions as well as timber, mining, and cannery lands in the Comox Valley, Baynes Sound, Hornby Island, Denman Island, Qualicum, Lasquiti Island, Sangster Island, Nanoose, and Texada Island. To the north, he surveyed at Black Creek, Oyster Bay, Campbell River, Savary, Hernando, and Quadra islands, Nimpkish River, Quatsino Sound, and many places in between. He surveyed the first townsites on what had been Native land at Comox, Courtenay, and Union Bay.

A mountain on the Forbidden Plateau and a group of lakes in Strathcona Park bear the name of this shadowy and controversial Victorian figure.

---

[4] Peter Murray, *Homesteads and Snug Harbours: The Gulf Islands* (Ganges: Horsdal & Schubart, 1991).

[5] Malcolm Lowry, *October Ferry to Gabriola* (Harmondsworth, Middlesex: Penguin Books, 1979).

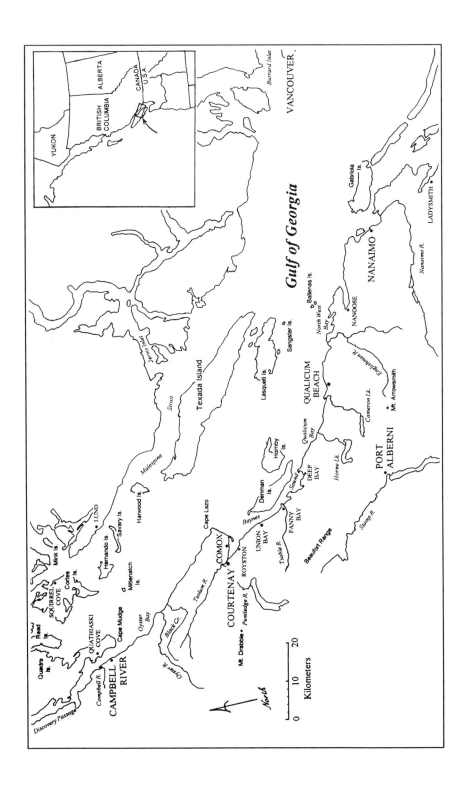

Introduction

Through this link of pen and paper, I stretch out my hand to you across the gulf of death, and my voice speaks to you from the silence of the grave.

FROM *She*, by H. Rider Haggard[1]

IN a collection at the Campbell River archives are 124 old pocketbooks. Unlike cheap pocketbooks of the paperback variety, they were not meant to be read quickly, thrown away, or left at the cottage for next summer. Rather, they are a surveyor's pocketbooks, sturdy and calf-bound, measuring roughly 4½ by 6 inches or 4 by 7 inches. They really were designed to be carried around in a pocket. They are of a high-quality, both in their construction and their contents.

And they have held up well. One or two are water-stained. The rest are well-preserved; indeed when taken from their archival folders and stacked one on top of the other they appear uniformly worn, like the well-thumbed volumes of some favourite novelist that have sat on the shelf in a quiet room for a century. Most of them have been marked with a big, bold, black, number of identification, suggesting that their owner, George Drabble of Comox, had arranged them into some sort of order, but any key to this numbering system has now been lost.

The saying goes that the truth is stranger than fiction, and a careful reading of the thousands of entries in these pocketbooks has revealed a story that a Victorian novelist might well have created. For the most part containing Drabble's careful handwritten surveys and notes, little about them suggests anything literary or even very personal, or that they were carried over some of the most rugged ground on the coast of British Columbia—often through some of the wettest seasons the region can offer. Their sturdy leather binding kept the rain away, and they spent most of their working lives secure in Drabble's own chest pocket.

Strictly speaking they are not pocketbooks but "field books," books used in the field by surveyors for technical notes. Drabble himself

---

[1] H. Rider Haggard, *She* (London: 1887; New York: Dover Publications reprint 1951), p. 22.

referred to them as his field notes, and they contain the informal working record of hundreds of surveys and other business conducted between 1873 and 1901. For thirty years Drabble drew straight lines, squares, and rectangles in the wilderness, all so that colonists and later arrivals might have access to land for their farms and industries. He drew exact lines around inhabited Native settlements which were then known—and are still known—as "Indian Reserves" in a settler domain.

George Drabble died at the Cumberland hospital at the age of sixty-eight in 1901. From his death until 1994 his field books were in the possession of at least three surveyors and were held by three archival institutions. Their earliest owner was Henry Collis, the Court Administrator in Cumberland who handled Drabble's estate. They next passed to Alfred King, a Cumberland surveyor, from whom they passed to another surveyor, Norwegian-born Vilhelm Schjelderup of Comox, who in the 1950s gave them to his articling student Gordon Wagner.[2] Wagner, who was responsible for their preservation, recalled that:

> I served my articles as a British Columbia Land Surveyor with Vilhelm Schjelderup and received my commission in 1952. Several years later I helped the Schjelderups move and we found a cardboard box and Schjelderup said, "Gordon, Alfred King, the land surveyor, gave me this box of stuff years ago. I have never taken time to look at the books it contains. You might like to have it."[3]

Wagner, recently retired from the profession, was captivated by the little leather books. "Over the thirty years I searched the fence corners, hacked my way through the blackberry patches, searched the logged off and well-burnt forest for the stumps of witness trees, I found many of the corner posts that George Drabble had set." Aware of their historical value, in the 1980s Wagner loaned the collection to the Courtenay and District Museum and Archives, and later to the Campbell River Museum and Archives, and the British Columbia Archives, without ever finding quite the right home for them. Eventually, to edit the field books, Wagner retrieved the collection, and in 1993 prepared a helpful guide.[4] In 1994 the field books were sent to their final resting place, the Campbell River Museum and Archives.

---

[2] British Columbia, County Court (Cumberland), Probate Files 1901-1917; "Personnel files," Buckham Collection; Dorothy I. Stubbs, *"All About Us." A History of the City of Courtenay* (Courtenay: c. 1965), p. 102 and John A. Whittaker, comp., *Early Land Surveyors of British Columbia* (Victoria: Corporation of Land Surveyors of British Columbia, 1990), pp. 56, 135.

[3] Gordon Wagner, ed., "Field Books of Comox Valley Surveys by George F. Drabble, Land Surveyor, 1870-1901," ts., Courtenay and District Museum and Archives (hereafter CDMA), 1993. Wagner told me that the box of field notes came from a shed, and that Schjelderup knew nothing about them, not even their author. Gordon Wagner, personal communication, July 1994.

[4] Gordon Wagner, "George Drabble," pp. 3-4.

In February 1993 Gordon Wagner wrote to me and asked if I would be interested in writing Drabble's biography. His letter and subsequent phone calls came weeks before I completed my doctoral dissertation, a task that had occupied me since the publication of my first book, a biography of the Comox naturalist Hamilton Laing.[5] Although I had never heard of George Drabble, I was anxious to get back to the real world and I accepted the offer. I worked closely with Gordon from late 1993 until the summer of 1994, when he was diagnosed with acute leukemia. He rushed to complete several projects, but the disease worsened and after a short and brave struggle he died at his home on 14 October 1994, aged eighty. This book is dedicated to him with appreciation and respect.

ꝏ

Soon after embarking on the project I wondered if I had made a mistake. I found an article written in 1962 by Mildred Haas, a grandaughter of settler Reginald Carwithen. Drabble, it seemed, was an anti-social misanthrope who took malicious pleasure in making early farmers climb the steepest part of Siwash (Comox) Hill to get to Comox wharf. Drabble wanted the Back Road to be the main road, but the people petitioned the government: "Drabble was mad, so he built the road up a very steep hill—said 'The people could damn well climb up for the rest of their lives!'"[6] I found this story, with a little more detail, in the comprehensive history of the Comox Valley, *Land of Plenty*, published in 1987:

> Drabble wanted to keep the Back Road as the main approach to the wharf, but the people petitioned the government for a road allowance on Comox Hill. A furious Drabble reportedly surveyed the steepest part of the hill for the disputed road, a severe hardship for farmers hauling livestock and produce to the wharf in lumbering oxen carts.[7]

I also found an article by Rene Harding entitled "Fallen Drabble lived alone with Queenie."[8] Harding, who had interviewed Gordon Pritchard of an early Comox family, termed Drabble "an Englishman who had fallen on hard times due to his penchant for alcohol." She continued:

---

[5] Richard Mackie, *Hamilton Mack Laing: Hunter-Naturalist* (Victoria: Sono Nis Press, 1985).

[6] Mildred E. Haas, "Our Early Pioneers," in D. E. Isenor, ed., "The Comox Valley. Its Pioneers," 1962, ms. copy in the Buckham Collection, BCARS.

[7] D. E. Isenor, W. N. McInnis, E. G. Stephens, D. E. Watson, eds. *Land of Plenty: A History of the Comox District* (Campbell River: Ptarmigan Press, 1987), p. 134.

[8] Rene Harding, "Fallen Drabble lived alone with Queenie," *Comox District Free Press* (hereafter *CDFP*), 28 October 1977, p. 7.

Drabble lived with his constant companion, a dog named Queenie. . . . Drabble did not encourage neighbours, especially lively young lads, who for their part had no reason to like the black frock coated old fellow whose suit and plug hat were relics of better days.

One day when Drabble was on his way home with Queenie at his heels he passed the Pritchard children and for some strange reason the dog turned around and bit young Walter. After that incident the children steered clear of old Drabble.

It struck me that the current image of Drabble owed much to the memory of someone who had been a young child in the last years of Drabble's life. Ben Hughes, in his *History of the Comox Valley* (1962) perpetuated the image of Drabble as a cranky old man:

There are many stories told of Drabble and most of them bear out the impression that he was not popular. One of these is that when he was living on what is now the Anderton Road at Comox, he had a couple of fierce dogs. A Courtenay man, who did not find much popular favour, complained about the rough reception he got from the canines. Drabble told him, "Don't worry, my dogs never bite anybody that is any good."[9]

I looked him up in the Akriggs' *1001 British Columbia Place Names* and found this story repeated, with the addition that Drabble was "a bachelor and a misogynist" (the Akriggs offer no evidence for this; they must have meant "misanthropist").[10] Drabble, it seemed, was a miserable old soul and an alcoholic with not even enough heart to treat the neighbouring children nicely; a man who cared little for the local farmers and their struggling oxen, let alone for his young neighbours. In one recent history he is described as a resident of the Elk Hotel, and in another he is identified as a resident of the Lorne Hotel.[11] I could see too that Drabble had entered Comox historical mythology, and I hoped that the original sources might offer a different interpretation.

The gist of the myth was that Drabble built a road up a steep hill, that he drank too much, and that on one occasion his dog bit Walter Pritchard—not pleasant perhaps, but all of them human-enough (or canine-enough) weaknesses. Nonetheless I wondered if the author of the sturdy field books was the same man described in these accounts.

Curiously, behind these perceptions lurked another interpretation in which Drabble—as Ben Hughes wrote—was seen as "a very impor-

---

[9] Ben Hughes, *History of the Comox Valley 1862 to 1945* (Courtenay: E. W. Bickle Ltd., *c.* 1962), pp. 44-45.

[10] G. P. V. Akrigg and Helen Akrigg, *1001 British Columbia Place Names* (Vancouver: Discovery Press, 1973), p. 54.

[11] Isenor, *Land Of Plenty*, p. 87; Judy Hagen, *Comox Valley Memories. Reminiscences of Early Life in Central Vancouver Island* (Courtenay: Courtenay and District Museum and Historical Society, 1993).

tant man in the little community," someone who through his surveys "left a lasting imprint on the district." Hughes also reported that Drabble may have been left a fortune by an English relation, but because he couldn't verify the story he named him the "mystery man," the "mysterious man of the early days of the Comox Valley."[12]

Other historians have recognized Drabble's importance: the authors of *Land of Plenty* and of a history of Comox schools paid tribute to him as a founder. Janette Glover-Geidt, Winnifred Isbister, and Helen Mitchell in their histories of Union Bay, Denman Island, and Campbell River treated his surveys seriously.[13] For the 1962 centennial of Comox, D. E. Isenor compiled an invaluable, yet unpublished, collection of articles relating to Drabble and his contemporaries entitled "The Comox Valley: Its Pioneers."[14]

Most importantly, at least one old-timer remembered Drabble with no obvious signs of animosity. Leo Anderton, member of an old Comox family, when interviewed in 1956, recalled as follows:

> I remember Drabble very well. He was a great friend of my family's. And he—he was a magistrate and surveyor and was a bachelor all his life and was quite a celebrated old character.
>
> "What did he look like?"
>
> Honestly, I couldn't tell you—it's too long—I—I think he was rather a short man. But that's the impression I had of him. But he was—he was quite a character. There were quite a few bachelors around Comox in those early days.[15]

Eustace Smith, a teenager when Drabble died, recalled that Drabble was usually called "The Judge" owing to his work as a magistrate.[16]

Despite these differing accounts and recollections, I found that the further I went into the past the more respectable, social, and human Drabble became. In 1897, for example, the editor of the Cumberland newspaper referred to Drabble as "an old and intelligent pioneer of singularly retentive memory," and solicited his views on early

[12] Hughes, *History of the Comox Valley*, pp. 42, 44.

[13] Dick Isenor, Margaret McGill, and Donna Watson, eds. *"For our Children:" A History of Comox Valley Schools [1870-1980]* (Courtenay: School Board District #71, [1980]), p. 16; Winnifred A. Isbister, *My Ain Folk. Denman Island 1875-1975* (Courtenay: E. W. Bickle Ltd., 1976), pp. 21-23; Janette Glover-Geidt, *The Friendly Port: A History of Union Bay, 1880-1960* (Campbell River: Kask Graphics Ltd., 1990); Helen Mitchell, *Diamond in the Rough. The Campbell River Story* (Aldergrove: Frontier Publishing Ltd., 1975), pp. 70-71, 75.

[14] Isenor, "The Comox Valley."

[15] Ben Hughes interview with Leo Anderton, 26 April 1956, p. 10, CDMA.

[16] B. A. McKelvie, "The 'S' Sign. A Biographical Sketch of Eustace Smith, Logger, Timber Cruiser and Forest Engineer," CDMA, p. 32.

Comox history. Drabble's 1901 obituary only adds to his mixed reputation. The list of his pallbearers, "all old time friends," reads like a *Who's Who* of early Comox and Courtenay: Robert Grant (blacksmith turned lumberman), Alexander Urquhart (farmer), Joseph Burnard Holmes (merchant), John McKenzie (blacksmith and Justice of the Peace), Joseph McPhee (labourer turned builder and merchant), and George McDonald (farmer and hotelier). He was buried at St. Andrews, the Anglican church cemetery at Sandwick, where the service was conducted by the Rev. Jules Willemar. The paper reported that:

> The casket was covered with beautiful floral tributes sent by his many friends. . . . At one time he was reputed fairly well off, but in later years misfortune overtook him and he died a poor man. Of kindly and charitable disposition, he was the first to extend help and aid to those in want or distress, and his many deeds of charity will not soon be forgotten.[17]

Here, it would seem, was a Jekyll and Hyde figure: a "fallen" figure valued by his contemporaries for his generosity, charity, and expertise, yet whom posterity has judged harshly.

I could see that I would have a lot of work to do if I hoped to find the real George Drabble beneath these contradictions, not to mention the cheap shots and plain innaccuracies. Like a furniture restorer, I would have to use the solvent of historical technique to dissolve later accretions and reveal the texture and quality of the wood beneath. Why, I wondered, were contemporary evaluations generally so praiseworthy and modern ones so negative? I found the origins of the two interpretations of Drabble in the writings of Comox Valley settlers Reginald Carwithen and Eric Duncan.

Carwithen, Oxford-educated and articulate, had little time for Drabble, who after all had been a working farmer in the English midlands before coming to Vancouver Island in 1862, and who did not come from the more established upper classes of England. An original Comox settler, Carwithen must also have known the true story of Drabble's immigration. At any rate, it was Carwithen who first blamed Drabble for building the road up Siwash Hill. In 1881 he wrote to a friend in England that:

> Our present road runs down past C. Green's Slough, and follows down the river crossing the lower sloughs, on a long continuation of piles, and along the beach slap through the rancherie, and worst of all thanks to Drabble up the very steepest part of that bluff on McCutcheon's old place; any duffer could have avoided it, only Drabble didn't want the road by the river, so he said he would pay us out by making us climb the hill. I'm afraid none of this will interest you but I dare think the Sywashes didn't even appreciate it.[18]

---

[17] Union *Weekly News*, 28 September 1897; *The Cumberland News*, 18 September 1901.
[18] Carwithen to Blaksley, 1 March 1881, Carwithen Correspondence.

Eric Duncan, on the other hand, was a self-taught Shetland Islander who came to the valley in 1877, some fifteen years after Carwithen and Drabble. Hard-working, thrifty, and teetotalling, he farmed at Sandwick, in the lower valley, and later became a postmaster, poet, and storekeeper there. He was an accurate and candid writer with a good turn of phrase, which in the 1920s and 1930s he directed into his memoirs which took the form of newspaper articles and books.

Duncan did not hesitate to identify the problem drinkers in the valley; he was, after all, a founding member of the Comox branch of the Lodge of Good Templars, a temperance society. He was the first to write that Drabble had a drinking problem. "Like many of the old-timers," he wrote, "he was much bothered by liquor." Duncan, however, presents a different and more plausible account of Drabble's road up Comox Hill. Owing to provincial land regulations, Drabble did the best he could with the road; he had no choice but to put the road up Siwash Hill owing to a provincial statute that prevented the government from surveying a public road through a settler's orchard and farm buildings. Duncan's original account makes no mention of the "fury" or "violence" attributed to Drabble by subsequent historians.[19]

Perhaps every society needs a cranky old bachelor figure, a misanthrope, a foil, someone whose overt misery serves to affirm other peoples' happiness—or to obscure their own failings.

Such contradictory views of Drabble are not resolved by the one surviving photograph of him. Taken probably in the late 1890s, a few years before he died, it shows Drabble sitting on a wooden chair with a cheap blanket for a backdrop. The blanket is held up by a piece of binder twine. The ground is littered with sticks, twigs, and other material, including a plank and the broken stem of a clay pipe. Drabble is wearing a three-piece wrinkled tweed suit and a bowler hat. He rests his left hand on his lap, clasps a knobbly walking stick with his right hand, and clenches a pipe between his teeth from habit or security. The image could have been taken by a travelling photographer on the grounds of the Comox Agricultural Fair; then again, it could have been taken outside the Lorne Hotel.

Eric Duncan preserved telling anecdotes about Drabble, who in appearance reminded him strongly of Victorian novelist Anthony Trollope. Drabble was familiar, Duncan wrote, with the works of the now-forgotten late nineteenth century English novelist, H. Rider Haggard. "When Haggard's *She* came out," Duncan recalled, "I heard that Drabble remarked: 'Such rot! and yet you can't help reading it.' Some one in

---

[19] Eric Duncan, *From Shetland to Vancouver Island. Recollections of Seventy-Eight Years* (Edinburgh: Oliver and Boyd, 1939), pp. 88, 116-17.

my hearing once asked him what he thought of the Bible. 'It will be well for most of us,' Drabble replied, 'if there is no truth in it.'" (In fact, Drabble was trustee of St. Peter's Anglican Church in Comox).[20]

To Duncan, Drabble was a "rather remarkable man," one of the most notable settlers in Comox and well-qualified to write the history of the valley: "Having a first-class education, he was afterwards magistrate, postmaster and provincial land surveyor, running all the farm lines and laying out most of the roads in the district. He lived till near the end of the century, and was often urged to write a history of the Settlement, but always refused."[21]

The real Drabble, then, was simply human, with faults and quirks in his character as well as redeeming features. In this book I search for the origins of the contradictory myths that surround him, follow his career as it intersected with the major developments in nineteenth century Comox, and discover why he was considered the ideal person to write the history of the valley. Sources for such an enterprise are varied. Few people kept their letters; very little private correspondence and only four Comox diaries (those of Reginald Pidcock, Mary Harmston, George Curtis, and William Duncan) survive from before 1900. Yet we know from Eric Duncan and others that the settlers were expert letter-writers; all of them came originally from homes elsewhere; they waited anxiously for their letters on "steamer day" at the Comox wharf— but few of their thousands of letters have survived. The two most important sources are Drabble's own field books and Eric Duncan's lucid recollections.

Many of the sources used in this book were generated by Drabble in the course of doing business, or notifying the government of commercial transactions. He took part in the great expansion of government in late nineteenth century British Columbia.[22] As surveyor, road superintendent, Government Agent, and Justice of the Peace, Drabble wrote frequently to Victoria, and many of his letters have survived at the Provincial Archives. The records of the Lands and Works Department are very rich and complete. His pre-emption surveys, complete with maps, are housed at the Surveyor General Branch in Victoria, and his Magistrate's returns and court records are in the papers of the Provincial Secretary and Attorney-General, along with his letters to the British Columbia Provincial Police. Fortunately, then, abundant material has survived for a book that is both biography and regional history.

---

[20] *From Shetland to Vancouver Island*, pp. 88, 298.

[21] Duncan, "Early Days and Early Settlers."

[22] See Daniel Clayton, "Geographies of the Lower Skeena," *BC Studies* 94 (Summer 1992), pp. 39-59.

Some late-nineteenth century usage requires explanation: Drabble and his contemporaries wrote "&c" instead of "etc;" and because most of them came from the British Isles, they spelled whiskey without an "e," called floods "freshets," wrote "gaol" for "jail," and generally used British spellings. At first they made little distinction between lumber and timber; lumber of course is the name given to timber after it has been sawn. When quoting from original sources I have retained Drabble's original spelling and punctuation, and I have made minimal use of the Latin "sic."

CHAPTER 1

Farmer Drabble of Nottinghamshire

*"In short," I replied, "thou hast found thy position one of
greater freedom and less responsibility."*

FROM She, by H. Rider Haggard[1]

ERIC Duncan was clear about two things: that George Drabble came from Derbyshire, and that he was a bachelor. The first statement was only partly right and the second, strictly speaking, was wrong. Drabble was born in Derbyshire, as were his parents, but he was married in Lincolnshire, to a woman from that county, and he lived with his wife and children in Nottinghamshire for six years before coming to Vancouver Island. Details of his life in England are scarce, and in their absence we must rely on church and census records to reconstruct his early life. None of these sources, however, prepare the reader for the startling circumstances of Drabble's 1862 departure from England.

Drabble was baptised at the village church of Barlow Lees, Derbyshire, about seven miles south of Sheffield, on 15 June 1833. He was born at Barlow too, but the exact date of his birth is unknown.[2] His baptism took place in the middle of the reign of King William IV, four years before Queen Victoria took the throne.

In Drabble's youth much of Derbyshire was agricultural, but in the early nineteenth century, towns like Sheffield encroached on the surrounding farmland and emerged as major industrial cities, specialising in the manufacture of steel, especially cutlery. In 1833 this growth was in full swing, and the population of Sheffield approached 100,000, up from 35,000 from 1821, and the city with its large workforce provided a growing market for surrounding farmers.

Drabble's father Thomas was born in about 1808 in the village of Dronfield near Barlow; his mother Eliza Fawcett was born in about 1813 at Norton, now a suburb of Sheffield. Both places then were rural villages. Barlow was also the home of George Drabble's grandparents,

---

[1] Haggard, *She*, p. 87.

[2] Joan Measham to Gordon Wagner, 30 September 1989; Great Britain, 1861 Census, Public Record Office (hereafter PRO), London, R.G. 9/2475, folio 11, page 15. All census information enclosed in Clare McMillan to the author, 27 May 1994.

Joseph and Mary Drabble; Joseph was a prosperous farmer at Moor Hall in the parish of Barlow.[3] Thomas and Eliza were married in February 1833 at Beauchief parish church, near Sheffield. The entry in the marriage register reads "Thomas Drabble of this Parish Liberty of Beauchief and Eliza Fawcett of the Parish said Liberty of Beauchief were married in this Church by Banns with Consent this Seventeenth Day of February."[4] Their marriage took place just four months before George Drabble was baptised, so Eliza would have been several months' pregnant at the time. Thomas was twenty-four or twenty-five years old; Eliza was nineteen or twenty. There is no evidence that they had any other children.

Thomas Drabble gave his occupation as "Labourer" at his son's baptism. This might seem an inappropriate occupation, but traditionally farmers' sons were identified in church records as labourers until they inherited their fathers' farms. Thomas Drabble was not a landless labourer; both he and Eliza were literate—they signed their names without difficulty on the marriage register—and his family occupied a small landowning niche somewhere between the gentry and the labouring class.[5]

Eliza Drabble also came from a secure farming background. Both her father George Fawcett and her mother Elizabeth came from Yorkshire, and both were born in about 1772. George Fawcett, his grandson's namesake, seems to have been a man of substance; in 1860 he was a farmer of Cockshutts, Norton, Derbyshire, just a few miles west of Sherwood Forest.[6]

George Drabble's early life and education are unfortunately shrouded in silence. He may have spent his childhood in Derbyshire, but by his late teens his parents had moved to Nottinghamshire. Thomas Drabble in 1857 was identified as farmer, and in 1860 and 1861 as Farm Bailiff (manager) at Winkburn, Nottinghamshire, quite near Sherwood Forest.[7]

---

[3] Great Britain, 1861 Census, PRO, R.G. 9/2472, folio 21, page 11; "Last Will and Testament of me Joseph Drabble of Moor Hall in the Parish of Barlow in the County of Derby," 14 July 1860, proved 5 October 1860. Information from Joan Measham to Gordon Wagner, 23 January 1993.

[4] Beauchief Marriage Register, Sheffield City Archives.

[5] Joan Measham to Gordon Wagner, 30 September 1989; John Creasey to the author, 1 June 1994.

[6] Great Britain, 1851 Census, PRO, London, entry for Norton; will of George Fawcett, 14 February 1860, proved 12 January 1863. Information enclosed in Joan Measham to Gordon Wagner, 15 October 1989 and 23 January 1993.

[7] Marriage of George Fawcett Drabble and Louisa Burnby, 25 August 1857, General Register Office (hereafter GRO), London; Great Britain, 1861 Census, PRO, R.G. 9/2475, folio 11, page 15; "Last Will and Testament of me George Fawcett of the Parish

Eric Duncan wrote that Drabble had a first-class education. Possibly this took place at a good grammar school, or in one of the new Victorian public schools. His name does not appear in the surviving records of surrounding schools. Drabble learned surveying and possibly engineering in Britain: later, when applying for the position of Land Recorder at Comox, he stated that he had worked in a land office in England for more than seven years, during which time he had worked on chain surveys in many parts of the country.[8] Drabble signed himself "C.E." for Civil Engineer, but it is not known when he received his training or where, and with whom he worked. He may have apprenticed in a land office and received his training while still a boy, say from school-leaving age of fifteen in 1848 until 1855, when he was twenty-two.

After his baptism, the first piece of solid information we possess is Drabble's marriage certificate, which shows that George Drabble, farmer of Ossington, married Louisa Burnby, of Temple Brewer, Lincolnshire, in the church of Wellingore, Lincolnshire, on 25 August 1857. They were married according to the Rites and Ceremonies of the Church of England by the Vicar of Wellingore, Rev. J. Peacock. Eliza's father was identified as Matthew Coulson Burnby, farmer.[9]

George Drabble in 1861 was married with two children and seven employees. The national census of that year shows him and his wife Louisa at Ossington, just over the western border of Lincolnshire in Nottinghamshire, and about twelve miles as the crow flies from Wellingore. Both were aged twenty-seven. George Drabble was identified as a farmer of 261 acres, employing two labourers and one boy. They had two children: Elizabeth Burnby Drabble, aged two, and Thomas Lambe Drabble, aged one. Also in the household were general servants Margaret Garland and Jane Heald, aged twenty-two and twenty respectively; John Brace, groom, aged thirty; three farm servants: William Branston, twenty-three, William Plummer, eighteen, and Samuel Johnson, fifteen. The farm boasted a shepherd, twenty-three year old John Sentance. By the standards of the day this must have been a prosperous farm.

About five miles away, to the east of Ossington, ran the Fosse Way, the famous Roman road connecting Exeter and Lincoln. Sixteen hundred years before, Roman surveyors had imposed their straight lines on the English landscape. Unlike the surrounding roads, which ran seemingly

---

of Norton in the County of Derby," dated 14 February 1860, proved 12 January 1863. Information from Joan Measham to Gordon Wagner, 15 October 1989.

[8] Drabble to Truch, 24 January 1870, in British Columbia, Colonial Correspondence (hereafter referred to as "Colonial Correpondence"); see F. M. L. Thompson, *Chartered Surveyors: the Growth of a Profession* (London: Routledge and Kegan Paul, 1968).

[9] Marriage of George Fawcett Drabble and Louis Burnby, 25 August 1857, GRO; Great Britain, 1861 Census, PRO, R.G. 9/2475, folio 11, page 15.

at random through the patchwork landscape of fields, farms, villages, and hamlets, the Fosse Way ran straight as an arrow through the countryside. It ran midway between Ossington and Wellingore; the Fawcetts farmed on one side, the Drabbles on the other.

Drabble held the dual occupations of farmer and maltster. Malt is a cereal grain that is kiln-dried after it has been germinated in water. A maltster is someone who makes or deals in malt; beer and whisky are the main malt liquors, and beer was a staple. According to John Creasey of the Rural History Centre at the University of Reading:

> Dual occupations were very common in England in the nineteenth century particularly where there was an element of seasonality to one job as in the case of malting, a winter occupation. Maltsters could also be grain merchants, coal dealers and brickmakers as well as farmers and there were cases of maltsters being millers as well. . . . The profession was particularly important in eastern England, in counties like Lincolnshire and Nottinghamshire close to the barley growing regions which provided their raw material and also the large industrial cities which required the ultimate product of malting, beer.[10]

The best millstones in England came from the peak district of central Derbyshire, only a dozen miles from George Drabble's birthplace.[11] Later, in Comox, Drabble constructed a waterwheel and grist mill.

A third child, Sophia (Sophie) Burnby Drabble, was born in March 1862, but unlike her elder siblings, Sophie was born at Farndon, Nottinghamshire, a village six miles from Ossington. When Louisa registered the birth she gave her residence as Farndon, and the occupation of her husband as "Maltster," but George Drabble was not present at the birth.[12]

When Sophia was only four months old, in July 1862, George Drabble did something quite out of character with the image of happy domesticity suggested by the church and census records. He left behind his wife, family, farm, and servants and boarded a sailing ship bound from Liverpool for Victoria, the capital city of Vancouver Island, the most distant colony in the sprawling British Empire.

The ship was the four-masted China clipper *Silistria* under Captain Jocelyn. The circumstances of Drabble's departure were, at best, impulsive, and at worst, foolish. In the 1920s Sarah Butler of Saanich, a passenger on the ship, recalled that her fellow passengers included:

> A Mr. Drabble who having been out with the crowd having a farewell dinner and coming to the boat to see the folks off in his silk hat and dress suit and

---

[10] John Creasey to the author, 1 June 1994, citing Jonathan Brown, *Steeped in Tradition: The Malting Industry in England since the Railway Age* (University of Reading: 1983).

[11] John Reynolds, *Windmills and Waterwheels* (New York: Praeger Publishers, 1970), p. 44.

[12] Birth certificate of Sophia Drabble, 4 March 1862, GRO.

feeling in good humour says, "Boys I am going with you," and made the trip with us being one of our early surveyors in Victoria.[13]

The *Silistria* left Liverpool on 11 July 1862 and arrived at Victoria, Vancouver Island, on 16 November 1862 after a four and a half month direct ocean voyage.

Drabble's reasons for his sudden departure may never be known. Marital discord may have contributed. Possibly he made a rash decision at a tipsy moment. He may well have been seduced by the reputed riches of the Cariboo gold rush. Possibly he had planned to emigrate, but not quite so soon or in such circumstances. Sarah Butler's statement that Drabble was "feeling in good humour" after the farewell party suggests that he had been drinking; if true, it would not be the last time that alcohol would figure in his actions. The farewell party may well have been on the *Silistria* itself. The ship left Liverpool at 5.30 p.m., so if Drabble had been celebrating with his friends prior to departure, he would have found himself on the Atlantic before he knew it. He may only have had time to write a quick letter to his wife telling her of his decision.

If he had second thoughts about leaving, he was out of luck. The vessel did not stop in Ireland or anywhere else; indeed in the whole voyage the passengers rarely saw land or other ships. William Lomas, Drabble's fellow-emigrant, wrote as follows in his diary on the first night of the voyage: "The feelings of an emigrant on leaving the shores of his native land must be felt to be understood. The thought of many dear ones whom you have seen, perhaps for the last time, will flash across your mind and do not tend to make the day a happy one."[14] It is easy to imagine Drabble waking up the next morning with a hangover and wondering where he was—and what he had done. So far as is known he did not return to England for twenty-five years. His wife died soon after he left, and his children never visited him on Vancouver Island.

---

[13] Sara Butler, "Reminiscences," BCARS. I owe this reference to Brad Morrison.

[14] William Henry Lomas, "Log of William Henry Lomas from Liverpool to Victoria on the Emigrant Ship Silistria White Star Line," BCARS.

CHAPTER 2

To the Uttermost Ends of the Earth

The sea is a difficult place to be
and the clouds conceal the mountains.

FROM *Clam Diggers to the Sand Bar*, by Tim Lander[1]

DRABBLE chose to travel to one of the furthermost colonies in the Empire: Vancouver Island and British Columbia were so distant that getting to them required the longest ocean voyage that could be taken from Britain at this time. Indeed, the colony of Vancouver Island was used by novelist Anthony Trollope to stand for the place at the uttermost ends of the earth. John Eames, the central character of Trollope's 1862 novel *The Small House at Allington*, sought to escape "hopeless entanglements and disappointments in love" and asked himself: "Had he not better go to Australia or Vancouver's Island, or—? "[2] The Comox Valley became the refuge for several characters like John Eames.

Two diaries have survived from the voyage of the *Silistria*: those of William Lomas and Edward Robinson. Though neither mentions Drabble, each provides detail that must have been shared by everyone on the ship. Two weeks after leaving Liverpool Lomas wrote that:

> The "Silistria" has never taken passengers before and therefore is very imperfectly fitted up and several things have been forgotten and lots of mistakes made. One is that the mustard and pepper have been sent *unground*, and no *mill* to grind with. The cooks are disgusting fellows, very dirty, and scarcely ever sober since we started. The doctor is a muff at his profession, and always drinking; his brother is a very nice fellow. It is strange what trouble some people will take to make fools of themselves. One saloon passenger has been drinking all evening and within an hour has had 13 quart bottles of ale (at 1/-) and is now as drunk as a fiddler.

Passengers and crew numbered altogether 297, including only twenty-one women and twenty-four children. Most travelled in the

---

[1] Lander, *To an Inland Sea*, pp. 35-36.
[2] Allan Pritchard, "The Shapes of History in British Columbia Writing," *BC Studies* 93 (Spring 1992), pp. 48-81.

Steerage and Intermediate sections, and only six patronized the Saloon cabins. Most were young men lured by fabulous reports of the Cariboo gold rush. Lomas, who was taking a shipment of trade goods to Victoria, passed the time reading Charles Dickens' *David Copperfield* and other books "of like sort." Edward Robinson, aged twenty, noted two weeks into the voyage that nearly all the passengers mustered on deck to sing "duets, glees, and songs, some of which were very well sung," including *The English Emigrants* and *Father's Love*. Lomas complained of the two-inch cockroaches, of the food ("The beef already stinks," he wrote four days out of Liverpool), of the brutality of Captain Jocelyn toward his crew, and of the other passengers ("A good many of the fellows are already wishing themselves home again. I can't think how many of them came to start at all. They will never do any good in Columbia, and only be a disgrace to the Old Country"). "The waves remind me of the hills between Sheffield and Manchester," Lomas wrote glumly when the ship was off the Falkland Islands.

Early in November, as the ship sailed through fog near Cape Flattery, Lomas complained of the foul drinking water and the rats:

> Many have spent all their money and are wondering what they shall do when they arrive. There has been at least £150 worth of drink sold on board. Several rats are found, dead, in the water casks. This adds considerably to the flavour.

As the ship sailed down Juan de Fuca Strait, both Lomas and Robinson commented on the forests around them. "The fine pine forests on either side appear never to have been touched by the hand of man," Lomas wrote on 15 November, and Robinson observed "altogether a very wild looking country." The *Silistria* arrived at Esquimalt on the following day, having made a near-record voyage from England of 128 days at sea.[3] The passengers inundated Victoria. A few went to the Mainland right away, a few continued on with the *Silistria* to Australia, but most spent an impoverished winter in Victoria living on odd jobs and waiting for the spring rush to the Fraser. Drabble was among the new immigrants in Victoria that winter.

୧୭

His family's response to his sudden departure has not been recorded. Whatever hope George and Louisa Drabble may have had for reconciliation or reunion were shattered just over a year later when, on 31 July 1863, Louisa died of typhoid fever at Newark-on-Trent. She was

---

[3] Lomas, "Log of William Henry Lomas;" Edward W. Robinson, "Log of Voyage from Liverpool to Victoria, Vancouver Island per Ship 'Silistria,'" BCARS.

thirty. She left behind three children: Lylie, aged four; Thomas, aged three, and seventeen-month old Sophie.[4]

On their mother's death the three children moved in with Louisa's father Matthew Burnby and his second wife Mary, who was twenty-two years younger than Matthew. They raised the Drabble children with their own two children, John and Mary Burnby. The Burnby and Drabble children—born in the space of six years—were brought up together as a single family at Crossburn House, Long Bennington, a town in Lincolnshire seven miles south of Newark-on-Trent.

With the help of a clue in one of Drabble's field books and the expert sleuthing in England of genealogist Clare McMillan, I located descendents of the five Drabble and Burnby children. Drabble's daughter Sophie used to relate how, on Louisa's death, Mary Burnby drove in a coach over to Ossington "to collect the children and servants and brought them back to be brought up with their second family" at Crossburn House. The 1871 census for Long Bennington shows Matthew Burnby, aged sixty-eight, "Retired Farmer Landowner" as head of the household, along with his wife Mary, aged forty-six, and their children, John, aged nine, and Mary, six. Also in the house were Eliza, twelve, Thomas, eleven, and Sophie Drabble, aged nine. They and the Burnby children were identified in the census as scholars. Household servants consisted of a governess, a housemaid, and a groom.[5]

The true circumstances of Drabble's departure were never revealed to his children. His descendents know very little about him. Sophie Drabble even had the story back to front: she believed that her father went to Vancouver Island out of grief at his wife's death: he "was so broken hearted he wanted to go away." Eliza, Drabble's other daughter, "never mentioned" her father. When contacted in 1995 with details of Drabble's departure, Eliza's grandson John Bemrose replied that he knew of the Drabble family, but he had never heard of George Drabble. His grandmother, whom he knew well, had never mentioned her father: "On reflection there appears to have been some reason for the silence."[6]

In 1995 Beryl MacNeill, Matthew Burnby's great-grandaughter, responded as follows to Sarah Butler's account of how Drabble came to Vancouver Island:

---

[4] Death certificate of Louisa Drabble, 31 July 1863, GRO, London. Louisa, according to family tradition, died of diptheria. Beryl MacNeill to Clare McMillan, 4 August 1994.

[5] The coach story is told in McMillan to the author, 29 July 1994 and MacNeill to McMillan, 4 August 1994; Great Britain, 1871 Census, PRO, R.G. 10/3544, folio 24, page 16.

[6] Beryl MacNeill to McMillan, 4 August 1994; John Bemrose to McMillan, quoted in McMillan to the author, 16 February 1995.

Neither my mother nor I had heard the story of George leaving in this way, but it would certainly explain why Matthew Coulson Burnby was reluctant for the grandchildren to go to their father. They were being brought up in a comfortable Victorian home and to send them to an uncertain future in an unknown wilderness must have been an awful decision to have to make.

According to heresay, Mary Burnby was a loving and kind mother, not at all like her bigoted husband. All the children loved her and I never heard a word against her.[7]

In Drabble's defence, Matthew Burnby looms to this day as something of a villain in the Burnby family. A successful landowning farmer, he succumbed to the great evangelical enthusiasm of Wesleyan Methodism in the early years of the nineteenth century. Brought up an Anglican, he converted and built a Methodist chapel at Long Bennington, and the Drabble children were brought up as strict Wesleyan Methodists.[8] He must have been a formidable father-in-law.

Drabble, meanwhile, need not have told anyone the true circumstances of his departure. If he was disgraced at home he was not necessarily disgraced in the colony: it was common enough in the mid-nineteenth century for the father of a family to embark on a sort of reconnaissance of the New World, to find some land, start a farm, and then, when everything was ready, fetch his wife and children. Drabble could have told such a story as this, with the uncomfortable parts censored. In 1869, when firmly settled at Comox, he wrote to the Lands and Works Department:

Will you be kind enough to inform me whether in the event of my going to England for the purpose of bringing out my Family you could grant me leave of absence for six or nine months from my Land without first having to pay for the Claim. My Journey would incur so much expense that it would be a great convenience if I could have the privilege of doing so.[9]

Although he received permission to leave Comox, he postponed his visit home in 1870, and his children never joined him.[10] He may have postponed his visit because Matthew Burnby refused to let his children leave England. Or the children simply may not have wanted to emigrate when they were old enough to do so.

A sad reality, then, lay behind the myths about Drabble's past. In Comox only vague rumours attended the details of his early life — rumours that contributed to his reputation as a "mystery man." Eric Duncan, postmaster in the valley, wrote that "Drabble's antecedents

[7] Beryl MacNeill to the author, 2 February 1995.

[8] MacNeill to McMillan, 4 August 1994.

[9] Drabble to Trutch, 2 November 1869, Colonial Correspondence.

[10] Trutch to Drabble, 8 November 1869, and Drabble to Trutch, 24 January 1870, *ibid.*

were doubtful. He was said to be a married man with a family, but his only link with the Old Land was his mother, who wrote and sent him money occasionally."[11]

With or without his children, Drabble would find abundant practical opportunities to apply his knowledge of farm management, milling, and surveying in a new colonial setting. Although he arrived in Victoria in November 1862, he did not move to the Comox Valley until the summer of 1864, when he applied for a section of land on a tributary of the Tsolum River, half a world away from Long Bennington.

[11] *From Shetland to Vancouver Island*, p. 88.

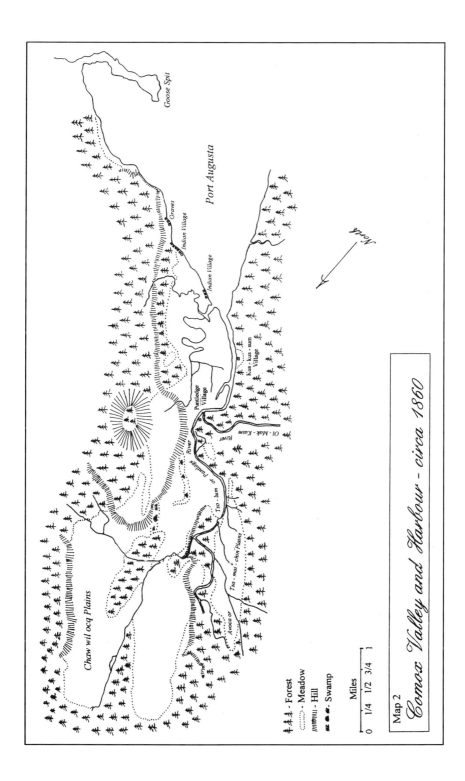

Map 2 *Comox Valley and Harbour – circa 1860*

Legend:
- Forest
- Meadow
- Hill
- Swamp

Miles
0   1/4   1/2   3/4   1

North

Goose Spit

Port Augusta

Graves
Indian Village

Indian Village

Puntledge Village

Chaw wil ocq Plains

Ol - Mak - Kum River

Kus - kus - sum Village

River
Puntledge or

Tso - lum

Avoca or

Tsa - mai - chin Plains

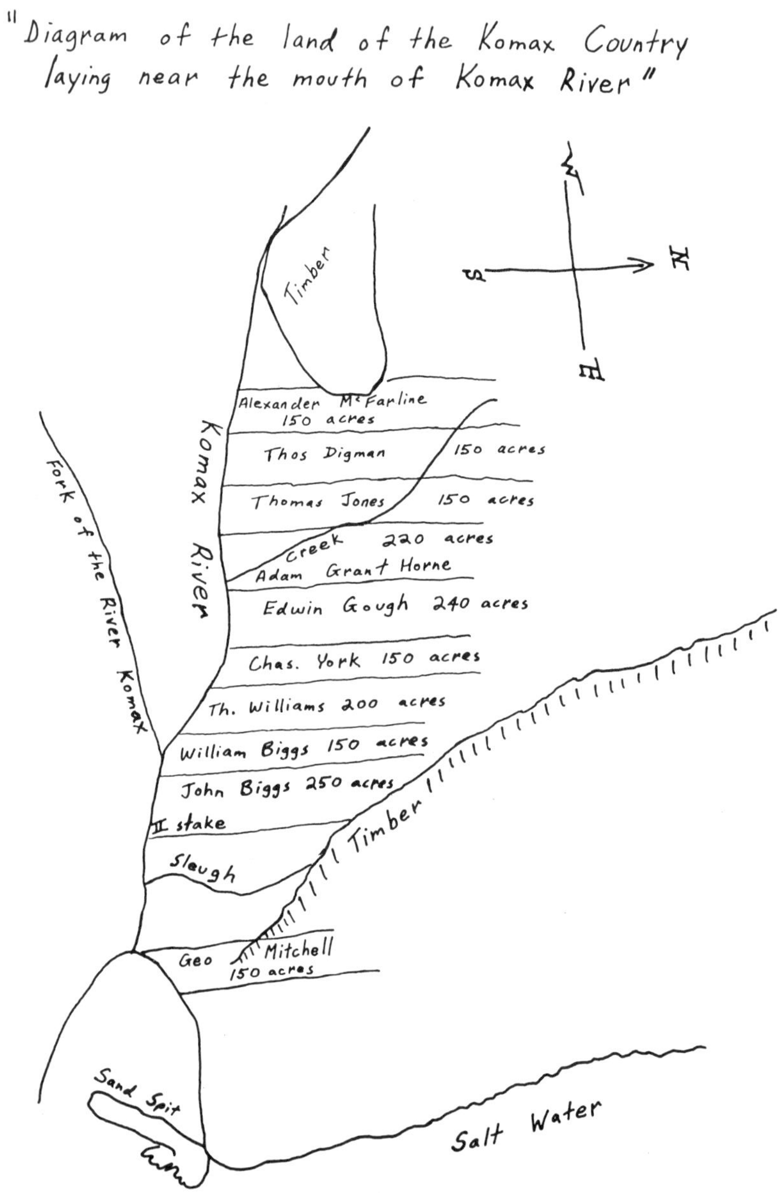

"Diagram of the land of the Komax Country laying near the mouth of Komax River"

Timber

Komax River

Fork of the River Komax

Alexander McFarline 150 acres
Thos Digman 150 acres
Thomas Jones 150 acres
Creek 220 acres
Adam Grant Horne
Edwin Gough 240 acres
Chas. York 150 acres
Th. Williams 200 acres
William Biggs 150 acres
John Biggs 250 acres
II stake
Slough
Timber
Geo Mitchell 150 acres

Sand Spit
Salt Water

Map 3
Comox Pre-emptions - June 1862

CHAPTER 3

Colonists and Apostles

Ye pinched and pent in cities, look at me,
I breathe the dewy freshness of the earth
while ye . . . jostle each other in the smoke and grime
For leave to labour at the beck of gold.

FROM *The Man with the Hoe,* by Eric Duncan[1]

DRABBLE and the other *Silistria* passengers came to a colony that had existed for less than fifteen years. The colony of "Vancouver's Island" had been created from the vastness of the Hudson's Bay Company western domain in 1849, three years after the Oregon Treaty had drawn the boundary between British and American possessions at the forty-ninth parallel. Fur traders from the whole region west of the Rockies moved to Victoria, the capital, where they bought land and settled down. For a few years Victoria was the only colonial settlement on the island, but in 1852 the company opened a little mining town at Nanaimo, staffing the place mostly with coal miners from the "Black Country" of Staffordshire. At the outset of the Fraser River gold rush in 1858, the colonial population of Vancouver Island amounted to less than 1,000 British colonists, while the island's Native Indian population stood at about 25,000. The colonists had not attempted to settle either of the most important agricultural districts on the island, the Cowichan and Comox valleys, owing mainly to their isolation.[2]

The name Comox appeared during a commercial relationship between English traders and seasonal users of the valley. The Lekwiltok people of Cape Mudge spent part of the year fishing at a river thirty miles down the Gulf; they called the place Comox, a name adopted by Hudson's Bay Company traders between the 1820s and the 1850s during their trade with the Lekwiltok.[3]

---

[1] Eric Duncan, *The Rich Fisherman and Other Tales* (London: The Century Press, 1910).

[2] Peggy Nicholls, *From the Black Country to Nanaimo 1854* (2 vols.) (Nanaimo: Nanaimo Historical Society, 1991 and 1992); Richard Mackie, "The Colonization of Vancouver Island, 1849-1858," *BC Studies* 96 (Winter 1992-93), pp. 3-40.

[3] Charles Edward Stuart, "Fort Nanaimo Memoranda," [Nanaimo Journal, 1 August 1855–31 March 1857], NCA; Walbran, *British Columbia Coast Names*, p. 104.

The company knew all about the agricultural riches of Comox: Joseph McKay of Nanaimo paddled up the Tsolum in September 1852, as did Governor James Douglas the following year. McKay made a short excursion into the prairies, which he noted were like those in Saanich, with Garry Oak on the ridges and rows of poplars along the river. "The bottoms along the course of the River are very rich, the Black mould in some places being more than Two feet thick." Douglas, similarly, concluded that "This valley is a fine agricultural district and contains more arable land than is found in any other known district of Vancouver's Island."[4] Though the potential was recognized, the Comox Valley was too distant from Nanaimo and Victoria and too close to the fearsome Lekwiltok for immediate settlement. It took a gold rush to increase the number of colonial settlers, and a smallpox epidemic to reduce the number of Native people.

Late in 1857 gold was discovered on the Thompson and Fraser rivers, and the following spring a massive gold rush began. The British government promptly established a colony on the mainland which Queen Victoria herself named British Columbia in 1858. For a while there were two colonies on the Pacific, each with its own governor, government, and capital city—Victoria and New Westminster. The colonies were united in 1866, with the island retaining the capital, and the mainland giving its name to both.

Victoria remained the principal city of both colonies. In 1861, gold discoveries were made in the Cariboo district, news of which took several months to reach England. A young, adventurous, footloose, and largely male population answered the call. They were attracted by articles in the English press, for example by Donald Fraser, the correspondent of the London *Times*. "I have not written so much on the subject of British Columbia of late," he reported in February 1862, "because the accounts which reached us throughout the summer and autumn were of so glowing a character and gave so superlative a description of the wealth of the upper gold country as appeared fabulous." Many miners, to escape the high waters and cold winters, migrated to the coast in the fall, swelling the population of Victoria and putting a strain on lodging and food facilities.[5]

---

[4] McKay and Douglas are quoted in Isenor, *Land of Plenty*, pp. 15-16; Richard Mackie, "Joseph William McKay," in Frances G. Halpenny, ed., *Dictionary of Canadian Biography* Volume 12 (Toronto: University of Toronto Press, 1990), pp. 641-43.

[5] *Times*, 5 February 1862, quoted in Jean Barman, *The West Beyond the West: A History of British Columbia* (Toronto: University of Toronto Press, 1991), p. 73. See also Dorothy Blakey Smith, ed., "Harry Guillod's Journal of a Trip to Cariboo, 1862," *BCHQ*, 19:3 and 4 (July–October 1955), pp. 187-233; R. Byron Johnson, *Very Far West Indeed: A Few Rough Experiences on the North-West Pacific Coast* (London: Sampson Low, Marston, Low, & Searle, 1872).

Anxious to promote farming and to retain the more respectable of the British immigrants and gold-seekers, the government of Vancouver Island initiated settlement in the Cowichan and Comox valleys. Victoria was crowded, and the authorities were anxious to divert some of the British immigrants from the gold fields to the island's agricultural lands. Governor James Douglas, when he met Englishmen armed with letters of introduction, advised them to avoid the gold districts and settle down instead to a farming life in the colony.

The colonial settlement of the Comox Valley began in the spring of 1861, when the *British Colonist* reported that a few people had gone there with the plan of starting farms. By September there were six settlers. "Parties who have been there report it as one of the best, if not the best, agricultural districts in the Colony. A belt of level land, well watered, is said to exist there, which spreads over an area eighty miles long, with an average breadth of twelve miles." The *Colonist* also reported, equally inaccurately, that the valley contained over 300,000 acres of rich farm land.[6]

It is fitting that these first Comox colonists were not attracted by gold; rather, they were Nanaimo coal miners who had come to Vancouver Island during the Hudson's Bay Company era. In 1861 and 1862 ten Nanaimoites staked claims between the harbour and the junction of Tsolum River and Portuguese Creek, a distance of about three miles. They were John and William Biggs, Thomas Dignan, Edwin Gough, Adam Grant Horne, Thomas Jones, Alexander McFarlane, George Mitchell, Thomas Williams, and Charles York.[7] (See map 3.)

All these men had come to Vancouver Island before the 1858 gold rush. The most senior was George Mitchell, a Scot, who had been a blacksmith at Fort Rupert, had served on the steamship *Beaver*, and arrived at Nanaimo in 1853. Adam Grant Horne, a native of Edinburgh, had come as a labourer with the Hudson's Bay Company on the immigrant ship *Tory* in 1851. Thomas Dignan was born in 1832 in Ireland, the son of a farmer. The other men, colliers and their sons—Gough, Jones, York, and Biggs—had come from England and Wales on the Hudson's Bay Company's *Princess Royal* in 1854.[8]

Only one of these men remained at Comox after 1862. This was George Mitchell, who claimed land on the harbour near the Indian

[6] *British Colonist*, 1 June, 13 September 1861.

[7] Isenor, *Land of Plenty*, p. 58.

[8] Walbran, *British Columbia Coast Names*, pp. 249-50; Murray, *Homesteads and Snug Harbours*, p. 135; June Lewis-Harrison, *The People of Gabriola: A History of our Pioneers* (Cloverdale: D. W. Friesen, 1982), pp. 19-33; Mark Bate, "Reminiscences of Early Nanaimo," *Nanaimo Free Press*, 9 February–18 May 1907.

village where, with his Native wife and children, he raised cattle. In June 1862 nine of these settlers recorded land at Comox.[9] A later newspaper recorded that there being "no communication with any market, other than by sailing boats, they became discontented, and left with the exception of one person, whose name was Mitchell, and who must be considered as the first bona fide settler in the district. He turned his attention to cattle raising and dairying, from whence the original stock of Comox was derived."[10] The others returned to Nanaimo or settled elsewhere. Dignan settled on Gabriola Island; Horne went into business in Nanaimo.

Apart from Mitchell, these Hudson's Bay Company men were soon replaced with settlers of the permanent kind favoured by the government. Gold seekers from Britain and the colonies arrived throughout 1862; the ships *Silistria*, *Tynemouth*, and others brought settlers from Britain, some of whom made their way to Comox between September 1862 and the spring of 1863. From San Francisco, other ships brought gold miners from Australia, New Zealand, Britain, and elsewhere. Whereas the 1858 gold rush had been largely American, the Cariboo miners were predominantly British.[11]

Several Comox settlers came on the steamship *Shannon*, which left Bournemouth in the spring of 1862. At San Fransisco the passengers boarded a coastal steamer for Victoria, where they arrived on 3 July. Among the passengers were two Anglican clergymen's sons, Reginald Carwithen and Reginald Pidcock (known to his friends as "Pid"). Also on board were Carwithen's cousin Harry Blaksley, son of an admiral, and their chums Harry Guillod and John Baily.[12] They were Drabble's friends and contemporaries. They and others became known as the "Twelve Apostles" of Comox. Carwithen had been at Oxford; Pidcock had worked in a London office. A distant British colony was hosting a spectacular gold rush, and they wanted a part of the action. In 1916 Harry Blaksley, then an old man, wrote to Carwithen's daughter concerning the voyage:

> When we left England on the 17th May, 1862, on the Royal Mail steamer Shannon, most of the boys had names given them without there being any meaning attached to them—Guillod went by the name Boiler, and Crockford we called Bottles; Bailey was called Snipe, and your father, Locust; but in

---

9 See B. H. Hunter to Pemberton, 3 June 1862, British Columbia, Department of Lands and Works, Vancouver Island Pre-emptions, 1861-1885.

10 Courtenay *Weekly News*, 28 December 1892, p. 1.

11 Smith, "Harry Guillod's Journal," p. 187.

12 *Ibid.*; Mildred Haas, "R. T. Carwithen and Cousin Blaksley," in Isenor, "The Comox Valley."

course of time the "t" was omitted altogether and he was always called Locus, both by Sywashes and white men; indeed I do not think there were many men who knew what his real name was; everybody liked him very much—both Indians and whites. As the Sywashes could not pronounce the letter "r" I went by the name of Hally; and whenever they met me they used to call out: "Klayhowya Hally mika tum-tum hyas kloche?"[13]

The most valuable contemporary account comes from Pidcock, who in 1868 wrote "Adventures in Vancouver Island," the story of his first year in the colony. Born in 1840, Pidcock turned twenty-one two weeks before arriving in Victoria. His friends were about the same age. After a month camping on the outskirts of Victoria he and his friend Harry Blaksley ("Fred" in the account) made a quick and disappointing trip up Bentinck Arm to Fort Alexandria, from where they intended to proceed to the gold district of the Cariboo.

They ran through most of their food crossing the Chilcotin Plateau. They proceeded on foot from Fort Alexandria toward the gold fields, but they met people who advised them to go no further. "We found many men returning with dismal accounts of the mines, and the scarcity and high prices of provisions. After a long discussion it ended by Fred and myself deciding to go back and the rest of our party went on the same morning."[14] In 1994 Pidcock's grandaughter, Ruth Barnett, told me that the last straw came when Pidcock and Blaksley met an Englishman, also the son of an Anglican clergyman, coming down the trail from the mines. "He was wearing nothing but a top hat—mad as a hatter."[15]

Pidcock and Blaksley returned to the coast, bought an Indian canoe at Victoria, and headed up the island. By now it was the fall of 1862. At Nanaimo they met a man who advised them "to go farther north & have a look at the open land at Comox which had lately been discovered and of which he had heard very good accounts." Near Nanoose they met two canoes of Comox Indians, who told them it was "one Sun to Comox if we had a fair wind & nearly two Suns if we had to paddle all the way. They said it was a very good place, everything was there that Indians could want and there was no place like it on all the Island; and indeed we found it to be so when we had been there a short time." Pidcock and Blaksley continued on their way. "The tide was in our favour & running very swiftly we made capital way & soon caught sight of the entrance to Comox Harbour or Bay, while we were still 10 or 12 miles off." They

[13] Blaksley to Jessie McQuillan, 12 July 1916, quoted in *Comox Argus* 17 March 1921.

[14] Reginald Heber Pidcock, "Adventures in Vancouver Island. Being an Account of 6 years residence, and of hunting & fishing excursions with some Account of the Indians inhabiting the island," (hereafter Pidcock, "Adventures in Vancouver Island"), pp. 26, 32.

[15] Interview with Ruth Barnett, 23 December 1994.

landed below the present location of the Anglican church at Sandwick Corner:

> Only one white settler was here then or at least had built a house. Others had just arrived on one of the Gunboats sent by the Government to encourage settlements & were exploring the open land & staking out their Claims. We went up the River as soon as it was high water and camped some distance up in fact almost as far as we could go. There are about 3000 acres of open land but so divided by strips of wood that you cannot see more than a small portion at once. The river divides it though not at all equally there being much more on the north than the south side. The land for the most part is covered with fern which grows to a great height on some parts and a blue berry something like our Bilberry grows in great quantities more or less all over it and these are gathered by the Indian Women about July and boiled & then spread into thin cakes & dried.[16]

These sons of the church left Comox in the fall and spent a happy winter hunting deer for the Nanaimo market. They camped at a little cove near Nanoose, shot deer in the forest behind, and supplied "mowitch" by the canoe load to the settlers and coal ships at Nanaimo.

Meanwhile Victoria was filling up with new arrivals and with men who had tried their luck at the gold mines. News travelled slowly in the pre-telegraph era, and eager miners continued to arrive long after the gold rush had peaked. Among them were miners from Australia, though none were actually Native Australians. All had come originally from the British Isles, but those who settled at Comox were known as "the Australians."[17] One of them was Shetland Islander William Duncan, whose nephew Eric Duncan recalled that there were two main groups of 1862 settlers of the Comox Valley:

> There were two bands, one of gold miners and sailors which came up from Australia, and another of emigrants from the British Isles which sailed around Cape Horn. The whole numbered about sixty, and all, except one Eastern Canadian named Bridges, were natives of the United Kingdom.[18]

The Australians, Duncan wrote, had been attracted by the Cariboo gold rush, but when they reached Victoria the fever had abated, and they were instructed by Attorney General Cary to try farming. Cary induced them "to take a look at the Valley, with the result that they went no further." Government surveyor Benjamin Pearse and Judge Matthew Begbie also advised young immigrants to avoid the Cariboo in favour of farming on Vancouver Island.[19]

---

[16] Pidcock, "Adventures in Vancouver Island," pp. 68-69.

[17] Rose Ann Milligan, "Fourth Prize Article," Union *Weekly News* 19 October 1897, p. 1.

[18] *From Shetland to Vancouver Island*, p. 86.

[19] Eric Duncan, [Draft Description and History of the Comox Valley, 1916]; Duncan, "Early Days and Early Settlers;" Captain G. R. Bates, "Narrative."

Immigrant miners were in a quandary in the fall of 1862. They could spent the winter—and their savings—in Victoria waiting for the new mining season, or they could inspect the land advertised by the government at Comox and elsewhere. Many were disillusioned with negative reports from the Cariboo, where Pidcock, Blaksley, and others had already tried their luck. Winter was coming on, and still there was time to stake a piece of land and build a cabin before the cold weather arrived. Reports of death from the severe cold in the Cariboo alarmed potential miners, who were easily persuaded to give up the idea of prospecting and take up farming instead.[20]

The government advertised for Comox immigrants in Victoria, and at the end of September about twenty names of intending settlers had been registered. By this time the Hudson's Bay Company immigrants of 1861 had abandoned the valley, except for Mitchell, and about fifty colonists accompanied Cary and surveyor Pearse on the *Grappler's* "Comox Expedition."[21] Carwithen and Baily were among them. Thirty years later George Drabble (who possessed the land records) recalled the circumstances of the trip:

> Early in September 1862, the Government dispatched the gunboat, *Grappler* up the coast, and due notice was given that any persons desirous to take up land in Comox would be given a free passage. The then Surveyor General accompanied them for the purpose of giving all the information and assistance necessary. A considerable number availed themselves of the opportunity, and from the second day of September to the twentieth day of December, 1862, thirty eight claims were preempted.[22]

Blaksley recalled that he "had the pick of the whole place; there was only one white man there then—George Mitchell, who lived down by the Bay, but plenty of Siwashes all painted and streaked, and no clothing but blankets." The first places to be taken up by the new arrivals were the Nanaimo miners' abandoned claims of the previous year. "Some 35 settlers have taken up claims in the vicinity of the Courtenay river and express themselves delighted with the prospect," a reporter wrote in October; "The land is of the richest character with scattered prairies from five hundred to a thousand acres, well watered, and abounding with game."[23]

[20] Bates, "Narrative."

[21] *Colonist*, 29 September 1862; *The Press*, 1 October 1862. See also Allan Pritchard, "Letters of a Victorian Naval Officer: Edmund Hope Verney in British Columbia, 1862-65," *BC Studies* 86 (Summer 1990), pp. 28-57; 36-37.

[22] Courtenay *Weekly News*, 28 December 1892, p. 1.

[23] Blaksley to McQuillan, 12 July 1916, quoted in *Comox Argus*, 17 March 1921; *British Colonist*, 10 October 1864, quoted in Hayman, *Robert Brown*, p. 152, n. 141.

Not all the settlers were pleased with the place. Some were what Eric Duncan called Birds of Passage, staying only a few months or a year before selling their claim to someone else; others, like an old-timer interviewed in 1897, needed a few weeks to form an attachment. "The first thought which struck him, after he had been here a day, was how he could best put in his time until the next boat would come and carry him away from this forsaken region. Eventually he bought a claim of one hundred and sixty acres; and now, said he, 'I assure you I had enough to do to divert my thoughts from emigration.'"[24]

◌◌

The *Silistria*, which arrived at Esquimalt on 16 November 1862 with Drabble among the nearly 300 passengers, threw Victoria into a state of emergency in the normally placid months of winter. The *Daily Chronicle* noted the ship's arrival, adding that "Our bachelors will no doubt be disappointed to learn that there are only 20 females on board, 18 of whom are accompanied by their 'worser' halves." The passengers were English, apart from about thirty Scots and thirty Irish. There simply was not enough work for all the men. "The passengers by the Silistria are for the most part sturdy laborers," editorialized the *Colonist*, "who are in most cases totally unprovided with means to carry them through the winter." These "able-bodied, sober, respectable-looking men" went around Victoria in groups of a dozen or more looking for work. Two hundred of them were broke, hungry, and destitute. "The English immigrants whom we have prayed for for the last five years, are here and in want. Shall we allow them to be starved out of the colony?" asked the *Chronicle*.[25]

They were not alone: about 1,000 out of the estimated 5,000 people in the city were out of work, and to make matters worse, more were expected from England. One recent arrival, "Veritas," complained that the English public had been deceived by "overdrawn and exaggerated statements" by correspondent Fraser of the London *Times* and by other books and pamphlets which had given the impression that Vancouver Island was an "Oasis in the Pacific."[26]

Within days the Lands and Works Department had hired about sixty passengers to work on the roads at Esquimalt, Metchosin, and Cedar Hill. Governor Douglas hired about seventy more to clear one of his ten-acre bush lots at Fairfield, and other landowners did the

---

[24] Mary Milligan, "Fifth Prize Article," Union *Weekly News*, 2 November 1897, p. 1.

[25] *Daily Chronicle*, 18, 23 November 1862; *British Colonist*, 17, 21, 22 November 1862. For a passenger list see *British Colonist*, 17 November 1862.

[26] *Daily Chronicle*, 22, 23 November 1862.

same.[27] Thanks to Governor Douglas, a few of the passengers went gold hunting, as the *Daily Chronicle* reported in December:

> Three of the Silistria's passengers have been sent to explore the Comax District for precious metals by Governor Douglas, who defrays their expenses from his private purse, and pays them $1.50 a day besides. The prospectors appear to be hardy, determined men, and if there is anything in the district worth finding, it is believed that they will find it.[28]

One of them may have been Drabble, but evidence is lacking.

Some of the passengers ignored the bad press and went to the interior in search of gold. One was Sam Cliffe, who went to the Cariboo, where he met Lincoln native Teddy Rollings, later the Comox shoemaker. "Rollings was an old pioneer," Cliffe stated on Rolling's death in 1898; "I first met him in 1863 mending gum boots in Cariboo. He had a claim on Sugar Creek."[29] Before the end of 1863 *Silistria* passengers, and others, were finding their way from Victoria to Comox. These included the Lincolnshire diarists William and Mary Harmston and their daughter Florence, who would later marry Sam Cliffe. The Harmstons had planned to go to to Australia but—Mary Harmston's great-great grandaughter Phyllis Currie told me—when they got to Victoria they "saw a notice on the dock that called attention to pre-emptions in the Comox district."[30] After dropping the passengers at Victoria, the *Silistria* proceeded with a cargo of Port Alberni lumber to Australia, only to disappear without trace in a tropical storm.

The government assisted in the new Comox settlement. Contractors started working on a trail from Nanaimo to Comox in December 1862. "From a man who has just come down," reported the *Colonist* at the end of December, "we learn that there are about thirty persons now living in the settlement."[31]

George Drabble may have visited the Comox Valley in that first winter, but his name does not appear in the land records for eighteeen months. He had been friends in England with the Harmstons, and he would follow them to Comox: to a new settlement consisting of men and women disillusioned with gold mining, physically separated from their pasts, and young enough to be optimistic about building for the future. All came to a region inhabited by Native people whose numbers had been decimated in the great smallpox epidemic of 1862.

---

[27] *British Colonist*, 21 November 1862; *Daily Chronicle*, 23, 24 November, 7 December 1862.

[28] *Daily Chronicle*, 11 December 1862, p. 3.

[29] *The News (Cumberland)*, 10 December 1898, p. 1.

[30] Interview with Phyllis Currie, 14 May 1994.

[31] *Colonist*, 27 December 1862.

CHAPTER 4

A Poor Country for Indians

> We entered Port Augusta (Comox Harbour) about 11 a.m.
> with a large convoy of canoes returning from fishing. On
> being told of my mission one of them, a wrinkled old woman,
> remarked "Ah Sir, you will see a fair country for white men,
> but the better for the whites, the poorer for the Indians."
>
> —Robert Brown, Comox, 20 August 1864[1]

THE first colonial settlers of Comox had a terrible advantage over the Native inhabitants of the Gulf of Georgia. In 1862, between April and December, thousands of Native people died in a great smallpox epidemic, which originated with a sailor from San Francisco. The disease arrived in Victoria in March, spreading north along the coast as Indians returned home from their work trips to Victoria. The disease was at first felt among the Haida and Tsimshian work camps at Victoria; by May it had reached Fort Simpson, and in June Native people at Nanaimo and the Lekwiltok of Cape Mudge were dying in scores. The *Colonist* reported that a hundred bodies had washed ashore on the coast north of Nanaimo, and people were still dying in the Cowichan area in December.[2] Although missionaries, government, and Hudson's Bay Company officials on the coast vaccinated many hundreds of Native people, mortality was very high compared to the settler community, where most people had been vaccinated.

Contemporaries asserted that the epidemic had converted Indian camps into graveyards, and some colonists predicted the total disappearance of the coastal people. More than a third of the Native population of Vancouver Island died. The epidemic left large tracts of the coast uninhabited just as the Cariboo gold rush brought thousands of colonists, including surveyor Drabble, to the region. "Still the same old story

---

[1] Hayman, *Robert Brown*, p. 110.

[2] *Daily Colonist*, 19 and 28 March 1862; Grant Keddie, "The Victoria Smallpox Crisis of 1862," *Discovery, Friends of the Royal British Columbia Museum* 21:4 (1993), pp. 6-7. See also Cole Harris, "Voices of Disaster: Smallpox around the Strait of Georgia in 1782," *Ethnohistory* 41:4 (Fall 1994), pp. 591-626.

of passing away!" wrote explorer Robert Brown after visiting a deserted village near Qualicum in August 1864.[3] "I don't know what God is doing," Bella Bella Indian Ham-chit told geologist George Dawson in 1878, regarding the disappearance of his people; "Klunas saghalie tyee Mamook." "Long ago he says they were like the trees, in great numbers everywhere."[4]

The first thing noticed by early Comox settlers was the devastation caused by smallpox. On their way by canoe to Comox in September 1862, Pidcock and Blaksley passed Village Point, Denman Island where there had been an inhabited Pentlatch village only three months before. "It has large quantities of Cedar Trees on it," Pidcock wrote, "& the Comox Indians make a great number of their canoes here. They used to live on it [until] some few months ago but the small pox which broke out in 1862 carried some of them off & they have never returned to it since." In 1864 Robert Brown camped at the same village and wrote that it must once have been very extensive "but is now quite deserted & nothing but the frames stand." The site of the old village was covered with a rich grass from the quantity of organic material but, Brown continued, "It still retained traces of its former grandeur—pickets, carved images, &c, & massive hewn cedar frames." Warfare with the Lekwiltok also contributed to the demise of the village. Thirty years later the village was still empty, an object of curiosity for visitors, one of whom wrote that: "The village has become deserted, like Sweet Auburn, but no poet like Goldsmith has arisen to sing its praise. A few potato patches are still discernible and mark with yearly receding lines the place."[5]

Like elsewhere on the Gulf of Georgia, the Native community at Comox had been ravaged in the fur trade era by disease, warfare, and dislocation. Native society was in crisis. In August 1864, during the salmon season when most Indians were present, Brown noticed the "great number of old men in the tribe and the small number of children. This must soon make the tribe very small."[6]

---

[3] Robin Fisher, *Contact and Conflict: Indian-European Relations in British Columbia, 1774-1890* (Vancouver: University of British Columbia Press, 1977), p. 116; George Woodcock, *British Columbia, a History of the Province* (Vancouver: Douglas & McIntyre, 1990), pp. 130-32; Hayman, *Robert Brown*, p. 108.

[4] Cole and Lockner, *To the Charlottes*, p. 83.

[5] Pidcock, "Adventures on Vancouver Island," p. 67; Hayman, *Robert Brown*, pp. 108, 110; Ranald McDonald, "Journal of the Vancouver Island Exploring Expedition," 7 June– 22 October 1864, Robert Brown Collection, p. 25; Courtenay *Weekly News*, 1 February 1893, p. 4.

[6] See Robert Galois, *Kwakwaka'wakw Settlements, 1775-1920: A Geographical Analysis and Gazetteer* (Vancouver: UBC Press, 1994), pp. 27-74; Hayman, *Robert Brown*, p. 114.

When the colonists arrived in Comox they encountered three groups of Indians: the Comox, the Puntledge (Pentlatch), and the Eucletaw (Lekwiltok), of whom the Pentlatch were nearly extinct. The Comox and Pentlatch were permanent residents, while the Lekwiltok came seasonally from Cape Mudge. The Comox did not refer to themselves as such at first; the Lekwiltok name "Comox" had been adopted by Hudson's Bay Company traders and then by settlers; it was, Robert Brown learned, originally a name of derision applied by the Lekwiltok.[7]

In 1864 explorer Ranald McDonald learned from a Nanaimo Indian named E-yees that the right pronunciation was "Koo-moox," and that their original name was Sa-thool-tuch. Captain Walbran called them the Sloslute; Brown noted that the proper name for the Comox tribe was Sae-luth. The Sae-luth name for the whole Comox country, Brown continued, was Pequodiem, and the Sae-luth had come originally from the north, where they had "broken or seceded from a tribe called the Ey-exen."[8]

After 1862 the Comox Indians (or Sae-luth) absorbed the remnants of the Pentlatch, who had been decimated by warfare and smallpox. Brown wrote that the Pentlatch village—about a mile up the river— was deserted and the site occupied by potato patches. His informant, "an old Puntledge," told him that the Pentlatch and the Comox had not been on friendly terms, but after smallpox and battle with the Comox, "the Puntledge became very few indeed & sought the friendship and alliance of their old Enemies the Comoucs for mutual protection & defence: & from that day they lived together." An early settler, probably Drabble, noted that Pentlatch lands were taken over by the new confederacy, "the Comox Indians taking possession of their lands and settling down on them."[9]

By 1864 the Pentlatch had abandoned their village on Denman, and the ten or twelve remaining people joined the Comox tribe. In 1870 only six remained, and when Franz Boas visited Comox in 1886 only

7 Hayman, *Robert Brown*, p. 123. On the Native people of Comox see also Isenor, *Land of Plenty*, pp. 24-56.

8 Hayman, *Robert Brown*, pp. 32, 105, 111, 123; McDonald, "Journal of the Vancouver Island Exploring Expedition," p. 25; Walbran, *British Columbia Coast Names*, p. 104. See also Courtenay *Weekly News*, 28 December 1892, p. 1; Dora Crawford, "First Prize Article," Union *Weekly News* 21 September 1897, p. 1; Franz Boas, "Myths and Legends of the Catloltq of Vancouver Island," *The American Antiquarian* 10:4 (July 1888), pp. 201-11. On the Eiksun see Homer Barnett, *The Coast Salish of British Columbia* (Westport, Connecticut: Greenwood Press, 1955).

9 Hayman, *Robert Brown*, pp. 122-23; see also p. 128; Crawford, "First Prize Article," Union *Weekly News* 21 September 1897, p. 1. On the demise of the Pentlatch see also Dorothy I. D. Kennedy and Randall T. Bouchard, "Northern Island Salish," in Wayne Suttles, ed., *Handbook of North American Indians* (Washington, D.C.: Smithsonian Insititution, 1990), pp. 441-52.

one family of Pentlatch speakers remained. The last of the Pentlatch was Joe Nim-Nim.[10] "They are not a numerous tribe," Pidcock wrote in 1868 regarding the Comox Indians, "& the Country does not properly belong to them but formerly a tribe called the 'Puntledge' Indians used to live here and a few families are here still but have amalgamated with the Comox though they have a different language and were formerly a very strong tribe."[11]

The Lekwiltok, the third Native group frequenting Comox, were the most southerly of the Kwakiutl, now the Kwakwaka'wakw. They possessed herring and salmon fishing sites at Comox. Pidcock recalled that at the beginning of November 1862, "a great many Indians began to come down from the Northern parts of the Island to fish for salmon & lay in their winter's provisions. They are a fine lot of fellows and belong to several different tribes all talking the same language peculiar to themselves." The Comox people were on friendly terms with the Lekwiltok; they went to a great potlatch at Cape Mudge in 1864, but the Lekwiltok fondness for whiskey often led to drunken brawls and violence at the Comox camp. Settlers viewed the Lekwiltok as a corrupting influence over the Comox Indians.[12]

In October 1865 Anglican missionary catechist Jordayne Cave Brown Cave reported that: "There are four tribes of Euclatore Indians the tribe that has come down is the Wawaka from Cape Mudge." These were the Weewiakay, one of the Lekwiltok, whose permanent villages were on Quadra Island. They had traditionally fished salmon and traded at Comox; indeed, in the 1860s their right to fish in the valley was confirmed by the Royal Navy and settlers who required their help as farm labourers. Their fearsome reputation was rarely alluded to at Comox after about 1870, and by 1881 ten Lekwiltok lived on the Comox Reserve. By the late nineteenth century the Comox Indians had been acculturated into the Kwakwaka'wakw, and by the 1980s there was only one remaining speaker of the Comox dialect.[13]

[10] McDonald, "Journal of the Vancouver Island Exploring Expedition," p. 25. On the amalgamation see also Isabelle Stubbs, "Indian History Recounted by Matriarch," *CVFP*, 30 October 1952; Rev. H. B. Owen, "Comox," in *Twelfth Annual Report of the Columbia Mission for the Year 1870* (London: Rivingtons, 1871), pp. 26-28; Boas is quoted in Isenor, *Land of Plenty*, p. 36; B. A. McKelvie, "The 'S' Sign. A Biographical Sketch of Eustace Smith, Logger, Timber Cruiser and Forest Engineer," CDMA, p. 28.

[11] Pidcock, "Adventures in Vancouver Island," pp. 79-80.

[12] *Ibid.*, p. 73. On the Lekwiltok see Galois, *Kwakwaka'wakw Settlements*, pp. 223-76. They "came regularly to procure salmon" at Comox: Owen, "Comox," p. 28; for the 1862 potlatch see Hayman, *Robert Brown*, p. 114.

[13] Cave to Colonial Secretary, 18 October 1865, Colonial Correspondence; *Daily Colonist*, 18 December 1865; Galois, *Kwakwaka'wakw Settlements*, maps 2.26 to 2.29 and p. 234; Kennedy and Bouchard, "Northern Coast Salish," p. 441.

The main amalgamated Comox village was on the harbour near the mouth of the Courtenay River. Agnes Edwards recalled that the village contained "seven immensely long potlatch houses."[14] In 1865 this village was made into a reserve for the surviving Indians of Comox, but neither it nor the old Pentlatch village site on the Puntledge were safe from land-hungry settlers. In 1870 William Duncan, Comox settler, tried to pre-empt the Puntledge village, and two years later Anglican missionary Jules Willemar applied unsuccessfully for part of the Comox Bay reserve. After much dispute between Duncan and the government, the Pentlatch village site was confirmed as an Indian Reserve in 1878, along with the Comox burial grounds on Goose Spit.[15]

For most of the late nineteenth century there were less than 100 Comox Indians. In August 1864, there were about seventy warriors; in 1870 the total population was about 100 Indians of all ages, and a careful census of 1876 found eighty-eight Comox Indians of whom forty-four were boys and girls. In 1864, the chief was Wacas, "a bold looking elderly man," and Nonmoncaas was a minor chief.[16]

The colonists, like the fur traders before them, replaced Native names with English or borrowed ones: the Sae-luth people became the Comox, Pequodiem became the Comox Valley, the Onymakqtam became the Courtenay River (after George Courtenay, a Royal Navy officer based at Esquimalt in the 1840s), and the bay in front of the Comox townsite was named Port Augusta after one of Queen Victoria's daughters. Brown was alarmed at the proliferation of English names; he called the naming of Courtenay River and Port Augusta "a needless and egotistical geographical pleonasm to flatter some unknown personages but as they are published it is better to keep them."[17]

∽

An empty landscape favourable to colonial settlement resulted from diseases like smallpox and the warfare that characterized the early and mid nineteenth century. Indian rancheries were deserted, and their survivors amalgamated with surrounding groups to whom they were

[14] Isabelle Stubbs, "Indian History Recounted by Matriarch," *CVFP*, 30 October 1952.

[15] McKinlay and Sproat to the Attorney General, 11 January 1878, Herald Street Collection; Anderson, Sproat, and McKinlay to A. C. Elliott, "Report of the Proceedings of the Joint Reserve Commission for the Settlement of Indian Reserves in the Province of British Columbia...." *c.* 1878, in British Columbia, Records Relating to Indian Affairs, 1876-1878.

[16] McDonald, "Journal of the Vancouver Island Exploring Expedition," p. 26; Owen, "Comox," p. 28; "Abstract of Census," included in McKinlay to A. C. Elliott, 4 January 1877, in British Columbia, Provincial Secretary, Records Relating to Indian Affairs, 1876-1878; Hayman, *Robert Brown*, p. 114, 123.

[17] Walbran, *British Columbia Coast Names*, pp. 115-16; Hayman, *Robert Brown*, p. 128.

related. Everywhere on the coast, middens and house remains indicated Native inhabitation; during the smallpox epidemic, people died on lonely islands where their bones remained for decades; people who had been travelling simply beached their canoes, set up emergency camps, pulled their blankets over themselves, and died.

On beaches near Comox blue trade beads can still be found by a patient searcher. This was especially the case at the turn of the nineteenth century when the beaches yielded many to settler children. Canoes constantly arrived and departed, deals were struck and canoes unloaded, and beads fell from canoe bottoms when they were beached and turned over for the winter. Some beads eroded from middens themselves, others came from burials, and all were collected by settlers' children like Leila Carroll: "Big bright blue many-sided beads, used by the Hudson's Bay Company in trading with the Indians were still to be found in the district. The holes were large enough for children to thread them on store string with their fingers. Soon after our arrival, we had found or acquired enough blue beads to make a string of them." [18] Almost a hundred years of trade and exchange were represented in these necklaces.

This was not all the collecting that went on. The shoreline was covered with Native middens, remnants of thousands of years of habitation and use. Drabble, when superintendent of Comox roads in the 1870s, helped himself to shell midden for road construction. In 1873 he specified that contractor Joe McPhee was to use shell heaps instead of gravel in the construction of the road near the Anglican Mission, and a few years later Drabble repaired the same piece of road with a "clam shell covering." Clam shells provided the plaster used in the construction of the Presbyterian church in 1877. In the next decade, ethnographers Adrian Jacobsen and Franz Boas collected skulls from the Comox waterfront—human remains that are still preserved in museum cabinets in Berlin and New York. [19]

Appropriation of Native remains went beyond names, beads, and bones, to include ownership of Native land itself. The Vancouver Island land laws did not allow settlers to claim inhabited Indian settlements. Main villages like the present reserve on the Dyke were retained as Indian land, but the act made available the whole of the rest of the coastline. Settlers' pre-emptions were often located on former Indian

[18] Carroll, *Wild Roses and Rail Fences*, pp. 12-13.

[19] British Columbia, Department of Public Works, Contracts, specifications, 1862-1909; Carroll, *Wild Roses and Rail Fences*, p. 141; Johan Adrian Jacobsen, *Alaskan Voyage 1881-1883. An Expedition to the Northwest Coast of America* (Chicago: University of Chicago Press, 1977), p. 79 (3 May 1882); Franz Boas, 15 November 1886, quoted in Isenor, *Land of Plenty*, p. 36; Douglas Cole, *Captured Heritage: The Scramble for North West Coast Artifacts* (Vancouver: Douglas & McIntyre, 1985).

village sites for the simple reason that such places possessed cleared land, fresh water, and safe anchorage. Indeed, the land acts permitted white settlement or commercial activity on most places used by Indians for resource procurement: clam and oyster beds, fishing stations, river courses, camas beds, hunting grounds for deer and waterfowl. Such places had been used for millenia for food procurement and some continued to be—to the consternation of settlers for whom possession of private property included rights against trespass.

Native land did not become settler land without some debate. In August 1864 Robert Brown discussed this issue while at Comox:

> Here as everywhere else the Indians are growling about payment for their land. The deer are fewer, and the berries are also & I noticed them cutting down the crab apple trees to get easier to the fruit. They never would do that before but now they think they may as well get as much out of their land as possible, as soon they will be altogether deprived of it. When travelling or sitting around the camp fire with them they always appeal to me on that subject & I assure you that it is no easy matter to answer the question satisfactorily when an intelligent [Indian] looks up in your face and asks "Had you no good land of your own that you come and deprive us of ours?"[20]

The British colonization of the Gulf of Georgia occurred when the Native population was approaching its nadir. Drabble was quite aware of the land laws regarding inhabited Native settlements, and he made a point of noting when a settler's land contained deserted or uninhabited Indian houses. Gulf of Georgia settlers found themselves in possession of places that had been until recently Native places. In a farmer's field on the island highway just north of Courtenay, for example, is an ancient camas bed, the purple flowers of which still bloom. In 1862 settler George Ford pre-empted the abandoned Indian fishing village of Kus-kus-sum on the Courtenay River. This village is now obliterated beneath Section 41 of downtown Courtenay, its name preserved only in archival documents. In 1864 Robert Brown noted that Kus-kus-sum was an "Excellent place for spearing salmon," though Ford caught them with a net.[21]

Modern-day settlers continue to find Native artifacts. The current owner of George Drabble's farm, Stan Rennison, found little slate arrowheads in his fields that were probably used for shooting birds. Eric Duncan noted that a great Douglas Fir at the back of the Duncan property at Sandwick had been used for a tree burial. At the foot of the tree were "fragments of a cedar-box and some dried up human bones, showing that the tree had been used as a repository for the dead." In

[20] Hayman, *Robert Brown*, p. 124. See also *Daily Colonist*, 10 February 1864.
[21] Hayman, *Robert Brown*, p. 112.

1878 Duncan had a close shave when the dead upper branches of the tree fell on him.[22]

The 1862 Comox settlers worked and traded with Indians and got to know them well. They learned Chinook, the trade jargon of the coast, a language in which Native men were known as "Siwashes" (a corruption of the French Sauvage) and women as "clootchmen," both of which became very derogatory before they went out of use. "In those far-off days," Blaksley recalled in 1916, "there were only a few Sywashes and their klootchmen about; Hyas klocheukkuk syya illyhee."[23]

The transition of ownership was not mutually agreeable. Much Native land was unilaterally pre-empted or otherwise seized. Irishman Fred Nunns at Campbell River wrote in his diary that the local Indians continued to regard his pre-emption as their property. The chief came to him and asked him if he really believed it belonged to him. At Nanoose, Portuguese settler John Enos resorted to theatrical magic to rid his pre-emption of its owners, who persisted in thinking it was theirs in 1863. Captain Walbran wrote that:

> Enos used to relate that when he first settled here the Indians living in the neighbourhood of his house were strongly opposed to his staying there, and as the Indians would not move away he used to play the ghost at night by flitting among the trees, dressed in white, and was successful in frightening them off his ground.[24]

The newer settlers held contradictory views of Native people: while on an economic level they valued their labour, on a social level they treated them with indifference, contempt, or racism. Eric Duncan—whose uncle and brother tried for forty years to pre-empt the Puntledge River reserve—called Native people "dull, phlegmatic, lazy." "The Indian, with salmon throwing themselves at his head, could take it easy and live on the natural resources of the country; and though such a life may have added to his bodily stature, it has dwarfed his mind." Duncan was not alone in his views. Fred Nunns, who had spent time in South Africa, commented that "The natives here are not up to the Kaffirs in any way."[25]

Just as in the days of the Hudson's Bay Company, commercial and working opportunities formed the main points of contact between settlers and Indians. Historians Blanche Norcross and Doris Tonkin noted that the farmers of the 1860s and 1870s "depended heavily on their Indian neighbours for harvest-time labour." While some Indians

---

[22] Interview with Stan Rennison, 1 June 1994; *From Shetland to Vancouver Island*, p. 162.

[23] Blaksley to McQuillan, 21 September 1919, quoted in *Comox Argus* 17 March 1921.

[24] Walbran, *British Columbia Coast Names*, pp. 521-22.

[25] *From Shetland to Vancouver Island*, p. 95; Fred Nunns Diary, 17 May 1888.

went to work for the settlers, it would be a mistake to assume that seasonal cycles did not continue. Brown, for example, noted the arrival of salmon in the Courtenay River in August 1864, and commented that "The salmon season is all round the Coast a season of joy and merriment. All the wanderers come back to the tribe."[26] The Comox Indians continued to potlatch, their ceremonies drawing the odd comment and description from settlers or visitors like W. W. Walkem, William Halliday, and Mary Harmston.[27]

Good relations existed between some newcomers and the Comox Indians. Perhaps a dozen early settlers intermarried or lived with Native women. Norcross and Tonkin wrote that "very real friendships" emerged in spite of quarrels over fences and livestock: "As the white population increased and became less dependent on the Indians, the two races grew apart and only the older people on both sides preserved the friendly contact."[28] English settlers like Carwithen and Blaksley gave names like Sam, Buckskin, Big Maly, and Old Polly to Native people at Comox, and lasting friendships developed. Unfortunately, the Native people of Comox did not leave corresponding views of the 1862 newcomers—lost men of eccentric habits and strange character.

[26] E. Blanche Norcross and Doris Farmer Tonkin, *Frontiers of Vancouver Island* (Courtenay: Island Books, 1969), p. 43; see also Rolf Knight, *Indians at Work: An Informal History of Native Indian Labour in British Columbia* (Vancouver: New Star Books, 1978); John Lutz, "After the Fur Trade: The Aboriginal Labouring Class of British Columbia, 1849-1890," in *Journal of the Canadian Historical Association* 3 (1992), pp. 69-95; Hayman, *Robert Brown*, p. 119.

[27] [J. W. McKay], "Fort Simpson in the Forties," [narrated 1876], in Walkem, *Stories of Early British Columbia*, pp. 75-86; W. M. Halliday, *Potlatch and Totem and the Recollections of an Indian Agent (London and Toronto: J. M. Dent & Sons,* 1935), pp. 124-27; Harmston Diary, 8 July 1884.

[28] Carwithen to Blaksley, 24 February 1884, Carwithen Correspondence; Norcross and Tonkin, *Frontiers of Vancouver Island*, p. 43.

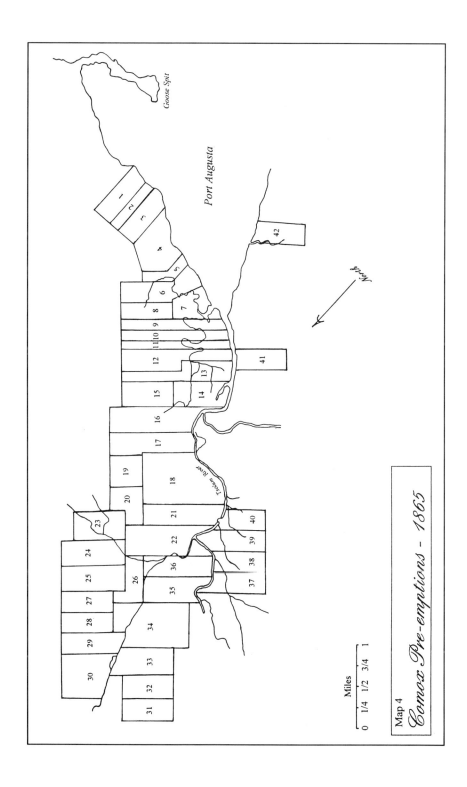

Goose Spit

Port Augusta

North

1
2
3
4
5
6
7
8
9
10
11
12
13
14
15
16
17
18
19
20
21
22
23
24
25
26
27
28
29
30
31
32
33
34
35
36
37
38
39
40
41
42

Tsolum River

Miles

0   1/4   1/2   3/4   1

Map 4
Comox Pre-emptions – 1865

CHAPTER 5

Lost Men in a New Land

There are no more maps.
Can I expect
log cabins in a clearing,
and a hermit, or a crone,
or perhaps
the remnants of a well
where gold was drowned,
or just incessant forest?

FROM *Last Song*, by Robin Skelton[1]

THE gold rush era was a time of great transiency. Many thousands of people arrived, but perhaps one in ten stayed. Drabble was one of those who remained, but he is absent in the historical record for the first eighteen months of his time on Vancouver Island. His whereabouts are unknown between November 1862, when the *Silistria* arrived, and September 1863, when he is known to have bought a dog in Victoria from a man named Smith. His shipboard friends are easier to trace: William and Mary Harmston staked their Comox claims in March 1863, and Sam Cliffe went to the Cariboo in 1863. Drabble may have been one of the *Silistria* passengers sent by Governor Douglas in December 1862 to explore the Comox District for precious metals, or one of the three men who helped survey the trail to Comox in March 1863, but names are lacking.[2]

The only clue to his activities during this year and a half comes from Sarah Butler, another *Silistria* passenger, who recollected that Drabble was "one of our early surveyors in Victoria." While no evidence has been found that Drabble worked in Victoria, it is likely that he did so. He possessed three important and marketable skills: surveying, engineering, and farm management—skills that separated him from the "sturdy

---

[1] Robin Skelton, *Landmarks* (Victoria: Sono Nis Press, 1979), pp. 85-86.
[2] *Daily Chronicle*, 11 December 1862, p. 3; "Roads and Bridges, Nanaimo to Comox," Herald Street Collection.

labourers" of the *Silistria* and would have been in considerable demand. Later he displayed a first-hand knowledge of the flood patterns of the Cowichan River, so he may have surveyed there, perhaps with a government party.[3] His fellow passenger William Lomas settled at Cowichan in February 1863. Drabble may have settled briefly there, but the sources are silent.

The news of Louisa Drabble's death on 31 July 1863 would have reached him two or three months later. One would like to think he returned to England to be with his children, but this was not the case. He was in Victoria in September 1863 when he bought a dog from a man named William Smith, and the following April he was present at a curious case involving the ownership of the same dog. According to Drabble's daughter, Sophie (who lived until 1956), at about this time Drabble borrowed money from his father-in-law, Matthew Burnby. Sophie told a family member that Burnby had "lent monies to George to start up in the New World with the proviso that monies would come back to the children, but according to Aunt Sophie, little did."[4]

Drabble first appears in the Comox sources in June 1864 in connection with the government survey of the Comox Valley. William Ralph and his party established a base line and surveyed lots. Settlers had complained of the lack of an accurate survey; they could not tell if their buildings were even on their own land. Drabble's name appears on the front cover of Ralph's field notes at the Surveyor General's Branch, and Drabble had his own copy of Ralph's survey, which he occasionally consulted.[5]

Drabble's name next appears a few weeks later, in July, when he applied for a vacant 100 acre pre-emption—Section 29 on the 100 acres of Land in 26 × 29 north bank of Portuguese Creek. (See map 4.) "I shall be obliged," he wrote to the Surveyor General, "by your requesting for me 100 acres of Land in Comax lately pre-empted by Mr. Harney—& now vacant." However, three months later, in October, the Comox Land Recorder James Robb notified the Lands and Works Department that Drabble was "leaving the district," and Drabble subsequently sold his claim to Section 29 to Robert Ritchie. Drabble left Comox because he got work in Nanaimo as a farm bailiff.[6]

[3] See Drabble to F. G. Vernon, CCL&W, 8 December 1875, *British Columbia Sessional Papers* (1877), p. 532.

[4] BCARS C/AA/30.3N/23. Beryl MacNeill to Clare McMillan, 4 August 1994.

[5] John Booth Good to Douglas, 23 September 1863 and Pemberton to Ralph, April 1864, Colonial Correspondence; William Ralph, "Field Book of the Survey of Comox," env. 49, Drabble Papers.

[6] Drabble to Surveyor General, July 1864; R. C. Coleman to Surveyor General, 24 September 1867, British Columbia, Department of Lands and Works, Vancouver Island

Drabble is next found in March 1865, when he and 150 other Nanaimoites signed a petition addressed to Vancouver Island Governor Arthur Kennedy asking that the old Hudson's Bay Company bastion be used no longer as a jail. Among the petitioners was Drabble's future Comox business partner Joe Rodello. "During four or five nights of the past week," the petitioners wrote, "in one of which the thermometer stood 33 degrees below freezing point, two white men and a sick Indian were locked up in the bastion, which is quite open to the weather."[7]

Two months later, in May, Drabble appears as the manager of a large farm near Nanaimo belonging to Judge William Hales Franklyn. Born in Kent, England, in 1816, Franklyn had captained a steam transport during the Crimean War and in 1860 had been appointed Stipendary Magistrate at Nanaimo. Franklyn enjoyed the rural life at his Nanaimo farm named "Cobtree." In May 1865, he prepared a "statement of the Settlers & of the Farming operations in and around Nanaimo." Such farms supplied produce to the Nanaimo miners and their families. Franklyn listed "Drabbles" as manager of his own farm. Cobtree possessed 300 acres capable of cultivation, 100 acres of pasturage and hay land, fifty acres under fence, and forty acres actually under cultivation—of which seventeen acres were devoted to oats and the rest to turnips, "sweedes," wheat, peas, potatoes, and "tares" (beans). Cobtree boasted sixty-seven head of cattle, forty pigs, thirty-five sheep, eight work oxen, and five horses, as well as a barn and five dwellings or outhouses. The whole operation was run by Drabble, five permanent labourers, and a number of casual workers.[8]

The position of farm manager gave Drabble the opportunity to do some surveying and road construction. In July 1865 the *Nanaimo Gazette* reported that "Mr. Drabbles, foreman at the farm of Captain Franklyn, J.P., has made a road from Prospect Bay to the farm, a distance of several miles, with his own farm labourers. He has as fine a carriage on the road as we have seen anywhere in the colony." Drabble's friends must have been confused as to his wherabouts, for in June 1865 there were two "unpicked up letters" for him at the post office in Victoria.[9]

Although he had sold title to his pre-emption to Ritchie, he maintained his connection with Comox, and when Franklyn left Nanaimo to

Pre-emptions, 1861-1885; Richard Hurford, "Old Ms. Record Book of Land Sales in the Comox District," British Columbia, Department of Lands and Works, Comox Land Registers, 1862-1933 (hereafter "British Columbia, Comox Land Registers").

[7] Victoria *Colonist*, 20 March 1865, p. 2.

[8] Franklyn to Henry Wakeford, 17 August 1864; Franklyn to Colonial Secretary, 27 May 1865, 8 June 1865, Colonial Correspondence.

[9] *Nanaimo Gazette*, 17 July 1865, p. 2; *Vancouver Times*, 15 and 23 June 1865, p. 3.

become Chief Civil Commissioner of the Seychelles Islands, Drabble returned to Comox for good. "Drabbles called," Mary Harmston wrote in her diary on 23 April 1866.[10]

∽

Drabble, like the other early settlers, was struggling to find his feet in a rural economy. A powerful agrarian ethos was at work. English views on the value of farming were transplanted to the colony and took on a new relevance during the gold rushes, when politicians extolled the virtues of a sedentary farming life. Farmers were to be in the vanguard of settlement. "Get settlers into British Columbia," the *British Colonist* editorialized in 1860, "and they will raise provisions, make roads, and generally develope [*sic*] the resources of the country." In 1862, publicist Edward Mallandaine wrote that wild land "tenanted only by the bear, the wolf and deer" had no value, but land "obtained gratuitously by industrious men" and made to produce the fruits of the earth was not only valuable but enhanced the value of the land around it.[11] Indeed, in this strange new colony—peopled by Indians who lived largely on the resources of the sea—the soil offered a familiar link with the past and a comfortable vision of existence.

Vancouver Island settlers were guided by liberal new pre-emption laws. In September 1862 the government passed the Vancouver Island Land Proclamation, which replaced all previous land acts and set forth the conditions under which Crown lands could be pre-empted: that is, occupied and improved in advance of survey and ownership. Applicants had to be British subjects or aliens who had sworn the oath of allegiance. A single man could claim 100 acres. A married man whose wife was resident in the colony could claim 150 acres, and he could claim an extra ten acres for every child under the age of eighteen—a clause that accounts for the irregular rectangular shapes of Comox pre-emptions. The claimant had to place posts at the four corners of his claim ("stake a claim") and send a description and a rough sketch of the land to the Surveyor General or local Land Recorder. After two years' permanent occupation, the applicant was entitled to purchase the claim for the miminal sum of $1 an acre, at which time he would receive a Crown Grant to the land.

The act stipulated that the applicant had to register his claim with the Land Recorder within thirty days of occupation. It also stipulated

---

[10] Harmston Diary, 23 April 1866.

[11] *The Weekly British Colonist,* 14 January 1860; Edward Mallandaine, *First Victoria Directory comprising a general directory of Citizens* (Victoria: Hibben and Carswell and Herre, 1860), p. 15. I owe these references to Ruth Sandwell.

that the claimant was entitled to sell, mortgage, or lease the claim before he had received the Crown Grant, but that if he were absent from the claim for more than two months, the Land Recorder could revoke the claim.[12]

Commentators were prone to overstate the quality and potential of agricultural land on Vancouver Island, but there was a decided opinion that what good land existed should be put to the plough—and in Comox there was plenty. British colonists had come from a country where land ownership was a privilege enjoyed by a very small elite, and they needed little convincing that farming was superior to gold-mining.[13]

The first farmers of Comox felt their isolation and asked for assistance with roads, mail service, and cattle. In January 1863, thirteen settlers petitioned the colonial government for a shipment of seeds and cattle. Comox, they wrote, had been "a wild waste undisturbed by aught but the howl of the wild Beasts or the formal tread of the Deer and Elk" until a few months previously. They wanted to transform the settlement into "a fertile Valley teeming with gladness, the permanent and happy home of the sturdy farmer," and they asked in their Dickensian language for some sort of outside communication:

> As a voyage to this place in the spring time of the year in those small sailing vessels is very precarious as well as expensive, and as many of the settlers here are of limited means having only enough to make an humble beginning, if they had a cheap and safe mode of obtaining a yoke of Oxen, a plough and a few seeds, they may become cultivators of the soil instead of wanderers in the Gold regions of Cariboo.[14]

In April a correspondent complained to the *Colonist* that great discontent prevailed among the residents "about the apathy which the Government has displayed towards them in not affording mail communication with this City. For several months during the winter the people have been shut up there without receiving any letters or papers, and some of the inhabitants are so thoroughly disgusted with the treatment, that they are thinking of leaving the place altogether." In response to these complaints and requests, the government sent the steamer *Emily Harris* with a load of Shorthorn Durham cattle from the Cloverdale

---

[12] *A Collection of Public General Statutes of the Colony of Vancouver Island, Passed in the Years 1859, 1860, 1861, 1862, and 1863* (Victoria: British Colonist Office, 1866), pp. 201-08.

[13] "The curse on British Columbia used to be that it had too many miners and not enough farmers." Lowry, *October Ferry to Gabriola*, p. 201.

[14] Petition of 23 January 1863 to Governor Douglas, reproduced in *From Shetland to Vancouver Island*, pp. 110-11.

Farm of William Fraser Tolmie. "She came as close as possible to the Indian village," Duncan wrote, "and there the cattle were dumped overboard and steered to the beach by canoes."[15]

Who were the first colonists of Comox, the people with whom Drabble threw in his lot, and how successful were their farms? At the beginning of December 1863 the thirty-three settlers of Comox had pre-empted almost 4,000 acres, but they had placed only forty-nine acres under cultivation and fenced a further sixty-three acres. They had also built twenty-four log houses and nine barns worth a total of $4,900.[16]

One visitor has left a sharp analysis of the early settlement. In August 1864, naturalist Robert Brown toured the new colonial settlements on the Gulf. While praising the Comox Valley for its fine land, he observed the settlers' poverty and their lack of enthusiasm and knowledge of farming. He blamed the gold rush for attracting the wrong sort of immigrant to the Colony. "The Settlers of Comoucs are in general a more enterprizing set than the Cowichan or Chemanus farmers, but still I notice the same apathy and fear of going into things too heavily. The same fear of the Country 'caving in' and all alike afflicted with the 'fearful crime' of poverty."[17]

"I cannot help noticing," he continued, "the want of confidence in the stability of the Colony manifested by most of the settlers and a 'Waiting for something to turn up' Micawber sort of disposition." (Micawber was a figure in Charles Dickens' *Great Expectations* who teetered on the brink of poverty, while always remaining optimistic in his unworkable schemes). Most of the settlers north of Victoria wanted only "a log shanty, a pig, a potato patch, Kloochman and a clam bed!" And Brown—the son of a farmer—continued:

> This is easily accounted for, most of the Settlers being either men with no business & totally unacquainted with farming: Men who came here attracted by the gold-fever & got their eyes jaundiced by the Cariboo failures, prodigal sons who are just waiting to get reconciled to their families, or to go home having mistaken their vocation. The few who have been really bred to farming are the men who are doing most, but the country is new and it is wrong to compare it with old established Colonies.[18]

The settlers seemed to attract almost as much interest as the valley itself. They were worldly, experienced, green, impoverished—depend-

---

[15] *British Colonist*, 2 April 1863; Duncan in *Comox Argus*, 3 August 1933; Flora McDonald, "Second Prize Article," Union *Weekly News*, 28 September 1897, p. 1.

[16] Pearse to Colonial Secretary, 12 January 1864, Herald Street Collection.

[17] Hayman, *Robert Brown*, p. 121.

[18] *Ibid.*, p. 122.

ing on who you look at and when. Some of them shared a common past in the gold fields of Australia and British Columbia; others a common past in the estates and drawing rooms of England. They were a microcosm of British society. Some had come from English universities; some from factories in the English midlands; some from dirt-floor cottages in the Shetland Islands. They came from almost every county in England and Scotland. The first "Canadians" to discover Comox were adventurous Maritimers who arrived in the 1870s, and it took the completion of the Canadian Pacific Railway to bring any numbers of Ontarians to the valley.

In the 1920s, Eric Duncan embarked on his memoirs after reading a newspaper article stating that the "pioneers" of the Comox Valley had come from the Maritimes. Duncan was offended at this perversion of historical reality. "As far as I could gather," he rebutted, "the only Eastern Canadian among them was Charles Bridges, an Ontario man." Most settlers were English, "with a sprinkling of Scotch and Irish."[19] Duncan was right: the settlement of the valley took place in a colonial and Imperial rather than a narrowly Canadian context: far from being a Canadian colony, Vancouver Island was part of a larger Pacific and Imperial world. Duncan noted that ten of the 1862 settlers had been in the Australian gold rushes: Scotsmen William Duncan, Alexander Brown, John Wilson, and Robert Ritchie; Irishmen John Fitzgerald, Adam McKelvey, and James Clarke; Englishmen Charles Green and George Ford, and Salven Gunderson, a Norwegian.

William Duncan, from the Shetland Islands, selected his land soon after Mitchell. His nephew Eric recalled that William, a sailor on an English vessel, had deserted in Australia, mined for gold there without profit, and finally settled on what Shetlanders called "the backside of America"—Vancouver Island. William was a stubborn bachelor, a litigious man who didn't let clumsy prose stop him from writing numerous letters of complaint to the government. "All I have to say," he wrote in 1879, "is that i was the first man that put in Peags in Comox to take a farm except one man that was living with the Indians i gave up gold Diging for to make my hom in Comox."[20]

A whole batch of relations followed William Duncan from the Shetlands, mainly in the 1870s: brothers Oliver and Robert, Oliver's wife Robina, nephews Eric, William, and Robert Duncan. Their cousins the Mansons also came. Other Scots were Alexander Brown, from Nairn; John Wilson, from the Scots borders; and Robert Ritchie, who had been

[19] Duncan, "Early Days and Early Settlers;" "Comox District Fifty Years Ago."
[20] *From Shetland to Vancouver Island*, p. 70; William Duncan to CCL&W, 6 January 1879, British Columbia, Department of Lands, Correspondence Inward.

a baker in Glasgow before going to Australia. The "Irish Australians" were John Fitzgerald, who was later joined by his Scots wife Anne and his Australian-born son Joe; Adam McKelvey, who was later joined by his son Stafford; and the eccentric James Clarke. The English were Charles Green from Berkshire, who had come up from Australia with William Duncan; Green's nephew Thomas Beckensell, and George Ford from Gloucestershire, "sailor and Australian."[21] A settler of unknown gold rush antecedents was "Portuguese Joe," who lived at the headwaters of Portuguese Creek. This was probably John Enos from the Azores, who moved to Nanoose in 1863.[22]

The second large group of settlers had come directly from Britain in 1862 and had never been to Australia. A few visited the Cariboo, but most went more or less directly to Comox after arriving from England. Some of the so-called "Twelve Apostles" were among this crowd, including Pidcock, Carwithen, Baily, James Rees, and Blaksley, most of them from the south of England. Others who came directly from Britain were James and Isabella Robb (from Aberdeen and London respectively) and, from the Midlands, William and Mary Harmston, and later their friends George Drabble and Sam Cliffe.

The gold miners included some real oddballs and eccentrics. "The British Isles beget bizarre sons," novelist Malcolm Lowry wrote, "and examples of her most fabulous were to be found in Canada." Take Irishman James Clarke, an 1862 arrival, whose "bachelor surroundings were of the roughest." Clarke's bushy hair and white, freckled skin reminded Eric Duncan of "Life in Death" in Coleridge's *Ancient Mariner*. He lived in a log hut, and his only kitchen utensils were a big spoon and a butcher knife.[23]

Take Henry Wilson Ross, an early arrival from Liverpool, who farmed on the Upper Road. He was, Duncan recalled, "of small stature, scarcely over five feet, with a great white beard, and the writer has a vivid remembrance of the queer figure perched astride of a huge ox, on the way to the Comox wharf for mail and supplies. Ross said he went home to his animals with the same pleasure that other men took in returning to their wives."[24]

---

[21] *From Shetland to Vancouver Island*, pp. 90, 93, 97, 98, 100, 101, 103, 105; Barbara Marriott, "The Duncans," and Mildred Haas, "The Fitzgeralds," in Isenor, "The Comox Valley."

[22] Eric Duncan, letter to Comox *Argus*, 7 April 1921; see also Walbran, *British Columbia Coast Names*, pp. 521-22; British Columbia, Department of Lands and Works, Vancouver Island Pre-emptions, 1861-1885.

[23] Lowry, *October Ferry to Gabriola*, p. 14; Duncan, "Comox District Fifty Years Ago;" "Early Days and Early Settlers in Comox Valley."

[24] Duncan, "Early Days and Early Settlers."

Take William Duncan who, his nephew Eric recalled, was a terrible cook. His bread was his crowning atrocity. All he used was flour and sodium bicarbonate, and "his loaves were the size and shape of half a brick, and pretty nearly as solid. Even my strong young teeth got stuck in them. They were like hard rubber on the outside, and the inside soft and raw." "William Duncan is no cook," another settler concluded, "makes poor bread—very poor bread—a man can't live on it." To combat his chronic heartburn, William drank sarsaparilla and American patent medicines, but he died on the Gulf in 1883 while taking a load of potatoes to Victoria. According to his doctor, John Ash, William was "A good man, spoiled by a bad, abused stomach."[25]

Prominent among the settlers were the well-educated sons, prodigal and otherwise, of middle and upper class families, whose careers resemble those in English fiction: Reginald Carwithen, Reginald Pidcock, Harry Blaksley, John Baily, William Musters, and Henry Maude. Baily settled at Comox in August 1862, but returned after about ten years to take over his father's business; later he became mayor of Glastonbury, Somerset, in the middle of Thomas Hardy's Wessex. When he married he gave his wife a ring made from a gold nugget from British Columbia.[26]

The immigration story of William Chaworth Musters (1839-1906) seems to have been plucked from a Victorian novel. Musters was the eldest son of Lady Chaworth and Rev. William Musters Musters, rector of Colwick and West Bridgford in Nottinghamshire. He arrived in Comox in about 1864, aged twenty-five, after resigning his commission in the 96th Foot Regiment. He had eloped with Lucy Byron, the daughter of a bricklayer from the town of Nottingham, and she had borne him a child. Rather than abandon her, he emigrated, and she joined him; they were married in July 1867 at Christ Church Cathedral, Victoria. They settled at Comox—the outer edge of settlement of the outermost British colony—where they had five more children. Lucy, who was a midwife, died of "child-birth fever" just seventeen days after her last child was born in August 1875. Musters then sold his land, auctioned his farm, stock, and possessions, and returned to England with his eldest five children.[27]

[25] *From Shetland to Vancouver Island*, pp. 139-40; 169-70.

[26] Margaret Biscoe, "John Baily, Pioneer of '62," [unidentified newspaper clipping, *c.* 1964], CDMA.

[27] W. R. Lewis, "William Chaworth-Musters," ms., 1995; Musters to Surveyor General, 17 August and October 1864, British Columbia, Department of Lands and Works, Vancouver Island Pre-emptions, 1861-1885; Elizabeth Forbes, *Wild Roses at their Feet: Pioneer Women of Vancouver Island* (Vancouver: Evergreen Press, 1971), p. 134; *From Shetland to Vancouver Island*, pp. 197-98.

Musters, with his large family and private fortune, was an exception. All but two of the 1862 settlers were single men, and most stayed that way.

The first two Englishwomen in Comox were Isabella Robb from London and Mary Harmston from Lincoln. Robb prided herself on being the "first white woman" in the settlement: Harmston, the diarist, was the second.[28] Robb, the matron of the brideship *Tynemouth*, arrived in 1862 in charge of "sixty marriagable lassies" and her own three children. After a few weeks in Victoria, she, her husband James, and her youngest daughter made the trip to Comox. "They made the journey in a sloop, and took with them their feather beds, a chest of drawers, a china tea set, two brass candlesticks, and some pewter pots." "The land was covered with forest down to the water's edge." At first they camped between the four walls of a small log cabin, using a large bedsheet as a roof.[29]

The Harmston story involved a bear and a barrel of molasses. The Harmstons and their daughter Florence came up the river on a rowboat after being delivered by a sailing ship. They unloaded their belongings on the shore and made numerous trips back. "On arriving back for their other supplies, they found that the bears had destroyed everything — some of the boxes had been pushed into the river." They rolled a barrel of molasses up the trail, but they got tired of shoving it along in front of them and left it, and every time they needed some molasses they'd go back for some. William Harmston planted an avenue of trees at his farm, known among the utilitarian settlers as "Harmston's Folly;" Robert Brown, however, considered that "It is rather a specimen of his good taste."[30]

Some settlers kept their land at Comox solely as a *pied à terre*; as a lodging for seasonal use when they were not at the gold mines — though they ran the risk of having their claims jumped if they were away for too long.[31] John Marwick, Patrick Murphy, James McNish, and Charles Fletcher, for instance, held their places in "The Swamp" in a partnership. "One of the four," Drabble recalled, "generally Murphy, kept the places while the other men hunted gold on the outside. These were the days of the Cariboo gold excitement, and miners were getting $10 a

[28] McDonald, "Second Prize Article."

[29] N. de Bertrand Lugrin, *The Pioneer Women of Vancouver Island* (Victoria: The Women's Canadian Club of Victoria, 1928), p. 156.

[30] Mildred Haas, "The Harmstons," in Isenor, "The Comox Valley;" Forbes, *Wild Roses*, pp. 125-26; interview with Phyllis Currie, 14 May 1994; Hayman, *Robert Brown*, p. 113.

[31] Hayman, *Robert Brown*, p. 152, n. 142.

day." Another old Australian miner who couldn't get gold out of his system was Salven "Oliver" Gunderson, who drowned in about 1868 in the Skeena River on his way to the Omineca gold fields to try and raise some capital.[32]

The old Australians had been wandering for years and longed for the sedentary, settled life some of them had left in Britain ten or fifteen years before. They appreciated the value of farming, even if at first their enthusiasm sometimes exceeded their experience. Poverty, isolation, and ignorance contributed to the valley's primitive farming character. William Beach—who had worked in an English factory as a boy—planted his first crop of onion multipliers upside down. They eventually grew just the same. Eric Duncan's father Robert had never seen a tree before getting off the boat in Victoria from the Shetlands, and neither of his uncles (William and Oliver) had handled an axe before coming to Vancouver Island: "To the last they cut their trees beaver-like, all round about."[33]

The most striking aspect of Comox in the 1860s was its maleness. Two Englishwomen were surrounded by forty-odd "bachelors" washed up from the gold regions of the world. Most were almost middle-aged, and if they were thinking of marriage they had come to the wrong place. The male-female ratio in the colony was severely skewed in favour of women. The brideship *Tynemouth* hardly made a dent in the problem. Colonial Vancouver Island was quite unlike the American western "frontier" where covered wagons containing nuclear families rolled westward to colonize a new land. The typical immigrant to Vancouver Island in the gold rush era was a somewhat hard-boiled single man aged anywhere from twenty to fifty years and chronically short of cash.[34]

One or two of the settlers (Drabble was certainly one) had left women or families behind somewhere; several of the younger ones (Carwithen, Pidcock, Guillod, Rees) married respectably in the next decade or so, but the Australians were content with their own company. So few settlers had children that a school was not organized until 1869, and according to Eric Duncan it had to be packed with "half-breed" children from Victoria to make up the required attendance of fifteen (Samuel Crawford, the schoolmaster, kept them on his farm). As late as

---

[32] Courtenay *Weekly News*, 11 January 1893, p. 1; Duncan in *Comox Argus*, 3 August 1933; *From Shetland to Vancouver Island*, p. 98; Hayman, *Robert Brown*, p. 113.

[33] Mildred Haas, "William Beech," in Isenor, "The Comox Valley;" Duncan, *From Shetland to Vancouver Island*, pp. 73, 179.

[34] For a differing view of the colonial sex ratio see John Douglas Belshaw, "Cradle to Grave: An Examination of Demographic Behaviour on two British Columbia Frontiers," *Journal of the Canadian Historical Association* 5 (1994), pp. 41-62.

October 1871, only ten of the sixty settlers had families,[35] and the first marriage in the valley was that of Florence Harmston and Sam Cliffe in 1872—a full ten years after the valley was settled, and eight years after the Anglicans built the log church.

Some of the early settlers lived with—and subsequently deserted—Native women. In August 1864 Robert Brown noted caustically that Native women were a good influence on their shiftless partners: "Three or four are married and several cohabit with native women who, it ought to be said to their credit, look closely to the interests of their 'husbands' & in more than one instance which I could mention have been the best Counsellors of their unworthy mates." A census of 1865 showed six settlers neither married nor single but "Cohabiting." One of them was James McNish, who staked a claim in December 1862. An oldtimer recollected that McNish, a very social man, had married an Indian woman out of sheer lonliness, but as "white" women arrived, "the inequality of his wife's position became more glaring, [and] he put aside his dusky mate and went east for a suitable bride." On his way home he died at San Francisco.[36]

Among those who married Native women were George Ford and Henry Horatio Maude. Both left the valley in early days to raise sheep on Hornby Island—safe from the predatory cougars and wolves that prowled the valley. Maude was a member of a prominent Devon family, "a connection of the late General Maude of Mesopotamia." Duncan recalled that both Ford and Maude married Indian women, and—he added significantly—"stuck by them." In 1870 Magistrate Spalding of Nanaimo gave up on trying to collect Maude's road tax, saying he was "merely existing with the assistance of an Indian woman and her Father on a part of Hornby Island more than twenty miles distant, he was to my own knowledge without a shilling."[37]

The early settlers experienced a high mortality rate, several of them meeting with a violent death. Their instability may have had something to do with their lack of female company, if surveyor Benjamin Pearse is believed. A frequent visitor to Comox in the 1860s, Pearse had no doubt that a lack of the "female influence" was to blame for the ills that afflicted these transient male colonists, and in 1900 he ventured that: "The ladies were then as now, charming, and many of them beautiful. One can trace the immense influence for good of the ladies, to those

---

35 *From Shetland to Vancouver Island*, p. 210; James Richardson's 1871-72 notebooks, copy in Buckham Collection.

36 Hayman, *Robert Brown*, p. 121; J. C. B. Cave, "Census," reproduced in Isenor, *Land of Plenty*, p. 64; Courtenay *Weekly News*, 11 January 1893, p. 1.

37 *From Shetland to Vancouver Island*, pp. 100-01; Murray, *Homesteads and Snug Harbours*, p. 173; Spalding to Colonial Secretary, 8 August 1870, Colonial Correspondence.

who submitted themselves to it; for those, alas! who shunned it, what can now be said?"[38]

George Mitchell and Henry Harrup were shot to death in drunken brawls; John Holder committed suicide in a fit of delerium tremens. William Brewster joined Waddington's road party in 1863 and was killed in the "Chilcotin Massacre." In August 1867 two settlers, Sydney Rennell and William Todd—who had been "residing in and about Comox since February last"—were drowned when their canoe capsized near Bute Inlet; Christopher Morley, a third member of the canoe, managed to swim to shore.[39] Settlers Henry Hargreave and William Harmston died from natural causes, as did road builder Miles Titus. With so many deaths through accident, murder, sickness, or suicide in less than a decade it is little wonder that Blaksley and Baily returned to England when they came into their inheritances.

The population of the valley in the gold rush years was highly transitory, and at first more people left than stayed. There was a high turnover rate of pre-emptions in the 1860s, caused by men dying, going home, returning to the gold fields, or finding work elsewhere in the colony. In the end, however, the constant buying and selling of pre-emptions selected for genuine farmers and productive farms. It was too early for Robert Brown to draw conclusions about the settlers' helplessness. In the 1860s and 1870s there was enough good land in the valley to support both an agrarian vision and a competent farming population.

[38] Benjamin William Pearse, "Early Settlement of Vancouver Island," BCARS.

[39] Courtenay *Weekly News*, 28 December 1892, p. 1; Spalding to Colonial Secretary, 13 August 1867, Colonial Correspondence.

CHAPTER 6

Land of Plenty

And down the lagging ages subtle brains
Have multiplied inventions numberless
Evil and good, but none to supercede
My trusty hoe.

FROM The Man with the Hoe, by Eric Duncan[1]

THE settlers' real concern, of course, was farming. The valley land was excellent. Robert Brown raved about its beauty and agricultural potential; he had "rarely or ever, even in England, seen more lovely situations for homes to men willing to go into their work with heart and spirit." Farms were capable of producing everything a farm could: "Monster potatoes, onions as large as Spanish ones, parsnips, wheat and oats full headed, and sound turnips, splendid butter & milk are productions of this most beautiful Valley."[2]

Land-clearing was the first task that faced the 1862 settlers. The lucky ones were those who pre-empted Indian settlements, like Robb and Ford; such places were clear, at least on the waterfront, possessed a fresh water supply, and underfoot contained an accumulated compost and fish midden which provided a rich soil for vegetable crops. (Indeed, so much salmon and fish oil were deposited that modern archaeologists excavating village sites find their hands and clothes covered with a deep black, organic, almost impenetrable oily sheen). James Robb's pre-emption, on what is now the Comox waterfront, included an Indian village site where Frederick Whymper and Robert Brown found a good vegetable garden in 1864. Isabella Robb apologized to Brown for having nothing better to offer than garden vegetables:

> "Mowich" (deer), she said, was scarce just now. Formerly there was "hyou" (plenty) but now the "Siwashes" (Indians) brought in little and wanted for that little *hyou chickamin* (plenty money). Mrs. Robb is an Englishwoman and

---

[1] Duncan, *The Rich Fisherman.*

[2] Hayman, *Robert Brown*, pp. 111, 120-21. On early farms see also Isenor, *Land of Plenty,* pp. 57-96.

69

of course with all a Britisher's contempt for savages, but like all others out here mixed in her conversation Indian Jargon. His [*sic*] garden is on the site of an Indian Village which must at one time have extended from here to where Mitchells' Farm house now stands.[3]

Other settlers had to start clearing right away, but this was straighforward in the "openings" of prairie land that extended seven or eight miles up the Tsolum and its tributaries. William Duncan's Section 17 at Sandwick was, in 1862, "nearly all good land; compared with a Shetland croft it was an estate. It was naturally open except for berry and rose bushes and a heavy growth of fern." Around the valley openings were clumps of Garry Oak and Douglas Fir, while along the river bottoms were strips of alder; the scenery was picturesque and park-like, as geologist James Richardson found. "The open country, in its natural state, is mostly covered with a growth of ferns, which sometimes attain a height of ten feet, with stems three quarters of an inch in diameter, and roots descending to a depth of three feet. These roots the native Indians prepare in some peculiar way for winter food, and excavate deep trenches to obtain them."[4]

Years later Eric Duncan wrote that the thickly matted fern roots made ploughing very difficult; "though, as they kept the soil loose and porous, enormous crops of splendid potatoes were raised in the early days, and even now it is claimed that Vancouver Island can beat the world in that line. I knew a man who for five years in succession raised ten tons to the acre on the same piece of land without manure; but it is only fair to add that it yielded him nothing but sorrel for a long time after." Some settlers simply fenced in their pigs and let them search for roots, thus more or less preparing the ground for a first crop of potatoes. Tillage, Drabble recalled, was "accomplished by the aid of hogs, which being fenced in upon a small tract of land would root and pulverize the soil so that either a crop of potatoes or oats could be grown with great success." Rounding up these half-wild pigs was no fun; indeed to the end of his life John Baily, Mayor of Glastonbury, carried a scar on his hand where a wild pig had bitten him. Another who specialized in hog-cultivation was 1862 settler William Beach. "In early days huge droves of swine helped with the ploughing," Duncan reflected, "and Beach never forgot that. He advised new-comers to get all the land they

[3] Whymper, "Journal," p. 18; Hayman, *Robert Brown*, pp. 111-12.

[4] James Richardson, "Report on the Coal Fields of the East Coast of Vancouver Island, with a Map of their Distribution," in Geological Survey of Canada, *Reports of Explorations and Surveys 1871-72* (Montreal: Dawson Brothers, 1872), pp. 73-100; 94-95; *From Shetland to Vancouver Island*, p. 76.

possibly could under crop, no matter how roughly: 'Scratch, or burn, or blacken the surface somehow, and throw in your seed.'"[5]

Most settlers put in a crop of potatoes immediately and afterwards attempted mixed farming, that is, a combination of arable and livestock farming. On his bottom land at the junction of Tsolum River and Portuguese Creek, Irishman Adam McKelvey grew potatoes "as big as yer fut." The Comox Indians, probably in the 1830s, had acquired the cultivation of potatoes from the Hudson's Bay Company at Fort Langley, and they became the mainstay of the early settlers and Indians alike.[6]

The Duncans were the main potato producers in the valley, supplying Native people, settlers, and later the Union mines with excellent tubers. Native women were prominent in the potato harvest at the Duncan farm, their standard pay for a day's work being a bucketful of potatoes worth about ten cents. Eric Duncan described the potato trade in 1878 at his uncle Oliver's farm on the bank of the Tsolum:

> His only hired help besides myself were Indian women to help in the potato harvest. Their tools were big clam shells or flat-pointed sticks, and half a dozen of them would come, marshalled by a man, who, as soon as he got them to work, would recline majestically in a fence corner on his blanket till near noon, when he would start a fire and cook a good supply of potatoes and salmon.

> He also saw that the women were properly paid at night, each getting a bucket of potatoes, though they often added a little to this by having some of their many skirts stitched together at the bottom, thus forming sacks into which they dropped on occasional extra large potato, for which they had a weakness, irrespective of quality. I often pitied these women on white frosty mornings when I saw how eager they were to get their broad, brown, bare feet on freshly turned soil.

Oliver Duncan, like other farmers, profited by selling these same potatoes back to Comox and Lekwiltok Indians in the winter:

> His chief customers were Indians, who came up the river in canoes to his barn, and they were not confined to the Comox tribe, for Euclatas from Valdes [Quadra] Island and Campbell River were also supplied. These were a hardier looking people. The Indian did not understand weighing, but he knew the bucket. An iron bucket would not do, though holding more. It had to be the little, round, painted wooden bucket of the Hudson's Bay Co.

---

[5] Duncan, "Vancouver Island," pp. 366-67; Courtenay *Weekly News*, 4 January 1893, p. 4; Margaret Biscoe, "John Baily, Pioneer of '62," unidentified newspaper clipping [1964], CDMA; *From Shetland to Vancouver Island*, pp. 107-08.

[6] Norcross and Tonkin, *Frontiers of Vancouver Island*, p. 43; Duncan, "The Autumn in Comox Valley," *The Daily Province*, 1934, in Newspaper Cuttings and Scrapbook; Duncan, *From Shetland to Vancouver Island*, p. 103.

The Indian was very helpful in filling this bucket, shaking it, and always piling a few extra potatoes on top. Then Oliver would stand up and say: "Potlatch Chickamin" ["Give Metal"], the Indian would hand over a quarter, and the bucket would be emptied into his basket. The basket when full was emptied into the canoe, and this process would go on till the canoe was loaded.[7]

Fine crops grew in this land of plenty. Oliver and Robina Duncan disposed of their Shetland-style gridiron when they learned how to bake wheat-bread in an oven. George Mitchell's cattle formed the original herd, and the shorthorn Durham cattle sent from Victoria in 1863 added to the valley stock. In 1864 Blaksley and Baily walked to Victoria to buy some young cattle, which they took back to Comox by boat. Cows, of course, meant milk and butter, and Mitchell produced both at his farm. Oxen did all the ploughing until the mid 1860s, when Musters brought the first horses.[8]

Chickens and geese, while desirable, were at first difficult to protect from predatory ravens and raccoons, but finally Liverpudlian Henry Ross mastered the technique and became the first regular poultry man in the valley. Pigs provided ham, pork, and bacon, but they were prey to cougars, and eventually the great number of unfenced feral pigs became a nuisance to the farmers. In 1869 the settlers petitioned Victoria for Comox to be made a "fence district," that is, a district with obligatory fencing of livestock, as Eric Duncan noted:

> These were mostly Yorkshires, and whole drives of them ran at large, marked like cattle (the law being that they must be fenced out), rooting up the roadsides, eating salmon from the rivers, and camping in the woods under trees, where they carried heaps of fern in their mouths to make their beds. Sometimes a herd of them would be penned on a patch of rough, stony land which they would turn over so effectively to get the fern roots that that it only needed harrowing to be fit for seed. When they were about a year old, several of them would be captured and fed for a month or so on milk, and with peas and potatoes boiled and mashed together. They were then ready for the market, which was entirely dependent on colliery Chinamen at Nanaimo, to whom they were shipped on foot and sold at six and seven cents a pound.[9]

---

[7] Courtenay *Weekly News*, 28 December 1892, p. 1; Ede Anfield, "Pioneer Woman Remains Remarkably Young at 94," *CVFP*, 18 April 1956; *From Shetland to Vancouver Island*, p. 154.

[8] Hayman, *Robert Brown*, p. 112; Whymper, "Journal," pp. 18, 25; *From Shetland to Vancouver Island*, p. 75; Blaksley to McQuillan, 12 July 1916, quoted in *Comox Argus*, 17 March 1921; Lugrin, *The Pioneer Women of Vancouver Island*, p. 159.

[9] Hayman, *Robert Brown*, p. 121; Duncan, "Early Days and Early Settlers;" H. P. P. Crease, "On Comox Settlers' Petition to be erected into a Fence District," 14 April 1869, in British Columbia, Attorney General, Correspondence 1864-1879; *From Shetland to Vancouver Island*, p. 134.

So many Comox Valley pigs reached Nanaimo that the valley became famous for them. In the 1870s Thomas Humphreys was elected M.L.A. for Comox even after referring to the settlers as "chaw-bacons."[10]

Cattle, oxen, and horses, of course, required winter feed, especially hay, which grew so abundantly in the meadows at the mouth of the Courtenay River that as early as 1864, farmers exported it to Victoria and Chemainus. Cattle required hay and other house feed from the end of November to the middle of April. In 1873 there were only three mowers in the valley, and most farmers cut their hay with scythes. At the Duncan farm all the haying was scythe-work, and Oliver, Robina, and Eric Duncan went from haycock to haycock loading them onto a flat cart drawn by an ox.[11]

By 1870 the valley possessed some fine farms. George McFarlan, for example, bought and amalgamated three farms that had belonged to Cariboo gold miners Fletcher, McNish, and Murphy on "the swamp"— the flats where the Tsolum flooded every winter. McFarlan's 450-acre farm became the Urquhart and finally the Farquharson farm. When geologist James Richardson visited in October 1871 he recorded that McFarlan's oats produced 2,000 pounds to the acre, barley from 2,500 to 3,000 pounds, peas 3,000 pounds, wheat 2,000 pounds. Two-and-a-half acres could produce five tons of hay or twelve tons of marketable potatoes. "Mr. McFarlande says the potatoes litterley [*sic*] cover the ground, he has got 60 to 65 good sized marketable potatoes from one stalk." McFarlan grew turnips for his fifty head of cattle and horses, and his eight cows gave an average yield of 150 pounds of butter a cow a year. "Fruit of all kinds thrive remarkably well such as Pears, Apples, Cherries, Plums, Raspberries, Red & black Current."[12]

Despite the abundance, settlers' lives were marked by isolation and simplicity. "They kept close to the land and lived from it," Duncan recalled, and he described the rough, almost peasant-like, clothing worn by the settlers:

> The standard in men's working garb in the seventies was brown canvas or blue denim, and underwear was immaterial. There were no factory-made underwear nor mackinaws, and no money to buy them if there had been. In a bitter January a strip of Hudson Bay blanket folded into the shape and size of

[10] Reksten, *The Dunsmuir Saga*, p. 79.

[11] Hayman, *Robert Brown*, pp. 121, 152, n. 141; Richardson's 1871-72 notebooks; *The Daily Standard*, 27 May 1873, p. 3; *From Shetland to Vancouver Island*, p. 149.

[12] Duncan, "Early Days and Early Settlers;" Richardson's 1871-72 notebooks. See also Richardson, "Report on the Coal Fields of the East Coast of Vancouver Island," pp. 73-100.

a grain sack, with the sides sewn up with sack twine, leaving armholes at the corners, and with a slit in the middle of the bottom to pass the head through, gave great comfort as an undershirt, while pieces of flour sacks often served for socks.

Women's and children's dresses were manufactured at home from print, gingham, wincey and flannel, bought by the yard, and they had woollen stockings and strong wide-heeled shoes.[13]

Some settlers lived in what was little more than poverty, as Michael Manson noted on his arrival from the Shetlands in October 1874. He was on his way to the wharf with his uncle, Oliver Duncan, when they passed an extraordinary woman:

> There were very few people in Comox at that time, but as we passed one farm the Wife of the Farmer who was out digging potatoes in the field saw us coming and having heard that I was on the way out she was anxious to see what I looked like so she came down to the road to see us. Her face had the appearance of not having been washed for a week, she had on a pair of long leather boots up to her knees, and what probably had been her husband's wedding coat, a black dress coat less one of the tails which apparently had been torn off, so that on the whole she would have made a very good scare crow.[14]

The first settlers had no horses, no wagons, and very rudimentary roads; to get their goods to and from the harbour they dragged them over the ground in sleighs drawn by oxen. "Sleighs were the only vehicle used in the early days," Drabble recalled, "until one of the more enterprising settlers built a cart and sawed two immense wheels off a large spruce tree. This was the envy of all his neighbours until through wear and want of lubrication the scream of the envied vehicle suggested the idea that efforts should be made to secure something more modern in its mechanism and silent in its movements."[15]

In 1877, when Eric Duncan arrived, farming equipment was still as primitive as the lodging and clothing. "There were only two horse teams in the Valley, the rest being huge oxen. There were a few wagons and one buggy owned by the Hudson's Bay storekeeper; but most of the vehicles were home-made carts, and sleighs, or drags. Ploughs were the wooden ox-ploughs with wheels, long beams and short stilts, and all the harrows were home-made except the teeth."[16]

---

[13] Duncan, "Winter in Comox Valley," *The Daily Province*, 1930 or 31, Newspaper Cuttings and Scrapbook.

[14] *From Shetland to Vancouver Island*, p. 154; Michael Manson, "Sketches from the Life of Michael Manson," pp. 2-3.

[15] Courtenay *Weekly News*, 4 January 1893, p. 4.

[16] *From Shetland to Vancouver Island*, p. 133.

Predatory animals and distance from market were the two main problems confronting this farming oasis. Wolves and cougars drove settlers like Maude and Ford to Hornby Island. Packs of wolves ranged openly across the Comox prairies in early days, and—Drabble recalled—they pursued the only donkey ever sent to the settlement, eating him for lunch "exactly at noonday." Eric Duncan noted, interestingly, that wolves howled and played with the settlers' dogs.[17]

Cougars, known as panthers on Vancouver Island until well into the twentieth century, were a greater problem, for they hunted alone and silently and preyed at random on most livestock and household cats and dogs. One of the earliest cougar references dates from July 1867, when William Harmston wrote in his diary: "Self & MacFarlane killed a *panther* on the 4th—great excitement." A well-known cougar story concerned Shetlander Robina Duncan. She was a "tiny woman with a brave spirit," Margaret Biscoe recalled; "We often heard the story of her finding a panther holding a pig and of her order 'Drop that pig!' The panther obeyed and fled." Eric Duncan recorded the story as follows:

> One day my aunt, hoeing potatoes in a field, was puzzled by the persistent squealing of a small pig in the bush alongside. Climbing the fence, she went towards the sound, and saw a cougar sitting on his haunches holding up the pig to his mouth like a squirrel with a fir cone. She advanced, waving her hoe and calling out, as she would have done to a fence-breaking cow, and the surprised brute dropped his prey and slunk off. The pig, though badly mauled, survived.[18]

Cougars could be controlled by baiting a deer carcass with strychnine, and the head earned a bounty. Wild pigs fought running battles with the big cats. "Cougars killed calves and carried off small pigs," Duncan recalled, "but they could only do this in the absence of the parents, for both cows and sows could be trusted to defend their progeny." Cougars descend to the valley farms to this day.[19]

Good land without accessible markets, of course, got the farmers nowhere, and until Robert Dunsmuir opened the Union Mine in 1888, the only way to dispose of Comox farm produce was by shipment to Nanaimo or Victoria. In the 1860s farmers sent butter and eggs to merchants in Victoria by the infrequent vessels servicing the settlement, and in exchange received finished goods such as ploughs. In June 1864 a Comox farmer (probably George Mitchell) sent a hundred pounds of

---

[17] Courtenay *Weekly News*, 8 February 1893, p. 1; Hayman, *Robert Brown*, p. 121; *From Shetland to Vancouver Island*, p. 133.

[18] Harmston Diary, 4 July 1867; Margaret Biscoe, "Mrs. Oliver Duncan," in Isenor, "The Comox Valley;" *From Shetland to Vancouver Island*, p. 135.

[19] *From Shetland to Vancouver Island*, p. 133.

butter, put up in kegs, to Victoria, and in May 1867 Mary and William Harmston sent forty-two pounds of butter and twenty-two dozen eggs to a Victoria merchant.[20]

The Duncans sent two-pound rolls of butter to Nanaimo and Victoria, but such exports were not without their problems. "One Victoria dealer said that, if he was in the oil business, he might handle it for axle grease," Eric Duncan recalled; "Cold storage was unknown and a bachelor farmer who sent down a consignment got it back a month later in poor condition. He tried to restore it by melting it over, and I saw a coal oil canful which had been thus treated, but the treatment was hardly a success."[21]

Another problem was that farmers who sent produce to Victoria or Nanaimo by the infrequent steamer had to take whatever payment the buyers at the other end could offer, and they had to pay freight charges. Buyers picked up Comox produce at the wharves in Nanaimo or Victoria and sold it for what it would fetch. Captain William Raymond Clarke of the *Douglas* was involved with this. William and Oliver Duncan got tired of consigning their goods to this uncertain market, and in 1866 William rented a house in Victoria and spent the winter there selling foodstuff sent down to him by Oliver. "But when spring came and William returned," his nephew recalled, "he brought no money, for all profits had gone in defraying expenses, and he said that, after all, farm life was best, as things grew while you slept."[22]

Comox farmers complained of the amount of cheap American produce available in the colony. The bulk of the flour and feed came from Oregon, often by sailing vessel, while many other grains came from San Fransisco. Ships from Puget Sound and the Columbia River flooded the island with produce, and Vancouver Island farmers campaigned for a tariff on such imports. "American produce from Puget Sound more than competes with them," Brown wrote in 1864:

> They complain sadly of the want of a market for their produce, the non-tariff on imported produce working most disastrously to the interests of the island farmers—the farmer having all uphill work, having to compete with our neighbours in Puget Sound, California & the already cleared and settled up farms, the cheaper rate of most necessaries of life, & the better access to a market.[23]

---

[20] Duncan, [Draft Description and History of the Comox Valley]; Harmston Diary, 24 December 1865, 22 April and 29 May 1867; *British Colonist*, 14 June 1864, quoted in Hayman, *Robert Brown*, p. 152, n. 141.

[21] *From Shetland to Vancouver Island*, p. 152; "Comox District Fifty Years Ago."

[22] *From Shetland to Vancouver Island*, p. 71-72.

[23] Duncan, "Comox District Fifty Years Ago;" Hayman, *Robert Brown*, pp. 113, 121-22.

Indeed, the "tariff question" remained a major political issue in British Columbia right through the 1860s and up to union with Canada.[24]

There were other problems. Communication with Victoria and Nanaimo in the 1860s was scant and irregular. Settlers were connected with the outside world by means of Indian canoes and occasional ships, the most regular of which were the Victoria-based steamer *Emily Harris*, Captain Chambers, and the sloop *Alarm*, Captain Kendall, which carried letters, goods, and passengers. In the mid 1860s the government steamer *Sir James Douglas* started monthly visits to Comox, and this vessel remained the settlement's lifeline into the 1870s. Captain of the *Douglas* was William Clarke, formerly chief gunner of H.M.S. *Forward*. He carried mails, merchandise, and passengers to Comox, and in return took livestock and farm produce to Nanaimo and Victoria. Comox did not yet have a wharf, so the *Douglas* anchored in the bay and unloaded goods and passengers into canoes. Because the water was shallow for some distance from shore, the Comox Indians carried the passengers on their backs to high ground. In about 1870 the *Douglas* began fortnightly visits to Comox.[25]

These vessels provided goods to the three merchants of Comox. English-born John ("Jack") Hart ran a store near the Indian Reserve and brothers Charles and William Burrage, also from England, started another store nearby. Hart sold liquor but the Burrages did not. They supplied the settlers with goods and also carried on a very considerable trade with the Comox and Lekwiltok Indians. During the winter, Brown wrote, "they sometimes trade tons of deers hides alone and Burrage is said on one occasion to have sold 3 tons of flour to the Indians in as many days." All three merchants were active by the fall of 1863.[26]

Jack Hart kept a bar at his waterfront shack, and the liquor he dispensed caused numerous fights and several deaths. In December 1864 Captain Franklyn wrote that Hart had been "notorious as a Whiskey seller, to both Whites, and Indians, for several years past; in 1858 in the Fraser River, and in 1862 at Stikeen, where the Miners threatened to hang him if he did not desist, in consequence of the danger of allowing the Indians to become intoxicated." Hart's store

24 Daniel Marshall cited in Sandwell, "Peasants on the Coast," p. 5, n. 12.

25 Duncan, "Early Days and Early Settlers;" *From Shetland to Vancouver Island*, p. 166; [Draft Description and History of the Comox Valley]; Courtenay *Weekly News*, 28 December 1892, p. 1; McDonald, "Second Prize Article;" *Colonist*, 21 January 1951, pp. 11-12; Crawford, "First Prize Article," p. 1; B. W. Pearse, "Public Notice" about steamer, Colonial Correspondence; Courtenay *Weekly News*, 28 December 1892, p. 1. On shipping see also Murray, *Homesteads and Snug Harbours*, pp. 180-86 and *Land of Plenty*, p. 377.

26 Courtenay *Weekly News*, 4 January 1893, p. 4; Hayman, *Robert Brown*, p. 112.

at Comox was within fifty yards of the Indian Reserve, and here he and his partner John Holder, also an Englishman, sold ale by the case and beer by the keg. In December 1864 Franklyn fined Hart about $600 for allowing whiskey from his store to be consumed on the Indian Reserve.[27]

Four violent incidents occured between 1866 and 1868, all of them stemming from liquor bought from Hart and Holder. Three of them resulted in death. In the first, in December 1866, a Comox Indian named Horne was injured by one Malkamalis. Horne gave a deposition at Nanaimo via interpreter John Sabiston. "On or about the 21," Horne stated, "we were having a feast at the house of 'Looking Glass' we were drinking, I took one glass and refused to take more, Looking Glass, Malkamalis Tom and his Clootchman, began to quarrel with me, Malkamalis bit part of my nose off, I then got away, Looking Glass got the liquor from John Holder at Harts whisky store, I then came down to tell the Tyhee."[28] The second incident occurred only ten days later, on 31 December 1866, when John Holder mortally wounded Henry Harrup, a Comox settler of 1862. Three weeks later, shortly before he died in hospital in Victoria, Harrup gave the following deposition to Judge Augustus Pemberton, adding that "I am aware that there is no chance of my recovery:"

> On monday night the thirty-first of December last I went over to John Holder's house at Comox in the Colony aforesaid to relieve a man named Charlie Coulter who was attending to Holder who was suffering from delerium the effect of drinking, when I saw Holder he had an iron bar which he flourished about, and said some body was trying to get into the house, he afterwards took a revolver and commenced firing the barrels off at random the last one he fired off at me and the bullet entered my left side at the same time he said "I have one barrel left for you" or words to that effect; I laid down under the counter and Holder threw some blankets on me, he continued firing a musket off in the house during the night.

> I have never quarrelled with Holder, I do not think he bore me enmity, I believe he was perfectly delerious at the time he shot me; I told Coulter to go and fetch Mr. Robb he sent some Indians for him and he Robb found me bleeding in the house.

After Harrup's death an inquest was held, at which Charles Coulter, Holder's neighbour, stated that he had taken care of Holder for two or three days before he shot Harrup. Holder "had the horrors, he acted as

---

27 *From Shetland to Vancouver Island*, pp. 95-96; Courtenay *Weekly News*, 4 January 1893, p. 4; Franklyn to Colonial Secretary, 13 December 1864, and petition *c.* February 1865, Colonial Correspondence; British Columbia, Attorney General, Documents, 1857-1966; Hayman, *Robert Brown*, p. 112.

28 Franklyn to Colonial Secretary, 31 December 1866.

78

though he was not in his right senses, he had been drinking very freely." His hands trembled when he tried to touch things, and after he shot Harrup he asked Coulter, "what woman was that lying there?" The jury's verdict was "Guilty of manslaughter whilst in a state of temporary insanity."[29]

The third incident, in October 1867, concerned the death of George Mitchell, formerly a blacksmith at Fort Rupert and Nanaimo, and the last remaining settler of 1861. At the Nanaimo inquest, Mitchell's partner Mary, a Native woman, stated that she had lived with him for about twenty years and that he was a "great drunkard." His friend Peter McClusky, formerly a labourer with the Hudson's Bay Company, stated that he had known Mitchell for twelve or thirteen years, and that Mitchell had been drunk on alcohol bought from Hart and Holder. In a drunken craze and unprovoked, Mitchell had levelled his gun and fired three shots at close range at an Indian named Peter; all the shots had missed, but Peter fired back and critically wounded Mitchell, who died in a canoe while being taken to Nanaimo for medical treatment. The court concluded that Peter had fired in self-defence and he was released, and lived for many years at Comox.[30]

The fourth incident happened in July 1868 when John Holder—having been released from jail in Victoria for killing Harrup—drowned himself in a fit of *delerium tremens* on the beach in front of Hart's store. Holder took his clothes off and remained outside for much of the day, talking to himself. In the evening, after much urging, Hart got him to return to the cabin. "He was sitting on his bed for about 10 Minutes," Hart wrote, "when he began to dress himself, he said, there were a Man burning in the bush and he is going to help him out, I was laing in bed reading until I fell asleep." At seven a.m. Hart was having breakfast when "I looked out and saw from the distant a blue shirt which I recognized as Holder's, I went to the spot and found the deceased laying with his fase in the water, as the tide just run out." Hart found a suicide note from Holder addressed cryptically to "Dear ever for with me," in which he confessed that he had been "continually in Broils and took drink killed Indian at Comox and more."[31]

Such a place needed a church. Between 1862 and 1864 Comox was visited occasionally by the Anglican rector of St. Paul's, Nanaimo, Rev. John Booth Good, and by his catechist J. C. B. Cave, and in fall of 1864

---

[29] British Columbia, Attorney General, Documents, 1857-1966.

[30] Spalding to Colonial Secretary, 25 May 1868, Colonial Correspondence; see also British Columbia, Attorney General, Record Book for the Nanaimo Coroner's Office, 1866-1905; Crawford, "First Prize Article;" Courtenay *Weekly News*, 28 December 1892, p. 1.

[31] Spalding to Colonial Secretary, 8 August 1868, Colonial Correspondence.

the settlers organized a bee and built a log church at Pidcock's Landing on Section 17. Blaksley, Carwithen, Pidcock, Baily, William Harmston, William Duncan, Musters, Beach, and William Machin helped build the church and a two-roomed "little log shanty" that served as Cave's parsonage.

Cave served at Comox as a layman until 1867, when he left to be ordained a deacon. Farmer James Rees, born in Wales and educated at Oxford for the Anglican ministry, preached occasionally, as did visiting Nanaimo clergy and lay readers until 1871, when former Roman Catholic priest Rev. Jules Xavier Willemar became the first permanent Anglican minister at Comox. Willemar found the log church in a state of great disrepair. "Ferns grow between the boards of the floor," he reported; "cobwebs are seen everywhere; the windows are wanting at least half-a-dozen panes of glass, and there are so many apertures that it would be nearly as good to have service in the open air, and it is scarcely worth repairing." Instead of tearing it down, however, Willemar fixed it up, and it was finally replaced in 1877 with the present St. Andrew's Church.[32]

Most settlers came not to shoot each other at the "whisky shops" on the waterfront but to shoot deer, elk, and geese, and of course to farm in the Tsolum River valley behind. The 1862 settlers had little in the way of livestock, so they relied on local supplies of deer, salmon, and wildfowl, some of it traded from Indians and some procured by themselves. Early settlers were uniformly impressed by the abundance of this "Land of Plenty." John Booth Good recollected "the ample provision which we had soon spread out on the natural table of the wilderness" during his 1864 visit, and Eric Duncan contrasted the poverty and greyness of the Shetlands with "Nature's wild profusion, broadly sown" that he found in the Comox Valley.[33]

Subsistence was the concern of Pidcock's "Adventures in Vancouver Island," subtitled "Being an Account of 6 years residence, and of hunting & fishing excursions" (1868). Young sportsmen like Pidcock, Drabble, and Blaksley hunted for subsistence at Comox, but they were also aware that hunting of any kind was a privilege enjoyed by very few in Britain, where most outdoor sports were restricted to landowners and their friends. Severe penalties against poaching kept the masses at bay. Even privileged immigrants like Blaksley, Carwithen, and Pidcock, com-

---

[32] *Courtenay Weekly News*, 4 January 1893, p. 4, 8 November 1893, p. 1, 22 November 1893, p. 1; Hayman, *Robert Brown*, p. 112; John Booth Good, "The Utmost Bounds of the West," ms., BCARS; Blaksley to McQuillan, 21 September 1919, quoted in *Comox Argus*, 17 March 1921; Bill Newman, "The Reverend Jules Xavier Willemar;" Mildred Haas, "James Rees 1842-1908," in Isenor, "The Comox Valley."

[33] Good, "The Utmost Bounds of the West," pp. 24-25; Duncan, *The Rich Fisherman*, p. 7.

ing from the upper middle class, had only limited access to hunting, shooting, and fishing; none of them came from the mainstream landed gentry or aristocracy. They may have had relations and friends with country estates, or they may themselves have rented a stretch of river for a week or two of fishing a year. In Comox, these settlers had their first real opportunity to hunt and shoot to their hearts' content, and Pidcock recollected the ease with which he and Blaksley ("Fred") obtained wildfowl in the fall of 1862:

> Soon after we arrived at Comox the wild fowl began to come in in great numbers. The Geese would fly in great flocks just at sundown not 10 yards over our heads & great was the execution Fred did amongst them. They were very fine birds in good condition & weighed from 9 to 14 lbs so that 4 or five of them were quite as much as a man cared to carry. The ducks of all kinds were in myriads & afforded excellent sport especially when it was blowing pretty fresh out at sea as it drove them inland.[34]

The number of deer was almost incredible for such a small expanse of country, Pidcock continued: "When the fern began to die away they began coming out on the Prairie in small herds and were very easily shot." Both in the Cariboo and on Vancouver Island, Pidcock met Canadians who condescended to him because he was young and English and supposedly green. Pidcock put them in their place with his superior ability with rifle and shotgun. At Comox he encountered a "Canadian Englishman," "a gentleman by birth & education," who despite his many years in Canada and regular boasting of his hunting prowess simply could not shoot a deer or a duck. He fired at many but never hit one—though he claimed he had wounded several.[35]

Elk habitat was a few miles up the river at the "little prairies" or "elk patches" where Pidcock, Carwithen, Blaksley, Drabble, and others hunted. In 1862 the Comox Indians told them not to hunt at the elk patches, but settlers ignored them, as Pidcock recalled:

> The Indians said there were plenty of Elk at the head of the prairies but were very loath to show us where their haunts were so Fred & I determined to go ourselves. We first walked up a trail that ran up toward the head of the prairie till we came to the edge of the forest and we had gleaned from them that by following a stream up some little distance we should come upon some more land & that there we should in all probability see signs of Elk.[36]

◌◌

---

[34] Pidcock, "Adventures in Vancouver Island," pp. 74-75.

[35] *Ibid.*, pp. 69, 76-78.

[36] Pidcock, "Adventures in Vancouver Island," p. 75; Carwithen to Blaksley, 2 December 1885, Carwithen Correspondence; *Comox Argus*, 15 July 1953.

This, then, was the place Drabble chose as his home in the 1860s. Despite the problems of markets, whiskey traders, and predatory wild animals, Comox became the agricultural centre of the northern part of the Gulf of Georgia. Drabble tried to solve one of the main problems of farming in the valley in the 1870s by building a grist-mill so that settlers would not have to import American flour. Even so, Comox farmers would have to wait several decades for a secure local market.

CHAPTER 7

Farmer Drabble of Comox

Just here the river bounds
The cultivated ground;
Far stretches, on the other shore,
The wilderness profound.

FROM *A Bull Song*, by Eric Duncan[1]

DRABBLE returned to Comox in 1866 when Captain Franklyn got the job in the Seychelles Islands. Settlers had claimed much of the best prairie land in the lower valley, but these colonists were both transient and impoverished, and pre-emption claims occasionally became available. Potential settlers were reluctant to claim the heavily-timbered land on the edges of the valley because all clearing had to be done by axe or auger. This was the era before cross-cut saws. Title, however, was fluid, owing to death and departure, and as soon as a pre-emption became available, someone was there to obtain a Certificate of Vacancy from Comox Land Recorder James Robb.

Between 1866 and 1870 Drabble was something of a Comox transient. He held three pre-emptions in these years. At first he lived with Pidcock and hunted deer and wildfowl; in 1867 he worked as William Musters' farm manager; in 1868 he got his own farm, which he sold two years later when he had the chance to buy Musters' fine farm on Portuguese Creek.

For a time Drabble's activities were linked to Pidcock, who made a living hunting and selling deer, elk, and wildfowl. He had started this profession with his chum Harry Blaksley over the winter of 1862-63, when they hunted deer at Nanoose for the Nanaimo market, and he continued at Comox. William and Mary Harmston, for example, in 1865 and 1867 recorded numerous purchases of "Mowitch" from "Harry" and "Pitcock."[2]

---

[1] Eric Duncan, *Rural Rhymes and the Sheep Thief* (Toronto: William Briggs, 1896), 17-18.

[2] Harmston Diary, *c.* 10 February, 21 September and 24 December 1865, *c.* 5 February 1867.

In about 1865, however, Blaksley went back to England, and when Drabble returned to Comox he became Pidcock's hunting partner. In 1866 or 1867 Drabble and Pidcock went elk hunting on Salven Gunderson's Section 21 (later Archibald Milligan's farm) where they shot the very first horse in the valley—one belonging to Musters. Their error provided the material for a favourite Comox hunting story. Four versions survive, spanning almost a century, and they reveal a good deal about the evolution of the "Drabble the misanthrope" myth. The first was recorded in the Courtenay *Weekly News* of January 1893:

> It is said two nimrods out hunting one day shot the very first horse imported into the district, mistaking it for an elk. Each avowed that he planted the deadly missile, and frantically rushed to succure [*sic*] the game, when the mistake was found. Then each tried to give credit to the other, when an altercation took place and each one declared that he pulled the trigger to kill if it was an elk and to miss if it was anything else; and so the matter stands to this day.

The second version, "A Comox Story," appeared in the same newspaper four years later; it may even have come from Drabble:

> One day two of the farmers were out with their rifles looking for big game. Luck was with them until as night was approaching, when on their way home they heard a slight noise ahead of them, and saw what appeared to be the head of a wild animal partly above a bush. They were both expert shots, and fired instantly. The beast fell heavily.
>
> "Now!" said farmer No. 1, "That was my shot."
>
> "And mine also," replied Farmer No. 2. "I never miss my game at that distance."
>
> "But I," retorted No. 1, "fired first."
>
> "Not by a jug full. I claim the game," and No. 2 scowled fiercely.
>
> In a short time they reached the bush, and there—was a neighbour's horse stone dead.
>
> They looked at it silently for a moment, when No. 1 remarked, "Yes, it was your shot which did the business and the owner will want $100 damages."
>
> It was finally agreed to say nothing about it, and it was a long while before the news leaked out, when they jointly made reparation.

The third version, dating from 1950, adds the information that Drabble and Pidcock were pitlamping. The story was told by timber cruiser Eustace Smith who came to the valley as a boy in 1887:

> The story goes that Mr. Pidcock and Mr. Drabble, who was a surveyor, went hunting elk on the lower prairie with a night lamp,—one holding the lantern and the other the gun (It was Milligan's farm). They saw a large pair of eyes staring at them, and Mr. Drabble fired. Down went the animal. Mr.

84

Pidcock said, "We killed an elk," but Mr. Drabble said "I killed an elk!" stressing the I. When they finally reached the animal Mr. Drabble said, "We killed a horse." Mr. Pidcock said, "You killed a horse!"

The final version, written for *Land of Plenty* in 1987 and based on Smith's story, is notable for its new interpretation of Drabble, who is now portrayed as an old curmudgeon slow to give credit and quick to seek praise. Instead of two friends and neighbours out hunting in a common enterprise, as in the previous stories, and together admitting and laughing at their mistake, now we have a cranky Drabble and a level-headed Pidcock:

> A crusty character, Drabble had a knack of rubbing people the wrong way. He once went out elk hunting at night on the lower prairie with Reg Pidcock. Pidcock held the lantern while Drabble carried the gun out in the darkness that surrounded them. The light caught a pair of shiny eyes staring in their direction. Drabble fired and they heard an animal fall. "We killed an elk!" cried Pidcock. "I killed an elk," Drabble corrected him.
>
> When they approached the elk, Drabble surveyed it for a moment by lamplight, then turned to Pidcock and said, "We shot a horse!" "You shot a horse," returned Pidcock.[3]

Pidcock's hunting experiences culminated in 1868, when he wrote "Adventures in Vancouver Island," subtitled an "account of hunting & fishing excursions." It is possible that Drabble was involved with the preparation of Pidcock's manuscript, which reveals a sense of escape from the trammels of Victorian England and an exuberant appreciation of the colony. Pidcock described for an English audience the Vancouver Island method of making a bed in the wilderness. The hunter cut the branches from a small hemlock or pine and piled them into a thick layer of brush:

> When it is thick enough, which is when he cannot feel the ground underneath, he spreads his Blankets on the top, takes off his clothes with the exception of his shirt and lays himself down on his bed of branches and has such a nights rest as it is not the lot of many persons to enjoy. He has his boots and coats for a pillow, perhaps puts his pipe in his mouth and takes a look at the fire outside the tent door which makes him feel warm for the rest of the night and never wakes till morning. Nobody who has never led this life can have any idea of the intense enjoyment one feels in going to bed after a hard days work in this manner.[4]

---

[3] Courtenay *Weekly News*, 4 January 1893, p. 4; Union *Weekly News*, 23 March 1897, p. 1; Eustace Smith, "Eustace Smith—1950," [memoirs], CDMA, pp. 6-7; Isenor, *Land of Plenty*, p. 87.

[4] Pidcock, "Adventures in Vancouver Island," p. 10. See also Good, "The Utmost Bounds of the West," pp. 24-25.

Around this time John Baily organized a barn-building bee on his Section 34, and it too generated a story about Drabble. A bee was a social gathering organized for a specific communal task. Barns, the most important farm buildings, provided shelter for livestock and permitted the storage of hay and other winter feed. Etiquette held that a farmer could request not a house-raising but a barn-building bee, owing to the size and weight of timbers required. Eric Duncan related that most of the neighbours gathered for Baily's bee, "and Drabble, being the oldest man, was appointed cook for the occasion. At night the crowd congratulated him on his culinary ability, and especially on a splendid cake he had made. 'Yes,' he said, 'it ought to be good when I put two large eggs into it.' But he confessed later, that, unknown to Baily, he had added ten eggs more."[5]

∽

His land dealings got Drabble into hot water in 1867. In that year he claimed Section 15, consisting of ninety-three acres roughly where the Back Road now intersects with Ryan Road. This parcel of land had been held first by Henry Hargreave. On Hargreave's death in March 1866 it was claimed by John Holder, who went to jail that December for killing Henry Harrup. In jail, Holder was unable to maintain possession, and Drabble obtained a Certificate of Vacancy late in 1866.

Drabble's claim was controversial. In September 1867 James Robb informed Benjamin Pearse, acting Surveyor General, that Robert Cameron Coleman had challenged Drabble's right to Section 15. "This land is now applied for by Mr. Coleman;" Robb wrote, "I have declined to give him a certificate of vacancy in the usual manner, because Mr. Drabble lives in the Settlement, & I think visits the land once in two months—he does not in my opinion occupy the land in a bona fide manner." At the same time Coleman informed Pearse that Drabble planned to return to England and held that land for speculative purposes:

> Some time in 1866 Mr. Drabble received a certificate of vacancy for a claim previously held by Henry Hargreaves, but then claimed by John Holder who did not reside on the claim.
>
> I understand that Drabble *has never had his claim recorded* at the *land office*, and if he has, he has *not* had it recorded *here* as the Land Act 1862 Clause XXV requires. Neither *does he reside on* the claim but either lives with Pidcock and goes shooting or hires out to Musters as he at present is. He only visits his claim *at rare intervals* in order to have room to *pretend* to hold it and chops a

---

[5] *From Shetland to Vancouver Island*, pp. 88-89. On "bee" etiquette see C. Dubois Mason to Crease, 4 November 1886, Crease Collection.

log or so and then leaves it for two months. He *has offered it for sale* as he does not intend to permanently live in this country. He, in my opinion, and in that of others here, merely holds a claim to this land as a speculation as he formerly took up a claim here in the same manner and sold it to Robt Ritchie who now holds it and this contrary to law as he has no certificate of improvements.

I beg to *apply for this claim* and hope that you will take these various circumstances into consideration, which can bear to be enquired into if need be — and grant it me.

Drabble learned of Coleman's intentions, and the very next day (25 September) he scribbled a note to government surveyor Edward Mohun:

I am not coming down on the Steamer to day. If you will be kind enough to "Record" my claim in Victoria immediately on your arrival I shall be extremely obliged as I am afraid lest that "G.J.L.C." of a Coleman may be asking Finley to try & get it recorded for him. I sent down the Certificate of Vacancy long ago by "Neale" of the Douglas but have never heard anything about it since, but you will be able to explain it to Mr. Pearse & return the record by next Steamer, if you will do me this favour I shall be under great obligation. Mr. Carwithen will give you $2 for me.[6]

Just what Drabble meant by "that G.J.L.C." is not known, but it is likely that the last two initials stood for "Lying Coward." The Land Office, however, backed Coleman over Drabble; Robb declared Section 15 vacant on 18 December 1867 and awarded it to Coleman the next day. It was, however, an unlucky piece of land: Hargreave died in 1866, Holder committed suicide in 1868, and Coleman himself died in 1873.

Undeterred, Drabble continued his search for land. In 1868 he bought Section 20 on the Upper Prairie Road from Robert Ritchie, containing 100 acres. Shortly after moving there he applied for an adjacent fifty acres under the terms of the Land Act. He informed Pearse that only forty acres of Section 20 were clear, of which only twenty-five acres were ploughable, "therefore the piece of Land in question being contiguous to mine & for the most part clear & free from stones I am anxious to acquire, as I do not think of leaving the Colony & intend to make Comox my Home." Drabble abandoned this plan when his neighbour Salven Gunderson told him he had already applied for the fifty acres, but had been unable to pay for it. "The recent Floods have done him a great deal of damage in his low Land," Drabble told Pearse, "& if he had not the additional fifty acres of high ground he

---

[6] Robb to Surveyor General, 17 September 1867; Coleman to Surveyor General, 24 September 1867; Drabble to Surveyor General, 25 September 1867, British Columbia, Department of Lands and Works, Vancouver Island Pre-emptions, 1861-1885.

considers his Claim of little value therefore I wish to withdraw my application as I should be sorry that he shd. think I was acting unneighbourly towards him."[7]

In November 1869 Drabble applied for a six- to nine-month leave of absence from his pre-emption claim in order to go to England "for the purpose of bringing out my Family." Although his request was conditionally granted, Drabble postponed his visit home, perhaps because the following spring he was able to buy Section 36 from Musters. This fine farm consisted of 132 rolling and well-watered acres stretching from the Tsolum to Portuguese and Finley creeks.[8]

Harry Blaksley had claimed the land in September 1862, but when he returned to England it passed to Edward Goldsmid and finally to Musters and Drabble. The history of the property was contained in an article published in the Courtenay *Weekly News* in 1893. The editor interviewed Drabble, who related that:

> Some 25 years ago, more or less, Harry Blaksley, the son of Admiral Blaksley, visited Comox and was so impressed with the beauty and promise of the country that he determined to make his home here. Passing up the valley, as far as the present site of Courtenay, he turned to the right and followed along the ridge above what is now the Upper Prairie road until he came to a small stream which he followed down partly across the valley to its junction with Tsolum River.
>
> Near this point he observed another stream which empties into the Tsolum, and runs north west from the first described creek. From the Tsolum River and running back for some distance these two streams form a figure resembling a bird's head and neck, the enclosed piece being naturally well drained and of great fertility. Blaksley selected a quarter section which embraced this strip. The Middle Prairie Road passes through this ranch, leaving about 25 acres lying between it and the Tsolum River. Wm. Harmston's place bounds it on the east. Blaksley put up the present residence and entered vigorously into the work of clearing.

After being there for several years Blaksley's interests required his presence in England. Musters bought a new farm on the Upper Prairie and transferred title to Drabble in March 1870.[9]

On the old Musters farm Drabble erected the first grist mill in the Comox Valley, a bold undertaking that met with mixed success. At first

[7] Hurford, "Old Ms. Record Book;" Comox Land Registers; Harmston Diary, 30 March 1866; Drabble to Pearse, 30 November 1868 and 9 February 1869, Pearse to Drabble, n.d., Colonial Correspondence.

[8] Drabble to Trutch, 2 November 1869 and 24 January 1870, Colonial Correspondence.

[9] Courtenay *Weekly News*, 9 August 1893, p. 1; Comox Land Registers, p. 23; Hurford, "Old Ms. Record Book;" Drabble to Trutch, 24 February 1870, Colonial Correspondence.

sight the valley needed a grist mill to grind wheat, barley, and other cereals into marketable products. In 1870, for example, John Wilson obtained six tons of spring wheat from a four-acre crop, and in 1874 he, Adam McKelvey, George McFarlan, and William Thompson owned threshing machines which saw communal use. McFarlan thrashed grain for his neighbours with a horse-drawn portable treadmill.[10]

The valley lacked, however, the means of grinding grain into flour on a large scale. Sending wheat to be ground in Victoria or elsewhere was slow and time-consuming. Shipments were hindered by distance and infrequent steamer service. "In those days communication was made by small schooners bringing the mails about once a month," Duncan wrote, "with scanty supplies of groceries and flour . . . but their regularity could not be depended on, so it was little wonder if Drabble thought a grist mill would pay." Drabble, unknown to Duncan, had been a miller and maltster in England, and he knew what was required. Perhaps he also thought longingly of the time he had made beer from malted barley. A mill was a sign of rural civilization. It gave settlers the hope of providing the foods that farming districts should properly provide. Like others in early British Columbia, Drabble may also have resented cheap American imports of flour, and sought a local alternative.[11]

Moreover, Drabble had good economic reasons to stay in Comox. He had decided to make the place his home, with or without his children, and in 1873 he was made a Justice of the Peace. New workers and farmers were arriving, a wharf was planned for Comox, and road work was going ahead. Mining exploration was on the increase. Drabble's farm was accessible by cart and horse.

Drabble dammed Finley Creek to create a small reservoir. "To my dam," he wrote in his notebook on 16 October 1873. Stan Rennison, current owner of the farm and grandson of the man Drabble sold it to, told me in 1994 that Drabble hired Chinese workers at fifty cents a day to build the earthen dam with shovels and wheelbarrows. A diverter and sluice gate sent the water into a wooden flume. Still visible at the bottom of Finley Creek is the cedar bed log from the sluice gate. From the flume the water flowed down a trench cut through a field and into a second flume, which emptied the water onto the mill wheel.

Unfortunately the mill did not work as well as planned. "Owing to the

[10] *From Shetland to Vancouver Island*, p. 87. On McFarlan's, Wilson's and Thompson's machines respectively see James Richardson's 1871-72 notebooks; *The Daily Standard*, 27 October 1873, p. 3; and Manson, "Sketches," p. 3.

[11] Duncan, Notes from Sandwick Store Cashbook; Willard E. Ireland, "Early Flour-mills in British Columbia. Part 1," *BCHQ* 5:2 (April 1941), 89-111.

lack of water during the dry season," Drabble recalled in 1893, "it could not be operated over seven months of the year, nevertheless it was of great convenience." Finley Creek—at least now—is a mere trickle for much of the year, and the water in Drabble's earthen dam would have seeped away in the hot summer sun. This must have been frustrating to Drabble after his high expenses and expectations.

The mill, which stood for seventy-five years, dominated the property, but little now remains. In the 1930s Stan Rennison and his father filled in the ditch so carefully that it is no longer visible. In 1946, soon after returning from the war, Stan toppled the mill with a stump-puller. "It wasn't safe even for cows." It was a high building, up on stilts. It had an eight to ten foot ceiling and a hipped roof above that. It would have been a long drop from the top of the roof to the creek bed. Stan was "scared as blazes to go up there." The large main floor was originally a storage space for wheat and flour, but the Rennisons converted it into a garage, first for wagons and then for cars. The floor level was at the same height as the road, and the Rennisons parked four cars inside when it was still safe. Much of the mill machinery remains at the Rennison farm; the millstones are at the Courtenay Museum, and the main shaft was incorporated into the Field Sawmill in the 1930s.[12]

Drabble's farm contained more than a grist mill. His 1874 Certificate of Improvement reveals that Blaksley's house still stood; it measured 34 × 21 feet. The original house, according to later owners, was built of logs and consisted eventually of three or four bedrooms as well as a kitchen and living room. Other buildings were a barn, measuring 42' × 16', a 28' × 14' cattle shed, and an 18' × 24' stable. The farm house was demolished in the 1940s, but other original buildings remain on the Rennison farm. Eight acres had been fenced in with 2,000 rails, and Drabble had completed his 30' × 20' mill building, valued at $350, while the total value of improvements was $1090. In December 1874 Drabble paid the pre-emption price of $132—a dollar an acre—and the land was his. It had taken the labour of four owners and twelve years to turn this Comox pre-emption into a Crown Grant.[13]

The everyday workings of his farm in the fall of 1873 are preserved in one of Drabble's farm notebooks. He built a bridge—"Drabble's Bridge"—over Portuguese Creek. He bought and sold cattle and pigs.

---

[12] Notebook, p. 9, env. 89 (16 October 1873); Courtenay *Weekly News*, 9 August 1893, p. 1; interview with Stan and Betty Rennison, 22 April 1994, and with Stan Rennison, 1 June 1994.

[13] Courtenay *Weekly News*, 9 August 1893, p. 1; Stan and Betty Rennison, "William Coates Rennison;" British Columbia, Department of Lands, Certificates of Improvement 1871-1887; Comox Land Registers, p. 23. Drabble received his Crown Grant for Section 36 on 19 February 1875.

He hired Louis at $1.25 a day for hunting, fencing, harvesting oats, fetching pigs, and surveying:

> 10 September. "Keep of oxen @ 55c per day from August 15th to Sept 5 = 22 days."

> 1 October. "Sold Williams 3 Heifers Cob, Tooley, and Whiteface. $27.50 each. $82.50."

> 29 October. "Finley for Beef on a/c $2.00."

> 3 December. "Cash of W. H. Thompson on a/c of Cattle Keeping 5$."

> 5 December. "Fetched 2 Pigs from C. Bridges. [Alphonse] Pelons Pig hauling. Cash 1$."

> 10 December. "Williams fetched away 3 Heifers."

> 11 December. "Bought Brindle Steer from Musters 20$ for lumber."[14]

Farmer Drabble took an active part in local events. In December 1872 he was elected first vice-president of the newly formed Comox Agricultural Society, and he and others set about planning an agricultural hall. In August 1873 schoolmaster Samuel Crawford noted the society's activities in a letter to the *Victoria Standard*:

> The Comox agricultural society held a special meeting on Tuesday, the 19th inst., for the purpose of arranging about building an agricultural hall, on the ground donated to the society by J. Wilson, Esq. A committee consisting of Messrs. Pidcock, Wilson and Drabble, was appointed to report at next regular meeting, September 6th. We will not be in a position to hold an exhibition this fall, as our ground is not enclosed, and the hall will require all our attention. We believe in doing one thing at a time, and doing that well.[15]

Construction continued through the fall and early winter of 1873. In October, Crawford noted that Dr. John Ash, the local M.L.A., sent up "four splendid lamps for the use of the Agricultural Hall" by steamer from Victoria. Meetings were held at the school until the hall was fit for occupation. A crisis of unknown origin occurred in October which led to Drabble's resignation, as shown by these 1873 notebook entries:

> 9 October. Resigned as Vice President of Comox Ag. Society.

> 11 October. Sunday. Countermanded all orders on behalf of Agl. Society this day.

> 12 October. Wrote Capt Clarke not to bring up any bricks Shingles or Lumb. on a/c of agricultural Society. Also wrote Standard Office to send up Plan of Hall. Also wrote Bateman saying the Building of Hall was postponed in consequence of wet weather &c.

---

[14] Envs. 89 and 96, Drabble Papers.

[15] *The Daily Standard*, 1 September 1873, p. 3. For a sketch of the Agricultural Society's lands see env. 127, Drabble Papers.

18 October. Attd an agricultural meeting held at the School, which termi-
nated in a disgraceful row, W. R. Robb taking off his coat & challenging to
fight &c &c. Ordered School Master to close up School room.[16]

The hall was incomplete when the society met next on 6 December.
Crawford ignored the trouble witnessed by Drabble and noted in his
next letter to the *Victoria Standard* that the schoolhouse meeting had
been "very successful and pleasant:" Harry Guillod was elected president, Sam Cliffe vice-president; Jules Willemar, treasurer, and Samuel
Crawford, secretary. Despite this promising start, this first agricultural
society was defunct by 1883, and went into hibernation until its reincarnation in the next decade.[17]

Drabble also worked as a land agent and farm auctioneer—undoubt-
edly a continuation of his work as bailiff. In November 1875 he auctioned William Musters' domestic and farm furnishings on Musters'
return to England after his wife's death. Drabble divided the material
from the farm (Section 52) into cattle, steers, yoke of oxen, pigs, feed,
"implements &c.," household furniture, and dining room, and he
recorded the names of Musters' cows: Jenny and calf, Violet, Trinket,
Strawberry, Nancy, Clubfoot, Blossom, Ruby, and White Cow. Alex
Urquhart, Thomas and John Piercy, Reginald Carwithen, and Henry
Greaves bought the cows for about $40 each. Steers named Bright,
Rover, Prince, Ranger, and Billy sold for about $20 each, and a valuable
(and nameless) yoke of oxen went for $130.

Drabble sold a batch of Musters' timothy hay and another of oat hay.
Implements consisted of an American plough with two shears; two
cultivators, one with a double mould board and seven shears and the
other with a single mould board, six shears, and seven points; two hay
forks, one grubber, two picks, two hoes, one garden rake, one manure
fork, one spade, one scythe, two "snaiths," one billhook, one bucksaw,
two handsaws, one ripsaw, one broad axe and flail, one adze, one
square, one axe handle, one hay knife, one harrow, one wheelbarrow,
and four augers.[18]

Drabble gradually became a Jack-of-all-trades, specializing in anything rural and managerial. Such a role came naturally: his father had
been a farm bailiff in England, and he had been manager of Captain
Franklyn's farm in Nanaimo. In 1871, for example, he acted as land
agent when John Wilson leased his large farm (Sections 34, 50, and 51)

[16] *The Daily Standard*, 27 October 1873, p. 3; env. 89, Drabble Papers.
[17] *The Daily Standard*, 22 December 1873, p. 3; Isenor, *Land of Plenty*, p. 120.
[18] "Muster's sale," env. 97.

to Scotsman and former sailor Alexander Urquhart, with whom he had a farming partnership.[19]

In the mid-1870s both Wilson and Drabble left their farms for the greener pastures of trade and, in Drabble's case, surveying. Wilson found his niche as a travelling trader, a commission merchant and intermediary between the farmers and the buyers, and he sold his fine farm to Maritimers Samuel Crawford and Matthew Piercy. Marketing their produce had been the great problem of Comox farmers in the 1860s and 1870s, and no solution was found until Wilson took produce to merchants in Nanaimo and Victoria on the *Douglas*. The start of fortnightly steamer service and the building of the Comox wharf in 1875 gave Wilson the boost he needed. He marketed the Duncans' beef, cattle, pigs, and butter in Nanaimo and Victoria, shopped for settlers, and did other errands. In 1881 Carwithen noted that Wilson had "a pretty good thing" as agent on the steamer and he had diversified into liquor. "Jack Wilson is making more money than anyone on the coast, keeps the bar on the boat and his woman on the shore end of the wharf with 2 or 3 red-headed youngsters."[20]

While on the farm Drabble got involved with the construction of the first school built north of Nanaimo. Requests for a government school had started in about 1865, but they had gone unheeded, probably owing to a scarcity of non-Native children. The settlers had taken matters into their own hands and started a school without government assistance in a log building on the Anglican mission property. Oxford-educated farmer James Rees was the first teacher at this school.

Pressure for a government-assisted school mounted, and in 1869 the settlers successfully petitioned Governor Anthony Musgrave for a grant. In March 1870 Adam Horne, Secretary of the Comox School Board, announced that the board had selected Robert Coleman as teacher; he had, Horne stated, "given very great satisfaction to the fathers of families whose children he has been teaching during the past winter." The settlers contributed $200 of their own money toward school costs. Horne noted that the board was considering building a real schoolhouse because Rev. Henry Owen wanted his church back.[21]

[19] Duncan, "Comox District Fifty Years Ago; *Victoria Standard*, 18 December 1871, p. 2; *From Shetland to Vancouver Island*, pp. 231-33; Mildred Haas, "Alexander Urquhart and Wife," in Isenor, "The Comox Valley;" Forbes, *Wild Roses*, pp. 127-29.

[20] Duncan, "Early Days and Early Settlers;" *From Shetland to Vancouver Island*, pp. 98, 155-56; Ede Anfield, "Radfords Here Before Roads or Bridges Came," *CVFP*, 7 March 1956; Carwithen to Blaksley, 29 August 1880 and 1 March 1881, Carwithen Correspondence.

[21] Isenor, *"For our Children"*, pp. 6-7; Crawford, "First Prize Article;" Alex C. Garrett to Colonial Secretary, 4 November 1869 and Horne to Colonial Secretary, 31 March 1870 in BCARS Vertical File "Comox schools."

Gradually the school became a reality. The government gave a grant in 1871 toward the construction of a school, and Anglican Bishop George Hills donated an acre of Mission property on the Upper Prairie Road. Between 1872 and 1876 Drabble, along with John Wilson and James Robb, served on the Board of Trustes. The school continued at the log church until 1873 when Drabble, as board chairman, initiated construction of a new school. His youngest daughter Sophie was only ten years old and he may well have entertained hopes of bringing his children out from England.

In the spring of 1873 the board selected Victoria architect Edward Mallandaine as architect and settler John Brown as builder. Lumber arrived from Sayward's mill at Shawnigan Creek. By the end of August the new Mission School—a "very substantial and commodious building for the money," a "plain, high, barn-shaped edifice"—was ready for use. Samuel Crawford, a Nova Scotian with a first-class teacher's certificate, opened the school on 1 September 1873 with fifteen pupils and on a salary of $50 a month.[22]

Drabble's earliest surviving notebook contains details of construction. Horne of the Hudson's Bay Company gave the school a gratuity of $5. Drabble supplied contractor Brown with paint, wallpaper, window blinds, roof spikes, and eight and a half pounds of shingle nails. In December he posted a notice for tenders for four cords of firewood to be delivered to the school. He hired Indian Dick at the school for four days at $1.25 a day, perhaps for cutting firewood. He ordered one dozen Spencerian Copy Books for the school.[23]

In October 1873 John Jessop, Superintendent of Education, visited the school and held an examination, but to Drabble's mortification only four pupils came. Jessop, constrained by the schedule of the *Douglas*, spent a week in Comox, and lectured at the new schoolhouse on the subject of "Popular Education." Crawford noted that "G. F. Drabble, Esq., occupied the chair, and conveyed the thanks of the meeting to the speaker. Jessop is the right man in the right place."[24]

Drabble calculated that the cost of running the school was $60-$70 per student, and he and the trustees passed a bylaw in accordance with the Compulsory Education Act. "We regret to say the attendance for the

[22] British Columbia, *Sessional Papers*, 1872-76; *The Daily Standard*, 18 March, 27 May, 25 August, 1 September 1873. (I owe these references to Brad Morrison); *From Shetland to Vancouver Island*, p. 210; Isenor, *"For our Children,"* pp. 6-7; Crawford, "First Prize Article," p. 1; env. 89.

[23] Env. 89, Drabble Papers.

[24] Env. 89, Drabble Papers; *The Daily Standard*, 27 October 1873, p. 3. On Jessop see Patrick A. Dunae, "John Jessop," in Cook, ed., *Dictionary of Canadian Biography*, Vol. 13, pp. 511-16.

past year has been small as compared with the number of children in the Settlement of School going age, & fervently hope that Parents in this District will consider the great advantages to be derived by giving their children a sound Education & that at the next annual meeting we shall be able to report more favourably on this point." Drabble paid for book prizes at the annual awards day and remained on the school board until 1876.[25]

The school, near the Anglican church and a short walk up from the river, became the meeting place of the valley. Pidcock founded the Comox Literary Institute there in December 1873 with twenty-five members present. He applied for government money to buy books and erect a suitable building. Later, both the Literary Institute and the Mechanics' Institute (which also lent books) were absorbed by the Athletic Club of Courtenay.[26]

Over the winter of 1875-76 Drabble broke with his past and sold his farm. It was no accident that the building of the Comox wharf in 1875 coincided with his decision. The wharf assured the continued growth of the valley; no longer would passengers have to row out to passing steamers or hoist livestock into their canoes. Now settlers would have a favourable first sight of Comox from the long and picturesque wharf. The Baynes Sound mine was about to open, business propects were favourable, and Drabble was beginning to dabble in trade. Most importantly, in 1873 he had been appointed Superintendent of Public Works, Justice of the Peace, and Collector of Votes for Comox District. Since 1873 he had resumed his old profession of surveying—a handy skill to possess in a new community. Thus he had both public and private sources of income to fall back on, and he no longer needed his farm. He changed and adapted to new circumstances.

Drabble bought nothing from the Musters sale in November 1875 except three hides. This was because he had just sold his own farm and mill to William Rennison, a foundry man from Yorkshire, who was registered as owner the following August. Views vary as to the reasons for Drabble's sale. Eric Duncan wrote that he sold the farm because he was chronically short of cash, and that because the mill did not pay "he dropped it, and with it all other manual labour." Drabble's own explanation for the sale of the property is rather more specific and plausible, as he told the editor of the *Weekly News* in 1893:

---

[25] Env. 89; Victoria *Daily Standard*, 4 January 1875, p. 2. In 1881 the school trustees fined Matthew Piercy $10 for refusing to send a child to school: James Robb to Provincial Secretary, 23 October 1882, Provincial Secretary, Letters Inward, 1872-1910.

[26] *The Daily Standard*, 22 December 1873, p. 3; Pidcock to Provincial Secretary, 17 December 1873, Provincial Secretary, Correspondence Inward, 1871-1892; Courtenay *Weekly News*, 11 October 1893, p. 1.

One season the winter was unusually severe and the snow lay heavy o'er "vale and brae" and Drabble grew discontented. W. Rennison, who was anxious to procure the place, and had previously enquired the price, came out to make a call, wading, for the purpose, through the deep snow up to his hips. He remained to lunch and talked of everything but the object of his visit. He finally left, went a few rods, came back as if something had occured to him, and said "By the way have you still a mind to sell this farm?" Yes said Drabble, "I'm disgusted with it. If you want it, now's your chance." The result was Rennison bought the place at a bargain and Drabble has ever since abused himself for selling at so low a figure, a ranch magnificently watered, naturally drained, and every way desireable.

Rennison operated the mill for a while, but it gradually fell into disuse as dealers brought in feed from outside. "Rennison a blacksmith, owns your old place, and same house yet," Carwithen later told Blaklsey.[27]

Drabble started surveying even before he sold the farm. His earliest surviving work dates from September 1873 when, for $4 a day, he surveyed the pre-emption claims of Michael Donohue, W. H. Thompson, David Williams, and Joseph Pelon at Point Holmes, a couple of miles east of the Comox townsite.[28]

He always had one of his leather-bound field books in his pocket for general use—books that contain rough material on the development of physical and social structures in Comox, for example memos concerning the dates of upcoming provincial elections, notes relating to his work with the school, church, and agricultural boards, and lists of letters written and memos concerning robberies and other crimes.

Early settlers generally chose land fronting on the ocean or a creek or river. For coastal surveys, Drabble and a chainman typically started at the front of the property and walked westard into the woods carrying a sturdy compass attached to a Jacob's staff. They measured their way around trees without cutting them down. Then they turned north and walked for the same distance, turned east for the same distance until they returned to what Drabble called the "sea beach," when they turned south and followed the beach to the "point of commencement," having legally delineated a giant 160-acre square in the wilderness, forty by forty chains square.

On his first survey Drabble found his way to the sea beach of Thompson's land south of Cape Lazo. Here he took his bearings from a small tree on the Denman Island spit, and another from the end of Entrance Point, Denman Island. Then he surveyed in a northerly direction across

---

[27] Stan and Betty Rennison, "William Coates Rennison;" *From Shetland to Vancouver Island*, p. 87; Duncan, Notes from Sandwick Store Cashbook; Courtenay *Weekly News*, 9 August 1893, p. 1; Carwithen to Blaksley, 10 May 1885, Carwithen Correspondence.

[28] Env. 89, Drabble Papers.

Cape Lazo. He made his way inland, crossing bush, sand hills, swamp, swamp willows, open sandy land, timber land, and another swamp. The next day, deep in the interior of the cape, he splashed into another swamp. "Discontinued too much water in Swamp," he wrote; "To be continued."[29]

In early years Drabble hired a Native assistant, someone to help paddle the canoe and hold the chain while Drabble took bearings and wrote his field notes. In the front of his Point Holmes field book he wrote: "4 Indians 2 dys. 1 Indian 1 dy." "Indian pr. Canoe to Deep Bay $2.50," he wrote in December 1873 after surveying for Dr. Ash. He stayed with settlers, or camped out. In April 1876 he made a list of necessary foodstuffs and utensils in preparation for a survey: flour, tea, sugar, yeast powder, bacon, suet, pepper, soap, candles, frying pan, cups & plates, spoons & knives, matches, tea pot, 16 lbs bacon, 1 sack flour. Tom or Thomas (probably Beckensell) was along on this survey for $2 a day.[30]

When he got back to Comox, he transferred the survey information into clean field books for transmission to the Lands and Works Department. When he ran out of his favourite leather-covered books, he went to one of the Comox storekeepers for an emergency supply of account books. Once, he got a batch of butcher's books, six by three by three and a half inches, the cover showing an engraving of a butcher at work in his shop. "Always Bring this Book. Mr. — Dealer in Choice Beef, Mutton, Lamb, Veal, Pork, Hams, Bacon, Corned Beef, Tongues, etc. Poultry & Game in Season." He always included a small sketch map in his field notes, and ordered his tracing paper and other stationery from Thomas Hibben in Victoria.[31]

Drabble found himself in hot water a couple of times in the 1870s. In January 1876 William Duncan, one of the most litigious and bad-tempered of the 1862 bachelor settlers, complained that Drabble had short-changed him when he surveyed his land on the Tsolum (Section 16). "No man likes to have a Smaler Clame of the sam number of acars then his Nighbour," Duncan complained to the Land Office; "The Chains or the Cheners most be wrong as the tow former Surveyors that was hear Cour spounded alike. The Instruments that Drabble have is poor ones." Duncan hired Drabble anyway to survey the old Pentlatch village site at the junction of the Puntledge and Tsolum rivers. Other settlers had always considered this an Indian Reserve, but it had not yet been surveyed as such. In 1878 Indian Commissioners Archibald

---

[29] Env. 58, Drabble Papers.

[30] Envs. 58, env. 89, 97, 116, Drabble Papers.

[31] Env. 89; on Hibben see Walbran, *British Columbia Coast Names*, pp. 242-43.

McKinlay and Gilbert Sproat visited Comox and wrote that Duncan, though he knew it was a reserve, "nevertheless for some reason employed Mr. Drabble of Comox to survey this piece of land, but Mr. Drabble, knowing it to be an Indian settlement, so marked it on a sketch attached to his field notes." Duncan did not succeed in securing this land.[32]

Duncan also quarrelled with his brother Oliver over the ownership of Section 16. They called in Drabble to survey their land into halves: "Then they divided up the land," their nephew Eric recalled, "Drabble ran a line from top to bottom of section XVI, and William took the south side; but, as the buildings were all on the north side, Drabble divided the ground on which they stood into lots, the lines of which ran through the centres of the dwelling-house and barns. . . . Those lots puzzled many people." Oliver's title deed was "a relic of the past, being in Drabble's neat handwriting, and with the great, plain, clumsy signature of Oliver."[33]

In the mid-1870s, then, Drabble's activities expanded enormously, making a farm perhaps more of a liability than an advantage. He was a Justice of the Peace, Superintendant of Roads, and a private surveyor. He and Joe Rodello may already have embarked on their commercial partnership, and Drabble had started dealing in potatoes and lumber. The new wharf at Comox Landing was an ideal place for a house and an office. All these activities required his presence at James Robb's Comox townsite. Drabble's rustic lifestyle at Blaksley's old farm ended in 1875 as his work as surveyor, road superintendent, Justice of the Peace, and trader increased.

It was, therefore, economically feasible for Drabble to dispose of his farm. He also showed good business sense: the mill worked only seasonally, imports of cheap American flour continued, and mining and forestry projects started up in the 1870s. The future prosperity of the valley lay as much in farming as in these new industries which, along with road building, would require his surveying and engineering skills. His farm represented his past while the opportunities around him represented his future.

---

[32] Duncan to CCL&W, 6 January 1876, Department of Lands and Works, Correspondence Inward, 1871-1918; McKinlay and Sproat to Attorney General, 11 January 1878, Herald Street Collection.

[33] *From Shetland to Vancouver Island*, pp. 164, 264.

Recreation of Drabble's gristmill by Ron Egan.

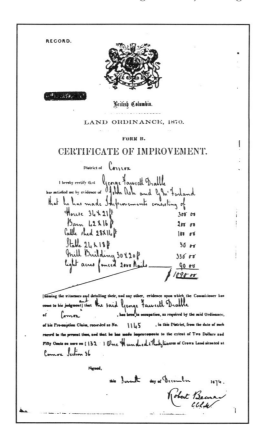

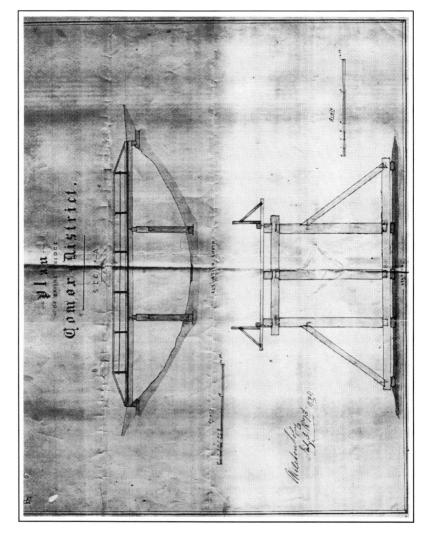

Drabble's design for the Ravine Bridge on the Back Road, Comox.

CHAPTER 8

Superintendent Drabble

Ye herding fools, come out where there is room,
Come out, and fill the earth's waste places up,
Make howling deserts laugh with running brooks,
Turn sombre woods to green rejoicing fields.

FROM *The Man with the Hoe,* by Eric Duncan[1]

WHEN Drabble parted with his farm on Portuguese Creek, he severed his connection with a profession that he had pursued since his youth and that his father and both of his grandfathers had followed. He may have sold the farm because the creek was short of water or because he was short of cash, as Eric Duncan asserted, but by 1875 he had several other ways of making a living. The wider opportunities available to him in Comox were impressive, and when confronted with them, Drabble chose to leave the profession of his youth behind. In the 1870s he put the valley's road and bridge system in place; more than anyone else, Drabble created the nineteenth century transport system of Comox that sped the settlement of the valley in later decades.

In the early 1860s the colonial Department of Lands and Works, which oversaw all road, trail, and bridge construction on the island, decided to build a road from Victoria to Comox. This was to be a grand colonial enterprise, somewhat akin to the Cariboo Road on the mainland. Roads in the colony were named, in the British fashion, after their destination, and north of Cowichan this was known as the "Comox Road." In July 1862 Joseph Pemberton, the Surveyor General, secured $25,000 for the construction of the road, and in December a party under William Ralph started to blaze a trail from Nanaimo to Comox.[2] It soon became clear that a proper fifteen-foot wide wagon road would be too expensive, and Pemberton settled instead for a narrow "Bridle Trail," but even this—in the dense forest and numerous flood-prone

---

[1] Duncan, *The Rich Fisherman.*
[2] "House of Assembly," *British Colonist,* 24 July 1862; Nanaimo-Comox Trail Accounts, Herald Street Collection.

rivers on the western shore of the Gulf of Georgia—would prove too difficult to construct and maintain.

By May 1863 a gang of men employed by the contractor, Malcolm Munro, had completed a "first-class trail" between Nanaimo and Comox, complete with bridges over rivers and creeks. Within months Munro's work had been ravaged by floods and storms, and in January 1864 surveyor Pearse reported that the trail was blocked by windfalls, and there was "great reason to fear that the whole will be impassable in a very short time from the same cause." A few months later Pemberton scrapped the proposed wagon road to Comox because it would cost $70,000 and the colony was broke. In the end this grand project, the Comox Road, was completed from Victoria only as far as Chemainus, and the bridle trail to Comox was open only briefly before it was ruined by windfalls and washouts. When Robert Brown came up island in August 1864, he found only one of Munro's bridges remaining—a "pretty bridge" spanning the Qualicum River. In 1893 Drabble recalled that the trail was so grown over with bush that it was difficult to tell where it was: "It was never of much use, as the freshets of the next season swept away the bridges along the trail and they were never replaced." The entire trail, even as near Comox as Baynes Sound, was abandoned under a myriad of fallen trees, and until the mid-1890s Comox could only be reached by sea.[3]

The Bridle Trail to Nanaimo did see some use during its short opening. Harry Blaksley made at least two trips down it for livestock. Once he walked with Indian guides to Nanaimo to buy a horse, which he rode back to Comox; on another occasion he walked all the way to Victoria. "There was only a trail then with the trees blazed here and there," he recalled in 1916; "Bailey was with me and we bought some young cattle there and took them back to Comox by boat." Drabble, in his later surveys in the region, marked the remains of the Nanaimo and Victoria Trail in his field notes.[4]

Though cut off from the outside world, the Comox settlers still needed roads, trails, and bridges. In January 1863 they petitioned the government for a road through the settlement and for bridges over the

[3] Hayman, *Robert Brown*, pp. 108, 151, n. 133; Pearse to Colonial Secretary, 12 January 1863, Herald Street Collection; Pemberton to W. A. G. Young, 25 April 1864, British Columbia, Department of Public Works, Contracts, specifications, 1862-1909; Courtenay *Weekly News*, 11 January 1893, p. 4; Ash to CCL&W, 13 July 1877, British Columbia, Department of Lands and Works, Correspondence Inward, 1871-1883.

[4] Carwithen to Blaksley, 29 August 1880, Carwithen Correspondence; Mildred Haas, "R. T. Carwithen and Cousin Blaksley," in Isenor, "The Comox Valley;" Blaksley to Jessie McQuillan, 12 July 1916, quoted in *Comox Argus*, 17 March 1921; see Drabble's 1884 survey for Thomas and Sydney Rabson, env. 126.

"several large creeks" that intersected the valley. Things moved slowly. In June 1865 the settlers again petitioned the government for a road, and the next month the government sent Superintendent of Roads John Trevasso Pidwell and a gang of men to Comox. Pidwell laid out a road from the schooner landing at Green's Slough to the Anglican Mission, another from the Mission to the Upper Prairie, and he blazed a trail from the Mission to the steamer landing at Robb's. He completed the Back Road survey only as far as Charles Burrage's claim next to the Indian Reserve because a beach road led around McCutcheon's Bluff to the Robb townsite. Settlers also used Burrage's private road from his store up to the Back Road. "For the present it is thought that the continuation of the [Back] Road towards Robbs will not be requir'd as all the settlers at that end of the district have a good road by the beach," Pidwell wrote. Two rough and makeshift log bridges were also built in the 1860s: one over the Tsolum River giving access to "McKelvey's country," and a small bridge over Portuguese Creek, known eventually as Rennison's Bridge.[5] (See map 5.)

In 1870 Drabble came to prominence in connection with Comox roads, and he remained the dominant force for a decade. James Robb was already Land Recorder, but he was unpopular with many of the settlers and resigned in 1869. In January 1870 Drabble wrote as follows to Chief Commissioner Joseph Trutch:

> I hear that Mr. Robb has had Notice from you to hand over the documents relating to the office of Land Recorder to Mr. Rodello for the present. If it is your intention to appoint any other person in the Settlement to that office I should feel obliged if you wd. confer the same upon myself & I wd. endeavour to show that your confidence shall not have been misplaced. Such an appointment wd. not be foreign to my abilities as I was in a Land Office in England for upwards of seven years during which time I had a great deal of Chain Surveying in many parts of the Country.[6]

Trutch, however, replied that Warner Spalding, the Nanaimo magistrate, would assume such duties. A month later Drabble, undeterred, drew up a petition asking that a portion of the Lower Prairie (Headquarters) Road be diverted from a section of low swampy ground which made it "almost impassable for carting produce in the winter." The next year the settlers, led by Drabble, censured Spalding for his neglect of

---

5 *From Shetland to Vancouver Island*, pp. 110; 114-16; Hayman, *Robert Brown*, p. 122; Vancouver Island, Colonial Secretary, Register of Correspondence Inward, 1864-1866 (27 June 1865); Pidwell to Pearse, 5 August 1865, Herald Street Collection; Harmston Diary, 26 and 28 July 1865. On early Comox roads see also Isenor, *Land of Plenty*, pp. 389-90.
6 Drabble to Trutch, 24 January 1870, Colonial Correspondence.

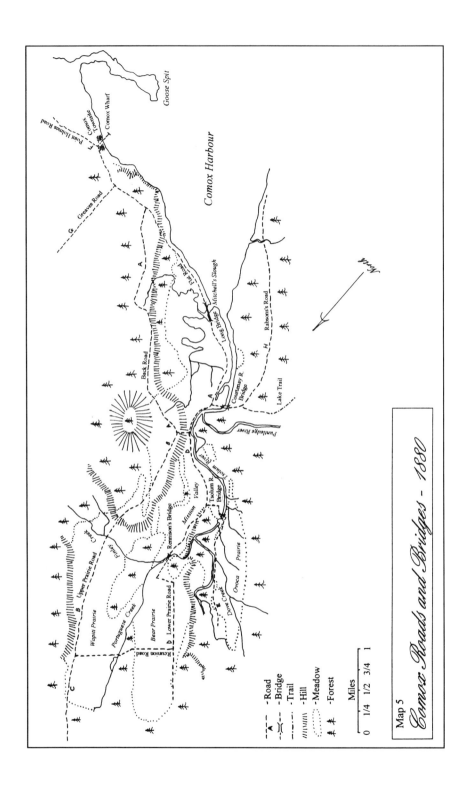

Goose Spit

Comox Harbour

Comox Wharf

Comox Towncite

Point Holmes Road

Greaves Road

G

Flat Road

A

Back Road

Mitchell's Slough

Long Bridge

Rabson's Road

H

Courtenay R. Bridge

A

Lake Trail

Puntledge River

Hill

A

Tsolum River

Mission Valley

D

Tsolum R. Bridge

Ococa Prairie

Renison's Bridge

Finlay Creek

Upper Prairie Road

C

B

Wapiti Prairie

Portuguese Creek

Lower Prairie Road

Bear Prairie

D

Dove Creek

Renison Road

C

North

Map 5

Comox Roads and Bridges – 1880

- Road
- Bridge
- Trail
- Hill
- Meadow
- Forest

Miles

0   1/4   1/2   3/4   1

the Comox roads and urged the government to build a new bridge over the Tsolum River and to extend the road through the Wapiti Prairie.[7]

Skilled farm labour was in perennially short supply, and in April 1872 John Wilson wrote to the Lands and Works Department, asking that the government hire men from outside the valley because "Farm hands in the Settlement are very scarce & should they be able to obtane employment upon the Roads at advanced wages the loss & inconvenience caused would be disastoures to the Farmers & endanger the harvesting of our crops in this far off locality where Labour is difficult to get at any Season."[8]

The government granted his request, and in June road builder William Hassard and his crew of sixteen arrived from Nanoose. They camped near the Mission and spent two weeks repairing the Back Road trail with a grader and oxen. They graded to a width of ten feet, installed culverts, removed stumps and standing trees, and repaired bridges. They bought goods and provisions from Horne of the Hudson's Bay Company and beef from John Wilson and Henry Ross. By the middle of July Hassard was down to twelve men, the others having gone to cut hay. Then he moved to the Upper Prairie Road which the settlers hoped would attract new settlers to the upper valley. Hassard and his men graded this road and extended a trail five miles up the valley from Gordon's. Hassard, however, found the settlers' herds of semi-feral pigs a nuisance. "I beg to remark," he told Pearse, "that pigs are rooting up the ditches and tail drains so that the work will not answer the purpose if they are allowed to do so."[9]

In 1871 the provincial legislature had passed a new road act, which defined the boundaries of the Comox Road District and established a mechanism for road maintenance and the collection of road taxes. Late in 1872 Drabble was appointed Superintendent of Public Works in Comox, and the legislature voted $5,000 for the repair of Comox roads. In 1873 he was made a Justice of the Peace, and therafter Comox was independent of Nanaimo's legal and government machinery.[10]

---

[7] Trutch to Drabble, 5 February 1870; [Drabble] to the Surveyor General, 22 February and 26 April 1870; Pearse to Drabble, 2 May 1870; Drabble to CCLW, 6 April 1871 and 11 April 1871, Colonial Correspondence.

[8] Wilson to CCL&W, 9 April, R. C. Coleman et al. to Pearse, 11 April, Pearse to Coleman et al., 18 April 1872, British Columbia, Department of Lands and Works, Correspondence Inward, 1871-1872.

[9] Hassard to Pearse, 22 May, 30 May, 3 July, 10 July, 6 August 1872; Coleman et al. to Pearse, 11 April, Pearse to Coleman et al. 18 April 1872, in British Columbia, Department of Lands and Works, Correspondence Inward, 1871-1872.

[10] "An Ordinance to provide for the Maintenance, Improvement, and Construction of Roads in British Columbia," The Laws of British Columbia (1871), pp. 382-86; Drabble

Drabble had worked on Captain Franklyn's road in Nanaimo, and his experience suited him for road surveying and building. Every spring he called for tenders for construction and repair, and settlers competed for this lucrative but demanding work, which required managerial skill and access to timber for cribbing, bridges, culverts, cordwood, and rocks and gravel for road construction. Two men emerged in the 1870s as the main valley contractors: John Wilson and Joe McPhee. Wilson was a travelling trader; McPhee was a recent and youthful newcomer from Nova Scotia, and both farmed before branching out into trade and construction.

Lumber and bridge building were Joe McPhee's specialties. Born in 1848 in Hants County, Nova Scotia, and the eldest of about thirteen children, McPhee went to Boston aged sixteen and worked his way across the United States, reaching Sacramento in 1869 on the first train from the east. He built railway snow-sheds in the Sierra Nevadas, worked at a Puget Sound sawmill, and came to Victoria, where he met trader Wilson—who brought him to Comox in 1872. McPhee at first rented Reginald Carwithen's farm while Carwithen was back in England; then he and Alex Urquhart "batched" and raised beef cattle at Fanny Bay, but after two years he moved to Comox, where he had already formed a road and bridge construction partnership with John Wilson.[11]

As Superintendent of Roads Drabble supervised contractors like Wilson and McPhee. He surveyed the lines for new roads, wrote specifications for work to be done, designed bridges, paid contractors and labourers, inspected all road work, and kept up a constant correspondence with the head office in Victoria. For this he was paid $170 a year.[12]

In 1873 Drabble, the new Superintendent, gave the roads alphabetical designations. Hassard had referred to them as "Section 1" and "Section 2," but Drabble changed these to alpabetical designations to avoid confusion with numbered land sections:

Section A.—Originally from Steamboat Landing to Grave Yard (now Back Road); later Section A was the road from the wharf to the Long Bridge.

Section B.—From Mission Junction to Gordon's Claim (Upper Prairie Road, now the Island Highway).

---

to CCL&W, 27 November 1872, British Columbia, Lands and Works Department, Correspondence Inward, 1872-1918.

[11] Interview with Bruce McPhee, 19 December 1994; Mildred Haas and Wallace McPhee, "Joseph McPhee," and Mildred Haas, "R. T. Carwithen and Cousin Blaksley" and "Alexander Urquhart and Wife," in Isenor, "The Comox Valley;" *From Shetland to Vancouver Island*, pp. 98, 231-33.

[12] J. A. Lavin, "B.C. Government Employees in 1876: An Index," *British Columbia Genealogist* 13:1 (March 1984), p. 21.

Section C.—From Gordon's Claim to Beach's Claim (Upper Prairie Road, now the Island Highway).

Section D.—From Green's Slough to Brown's Claim (Lower Prairie Road, now Headquarters Road).

Section E.—From Wilson's Junction to Thomas's Claim (now Dove Creek Road).

Section F.—From Steamer Landing (or "Rodello's Junction" to Point Holmes).

Section G.—Greaves' Road (now Anderton Road).

Section H.—Crawford's Road (road from the Mission to Little River, later abandoned).

Section I.—Rabson's Road. Courtenay River Bridge to Trent River (now the Island Highway south of Courtenay).[13]

In May 1873 the government called for tenders for work on Sections A through F. "Specifications may be seen at Mr. Drabble's, Comox, and at this office," wrote Chief Commissioner of Lands and Works Robert Beaven. Successful contractors were Joe McPhee, William Beach, James Somerville, and David Williams. McPhee's work on Section A included the construction of the Ravine Bridge over the creek that flowed down into the flats at the hairpin turn.[14]

The most notable dates in late nineteenth century Comox were 1874 and 1888. In 1874, Drabble supervised the building of the Comox wharf, the Courtenay River Bridge, and four new roads reaching to the north, south, and east of Comox; in 1888 Robert Dunsmuir opened the Union Mine. Comox road builders were fortunate that their M.L.A., Dr. John Ash, owned land locally, and that as a member of the cabinet he had much influence in getting grants for roads and bridges.[15]

Road work began in the early summer when the land and roads had dried out from the winter rains. Three wagon roads were new in 1874: Sections G, H, and I. All were to be fourteen feet wide. Section H, or Crawford's Road, did not prove permanent: Eric Duncan recalled that Crawford arrived in 1870 and settled at Little River on what became the Miller Ranch: "There being no other outlet for him at that time, the Government opened a trail which went up past the Anglican cemetery at Sandwick and mounted a very steep hill in the woods behind. This trail was never much used, and it was quickly obliterated by bush fires." Rabson's Road ran from the bank of the Courtenay River at Ford's old place (Section 41) as far as the mouth of Trent River. This is now the Island Highway running south of Courtenay. Duncan recalled

[13] *British Columbia Gazette*, 3 May 1873, p. 7. British Columbia *Sessional Papers*, 1873-77.

[14] British Columbia, Department of Public Works, Contracts, specifications, 1862-1909.

[15] *From Shetland to Vancouver Island*, p. 149.

that Section I was rarely used, was quickly blocked by trees, and that settlers Sydney and Thomas Rabson, Robert Scott, Peter Lindberg, and George Gartley communicated with the Comox wharf by rowboat. Money was also available in September 1874 for the construction of a crossroad—now Bridges Road—linking the Upper and Lower Prairie roads along the boundaries of Robert Ritchie's Section 29, John Baily's Section 50, and Charles Bridges' Section 33. It required four bridges: a sixty-foot bridge over "Bridges Creek," a simple ten-foot bridge over the "Creek in the Wood," a one-hundred-foot bridge over "Ritchie's Creek" (Portuguese Creek), and a thirty-foot bridge known as the Prairie Bridge.[16]

Later in 1874 two notable projects were initiated: a wharf at Comox and a bridge over the Courtenay River. "In 1874 a wharf was erected by the Government," Drabble told the local newspaper in 1893, "for the purpose of facilitating the shipping of produce and cattle, as heretofore freight was shipped alongside the steamers in canoes or boats, and cattle were made to swim and then hoisted with slings on board." The Royal Navy assisted in the preparations: in May 1874 Richard Hare, commander of H.M.S. *Myrmidon*, wrote the Lieutenant-Governor regarding "Erection of a Pier at Comox":

> I have the honor to acquaint you, for the information of the Works Department, that in compliance with your request, I sounded at Comox (on the Myrmidon's recent visit) for the most suitable place to erect a Pier, and I beg to state that I consider the best spot to be in a line with the Road near Mr. Rodello's House, where it will have to run out 90 fathoms from low water mark to admit a vessel of fourteen feet draught alongside.[17]

At the end of June a large contract, worth $3,300, was awarded to Joe McPhee, with John Wilson as surety. It called for a pier 1,015 feet in length, twelve feet wide between the handrails, and supported by forty-foot piles placed every twenty feet and cross-braced. Only the best Douglas Fir and cedar were to be used. The wharf itself, at the end of the pier, was to be sixty by forty feet with eight feet of water in front at the lowest tide.[18]

The wharf became the main asset of the village of Comox over the next few decades and gave Comox a commercial life well into the twentieth century, long after it had been eclipsed by the new town of

---

[16] Duncan, "Early Days and Early Settlers;" env. 96; *From Shetland to Vancouver Island*, p. 133; British Columbia, Department of Public Works, Contracts, specifications, 1862-1909.

[17] Courtenay *Weekly News*, 4 January 1893, p. 4; Hare to Trutch, 29 May 1874, British Columbia, Lieutenant-Governor, Correspondence 1871-1936; see also *British Columbia Gazette*, 27 June 1874, p. 115.

[18] British Columbia, Department of Public Works, Contracts, specifications, 1862-1909.

Courtenay. James Robb's Comox town lots finally started to sell, and the wharf served for visiting naval vessels, government steamers, and coastal traders and schooners. In the spring of 1875 the government, to recover some of the expense of construction, imposed a toll on livestock and freight. Beaven called for tenders for the lease of the wharf and the collection of tolls:

On Cattle, 25 Cents each.
"   Horses, 25 Cents each.
"   Pigs and Calves, 12 1/2 Cents each.
"   Freight, 50 Cents Per Ton.

Officers, servants, freight, and animals for the time being in the employ or the property of the Provincial Government to pass free.[19]

In the spring of 1874 Drabble surveyed and prepared specifications for a bridge over the Courtenay River. He chose a spot where the river narrows. Even today a person standing on the 5th Street Bridge on the same site will notice that the water above the bridge is rippled while below the bridge it is still. This is because the deep water ends right here; it is the head of navigation. It was also an important traditional fishing site of the Comox Indians: in 1952 Agnes Edwards remembered, as a young girl, fishing with her family for salmon and trout where the bridge now stands.[20]

Drabble's interest in the site was unrelated to its Native uses. The bridge would allow access to Pidcock's sawmill (then under construction), to Section I, and to the whole country to the west including the projected Union Mine. At the end of July 1874, Wilson and McPhee got the contract. The bridge was to be completed by 1 November.[21]

The bridge was supported by two ninety-two-foot spans resting on a centre pier of unbarked cedar piles. At each end was an abutment pier of twelve piles. The bridge deck was thirteen feet in width: wide enough for a wagon or a team of oxen. Most lumber on the bridge was to be Douglas Fir, "sawn fair and square to the specified size," and "free from sap shakes, knots, dry rot or any defect whatever." The roadway of the bridge was to be covered with three-inch diagonal planking. The underside was to be a full three feet higher than the record flood tide of 1865. "The entire workmanship on the superstructure of Bridge shall be of the first class, as any imperfect workmanship shall be rejected."[22]

[19] "Lease of Comox Wharf" (28 April 1875) in "Comox" Vertical file, BCARS.
[20] Interview with Bruce McPhee, 19 December 1994; Isabelle Stubbs, "Indian History Recounted by Matriarch," *CVFP*, 30 October 1952.
[21] Env. 127; Courtenay *Weekly News*, 11 January 1893, p. 4.
[22] *British Columbia Gazette*, 27 June 1874, p. 115; British Columbia, Department of Public Works, Contracts, specifications, 1862-1909.

Comox settlers attached their memories to the construction of these tangible manifestations of their enterprise in the wilderness. These structures provided settlers with occasion to recall their arrival in the valley, and their opening celebrations provided a sense of community. Florence Radford (née Cliffe) recalled that people danced on the bridge at its 1 July 1875 opening, and her brother Lou Cliffe recollected, in 1940, the events of sixty-five years before:

> When he was quite a small boy he came to the celebration of the opening of the first bridge across the Courtenay River, which was on the first of July. There was a great-to-do about. Joe Fitzgerald, Chas. Hooper, Bob Jones, "Handsome" Harry Huxton and others were busy broad-axing the timbers to go across the bridge so they would be smooth enough to dance on. For that was one of the big events of the day—the dance on the new bridge. It had been roofed in completely with small firs and dogwood trees in blossom and made a very pretty picture. The celebration started with a picnic at noon and was kept up all day until the early hours of the morning. "Handsome" Harry was one of the characters of the time. He was an Englishman, who had all the comic songs of the day on his tongue, and he was a great favourite at all the gatherings.[23]

Another of the bridge builders was Michael Manson, who earlier had worked on the wharf; another was John White, a twenty-one year old from Victoria who died instantly when a tressle fell on him.[24]

Fifteen-year old Isabella Piercy, a recent arrival from New Brunswick, also witnessed the opening. Men came from Victoria to officiate: "The official cut the white ribbon, which was made of paper, and with these words opened the bridge 'I declare this bridge open for travel from this day forward.' Tea and coffee and sandwiches were served to all on the Sandwick side."[25]

With the bridge complete there was a need to construct or improve the roads leading to it. In September 1874 George Gartley extended Section I from Ford's old place back to the new bridge site, and in May 1875 Thomas Piercy built the "Lake Road" from the bridge to Comox Lake and the Union mine, a distance of six and a half miles. The contract required a great deal of corduroy over the swamps along the way. Drabble described precisely how corduroy should be laid:

> The ground being previously prepared and brought to a level is to be covered with round or split logs (lying fair on the ground so prepared) not

---

23 Ede Anfield, "Radfords Here Before Roads or Bridges Came," *CVFP*, 7 March 1956; *Comox Argus*, 11 April 1940; see also Carroll, *Wild Roses and Rail Fences*, p. 31.

24 Manson, "Sketches," p. 3; Walbran, *British Columbia Coast Names*, p. 317; Victoria *Daily Standard*, 17 October 1874, p. 3.

25 Ede Anfield, "Pioneer Woman Remains Remarkably Young at 94," *CVFP*, 18 April 1956; Victoria *Daily Standard*, 3 April 1875, p. 3.

less than 8 inches in thickness laid even and closely spotted, to be well brushed and covered with earth brought to a level surface. No portion of edges of split logs to be less than six inches thick. Cedar to be used if obtainable within reasonable distance.[26]

The Lake Trail Road still leads from Courtenay to Comox Lake.

There was an obvious need to connect the new bridge with the new wharf at Comox, but here Drabble's plans fell foul of political forces beyond his control. He wanted to replace the Back Road as the main route between the Landing and the valley in favour of a new road slightly lower on the side hill. Such a road, while still entailing an uphill climb for the farmers and their oxcarts, would have represented a real improvement on the Back Road, with its steep hills and hairpin bends. Drabble surveyed this road in April and May 1875.[27]

Others in the valley disagreed. They balked at the idea of climbing any hill and wanted to follow the shore of Comox Harbour to the wharf. A group of settlers petitioned the government for a road along the tideflats to the landing. They were supported by John Ash, who happened to be Provincial Secretary. They wanted a new road almost at water level, starting at the bridge and running beside the Courtenay River, over the swamp and sloughs, straight through the Indian Reserve, and on to the steamer landing via the existing beach road. Such a route, while avoiding both the Back Road hill and the hill at Comox Landing, would require expensive bridging and trestlework over the tidal flats.

Political interference eroded Drabble's authority as road superintendent. Ash and the petitioners persuaded the Chief Commissioner of Lands and Works to drop Drabble's road plan in favour of the elaborate and costly road across the flats. In June 1875 Beaven called for tenders, and in July the contract to construct a wagon road between the new bridge and the wharf—worth close to $8,000 and incorporating the entire 1875 appropriation for Comox roads—was awarded to George Baker and Joseph Nicholson of Victoria.[28]

Drabble, perhaps reluctantly, found himself superintending the construction of what was called the Comox or Flat Road, the most notable feature of which was the "Long Bridge"—an elevated shoreline bridge over the slough, the swamp, and the tide flats. This road ran along the

[26] *British Columbia Gazette*, 29 May 1875, p. 131; env. 146; British Columbia, Department of Public Works, Contracts, specifications, 1862-1909.

[27] Env. 100. On the hazards of the Back Road see Courtenay *Weekly News*, 11 January 1893, p. 4.,

[28] British Columbia, Department of Public Works, Contracts, specifications, 1862-1909; Ash to Vernon, 11 July 1876, British Columbia, Department of Lands and Works, Correspondence Inward, 1871-1883; *British Columbia Gazette*, 27 June 1874, p. 115; 3 July 1875, p. 160.

outer edge of the estuary and over the mud flats and sloughs that separated the Indian Reserve from the main farming district of the Valley. The "swamp farms" in Sections 7 through 14 faced the estuary and were subject to seasonal flooding when the Tsolum burst its banks; high tides also brought salt water far into the farms via Mitchell's Slough and the smaller estuarial sloughs. An elevated roadbed placed on pilings seemed the best way across, as it would let the tides and the river floods wash underneath — and avoid any semblance of a hill.

The specifications called for 1,062 feet of continuous trestlework, a pile bridge 561 feet long, and no less than seven smaller bridges over sloughs and creeks. Part of the road went through patches of fir and spruce, some through "Open flat land" and some "Open shell bank," indicating that the estuary had seen extensive Native use. On the modern map, the Long Bridge extended from Field's Saw Mill to the Ocean Cement Silo, just west of the Indian Reserve.

Between July and November 1875 Drabble supervised the construction of the Flat Road. He recorded the daily wages of "Chinamen," "White Men," and "Indians." In August, eighteen Chinamen and six White Men were at work on the Flat Road, and toward the end of the project Drabble hired "2 Indians." Two camps were attached to this project: Nicholson's and Baker's.

Nicholson's road camp went up first, at the end of July, and remained open into November. Drabble recorded daily expeditures and personnel, the number of horses at work, and layout on grub and horse feed. The camp moved regularly to keep up with the progress of the road. Baker's task was to drive piles across the slough. Drabble and McPhee arranged for and supplied the timber. On 5 August Baker was "Fixing Pile Driver &c;" pile driving commenced two days later. Only White Men worked on the project, and they got $1.75 a day. Work continued into the winter: "Sunday Nov 14th frost heavy snow fall," Drabble wrote in his notebook. On the evening of 16 November the camp moved to Rodello's store at the landing and most men were released.[29]

Nicholson and Baker finished the Long Bridge before the end of the year, but they could not complete the road owing to the early onset of the rainy season and the absense of a local supply of suitable rock. For many years Comox farmers had been in the habit of clearing their land of rocks and stones and piling them on the edges of their fields for the road workers, who used them as fill or crushed them with sledge hammers for use as "Macadam," the mixture of broken stones ideal as a

---

[29] British Columbia, Department of Public Works, Contracts, specifications, 1862-1909; envs. 97 and 127.

road surface. Every November at the Duncan farm, when the ground was bare of crops, Oliver, Robina, and their nephew Eric Duncan "gathered and hauled stones on the hill-slopes of Section XVI, piling tons and tons along the roadside fences, from whence the road workers took them when wanted to reinforce the river banks." However, these river cobbles were hard, round boulders unsuitable for the surface of a road, and Drabble authorized Nicholson to use a mixture of fine gravel and clam shell ("shell gravel") found on the flats; this mixture, he wrote, did not make such a durable road as rock and gravel, "yet it makes a very compact and even one, and will stand all the traffic likely to pass over it for several years hence."[30]

Nicholson could not finish the road portion of the contract in time partly because his bid had been too low—and partly because the neighbouring farmers resented that he was not a "Comox man" and that he had hired Chinese workers. They refused to allow him to remove waste gravel from their farms. In June 1876 Drabble explained to Forbes Vernon, the new Chief Commissioner of Lands and Works, that:

> There is no doubt but that he [Nicholson] took the building of the road too low, and every difficulty is thrown in his way against getting his materials in convenient places, owing to a designing prejudice against him by the people here because he is not a Comox man, and that he is employing a great number of Chinamen to work on the contract; all of which is as ridiculously absurd as it was of the Government to attempt to build a road to foster the whims of such people, after I had written the then Chief Commissioner condemning it or any road for the like traffic with such an amount of bridges, where it could have been built in a more convenient location and upon the best possible ground for making a permanent highway, which would have improved annually at a very trifling cost for repairs, instead of the one now under contract, which will be an everlasting tax upon the people, one-tenth part of the entire length being over plank trestle-work and bridges.

In July, Vernon sent road-maker A. R. Howse up from Cowichan to report independently on the road. Howse found Baker's substitution of shell gravel for rock quite acceptable "owing to the nature of the ground," and he endorsed the road and Drabble's original plan for a road along the side hill:

> The original line marked out by Mr. Drabble was on the rising ground surrounding the prairie, and it is much to be regretted that such line was not

---

[30] *From Shetland to Vancouver Island*, p. 153; Drabble to F. George Vernon, 10 July 1876, *British Columbia Sessional Papers* (1877), p. 535.

adopted, as the soil is first-class for road-making, and although the distance is a little further, it would have saved at least 2,000 feet of bridging.[31]

Howse and Drabble were right in their opinions of the extraordinary Long Bridge. It started to tilt as the pilings sank. It was slippery when wet. It was a terrifying and dangerous place during floods and winter storms. Parents at Comox Landing refused to send their children to the Mission school during storms for fear that they would be blown out to sea. Rosemary Lowry (née Anderton) recalled that "Children walking over the 'Long Bridge' in those days were in danger of being blown off the bridge during a south-easter."[32] The bridge needed constant repair, by 1890 it was hazardous, and in 1895 it was replaced with a raised dyke road.

This was not the end of the trouble. Everyone in 1875—Ash, the petitioners, and Drabble—assumed that the road would run along the beach and along the waterfront to the Comox wharf. After all, there was already a shoreline road from the Indian Reserve and Hudson's Bay Company store to the wharf. They had not reckoned on the intransigence of James Robb, owner of the Comox townsite. They needed his cooperation, but he refused to let the road through his property, citing the provisions of the Land Act which prevented any government road from going directly through a settler's house and orchard. Drabble then had no choice but to build the road up "Siwash Hill," and by doing so he incurred the wrath of settlers like Carwithen, who thought he had spitefully "paid them out" for subverting his plan for a side hill road. Eric Duncan summarized the controversy as follows:

> The construction of the long trestle over the tide flats about 1875 let the settlers out by the lower road to the Hudson's Bay store, and to communication with the steamer by boat and canoe from the Indian beach, and the back road fell gradually into disuse, except on rainy days when the long bridge was too slippery for oxen. But the wharf was built shortly after, and now there was an agitation that the lower road should never leave the beach, but continue on around McCutcheon's Point to the wharf. But the main street of the Robb town-site ran straight up from the wharf and was designed to connect with the original road to the Valley. There was a provincial statute to the effect that though one-twentieth of a man's land could be taken without compensation for public highways, his orchard and his buildings were inviolable, and Robb had both across the line of the wished-for road. So Drabble had to do the best he could, and many a weary team of oxen struggled up the Siwash hill with their loads of pigs and potatoes, and then skidded down the steep

[31] Drabble to Vernon, 21 June 1876 and A. R. Howse to Vernon, 22 July 1876, *British Columbia Sessional Papers* (1877), p. 535.

[32] Rosemary Lowry, "Comox School, and Early Teachers," in Isenor, "The Comox Valley."

slope to the wharf (vastly steeper then than now) with the yokes rattling on their horns.[33]

Despite these problems, by 1876 the main road from the wharf to the Courtenay River was in place. For the next few years Drabble awarded contracts for work on all the Comox roads—but it was work for maintenance and extension, rather than new road-building. He selected contractors from among the local farmers, who knew the locale, possessed their own sources of rock and gravel, and hired their sons or neighbours. Road-making thus became an important source of government largesse in what was still largely a barter economy. One road worker was newcomer Eric Duncan, who in the fall of 1877 worked on the roads after scything hay in on the Duncan farm. When the hay was in, he recalled, "I was let off for a few days' work on the roads at $2.00 for ten hours, and as in Shetland my wages had been 50 cents for twelve hours, I thought I had struck El Dorado."[34]

Road work brought many benefits to the valley. Roads and bridges required timber, lumber, livestock, provisions, and the handiwork of tradesmen like blacksmith John McKenzie, who arrived in Comox in 1879. He worked there for ten years before moving to Courtenay, where generations of children watched him make bridge bolts at his smithy.[35]

∽

It was business as usual for Drabble in 1877. He spent a busy summer and fall supervising road and bridge construction and hiring cattle, oxen, and horses. In October, the road work nearly finished, he wrote to John Austin, clerk at the Lands and Works Department. "I send by this mail also an application for some time in my own hook."[36]

Perhaps as a result of his run-ins with the settlers, Drabble retired as Superintendent of Comox Roads over the winter of 1877-78. He was replaced by farmer Archibald Milligan, who Duncan remembered as a "hardworking Irishman, particularly liked by all who came in contact with him. He was road boss of the valley for several years, and stuck to the pick and shovel as hard as any of his men."[37]

---

[33] *From Shetland to Vancouver Island*, pp. 116-17.

[34] British Columbia, Department of Public Works, Contracts, specifications, 1862-1909; "Trail cutting to Mr. G. Grieves along Western boundary of James Reeses Claim," 25 October 1876, Herald Street Collection; Ede Anfield, "Pioneer Woman Remains Remarkably Young at 94," *CVFP*, 18 April 1956; *From Shetland to Vancouver Island*, p. 130.

[35] Carroll, *Wild Roses and Rail Fences*, p. 80.

[36] British Columbia, Department of Public Works, Contracts, specifications, 1862-1909; Drabble's field notebook, 5 June–29 October 1877, Buckham Collection; Drabble to Austin, 10 October 1877, Herald Street Collection.

[37] Duncan, "Early Days and Early Settlers."

Drabble, however, left an impressive physical legacy. There is ample reason for revision of Eric Duncan's statement that Comox roads were in a neglected condition in 1877 when he arrived. "None of the roads were graded," Duncan asserted; "even surveyed highways were mere tracks in the open and trails in the woods."[38] On the contrary, the valley possessed fine roads, wharves, and bridges, the result of fifteen years of labour, constructed with the best local materials and maintained at public expense—roads and bridges that made possible the rural settlement and urbanization of the valley in the late 1880s and 1890s. Drabble's work for the Lands and Works Department changed the physical appearance of the Comox Valley. His roads and bridges gave the farmers access to the wharf and to Pidcock's sawmill on the west bank of the Courtenay River, and eventually connected old Comox to Robert Dunsmuir's new mine beneath the Beauforts.

Perhaps maddened by petty politics, in the summers of 1878 and 1879 Drabble left Comox altogether and traded with Native people in the Gulf of Georgia. In March 1881 Carwithen wrote that "poor old Drabble" "might have continued doing odd jobs for the Lands & Works Dept but he fell out with them as well as the settlers."[39] Carwithen was right that Drabble had quarrelled with some of the settlers over the location of the Flat Road and over the Comox Hill controversy, but poor old Drabble was only forty-eight in 1881. He had many active years left as a trader, surveyor and magistrate—years when he made a name resolving conflicts between the very settlers he had apparently fallen out with. It was too late to write him off, as Carwithen was apt to do, for Drabble had twenty years ahead of him.

---

[38] *From Shetland to Vancouver Island*, p. 115.

[39] Carwithen to Blaksley, 1 March 1881, Carwithen Correspondence.

CHAPTER 9

Whiskey Bottles and Deer Hides

*And so we set out
to discover history
among the broken bottles
and sand dunes of the world.*

FROM *Clam Diggers to the Sand Bar*, by Tim Lander[1]

*E*VEN while operating his Portuguese Creek farm and supervising Comox roads, Drabble had embarked on yet another career: as trader. In 1873, just as he received his road work from the government, he started to deal in lumber and farm produce. Then at the end of the decade, he quit his work with the Lands and Works Department to become an Indian trader in the Gulf. In 1878, after the Siwash Hill controversy, he disappears from many of the public documents and reappears in his private notebooks as partner of the "notorious" Guiseppe Rodello, Comox constable, hotel keeper, bootlegger, and fur trader. For Drabble, this was a time of striking change and adaptation. He formed a union with a Native woman, "Drabble's Mary," with whom he had at least one child. He left behind farming, the profession of his youth, the memory of his wife, and the confines and strictures of farming in the Comox Valley for the larger, commercial, world of the Gulf of Georgia.

Drabble's trading activities must be placed against the background of events in the tumultuous 1860s, when Hart and Holder and the Burrage Brothers had traded furs and deerskins at their stores near the Indian Reserve. They had sold blankets and flour, and in the case of Hart and Holder, whiskey. In 1868, after Holder's death, Hart closed his store at Comox and moved to Victoria where he opened a curio business called the "Indian Bazaar." Here, for many years, he sold baskets, masks, and other paraphernalia to tourists.[2]

---

[1] Lander, *To an Inland Sea*, pp. 35-36.
[2] Tolmie to Lewis, 22 June 1868, HBCA B.226/b/35, fo. 936; Cole, *Captured Heritage*, p. 137; Courtenay *Weekly News*, 4 January 1893, p. 4.

His departure coincided with the Hudson's Bay Company's arrival. This venerable London-based company had lost its trade monopoly on Vancouver Island in 1849, but two decades later was still very powerful and active, though now primarily in shipping and retail in addition to the fur trade. The company had two aims in opening the store at Comox: to intercept the furs of "Northern Indians" before they reached the competitive Victoria market, and to supply the growing agricultural settlement of Comox with merchandise. The company brought to bear its own unique mixture of trading experience and English capital, though in the end these would be of little consequence.[3]

The company leased both Hart's and the Burrages' land and buildings at Comox and opened a store in the fall of 1868. Despite the apparent legality of transfer, some Native people at Comox believed that the company built its post on their land. In 1952 Agnes Edwards recalled that:

> The Hudson's Bay Company negotiated with the Indians for land on which to build a trading post. According to Indian tradition, promises were made that the land would be returned to the Indians in time. Rental payments were made in rolls of tobacco which the Indians prized highly. Despite the terms of the early agreement it is Mrs Edwards' belief that the land is still withheld from the Indians.[4]

When Hart left Comox, the company obtained his old store, which they placed in charge of Adam Horne, previously of Fort Simpson and Nanaimo. The company built him a dwelling-house with a large fireplace and chimney of English brick brought around Cape Horn, and Horne built a lean-to addition to Hart's old store. Settler Isabella Piercy remembered that the company's store was primarily an "Indian store," and Jules Willemar, who arrived in 1871, recalled that "storekeeping was a much more profitable business then than now and the Indian trade far more valuable." Horne was also a livestock dealer. He sold live geese.[5]

According to one visitor the Comox Indians had "implicit trust" in the company, and the patterns of trade and social contact between traders and Native people in the colony owed much to the company's

---

[3] Bissett to Grahame, 12 October 1870, HBCA B.226/b/44, fos. 673-74, 690; *From Shetland to Vancouver Island*, p. 99; Tolmie to Lewis, 22 June 1868, HBCA B.226/b/35, fo. 936.

[4] Isabelle Stubbs, "Indian History Recounted by Matriarch," *CVFP*, 30 October 1952.

[5] *From Shetland to Vancouver Island*, p. 99; Tolmie to Lewis, 22 June 1868, HBCA B.226/b/35, fo. 936; Ede Anfield, "Pioneer Woman Remains Remarkably Young at 94," *CVFP*, 18 April 1956; Courtenay *Weekly News*, 8 November 1893, p. 1; Mildred Haas, "Alexander Urquhart and Wife," in Isenor, "The Comox Valley."

precedent. Over its fifty years on the Pacific coast the Hudson's Bay Company had traded its high-quality goods and indispensible blankets to advantage. Blankets were the main unit of exchange on the entire coast, as geologist George Dawson noted in 1878:

> 2½ point blankets are the recognised Currency among the Coast Indians, now equal to about $1.50. Everything is worth so many blankets, even a large blanket Such as a 4 point, is Said to be worth so many *blankets* par excellence. The H.B. Co. & traders even take blankets from the Indians as money, when in good condition & sell them out again as required.[6]

The company's monopoly of the Comox market was very shortlived. In 1868 a trader arrived from Nanaimo to fill the gap left by Hart, Holder, and the Burrage brothers: Guiseppe (Joe) Rodello, a Native of Ivrea, near Turin, Italy. Rodello had been one of Garibaldi's soldiers in the wars for the unification of Italy.[7]

Rodello specialized in the fur trade and in general goods and hardware. In 1869 he held a liquor licence at Comox, but he relinquished it the next year when he became a constable and a British subject. By 1873 he was deeply involved with the fur trade at Comox in competition with the Hudson's Bay Company. In the same year the Provincial Secretary removed Rodello from his job of constable owing to his regular absences from Comox and large business dealings, which interfered with his official duties. Rodello wanted the job back; no one in Comox, he stated, had any objections to his being reinstated "on condition that I give up my trading which I am perfectly willing to do." "At the present time," he continued, "I have an opportunity of disposing of my business and such a change would be of great benefit to me." Rodello did not dispose of his business, but he did work increasingly often with Drabble; indeed Drabble wrote Rodello's letter for him.[8]

With canny foresight Rodello bought a building lot from James Robb at the landing across from the sandspit, and when the government built the wharf there in 1874, he was in an excellent position to wage commercial war with the Hudson's Bay Company. In November of that year he started his new store and ordered a large stock of goods to engage in the fur trade. In June 1875 Drabble measured Rodello's large lot (divided by the road leading to the wharf) at the Comox wharf; his

---

[6] [J. W. McKay], "Fort Simpson in the Forties," in Walkem, *Stories of Early British Columbia*, pp. 75-86; Cole and Lockner, *To the Charlottes*, p. 52.

[7] Env. 131, Drabble Papers; *From Shetland to Vancouver Island*, pp. 108-09; see also McDonald, "Second Prize Article," p. 1; Courtenay *Weekly News*, 4 January 1893, p. 4.

[8] Rodello to Provincial Secretary, 20 October 1873, Provincial Secretary, Correspondence Inward, 1871-1892.

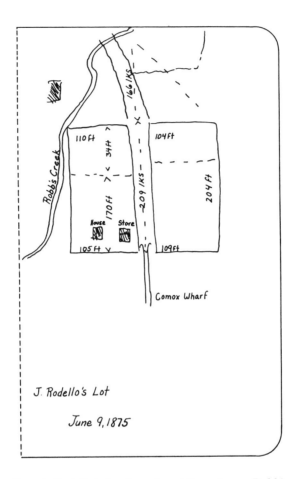

The sketch shows labels: 110 ft, 104 ft, 34 ft, 209 iks, 166 iks, 170 ft, 204 ft, Robb's Creek, House, Store, 105 ft, 109 ft, Comox Wharf, J. Rodello's Lot, June 9, 1875.

Joseph Rodello's lot (purchased from James Robb),
Comox Wharf, 9 June 1875.

sketch shows a house and store on the west side of the road. Between
1875 and 1880 Rodello served as Comox postmaster, a job with which
Drabble lent his assistance.[9]

Liquor was Rodello's other specialty. Michael Manson implied that
Rodello continued to deal in liquor even after he had given up his
license. Manson—later a Justice of the Peace on Cortes Island—arrived from the Shetlands in October 1874 and while helping to build
the Comox wharf, met "the notorious Joe Rodello, the Store keeper and
Postmaster, as well as the rank and file of the hangers on around the

[9] Williams to Charles, 16 November 1874, HBCA B.226/c/3; field notebook 3A, p. 36,
env. 127; Isenor, *Land of Plenty*, p. 131.

store where there was frequently a drink to be had as Rodello did considerable bootlegging there was no hotel at that time."[10]

Rodello's superior location, mastery of the fur trade, and perhaps his illicit liquor eroded the Hudson's Bay Company's position in Comox. As early as 1870 company officials had voiced concerns about their location in a rented building a mile and a half from Robb's townsite. "The goods can be delivered only in boats, and canoes, at high tide;" James Bissett wrote, "the cost of which is about $1.00 p. ton. In continuing the business, it will be subject for consideration, and in fact, would appear to be necessary to remove to the landing opposite to the anchorage."[11]

Soon Rodello joined forces with George Drabble, who started trading in the early 1870s. "Went to Point Holmes," Drabble wrote on 17 September 1873; "stayed at Rodellos all night." Ten days later he noted that for $15 he had bought from Rodello a bed, bedstead, a mattress, two window blinds, and 500 shakes. Drabble built a dwelling at Comox Landing, a simple office perhaps with a bed for overnight stays when he couldn't get back to the farm. Over the next few months he exchanged money and paid for postage at Rodello's, bought an axe ($2.50), socks ($1.25), and on two occasions tobacco ("Rodello for Tobacco 50 cts"), and through him arranged for a subscription to the Victoria *Standard*.[12]

Comox Landing was an ideal centre for Drabble's growing legal, road, and business dealings. He became a middleman between Victoria and Nanaimo merchants and the settlers of Comox. At first he was independent, but at the end of the decade he and Rodello joined forces. His 1873-74 notebooks contain a patchwork of references to Comox merchants and dealers: he paid Horne $192 on one occasion. He recorded transactions between his hired help Louis and Horne, and between Horne and Joe McPhee, who at this time was beginning his career as a contractor on government projects. More substantial were his dealings with Captain Clarke of the *Douglas*, with whom Drabble sent cereals to Victoria in exchange for lumber and manufactured products. Clarke, in the early 1870s, brought the *Douglas* to Comox from Victoria every two weeks, and through him merchants like Drabble and John Wilson ordered their goods; indeed this traffic was one of the things that eroded the Hudson's Bay Company's business at Comox.

He also sent agricultural produce to Victoria. On 3 December 1873 he noted "Indian Canoe bringing Bran &c $1.00;" two weeks later he

[10] Spalding to Colonial Secretary, 16 November 1869 and 4 March 1870, Colonial Correspondence; Manson, "Sketches," p. 3.

[11] Bissett to Grahame, 12 October 1870, HBCA B.226/b/44, fos. 673-74, 690.

[12] Env. 89, Drabble Papers.

noted that he had paid Captain Clarke 10$ on account of the "Bran &c.," and at the end of the year he made a memo "To Settle with Capt. Clarke for Bridge's Oats. 50 Sacks."

Lumber was his major transaction through Clarke. Pidcock did not get his sawmill going on the Courtenay River until about 1877, and there was a limited but lively local demand for lumber. In November 1873, Drabble received a shipment from the "Mills" of 31,702 feet of lumber. This was perhaps Sayward's mill at Shawnigan Creek, which had provided lumber for the first Comox school. The next shipment came from Sewell Moody's mill on the north shore of Burrard Inlet (Moodyville): in January 1874 he made the following note: "Amt of a/c for Lumber Shippd for which Capn. Clarke accepted Bill to Moody. Abt. 475$." That is, Clarke had picked up $475 worth of lumber at Moody's mill and delivered it to Drabble.[13]

In 1873-74 Drabble was engaged in the lumber trade, supplying rough lumber, scantling, battens, rustic, and T & G (Tongue and Groove) to fifteen settlers, most of whom took between one and five thousand feet, including a quantity of T & G for flooring. Most seem to have picked up the lumber themselves, but Drabble paid Joseph (Alphonse) Pelon $10 to transport 5,000 feet of Oliver Duncan's lumber. In 1876 Drabble and Horne formed a Comox branch of the A.O.F.—the Ancient Order of Foresters, a friendly society.[14]

Drabble also traded lumber to the region around Comox. On 15 November 1873 he noted that he had "Agreed with Capt. Jones to take Lumber to Denman Isld 3$ per thousand." This was probably James (Jemmy) Jones of the schooner *Industry*. Jones, a Native of Wales and a legend on the coast, had come to Vancouver Island in about 1854 aged twenty-four. According to Captain Walbran he could neither read nor write, "but trusted to a good memory in business matters." He agreed with Jones to take two tons of Oliver Duncan's potatoes to Victoria, but when Jones did not pay for them, Drabble asked Jones to deliver the money to Victoria lawyers Tyrwhitt-Drake and Jackson or suffer the consequences.[15]

The Hudson's Bay Company continued to worry about Rodello. "This person," a company official wrote in November 1874, "left Comox last summer with a large number of deer and other skins which he took to New York and sold, I am given to understand he did very well with them." Moreover, Hart's old store, built merely of one inch boards

---

[13] Env. 89. See James Morton, *The Enterprising Mr. Moody, the Bumptious Captain Stamp. The Lives and Colourful Times of Vancouver's Lumber Pioneers* (Vancouver: J. J. Douglas, 1977).

[14] Envs. 89, 96, 97, 127; see "Excursion" of Foresters, *Nanaimo Free Press*, 31 May and 10 June 1876.

[15] Walbran, *British Columbia Coast Names*, pp. 266-27; env. 89.

with battens over the joists, was rotting, and the company's three small storage houses were packed full of goods and furs. Horne recommended that the company move to the landing to compete with Rodello. Here they could build a "more commodious and stronger building" than the several small ones they then occupied near the Reserve. Chief Trader Robert Williams described the company's predicament in November 1874:

> Should you decide on building, I would recommend the giving up of the property now occupied, and lease or purchase, either can be done, a piece of land in a more suitable position. There is under construction, by the Government, at this place a long jetty or wharf and very shortly vessels instead of anchoring in the harbour will lay at the wharf and, in consequence, trade will centre around this landing, this would, in my opinion, be a far better business stand, and a great expense and loss of time saved; as it is at present we have to hire canoes, no other mode available, and take our goods from the steamer to the store a distance of 1 1/2 miles. Mr. Horne informs me, a piece of land could be leased near the wharf and on as equally favorable terms as the ground we now occupy.[16]

Amazingly, the company did not act on Horne's and Williams' sound advice, and closed the Comox store in November 1877, citing lack of profit caused by competition in the fur and retail trades. Traders Wilson, Clarke, and Drabble had done a good deal of business with the settlers, Rodello was adept at the fur trade, and the fortnightly visits of the *Douglas* allowed farmers to obtain their supplies directly from Victoria in exchange for produce.[17]

The overall result was that people started shopping at Comox Landing rather than at the Hudson's Bay Company's store. "My son and myself," Horne told Eric Duncan in 1877, "have stood a whole day behind that counter for one dime." The company thus lost a good opportunity to form a viable retail business in a growing settlement. In about 1878 Horne left the company and went into business in Nanaimo, where he continued to handle Comox farm produce.[18]

A few old Hudson's Bay Company families lent the young community a measure of stability—or at least continuity—that was otherwise lacking in the settler population. Old Shetland carpenter Gideon Halcrow built houses in the valley in the mid-1860, and Horne, his wife Elizabeth, and their children lived at Comox from 1868 to 1877. Horne's clerks at the store included his son Adam H. Horne and George Hamilton Blenkinsop. Later arrivals with Hudson's Bay Company connections included merchant J. B. Holmes, an ex-company employee

---

[16] Williams to Charles, 16 November 1874, HBCA B.226/c/3.

[17] Charles to Armit, 10 October 1877, HBCA B.226/b/48, fo. 407; B.226/b/52, fo. 4.

[18] *From Shetland to Vancouver Island*, pp. 99, 100.

from Kamloops; Comox policeman Walter Birnie Anderson, son of fur trader A. C. Anderson; and Eliza Parkin (née Malpass), matriarch of the large Parkin clan of the Comox Valley, who had arrived as a girl at Nanaimo from Staffordshire in 1854 on a Hudson's Bay Company immigrant ship.[19]

Rodello, having reduced the Hudson's Bay Company to dealing in nickles and dimes, lost no time in consolidating his position. He demolished his old house and store at the landing and, in 1877, built a new store and the Elk Hotel in their place. The Elk, built by Bruno Mellado, stood almost down on the beach. In the middle 1870s Rodello entered into an informal partnership with Drabble, who acted as his amanuensis; Rodello wrote poorly in English, and Drabble sometimes wrote (and signed) his letters for him. Having sold his farm to Rennison in 1875 and moved permanently to the wharf, Drabble became Rodello's associate in the fur trade and in his various government work. "Rodello bought the ground on both sides of the road at the head of the wharf," Eric Duncan recalled, "and built on the east side a large rambling store, and on the west the old original Elk Hotel. For a good many years he was storekeeper, hotel-man, constable, tax collector and postmaster, but he had the help of Drabble in the two latter offices, and about the time I came [1877], he rented out the hotel." The Elk Hotel became a Comox institution for some fifty years, a haven for hunters and fishermen, and a drinking establishment with a certain reputation among local loggers and miners. A later visitor described it as follows:

> The Elk had a wide carpeted stairway rising to a landing from the lobby then turning to a long hall and to rooms, many with broad windows facing out to sea. [It] stood back from the beach, where, on the wide, shaded verandahs guests lounged and talked about fish and lures and tackle, or just rested quietly, puffing pipes, while watching small steamers and fishing craft at the end of the long pier which stood on spindly piles.[20]

∽

Drabble's second surviving trade notebook dates from 1878-79. He had a store at Cape Mudge for the storage of dogfish oil, and almost all his customers were Native. Years later, Drabble's friend Walter Anderson recalled that Drabble had been "associated with the late J. Rodello in trading with the northern ports in early days."[21]

---

[19] Bill Newman, "The Reverend Jules Xavier Willemar;" Rhoda Beck, "Parkin Reunion;" for Blenkinsop and Horne Jr. see *The Daily Standard*, 17 February 1873, p. 3.

[20] Duncan, "Comox District Fifty Years Ago." The Elk was built by Bruno Mellado: see McDonald, "Second Prize Article," p. 1; *From Shetland to Vancouver Island*, pp. 108-09; Eric Sismey, "The Elk Hotel," *Colonist* (Islander) 1 April 1973, p. 7.

[21] *The Cumberland News* 18 September 1901, p. 8.

With the Hudson's Bay Company gone late in 1877, the entire Native fur trade of the northern part of the Gulf of Georgia was up for grabs. Drabble sought to buy furs from Native people at their villages in return for trade goods. Such an arrangement suited all concerned: Indians found a local source of goods and provisions, and traders intercepted furs before they reached Victoria's competitive, pricey, market. Drabble also traded for dogfish oil, a valuable commodity on the coast, in demand both as a fuel for lamps and as skid road grease — that is, as a lubricant spread on skid roads to help oxen or horses pull heavy logs to the water. Fish-oil lamps were also used underground by coal miners in the Dunsmuir mines. "The dog-fish is very abundant along some parts of the coast," Dawson wrote in 1878; "the oil extracted from the liver is readily sold to white traders, and constitutes one of the few remaining articles of legitimate marketable value possessed by the natives."[22]

In the spring, summer, and fall months of 1878 and 1879 Drabble traded out of Comox in association with Rodello, performing a middle-man role between the marketplace and the Native customers. He traded at Cape Mudge, Squirrel Cove on Cortes Island, and elsewhere. Michael Manson, who set up as an Indian trader on Cortes Island a few years later, recalled that the principal trade items were dogfish oil, deer skins, and furs. In return for such commodities as these, Drabble exchanged traps, ammunition, rifles, hooks, line, rope, and other hunting and fishing equipment, general hardware, clothing, and staple foodstuffs like potatoes, flour, and "saleratus" or baking soda: by the 1870s home-made bread was a popular domestic and potlatch item on the coast.[23]

Drabble obtained at least some of his trade goods from Victoria merchants via Captain Clarke of the *Douglas*. In April 1879, for example, he bought "1 Box 4 Suits Clothing 42 doz Collars Hooks & Eyes 3 doz Socks 8 Chemise 3 dz Handkerchiefs 12 Hammers" from Clarke.[24] He also traded blankets, the staple currency in the Native economies, and he received goods from merchants and traders Rodello, Horne (then of Nanaimo), J. Collins, and David Croll or Crowell.

By 1878 Drabble had started trading directly, in his sloop *Mermaid*, with the Native people at Cape Mudge and elsewhere. His custom-ers were mainly Salish-speakers from the Gulf of Georgia and Kwak-waka'wakw speakers from Cape Mudge and further north. In 1878 he traded dogfish oil from Quomshut of the "Queek Ranch," one of

[22] For an 1879 "New York Price List of Furs" see env. 141; for dogfish oil see Bowen, *The Dunsmuirs of Nanaimo*, p. 30; Cole and Lockner, *To the Charlottes*, p. 105; Pidcock, "Adventures in Vancouver Island," pp. 49-50.

[23] Manson, "Sketches;" Cole and Lockner, *To the Charlottes*, p. 89.

[24] Env. 141, Drabble Papers.

thirteen villages of the Kweeha, a Lekwiltok group inhabiting the Phillips Arm and Port Neville region. In the same year he did business with some 200 Native people including the Lekwiltok groups Kweeha, Weewiakum, Komenox, Hahamatsses/Waliltsma, and Weewiakay, who controlled Cape Mudge. He also traded with the Sliammon; "Clayous" (Klahous, a Salish-speaking group); Bute Inlet (Homalco); Harbledown Island (possibly Tlawitsis or Mamililikulla); and Fort Rupert (one of the Kwakiutl tribes). Among his prominent Native customers were Quocksister, Seaweed, and Chuckate from Cape Mudge; Quistetas and Quockquockelis from Queka, and from Salmon River Quinquolattle "alias Jim" and Sarcatzy. Drabble also traded with the scattered non-Native settlers, for example with Peter Berry and David Murray of Denman, and with Lars Olaf Backstrom and James Shields.[25]

In 1879 he got out of the fur and oil business and withdrew his operations to Comox, as he noted in his northern trading account book on 29 May 1879: "Sold Chuckite my Oil Shed at Cape Mudge to be paid in Oil 1.25 per Tin." Reasons for his withdrawal are unknown. Comox merchant J. B. Holmes, who arrived in 1884, believed that Rodello was too generous as an Indian trader. "He was a great friend of the Indians and could speak Chinook and several Indian dialects of the various tribes. He was a very clever trader with the Indians and enjoyed their confidence. He had been in business but owing to giving unlimited credit to the Indians he was unable to continue."[26] Drabble, as Rodello's partner, may have suffered from the same weakness, or he may have decided to return full-time to his surveying and legal careers.

Drabble, with Clarke, Rodello, and Wilson, was among the first to trade between the farmers of Comox and buyers in southern markets. As a farmer he was suited to such a role, but he left it to Wilson, another farmer-turned-trader, to grow wealthy selling Comox farm produce in Victoria on a commission basis.

Drabble's business partnership had ended before Rodello's store was destoyed by fire in June 1881. Eric Duncan recalled the fire as follows:

> Some three years after my arrival my employer and I, on bringing down a load of produce for shipment, found that Rodello's store had burned down the day before, and nothing was left on the site but a battered and blackened safe. The Robbs also had been put to much trouble to save their barn, as the sparks had flown there, and few people were around to help. The old gentleman [James Robb] was quite exasperated, and I heard him shouting to the arriving settlers, "Joe Rodello should be taken and lynched."[27]

---

[25] Env. 29; Galois, *Kwakwaka'wakw Settlements*, map 2.32, pp. 7-22; pp. 223-76 for identifications; Galois to author, 10 January 1995.

[26] Env. 29; Holmes, "Reminiscences."

[27] *From Shetland to Vancouver Island*, p. 130.

An inquiry was held: Rodello, Frank Collins, John Fitzpatrick, William Dingwall, Thomas Beckensell, and Joe McPhee gave evidence. A jury concluded that Rodello had not set the fire intentionally, nor had anyone else committed arson—though people had threatened on occasion to burn down his place. "A Jury called to enquire into the cause of Rodello's fire," Mary Harmston wrote in her diary; "decision cause unknown no blame attached to Rodello."[28]

Drabble's association with Rodello did not do him much good in the eyes of the yeomen of Comox. "I saw old Drabble the other day," Carwithen wrote to Blaksley in August 1880, he "has a hard time to scratch a living except by claiming relationship with some of the chiefs." A few months later he wrote again to Blaksley that "Poor old Drabble isn't worth much, barring a whale boat which he calls the sloop Mermaid."[29]

The meaning of these references is clear: Drabble was not doing well in trade, but on the positive side he had entered into some sort of relationship with a Native woman of chiefly rank. Her identity is not known. She may have been a daughter of Joseph, one of his Clayhous customers, from whom in May 1879 he had obtained deer skins. His account book reveals that in 1878 and 1879 he had accounts with Joseph, his wife, and their daughter Julia:

[Spring 1879]. "Julia. Clayous. .37 1/2"
[Spring 1879]. "Joseph (Julia's Father). Clayous. .50"
[Spring 1879]. "Julia. Clayous. 5.37 1/2"
[22 August 1879]. "Pd. Julia's Mother 1 Blanket. 1.25"
5 September 1879. "Pd Julias Mother 1 pr Blankets 3$"[30]

This, admittedly, is flimsy evidence on which to suggest a relationship, but in Comox persistent rumours indicated that he was involved with a Native woman. His wife Louisa, after all, had died in 1863, and his children remained under his father-in-law's inflexible rule in England, so he was not bound by local familial responsibilities or even by distant ones. His partner Rodello is known to have had at least one daughter by a Native woman.

In the 1950s, Mary Harmston's grandaughter Myra Thompson (née Cliffe) told Gordon Wagner a story about a woman named "Drabble's Mary." Wagner wrote as follows:

---

[28] British Columbia, Attorney General, Inquests, 1865-1937; Harmston Diary, 15 June 1881.

[29] Carwithen to Blaksley, 29 August 1880 and 1 March 1881, Carwithen Correspondence.

[30] Env. 141, Drabble Papers.

In the mid-fifties I was doing a timber survey for the Olympic Logging Company . . . Mrs Thompson was a great hostess and a wonderful cook . . . It was from her that I learned about George Drabble. Mrs Thompson was a Cliffe, a daughter or grandaughter of the original Sam Cliffe. Her first name was Myra. She had been born in the Lorne Hotel. We had the long summer evenings to visit and I plied her with questions about the early days in the Comox Valley. She told me about Drabble and the Native woman he lived with. Her name was Mary, Drabble's Mary. She lived with him in the green-shingled cottage on the Anderton Road.[31]

Certainly the name Drabble has persisted in the Native community. George Drabble and "Mary" had a son named John or Johnny who, through his mother, became a chief. "Old Man Johnny Drabble" built the hall on the reserve at Alert Bay. "He was a very active and progressive Indian," recalled James Sewid, "a very close relation of mine through my grandfather, Chief Sewid." His Native name was Tlagoglas, and William Halliday identified him as the orator at Awalaskinis's illegal potlatch of 1922. Halliday's book included a photograph of "The paid orator with coppers" (confiscated ceremonial goods).[32]

Chief Johnny Drabble had a daughter, Alice Rachel Drabble of Alert Bay, who married Thomas King of Wakeman Sound in the Anglican church at Alert Bay on 5 December 1933. Their two surviving children are Christine Bowbrick of Sayward and Harold King of Campbell River. In March 1995 I tracked down Bowbrick at "Charlie's Place," the Sayward restaurant where she works. We had a long and interesting conversation about her ancestors, but like Drabble's descendents in England she had never heard of her great-grandfather who traded in the northern Gulf one hundred and twenty years ago.[33]

---

[31] Wagner, "George Drabble," pp. 4-5.

[32] Personal Communication, Wadlidi Speck, 14 August 1994; James P. Spradley, ed., *Guests Never Leave Hungry. The Autobiography of James Sewid, A Kwakiutl Indian* (New Haven and London: Yale University Press, 1969), pp. 157-58; Daisy Sewid-Smith, *Prosecution or Persecution* (Alert Bay: Nu-Yum-Balees Society, 1979), p. 92; Halliday, *Potlatch and Totem*, pp. 28-29, opposite p. 32; see also Douglas Cole and Ira Chaikin, *An Iron Hand Upon the People: the Law Against the Potlatch on the Northwest Coast* (Vancouver: Douglas & McIntyre, 1990), pp. 120, 135.

[33] Letter from "Mary" to "Father John," 30 November 1992, "from Anglican Church Records in Victoria" (from Gordon Wagner, November 1993); interview with Christine Bowbrick, 13 March 1995.

George Drabble (1833-1901).
Photograph taken about 1895.

Elizabeth (Lylie), George Drabble's
daughter, *c.* 1885.

Crossburn House, Long Bennington, Lincolnshire. George Drabble's
children were brought up here by his father-in-law Matthew Burnby after
Drabble's abrupt departure for Vancouver Island in 1862.

L-R: George Drabble's daughter Sophie, his two granddaughters, Louie and Annie Bemrose, and one of his Burnby in-laws, *c.* 1910.

George Drabble's son Johnny Drabble (Tlagoglas) with confiscated ceremonial items at Cape Mudge, Quadra Island, 1922.

George Drabble's son Thomas Lambe Drabble of Great Yarmouth, Norfolk.

Reginald Carwithen's log and shake cabin, Comox Valley, 1870s.

Walter Gage's pre-emption, Kye Bay, Comox District, *c.* 1895.

Looking up the new government wharf, Comox, 12 October 1878. James Robb's house and barn are at the left, Rodello's house and store are at the wharf, and the government jail (white building at centre) is under construction.

Comox Valley road scene, *c.* 1900.

Part of the Colonization Road south of Oyster River, *c.* 1900.

Unidentified oxen logging team and skid road, Comox District, *c.* 1900.

Industry in the wilderness: The Baynes Sound Coal Company's wharf, Fanny Bay, 14 October 1878.

Loading coal at James Dunsmuir's shipping point, Union Bay, *c.* 1894.

Camp at unidentified location, possibly Gowlland Harbour, Quadra Island.

A fine farm in the Comox Valley; the Urquhart house and farm, 1912.

A view of Comox from the west showing the road from Courtenay, the Anglican church, Comox wharf, and Comox spit, *c.* 1900.

The Elk Hotel, Comox, *c.* 1910.

Sam Cliffe coming up the hill from Comox wharf with
three of his grandchildren, *c.* 1900.

Looking up the Comox wharf, *c.* 1900. St. Peters Anglican church is at the left;
the Elk Hotel and Holmes's store are on either side of the wharf, and at the top
of the road leading from the wharf is the Lorne Hotel.

Group at the Lorne Hotel, Comox, *c.* 1890. At the top of the stairs is the aged Lorne Hotel diarist, Mary Harmston.

Lorne Hotel group, 1888 or 1889. *L-R*: Maude Cliffe, Ed Millet, Florence Mary Cliffe, Sam Cliffe, Ted Cliffe, Jack McMillan, Florence Sophia Cliffe holding Samuel Hughes Cliffe, unknown, Tom Lever, Jimmy Derbyshire, Myra Cliffe, Jack Dore, Alfred Radford, Jack Rowe, John Hawkins.

View from Back Road, *c.* 1910, with the new town of Courtenay in the background.

View across the Courtenay River Bridge (now 5th Street), *c.* 1899. The large building at the left is Joe McPhee's store. The field of stumps is now Lewis Park, beyond which is the large Courtenay Hotel.

Looking across the Courtenay River, *c.* 1900, showing McPhee's store (bottom right), Drabble's trestle-bridge, McKenzie's blacksmith shop, and the Courtenay Hotel. The Lewis and Duncan farms lie in the distance.

Loading sacks at McPhee's store, Courtenay, *c.* 1905.

Building the Comox Dyke, 1895.

Building the Comox Dyke, 1895: horse teams and men.

Drabble's last major project: the new Courtenay River Bridge, 1900.
In the distance are the Riverside Hotel and McPhee's store.

Steamer Day at Comox, *c.* 1910, with the Elk Hotel at the right and a
group of old-timers contemplating the photographer, Walter Gage.

H.M.S. *Egeria* and H.M.S. *Algernine*, Comox Harbour, *c.* 1895.

The Beaufort Range from the Comox Bluffs, with a Royal Navy
vessel riding at anchor, *c.* 1890.

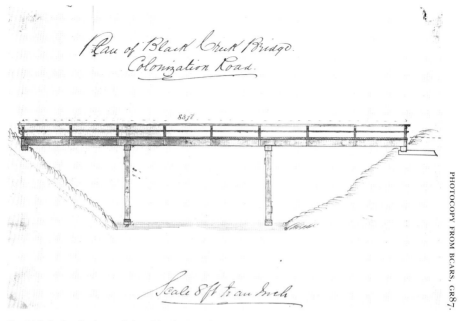

Plan of Black Creek Bridge.
Colonization Road.

83ft

Scale 8ft to an inch

Drabble's final plan of the Black Creek Bridge, Colonization Road,
18 November 1886.

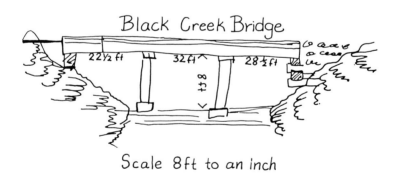

Black Creek Bridge

22½ ft   32 ft   28½ ft

8 ft

Scale 8ft to an inch

14 x 10 Stringers

13 ft   14 x 10
14   14   14
16 ft   10 x 15

Specifications for Black Creek
Bridge, side view and cross section,
3 November 1886.

COPIED FROM NOTE BOOK BY REAH THEOBALD.

CHAPTER 10

Magistrate Drabble

Raining all the last night.
First Snow upon the mountains.
—George Drabble, Comox Notebook, 9 October 1873[1]

D<small>RABBLE</small>'S shadowy private activities filled one compartment of his life; his public activities filled another—historically much more accessible—compartment. In 1873 he was appointed Justice of the Peace, a job he would fill until 1898 at Comox, where eventually he was known as "Judge Drabble" and "Nestor of the Bench." In 1872, when the decision was made to appoint him, he was already something of a pillar of the settlement: road advocate, surveyor, and an ambitious local farmer with a gristmill under construction. He had not yet embarked in business as a trader at Comox Landing, and had not yet entered into his partnership with the notorious Joe Rodello.

Having a resident magistrate in Comox was long overdue. Hart and Holder's whiskey selling had resulted in the death of three settlers and caused much distress locally. Segments of the settler and Native communities had given the valley a rough character since its founding; it was, after all, on the northernmost frontier of the colony. The Comox Indians were still recovering from the 1862 smallpox epidemic and from the loss of their hereditary lands, and the "whisky shops" on the Comox waterfront had offered an escape to elements of both the colonial and Native communities. A magistrate was needed to keep an eye on the whiskey traders and to regulate the visits of the Lekwiltok from Cape Mudge, who were considered a bad influence on the Comox Indians.

Nor was the settler community without the usual squabbles and disputes: in 1865, for example, William Duncan accused his neighbour Edward Goldsmid of "maliciously shooting & making away with two pigs." Two years earlier, the settlers had petitioned the government for a resident magistrate to settle minor differences. The petition, drafted by James Robb, read:

---

[1] Env. 89, Drabble Papers.

We the undersigned settlers of Comax being impressed with the great necessity for a resident officer of the crown to take cognizance of & adjudicate minor differences between the settlers and also to render legal any steps that may be considered necessary for their mutual protection, beg humbly to petition your Excellency to empower a resident to act as magistrate for the district.[2]

Robert Brown found the situation unchanged: "The settlers are loud in crying out for a magistrate & Indian Agent (in one office) to look to the enforcement of the law generally in the Settlement and to the management of Indian affairs between here and Fort Rupert."[3]

In the absence of a local magistrate, the administration of justice in the valley was the responsibility until 1873 of the Nanaimo magistrates, William Franklyn and Warner Spalding. Both had worked previously in the gold districts of the mainland, and both were fiercely overworked: in 1864 Franklyn complained that he was Stipendary Magistate, Harbour Master, Land Recorder, Coroner, and General Government Agent for the whole of Vancouver Island from Nanaimo north. His territory included Comox. Spalding, who succeeded Franklyn in May 1867, had orders to visit Comox each month, "or as often as the interests of the Settlers there should render it advisable."[4]

The Lekwiltok were regarded as the villains of the peace by the Comox settlers owing to their trade and consumption of whiskey. Selling liquor to Indians was illegal on Vancouver Island; in 1871, on joining Canada, the Provincial Government passed a law prohibiting the sale or gift of alcohol to Indians, and imposed a maximum fine of $100 on "any person selling, bartering, or giving, or attempting to sell, barter, or give intoxicating liquor to any Indian."[5]

This law was difficult to enforce on the labyrinthine coastline of British Columbia, where most Native villages were located, and without a magistrate or policeman it was difficult to prevent the likes of Hart and Holder from selling liquor to any buyer. References to the possession of liquor among the Lekwiltok of Cape Mudge are so numerous that it is hard to believe that they did not deal with it on a large scale — as they had dealt traditionally with slaves and other commodities. The Fort Rupert Indians, who stopped at Comox on their way up and down the Gulf, were also involved in this whiskey trade.

---

[2] Franklyn to Colonial Secretary, 10 March 1865, Colonial Correspondence; *From Shetland to Vancouver Island*, p. 137; James Robb, Petition to Governor Douglas, February 1863, [copy at CVMA].

[3] Hayman, *Robert Brown*, p. 124.

[4] McDonald, "Second Prize Article," p. 1; Franklyn to Colonial Secretary, 17 August 1864 and Spalding to Colonial Secretary, 6 November 1870, Colonial Correspondence.

[5] *The Laws of British Columbia* (Victoria: Government Printing Office, 1871), pp. 249-53.

The Lekwiltok fished for salmon and herring at Comox on a seasonal basis, and during their visits they apparently corrupted the Comox Indians. "Generally after the fishing is over," Pidcock recalled, "they all go & camp near the Ranch of the Comox Indians and very often they manage to obtain a supply of Whiskey from some Schooners trading up the Coast get drunk and seldom a night passed [November 1862] without some one of their number was shot or stabbed." The Comox Indians seemed largely innocent. "In Victoria we continually hear of the disorderly character of the Comoucs Indians," Brown stated, "but they suffer by the reputation of the Eucletaws who are often at Comoucs & continually drunk when quarrels are the consequence." A later writer, possibly Drabble, asserted that the Lekwiltok had corrupted the Comox Indians and encouraged them to steal from the settlers.[6]

The Lekwiltok moved to Comox in 1863 in large numbers for strategic and economic reasons—not just to annoy the settlers. They wanted access to the stores of Hart and the Burrage brothers, and they wanted to work for the settlers. Their motives were identical to earlier Native groups who had urged the Hudson's Bay Company to establish posts in their territories. In February 1864 a visitor noted that the Lekwiltok almost continuously had "a large force" camped on the Indian Reserve at Comox, amounting sometimes to over 300 and seldom falling short of 100. Over the next few years the Lekwiltok insisted that they had a right to visit Comox and work there.[7]

Several incidents occurred between the settlers and the Lekwiltok. In October 1864, for example, the litigious William Duncan wrote to surveyor Pearse as follows:

> I the undersined am compelled to trubell you at this time to let you know how I am trubled hear with the Indians the Ucoltoes have com and camped on my ground alongside of my garden and is selling the Potates and puling Down the fance, so that, the hogs and cattle is Destroying what they cant I have taken some of them in the act and the others cam and waleaked [walked] up with ther Bow Knives so you will see that my life as well as property is not save.

> Dear sir I know that this is not your business But as you in the Land Office is the only ones I know I hop that you will pay atinetion to this and try to send the gun Boat up to remove them of my ground as my crope is my only Dependence for Liveing.[8]

---

[6] Pidcock, "Adventures in Vancouver Island," pp. 81-82; Hayman, *Robert Brown*, p. 123; Courtenay *Weekly News*, 28 December 1892, p. 1.

[7] *British Colonist*, 18 February 1864, quoted in Hayman, *Robert Brown*, p. 154, n. 160.

[8] Duncan to Pearse, 17 October 1864, in British Columbia, Department of Lands and Works, Correspondence Inward from William Duncan.

Pearse noted that Duncan's land was not an Indian reserve, and that "the Indians complained of, live some 40 or 50 miles further up the Coast, and have always been a turbulent and warlike tribe. They are from Point Mudge (Euclataws)."⁹

The Lekwiltok worked for the settlers for low wages, especially in their potato fields and at harvest. In December 1864, Cave reported that the Lekwiltok had returned to Comox and stolen over a ton of potatoes, and Franklyn concluded that the disturbed state of Comox required the appointment of a magistrate to save the expense of sending constables from Nanaimo. The Lekwiltok had to be "removed" to Cape Mudge over the winter of 1864-65 with the aid of a gunboat.¹⁰

Things got very tense in 1865. Cave reported that a party of 150 Lekwiltok—prevented from visiting the potato fields at the old Pentlatch village on the Puntledge River—had threatened to kill a settler or settlers. In October a Lekwiltok drew a knife on William Harmston while trading or digging potatoes.¹¹

Such reports resulted in visits of H.M.S. *Devastation* and other warships, but the captains found to their surprise that the settlers were not nearly as concerned about the Lekwiltok as Cave and Franklyn. In November 1865, Denman and Franklyn visited Comox on the gunboat *Forward* and met with the settlers in heavy rain. They complained that Cave had not consulted with them before writing his alarming dispatches. "About 30 settlers attended," Denman reported, "of whom two-thirds appeared to be in favour of leaving the Euclataw Tribe undisturbed; they stated that their labour was of great importance to the Settlers and that there was no danger to be apprehended from them." Nonetheless Denman informed the Lekwiltok that they were welcome in Comox only between September and December, as these were the earliest and last dates of the appearance of salmon. He wrote that the "growing wants of the Settlers at Comox appear to me to require the labour of these people," and urged the appointment of a magistrate or policeman to maintain order.¹²

---

⁹ Pearse to Kennedy, 19 November 1864, Colonial Correspondence.

¹⁰ Cave to Franklyn, 5 December 1864; Franklyn to Colonial Secretary, 17 December 1864, Colonial Correspondence; Memo by Kennedy, 31 May 1865 on Pearse to Kennedy, 19 November 1864, in British Columbia, Department of Lands and Works, Correspondence Inward from William Duncan; Hayman, *Robert Brown*, p. 124; Barry M. Gough, *Gunboat Frontier: British Maritime Authority and Northwest Coast Indians, 1846-90* (Vancouver: UBC Press, 1984).

¹¹ J. M. Jones to Kennedy, 10 April 1865, C.O. 305; Cave to Colonial Secretary, 13 and October 1865; Franklyn to Colonial Secretary, 18 October 1865, Colonial Correspondence; Harmston Diary, 12 October 1865.

¹² Franklyn to Colonial Secretary, 4 and 13 November 1865; Denman to Kennedy, 14 November 1865, Colonial Correspondence; Kennedy to Colonial Office, 27 No-

Despite all these requests, a resident magistrate was not appointed until late in 1869, when Spalding found the settlers alarmed at robberies and assaults committed after the Fort Rupert tribe sold the Comox Indians large quantities of liquor. He recommended Joe Rodello who was, he wrote, "a most trustworthy and energetic man, and in every way suitable & who has on several occasions rendered me valuable assistance gratuitously." Spalding thought Rodello would make the liqour traffic a thing of the past in six months, but the Colonial Secretary balked because Rodello himself had a liquor license. Rodello promised to give up his license and take the oath of allegiance as a British subject.[13]

Rodello got the job, but he had his work cut out for him. Serious incidents had occurred in the 1860s. In August 1867, for example, an unknown white man was found dead on Hornby Island alongside the bodies of Nanaimo Indians named Quees-tan and Et-sat-sa. The coroner determined that they had killed each other in a "drunken row" on 27 August 1867. Only their bodies remained to tell the tale.[14]

Rodello did his job alone until 1872, when the long absence of a resident Justice of the Peace finally ended. In November 1872 Reginald Pidcock became the first Justice of the Peace, and he was joined the following April by George Drabble and James Robb. All three were then farmers: Pidcock and Drabble in the valley and Robb at Comox Landing. Robb, Eric Duncan recalled, was a man of masterful character who many thought dominated the bench, "but I never found him either unfair or unreasonable."[15]

Drabble—involved so extensively in valley affairs—was in many ways a logical choice. He was known to officials in the Lands and Works Department who were in constant touch with the Provincial Secretary's office. He may have listened to Captain Franklyn when he worked as his farm bailiff in 1865-66. Franklyn was, Captain Walbran wrote, "a fearless and impartial magistrate, and did much to check the unruly and lawless element, among both Europeans and Indians, during his official

vember 1865, C.O. 305. On Lekwiltok tillage of the soil see Milligan, "Fourth Prize Article," and Owen, "Comox," p. 28.

[13] Spalding to Colonial Secretary, 16 November 1869 and 4 March 1870, Colonial Correspondence.

[14] British Columbia, Attorney General, Record Book for the Nanaimo Coroner's Office, 1866-1905.

[15] British Columbia, Attorney General, Register of Justices of the Peace and dates of Commission, 1872-1875; *From Shetland to Vancouver Island*, p. 137; Duncan, "Comox District Fifty Years Ago."

career at Nanaimo." Drabble may have approved of Franklyn's Tory outlook.[16]

Magistrates' duties varied. They were expected to learn on the job, and through their close contact, discussions, and questioning of the circuit judges and the Attorney General's and Provincial Secretary's ministries, they gained a good practical knowledge of the law. They would have received copies of government forms and a manual entitled *Justice of the Peace*, by Richard Burn, but no other training or preparation was required.

Traditionally, in England, appointments were made chiefly on political grounds and from the landed gentry, that is, from landlords to the small farmers and general population of the English countryside. Justices of the Peace were not paid for their services; they were supposed to undertake the job from a sense of duty or *noblesse oblige*; their landed or private income would pay for their public obligations. They were not appointed on account of any legal knowledge: they were to use their common sense in judging cases. A stipendary magistrate, on the other hand, was paid for his services, and by the twentieth century was usually a trained lawyer.

Justices of the Peace dealt with lesser crimes. Their duty generally was to see that the peace was kept. They met four times a year in a court of Quarter Sessions, in which crimes were tried with or without a jury; they also, every week, heard petty civil offences in Courts of Summary Jurisprudence and tried them summarily without a jury, but at least two justices had to be present at a summary court and for the granting of liquor licences—which explains why three justices were appointed at Comox. Indictable offences had to be tried by a higher court, but even a person accused of such an offence was first brought before the magistrates, who made a preliminary inquiry before sending the person to a superior court in Nanaimo or Victoria. Most English legal customs pertinent to magistrates' duties were applied *holus-bolus* in the colony and were later modified to suit local conditions.[17]

By 1870 the government had built a court house at Comox about one hundred yards from James Robb's house. This building was used by Spalding on his regular visits to Comox, and also for general government work. When Pearse, for example, inspected the Comox roads in the spring of 1872 he asked Rodello to ensure that horses were "ready at

---

[16] *Gazette* notices, *Colonist*, 6 April 1873, p. 3; Walbran, *British Columbia Coast Names*, pp. 189-90.

[17] Tina Loo to the author, 9 August 1994; Louis Knafla, personal communication, January 1995; Egerton Smith, *A Guide to English Traditions and Public Life* (Oxford: Oxford University Press, 1953), p. 150.

Court House on the Thursday 9th May at 8 a.m." Late in 1872 Constable Rodello built a lockup at Comox made with logs from the Government Reserve east of the Landing (Section 87). Rodello stated that the lock up was required for Indians arrested for minor offences in the settlement. This "log-built cage," Duncan recalled, held prisoners until they could be sent to Nanaimo.[18]

Drabble began his magisterial duties in 1874 or 1875. He used his office near the wharf for legal purposes, as did Robb, Pidcock, and later Comox justices. Eric Duncan recalled that when he arrived in 1877, Robb and Drabble formed the magisterial bench of the district, Pidcock having resigned. Cases were held at the Comox Court House (which doubled as a jail), but they were also, Duncan recalled, "held almost anywhere."[19]

Rodello's log cage was not very secure, and Drabble and Robb continued to send Native people to Nanaimo for incarceration. "Returns of Convictions" kept by Justices Warner Spalding and Mark Bate reveal that a Comox Indian was almost constantly in residence at the Nanaimo jail in the 1870s. In the spring of 1875, for example, the jail held "Bob," Comox Indian, sentenced to fourteen days' imprisonment and hard labour for "Giving liquor to Ind." On 12 April 1875 an entry reads: "Four Comox Inds. Drunk & Disorderly. Fined 2-3$." A common offence among the "Whites" was "selling liquor to Inds."[20]

In 1877, the log cage at Comox was replaced with a proper jail which doubled as courthouse. In October 1875 Bishop George Hills offered a two-acre piece of land for a jail at the Anglican Mission at Sandwick, but Drabble did not take up his offer because, he wrote, it "lies so far off the Steam Boat landing and the Indian settlement where most of the disturbances have their origin." Drabble and Robb complained in July 1876 of the shady characters attracted by the new mining operations at Baynes Sound, a few miles south of Comox, and they asked for a jail to be built at the landing owing to the strain these people put on the legal structure. Drabble wrote that:

---

[18] Spalding to Colonial Secretary, 8 August 1870, Colonial Secretary; Pearse to Rodello, 18 April 1872, British Columbia, Department of Lands and Works, Correspondence Inward, 1871-1872; Rodello to Pearse, c. September 1872, British Columbia, Lands and Works Department, Correspondence Inward, 1872-1918; Duncan, "Comox District Fifty Years Ago."

[19] Drabble to Provincial Secretary, 18 August 1887, Provincial Secretary, Correspondence Inward, 1871-1892; Duncan, "Comox District Fifty Years Ago."

[20] Spalding and Bate, "Return of Convictions, 5 January 1875–30 December 1875" and "Return of Convictions, 4 January 1876–26 December 1876"; Spalding, Bate, and others, "Return of Convictions and Orders, 29 January 1877–28 December 1877," in British Columbia, Attorney General, Documents, 1857-1966; see also British Columbia, Nanaimo Magistrate's Office, Gaol Register, 1877-1884.

Since the Baynes Sound Coal Mining Co have commenced operations at their mine, it has been attended with an influx of unscrupulous characters several of whom have made Comox a rendezvous for the supplying Whisky to Indians, two cases have come before us during the last few days and been dealt with and a "warrant" issued for the arrest of a third.

During last week one man was convicted on a charge of supplying liquor and maltreating the Indians, the prisoner was sent to Nanaimo Gaol by canoe which entails considerable expense to the Government in consequence of there being no place of confinement with safety here. We therefore think it highly expedient that a Lock up should forthwith be erected.

The government promptly bought Lot 12 on the Comox Townsite, measuring 100×100 feet, from James Robb as the jail site and hired Drabble to survey it in July 1877. It was situated straight up the hill from the Comox wharf. In September Drabble awarded the contract to Thomas Piercy. The jail was to be finished by the end of November. "The contractor shall clear the said lot of all stumps roots and Brush." The lock up was to be made of ten-inch square logs "laid up close so as to make a perfectly weather tight joint, the corners to be dovetailed." Seven-inch spikes served as nails. "The building is divided into a court room 13 feet by 16 feet, and two cells 6 feet by 8 feet. A lavatory, &c., is also provided. The windows are securely barred and door fitted with a suitable fastening." The cells were secured with French Bramah locks "secured in the firmest possible manner to a metal plate in the outside by suitable screws."[21]

Between them, Drabble and Rodello almost monopolized government services at Comox. In the 1870s Drabble was not only Justice of the Peace and Superintendent of Roads, but Collector of Votes, Returning Officer, and Poll Clerk in the provincial elections. Rodello was Collector of Road Tax, Collector of Wild Land Tax, Constable, and postmaster. Drabble revealed his bellicose, "John Bull," Tory outlook in a January 1875 letter to the editor of the Victoria *Daily Standard*:

I was surprised to be an eye witness to a scene to-day that does little credit to our postal authorities and degrading to British progression, to see the mails on the arrival of the steamer Maude thrown upon the table of the Court House and the settlers and residents instructed to help themselves. Surely our Postal Inspector must attribute little importance to the distribution of Her Majesty's mails. Such a state of affairs is disgraceful and altogether anti-British.[22]

---

[21] Envs. 97, 116; Drabble to CCL&W, 22 November 1876, British Columbia, Department of Lands and Works, Correspondence Inward, 1871-1883; Robb and Drabble to Provincial Secretary, 19 July 1876, Provincial Secretary, Correspondence Inward, 1871-1892; British Columbia, Department of Public Works, Contracts, specifications, 1862-1909; "Report of Public Works," *British Columbia Sessional Papers* (1877), p. 289.

[22] Victoria *Daily Standard*, 12 January 1875, p. 3.

Drabble took his government work very seriously.

Comox was holiday-land for the upper echelons of the provincial judiciary. "In those days fishing was good on the Comox rivers, because then, as now, the farmers had no time for it," Duncan sarcastically recalled; "Therefore the leisured class of the towns, as well as the Indians, had good times. There was an individual known as Captain Spalding who came occasionally to hold County Court, but in reality to fish." Victoria Lawyers Montague Tyrwhitt-Drake and Robert Jackson, judges Henry Crease and John McCreight, and Lieutenant-Governors Joseph Trutch and A. N. Richards, all set up their tents on the deserted Puntledge River Indian Reserve in the 1870s and 1880s.[23]

Drabble was a personal friend of Judge Crease, who on one occasion sent him a Labrador puppy which so much resembled Venus, his deceased "favourite Bitch," that Drabble gave her the same name.[24]

When Drabble was trading in the Gulf he investigated cases requiring the attention of the law; indeed he may have been the only Indian trader on the coast who doubled as a judge. He kept track of legal infractions during his trading voyages on the *Mermaid*; for instance, in 1879, when he was trading at Cape Mudge, he made the following memo:

> March 30. Arso informs me that one Towate Indian named "Sepulka" together with 3 other Indians and 1 Woman Pootlas, Klacklakia (woman), Macwarkeles, one Indian Name unknown killed a Beast beonging to Mr. J. Hirst about 3 mos. ago.
>
> Apl 18. Went to Cape Mudge Indian Village & fetched 1 Box taken from Douglas Schooner and 1 piece of Copper (by Quocksister).
>
> Apl 18. Found a box in Quocksisters House marked J.M.P. Comox which he says is the Box containing the whisky given by Chukate to Indians at Matilpa and obtained from Douglas Schooner. Does not know how many bottles. Nimskunitim—Matilpa Indian brought the Box to Cape Mudge on the 14th Apl last past. 4 days ago.[25]

One of his many duties was to pay the bounty on cougars and wolves. "Strychnine $2.25," Drabble wrote in his 1875 field book; "Fawcett Panther $5.00." Drabble here referred to Thomas Fawcett, Government Agent at Nanaimo. He also kept the Comox legal machinery well oiled. The upstairs of Rodello's store served as Comox's unofficial second courthouse (it was more spacious than the courtroom in the jail), and when Rodello's fire of 1881 destroyed the handcuffs and nippers, Drabble wrote to the Provincial Secretary with the following request:

---

23 Duncan, "Comox District Fifty Years Ago."
24 Drabble to Crease, 18 December 1886, Crease Collection.
25 Env. 141, Drabble Papers.

I have the honor to ask you to be good enough to provide for use at Comox 2 pairs of Hand Cuffs one pair of Nippers and a Batten those used formerly were destroyed by fire at the time Rodellos Store and Court House were burnt.

Without these irons a Constable cannot execute his duty without frequently calling for extra assistance thereby incurring more expense.[26]

The 1870s, then, were years of transition and adaptation. Drabble left the farm behind him and found work as road superintendent, surveyor, merchant, Indian trader, and Justice of the Peace. From his new Comox office he held court and attended to his numerous public tasks.

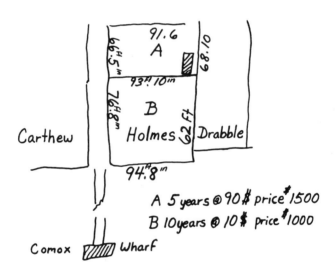

Measurements of Rodello's lots sold to Holmes
(Comox Wharf), March–April 1886.

---

[26] Envs. 89, 97; Drabble to Provincial Secretary, 21 May 1881, British Columbia, Provincial Secretary, Correspondence Inward, 1871-1892.

CHAPTER 11

Comox Village

The population has gained rapidly the last few years, and on steamer day, once a week, the wharf in front of Mr. Robb's is crowded with strange faces.
—Reginald Carwithen, 8 December 1887[1]

*I*NCREASED farming, mining, and trading in the Comox Valley and the northern Gulf required urban services unavailable in the countryside—a post office, courthouse, doctor, hotel, general and hardware store, blacksmith, shoemaker, and butcher. As a surveyor and magistrate, Drabble helped form such a village in the 1870s and 1880s. The valley in the 1860s had been a rural place, but in the following decades James Robb's Comox townsite became the urban centre for the northern Gulf region. Socially, this later urban phase was more stable than earlier: alcohol abuse and the illegal whiskey trade, while still prevalent, were not marked by the violence of the 1860s. Some of the younger settlers married in the 1870s, contributing to a stabler community than the earlier fraternity of washed-up and superannuated gold miners. They and their families provided, in turn, a demand for services that an urban centre could best supply.

In all his private and public capacities, Drabble was involved in the transition from rural to urban. He did everything from managing local elections to selling real estate. In the 1880s Comox became a place with a hinterland; a civilized place for the outlying work camps, for the mining camps on Baynes Sound, for the settlers of Hornby, Denman, Quadra islands, and Campbell River, as well as for the farmers of the valley. In 1886 Drabble bought an expensive new surveyor's transit to replace the old compass and Jacob's Staff he had used until then; now he could survey townsites with precision.[2]

James Robb had hoped to provide an urban centre as early as 1862, when he and his son William pre-empted 286 acres inside the Comox

---

[1] Carwithen to Blaksley, 8 December 1887, Carwithen Correspondence.
[2] Holmes to Hirst Brothers, 29 July 1886, Planta Collection, NCA. On the early history of Comox village see also Isenor, *Land of Plenty*, pp. 130-49.

Spit. "The Town site of course is on the Harbour," Robert Brown noted in August 1864. "Here a Mr. Robb with a laudable good faith in the country has pre-empted land though the site is principally bush: when he could have got good prairie as he came among the first about 2 years ago." Robb was fond of reminding people that he could have pre-empted the best open land in the valley, but as he told Eric Duncan, he let himself in for "a lifetime of hard labour among trees and stones in the hope of selling town lots; events did not move so quickly." Duncan listed the advantages of the Robbs' pre-emption:

> It was the only possible location in the Valley for a wharf at which steamers could tie up, as it was sheltered by a long sand spit from the prevailing south-easterly winds, and had good depth of water at all stages of tide (though needing a long stretch of trestle-work to get to it), whereas the shallow bay farther up, into which the river discharged, was completely exposed at all winds.[3]

Robb's land was solid timber except for an acre on the beach of naturally open field fenced with driftwood. Here, on what Robert Brown identified as an old Indian village site, James, Isabella, and their children grew vegetables, drawing their water from a creek that came down from the forest and passed under a bridge on Wharf Street on its way to the harbour.[4]

James Robb, appointed a Justice of the Peace at the same time as Drabble, had the ability to generate extreme and conflicting reactions. Merchant J. B. Holmes found him generous and open-handed: "One cannot speak in too high terms of the hospitality of the Robbs in those days; theirs was an open house and headquarters to all visitors in the settlement." By contrast, Reginald Pidcock in 1888 found Robb "as illiberal as ever."[5]

The building of the government wharf in 1874 was the catalyst of urban development at Comox. The Robbs' townsite then had the advantages of a wharf, a well-drained location facing the west and the Beaufort Range, a freshwater creek, a protected harbour, a post office, store, court house, and a road to the valley. In about 1875, Robb hired Drabble to survey part of his land into a townsite—the first such urban experiment north of Nanaimo. (See map 6.) In Drabble's original "Plan of the Townsite of Comox," the business section of the town was dominated by three streets with utilitarian names: Wharf, Front, and

---

[3] Hayman, *Robert Brown*, pp. 111-12; *From Shetland to Vancouver Island*, pp. 92-93.
[4] Duncan, "Early Days and Early Settlers."
[5] Holmes, "Reminiscences;" Pidcock Diary, 9 August 1888.

View. Behind were Victoria (named for the reigning monarch), while parallel with Wharf were Elizabeth Street (named for the Robbs' daughter, who married local politician D. W. Gordon), St. Andrew (patron saint of Scotland), Drabble, Gordon, Queen, Ingram, and St. Ann streets. Over the years, successive Comox town councils have replaced all these street names with ones more in line with their fancy, so that not a single original name remains.[6]

The "first and chief customer" for Robb's lots, Duncan wrote, was Joe Rodello, who in about 1870 bought two lots at the head of the wharf, where he built his store and, in 1877, the Elk Hotel. Later sales were as slow as Duncan recollected. In 1876 the province bought a lot for a jail, and a few years later carpenter John Fitzpatrick bought a lot at the corner of Wharf and View streets, where he built the Lorne Hotel, named after the Marquis of Lorne, Governor-General between 1878 and 1883. He leased the Lorne to Sam Cliffe in December 1883, and it has stood ever since as a hotel and pub.[7]

In 1880 Robb asked $300 for his town lots. Some felt this was a preposterous price to pay when dense forest covered the townsite, and when pre-empted rural land could be had for a dollar an acre. But Dunsmuir started to invest in the Baynes Sound coal properties soon afterwards, and suddenly the townsite had some appeal and Robb cleared the trees and surveyed more lots. In 1884 Carwithen—that caustic observer of valley life—remarked that "The Robbs have made their property at the wharf worth having now." Robb continued to clear the land and burn slash in the autumn when the weather was fine, as Mary Harmston noted from her top-floor room at the Lorne Hotel on 7 August 1885: "Robbs set fire to their chopping all along at the Back." "Robbs fire still burning" she wrote two days later.[8]

The Robbs had left their log cabin in 1878 for a modern house west of the wharf, but they could not sit back and take it easy on the proceeds of the stray sale of a town lot. Instead, their livelihood depended on their dairy farm, located on the land west of the wharf that they had so laboriously cleared. "Mrs. Robb did the milking and churning on the farm," Lugrin wrote. "As time went on they had a large herd of cows, and her butter was delicious and in great demand." Duncan noted that

---

[6] George Drabble, "Plan of the Townsite of Comox, BC," *c.* 1883, CDMA (Plan 104, Comox District).

[7] *From Shetland to Vancouver Island,* p. 108; env. 127; Robb and Drabble to Provincial Secretary, 19 July 1876, Provincial Secretary, Correspondence Inward, 1871-1892; "Historical Buildings, Comox, B.C.," Buckham Collection.

[8] Carwithen to Blaksley, 29 August 1880 and 9 August 1884; Harmston Diary, 7 and 9 August 1885.

James Robb may have sold a few lots, but to the day of his death his cows were his mainstay.[9]

Business at Comox was irregular until the mid-1880s. In 1877, Duncan wrote, the fortnightly steamer visit "brought the whole Valley to the Landing, but on other days it was practically deserted." The road from the Indian village to the beginning of the townsite was a lane with tall timber on both sides, and what is now Comox Avenue passed between the Robbs' stump-dotted pasture and the "forest-primeval."[10] This changed when Dunsmuir started his E&N railway (1884) and opened his mine at Union (1888). Landowners around Robb then divided their large parcels into smaller residential lots, pre-emptors took up the whole of Comox peninsula as far as Little River, and sportsmen discovered the Comox region and found congenial lodging at the Elk and Lorne hotels. More people moved to the region who in turn patronized the stores at Comox—and not just on steamer day.

The two most influential merchants of late nineteenth and early twentieth century Comox and Courtenay got their start in Robb's village in the 1880s: Joe McPhee and J. B. Holmes. Nova Scotian McPhee was an important transitional figure: he started at a Fanny Bay beef farm with his partner Alex Urquhart before getting into road and bridge-building and finally into trade. In 1878 he married New Brunswicker Isabella Piercy; Urquhart married Margaret Paterson, and both couples stayed in the valley. In 1879, McPhee left behind his road and bridge-building and started as a merchant at Comox. By doing so, he helped fill the niche left when the Hudson's Bay Company had closed its Comox store in 1877.[11]

Joseph Burnard Holmes was an Englishman in his late twenties who had worked for the Hudson's Bay Company at Kamloops, and in Nanaimo for another English immigrant, merchant Arthur Bullock, who asked Holmes to open a branch of his business in Comox. Holmes arrived in Comox in December 1884 with a stock of dry goods. His partnership with Bullock lasted until 1886, when he switched to Nanaimo merchants Thomas and William Hirst. At first Holmes rented Rodello's store; his letterhead advertised "Groceries, Provisions, Feed, &c." Holmes remembered with fondness his meeting with Rodello:

---

[9] Lugrin, *The Pioneer Women of Vancouver Island*, pp. 158-59; Duncan, "Early Days and Early Settlers."

[10] *From Shetland to Vancouver Island*, pp. 129-30.

[11] Carroll, *Wild Roses and Rail Fences*, p. 23; Forbes, *Wild Roses*, 127-29; Mildred Haas, "Alexander Urquhart and Wife," and Haas and McPhee, "Joseph McPhee," both in Isenor, "The Comox Valley;" Duncan, "Early Days and Early Settlers;" Courtenay *Weekly News*, 8 November 1893, p. 1,

> The history of early days would not be complete without mention of my landlord Joe Rodello, an Italian, who was the first constable. He was certainly one of the most kind hearted men one could meet. He was the friend of everyone and no stranger ever came to the district whom he did not help; if he could not get work he would make work for him.[12]

The upper floor of Rodello's store, Holmes recalled, was used both as an unofficial courthouse and as a place of worship by the Anglicans and Presbyterians. Holmes rented a room from James Robb after tiring of both the Lorne and Elk: "It was difficult to obtain board even at the hotels as the serving of meals was not what the hotel keepers were catering for," he recalled; "The bar was the profitable part and only those guests were sought for and acceptable who had a propensity for drinking and treating others." In the spring of 1886 Holmes bought from Rodello, for $2500, two lots at Comox wharf on the location of Rodello's old store that had burned down five years previously.[13]

In 1886 Holmes married a woman he met when visiting his sick mother in London; Ellen Holmes had been his mother's nurse. When he brought her to Comox the local men staged a traditional charivari — a noisy, mock serenade—for the couple. Led by logger Mike King, the loose and single working men of Comox seized the opportunity for a party, but the Tuesday-night celebration got right out of hand, culminating in cannon salutes and a burning barrel of tar. Mary Harmston witnessed the events from her vantage point in the Lorne Hotel and she was not amused; in fact, she was alarmed. She wrote in her diary on 17 February 1886 that: "Holmes & his Wife up the *men* have been Chivereeing them a more dreadful noise I never heard in my life they behaved more like Demons than men." Many years later Holmes recalled the charivari as follows:

> The charivari of the writer bringing his wife to Comox was one of the events of the early days. This was commenced in good will but owing to the distribution of considerable liquor, the participants lost control of themselves and started breaking windows and doors until nearly every window and door in the old store was wrecked. There was no wharfinger in those days and the warehouse was not locked and there happened to be a big barrel of tar there. This was siezed upon and distributed on the road from the top of the hill from the Lorne Hotel to the Elk and set on fire and the road was a mass of flames. They brought an old cannon from the Indian Reserve, loaded and fired it, which I presume was meant for a salute.[14]

---

12 Holmes, "Reminiscences."

13 *Comox District Free Press*, 26 October 1955, p. 14; Holmes, "Reminiscences;" envs. 131, 144; on the church service see Pidcock Diary, 19 August 1883.

14 Nellie Stewart, "Mrs. Ellen Holmes," in Isenor, "The Comox Valley;" Harmston Diary, 17 February 1886; Holmes, "Reminiscences."

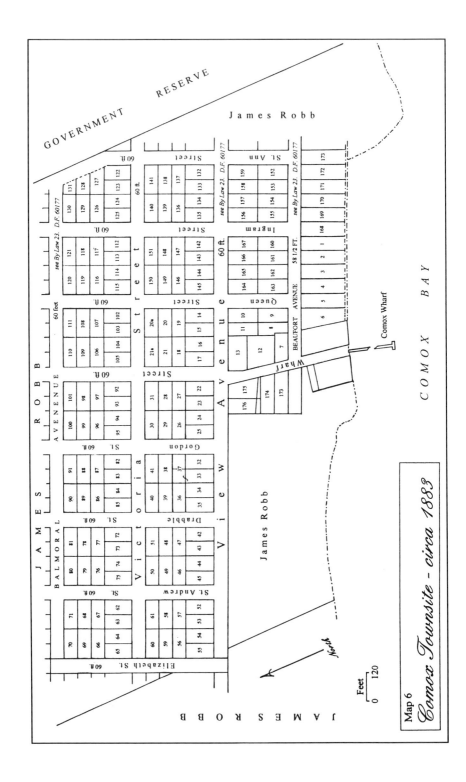

Map 6

Comox Townsite – circa 1883

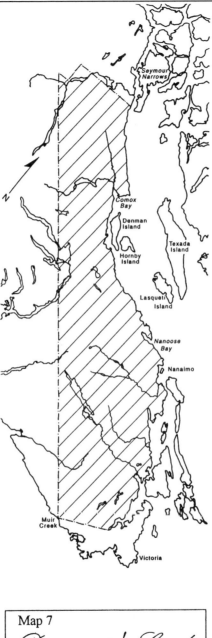

Seymour
Narrows

Comox
Bay

Denman
Island

Texada
Island

Hornby
Island

Lasqueti
Island

Nanoose
Bay

Nanaimo

Muir
Creek

Victoria

Map 7

Dunsmuir's Land
Grant - 1884

FROM DONALD MACLACHLAN, *THE ESQUIMALT & NANAIMO RAILWAY*

Holmes, as his account suggests, was a sober and conscientious merchant with work to do. From valley farmers he bought vegetables and livestock for shipment to Nanaimo. From the Duncan brothers, for example, he bought potatoes, oats, eggs, onions, and other vegetables. He sent farm produce down to the Hirst Brothers, who sold it to Nanaimo coal miners and their families. Butter was a staple product of valley farms, but it was not always of the best quality, as Holmes recalled: "There was little uniformity in the manufacture of the butter and some very indifferent butter was put on the market. I myself have handled butter which owing to its exposure and not being properly worked, realized only four (4) cents [a pound] at the soap factory."[15]

The Native trade continued as an important part of the commercial life of Comox in the 1880s. Holmes and McPhee took over where the Hudson's Bay Company, Rodello, and Drabble left off: Holmes bought furs, skins, and dogfish oil from Native hunters in the Gulf, and supplied them with blankets, hardware, rope, fishing line, and staple foods like flour, sugar, and baking powder. For example, in late November 1886 he wrote to his Nanaimo suppliers that: "I hope you will get a few fancy tea Blankets & send them to me to give away at Xmas. What do you think about Biscuits are they worth keeping, the potlaching season is soon coming off. The matches are something awful—the folks cannot get them to light." Later, Holmes recalled that:

> The bulk of business in those days was transacted with the Indians for there were a great number located on the "ranch" and the younger ones were mostly engaged in hunting and fishing and earned a large amount of money. Their products were readily converted into cash as the fur buyers were anxious to obtain the furs and the mine owners would buy all the dogfish oil that was offered. At potlach times at Cape Mudge there were large transactions in bales of 2½ point blankets, boxes of pilot bread, and barrels of sugar.
>
> It needed considerable experience to deal with the Indians as they were very artful. They would offer deer skins that had been dried in the sand and small stones adhered to the pelt so that they would weigh much more than they ought had they been properly dried. The Beaver, which was then bought from the Indians by the pound, was treated in a similar manner to obtain a fictitious weight.[16]

Holmes's daughter Nellie Stewart recalled that Indians camped near her father's store when they wished to trade. Deer skins were a favourite

---

[15] William Duncan Diary 1887-1889; 1891; Holmes, "Reminiscences." For shipments of farm produce to Nanaimo at this time see also A. G. Horne to Thomas Cairns, 26 August 1886, in Barraclough, "Selected Items."

[16] Holmes to Hirst Brothers, 25 November 1886, Planta Collection, NCA; Holmes, "Reminiscences."

item of trade until overhunting made it illegal for them to be shot for their skins alone. Over the winter of 1889-90, the record deep snow drove the deer down to the beaches around Comox, where Indians shot them from their canoes and killed them with clubs. They sold canoe loads of hides to Holmes and McPhee, who in turn shipped them down to a Victoria tannery where they were made into a fine chamois.[17]

Holmes also remembered the social life of Comox in the late 1880s and early 1890s. "Old timers will never forget the good old dances at the Elk," he exclaimed. The Elk was leased at first from Rodello by Nova Scotian John Carthew, and then by George Grant McDonald and his wife Dolena, from Nova Scotia and New Brunswick respectively, who brought with them their many daughters. Eventually Holmes had to close down his Port Augusta Hotel, licence and all, because he could offer nothing comparable to "George's pretty daughters." "I often told George a loaded gun would not prevent anyone obtaining a look at his pretty family." Nor could Holmes compete with George McDonald's and Sam Cliffe's stories:

> If our friend Charles Dickens had been in Comox in those days only his pen could have portrayed those two interesting personalities, G. G. McDonald and S. J. Cliffe and their gifted families, not forgetting the noted character G. F. Drabble. Money in those days was not much valued and with a little leisure and a fifty cent piece you could derive a vast amount of pleasure from the Yarns of the Proprietors of either the "Elk" or the "Lorne." In fact those yarns seemed to be the stock in trade or good will of the business and they seemed to compete with one another as to who could tell the most amusing Yarn. What often happened, refreshments in those days were 10c a drink and a bunch of five would would repair to the "Lorne" for one of "Sam's" yarns.
>
> Having entered and called for drinks, asking "Sam" to join and getting him in a good humour, would ask him if he had ever killed a deer. Sam would then relate how he stood on the wherefore day with his gun, looking over at Robb's turnip field toward the "spit" and saw a great big buck. He fired and still the buck's head was visible; he fired again with the same result. He thought there must be some fault in the sight of the gun, but he decided to get nearer the game and on going to the spot to where his aim had been centred found three dead bucks!! Often the number increased as he repeated the yarn. The air in those days was full of such yarns and hoaxes.[18]

The village's main problems were related to the excessive consumption of alcohol, such as fuelled Holmes's charivari. Then as now, whiskey drinking knew few boundaries of origin or class. "Rain," Mary

[17] Nellie Stewart, "Mrs. Ellen Holmes," in Isenor, "The Comox Valley;" *Comox Argus*, 24 February 1954.

[18] Holmes, "Reminiscences."

Harmston glumly wrote on 9 November 1881, "Boat day. A great deal of drinking at Bay." In 1883 Reginald Pidcock noted in his diary when he received a package from his brother-in-law Ashdown Green, a Victoria surveyor: "Ashdown wrote and sent us a box of odds & ends & three bottles whiskey which he said were good for rheumatism." Drinking was a problem on the whole coast, especially at the male-dominated work camps. Numerous empty bottles of "Eno's Fruit Salts," a hangover cure, are found at abandoned logging and mining camps. Teetotaller Eric Duncan identified ex-miner Adam McKelvey as one of the valley's confirmed drinkers. Appointed a Justice of the Peace in early days, his legal career was ruined by whiskey. "He was not a bad fellow when sober," Duncan recalled, "but when liquor was in him he became vicious."[19]

The patrons of the Lorne and the Elk were the main culprits. Mary Harmston found it hard to live upstairs at the Lorne, and got her revenge by naming the offenders in her diary. A month after her son-in-law Sam Cliffe took possession of the hotel, in December 1883, she wrote that "J.J. Hirst & others drunk all day," referring to English-born John Hirst, Nanaimo merchant, who was a frequent visitor to Comox. Many respectable Comoxians, but not Drabble, kept a running account at the Lorne Hotel, where they charged up whiskey by the bottle and glass.[20]

James Robb had no doubt as to the cause of the problem. His and Drabble's civil convictions nearly all related to the sale or abuse of whiskey. "It may be seen by this return that Whiskey is the root of nearly all the evils in Comox," Robb reported in October 1884; "There are two public houses here, & the way they are conducted is nothing less than infamous. I have not the least doubt in my own mind, that they connive at the Indians' obtaining whiskey." Things got so bad that Robb and Drabble revoked Sam Cliffe's Lorne Hotel licence, and Presbyterian minister James Christie wrote to Judge Crease that:

> Since licence in intoxicants has been withdrawn from the Cliff House, called the Lorne Hotel, the settlement has been an Entirely different place, quiet and orderly to a degree that never existed here before. Mr. Carthew, who keeps the only other licenced house in the place, is inclined to keep drinking within moderate bounds, and to prevent as far as he can any excess and has been compararatively successful.[21]

---

[19] Pidcock Diary, 23 May 1883; *From Shetland to Vancouver Island*, pp. 104-05.

[20] Harmston Diary, 15 December 1883; Sam and Florence Cliffe, Lorne Hotel Register 1888-1895, Private Collection.

[21] Robb to Provincial Secretary, 8 October 1884, Provincial Secretary, Correspondence Inward, 1871-1892; Christie to Crease, 9 December 1885, Crease Collection.

So prevalent was drinking that letters of recommendation contained remarks on the sobriety of the applicant. For example, early schoolteacher R. C. Coleman was "sober and industrious" and a doctor was described as a "sober married man."[22]

A scandal occurred in November 1884 when Constable Rodello charged Adam McKelvey, nominally a Justice of the Peace, with drunkeness and resisting arrest. Drabble and newly sworn magistrate Thomas Piercy fined him $10. Two months later Rodello, in his semi-Italian, reported to the Provincial Secretary on the state of affairss at Comox:

> I can also inform you that Comox District as been very orderly ever since my troble with the Justice of the piese and also only on Hotell now open it is kept by a good man John Carthew a large number of Indians are here at Comox of Different tribes calling on there winter Dances wich they are keeping me buizy night or day. A few hard cases have come up here from Nanaimo but they soon had to scip out from her in short notice.[23]

McKelvey's conviction resulted in the formation, in December 1884, of a local branch of the Lodge of Good Templars, a friendly society of British origin devoted to total abstinence from alcohol. Calling itself the Bateman Lodge, within three years it had thirty members. Surviving lodge journals contain news and stories by founders William Duncan (Jr.) and schoolteacher William Halliday. Women ("sisters") were admitted to the lodge and participated in its meetings. M.P. Anthony Stenhouse noted in 1886 that a "wave of temperance" had broken over the Comox District, in addition to a wave of immigration. In 1886, and again the next year, Comox residents sent petitions to the Legislative Assembly asking for a thorough revison of the laws relating to the liquor traffic. Public houses and other licenced places were then untramelled by opening and closing hours of any kind, and the petitioners wanted them to close between midnight and six in the morning from Monday to Saturday. On "Lord's Day, commonly called Sunday," they wanted pubs to close altogether. Drabble signed neither petition.[24]

"It will be our endeavour to fill our sheets with only the most chaste literature," wrote Good Templar Halliday in 1887, and as an example he contributed an "Essay on the use of Profane Language" to the

[22] *The Daily Standard*, 17 February 1873, p. 3; Hunter to Holmes, 25 December 1893, in Joseph Hunter, Correspondence Outward, 1893-1900.

[23] George Drabble, "Return of Convictions made by me for the half year ending December 31st 1884;" Rodello to Provincial Secreary, 19 February 1885, Provincial Secretary, Correspondence Inward, 1871-1892.

[24] "Minutes of Bateman Lodge No. 83," IOGT, 1884-1892; "Minute Book of Bateman Lodge IOGT," 1892-1895; [Halliday and W. Duncan, eds.], "The Bateman Journal," Volume 1, Nos. 1-10 (23 April 1887 to 31 December 1887), private collection; Stenhouse, "To the Free and Independent Electors of the District of Comox;" *British Columbia Sessional Papers* 1887, pp. 347-52; 1888, pp. 311-20.

Bateman Journal. The lodge succeeded in depriving the Lorne of its licence for two years but finally had to admit defeat, as Robert Duncan reported in November 1887: "We have tried to prevent the reopening of another saloon in the district and after two years contest have been defeated. The liquor men, who, a year ago, spoke of the lodge with respect and fear, now, if they do not actually despise us seem quite indifferent to our opposition."[25]

The lodge, as Eric Duncan's "Rural Rhymes" suggest, defended the valley's rural values against the urban, or at least decadent, values promoted by the "whisky shops" at Comox landing. It acted as much as a social club as anything, and its newsletter boasted its own personal advertisements. Two sisters offered their jokes for sale "wholesale and retail." A sample of advertisements from November 1887:

> Wanted—A Wife. We have heard of a brother who is wanting badly to get spliced. Any lady who has a temper that cannot be ruffled, an arm that is untiring, a slipper that will not wear out, and who will be contented to live on potatoes, beef, milk and bacon, will do well to apply. Address care of Bateman Journal Office.

> Lost, Stolen, or Strayed—Two hearts. Any information that will lead to their recovery, without being either broken or cracked, will be gladly received. N.B. The chances are that they will be found together.

> Found—Too many tracks from a number seven boot going to a certain house. We would warn the maker that such things should not be.[26]

The Templars were joined in 1893 by another lodge, the "Sons of Temperance," who despite their name also admitted women. Drabble belonged to neither lodge.[27]

People in Comox of all political stripes shared a common platform in the late 1870s and early 1880s: they were adamantly opposed to the E&N land grant, a massive tract running from Seymour Narrows to the head of Finlayson Arm near Victoria. (See map 7.) British Columbia's terms of union with Canada in 1871 had required the federal government to build an island railway; a large tract of land was set aside to compensate the builders of the railway, and land sales were frozen until a deal was struck. Comox people regarded it as a hindrance to the economic development of the District.

"This place has been filling in very slowly of late," Carwithen told Blaksley in 1881, "owing to the Dominion Govn't reserving the land for

---

25 Halliday in "The Bateman Journal," 1:1 (23 April 1887); letter to editor from "R.D.," 1:8 (5 November 1887).

26 "The Bateman Journal," 1:9 (3 December 1887).

27 *The Weekly News*, 22 March 1893, p. 1. On the Bateman Lodge see also Isenor, *Land of Plenty*, p. 408.

railway purposes so at present one can only obtain a squatter's right, and then eventually be called on to pay perhaps more than the old price of a dollar an acre." In the same year Drabble drafted a petition to the members of the provincial legislature which was signed by sixty-six Comox settlers. "The said reserve has very materially retarded the progress of settlement in our district and along the coast," Drabble wrote, "and has also been a barrier to the development of our extensive coal fields, thereby depriving us of a near market for our agricultural products, and relieving us from the many disadvantages under which we suffer from our present isolated situation from a remunerative market."[28]

In 1882, after the federal government backed out of the deal, Robert Dunsmuir stepped forward and offered to build the railway in return for the land grant—which was known to contain coal. Both levels of government then put together a very attractive package for Dunsmuir and his American partners. The prospect of such a deal alarmed the people of Comox, and in the spring of 1883 Jules Willemar and eighty-two other Comox electors—including Drabble, Carwithen, Cliffe, Robb, McPhee, and Pidcock—sent another petition to Victoria protesting the proposed Settlement Act, so-called because it was intended to settle existing difficulties between the province and dominion over the terms of union of 1871. The petitioners felt the act limited the public right "to purchase Agricultural, Timber and Coal Lands at any fixed price" and threatened to create "a monopoly in the chief resources of the Province." Their concerns went unheeded while, in 1884, construction of the railway went ahead. Carwithen reported to Blaksley:

A railroad is being built between Victoria and Nanaimo, the company getting a strip of land about 20 miles back from the coast as far up as the Euclatawville. Did anyone ever hear of a more scandalous bargain, the M.Ps apiece should be strung up. Victoria and its neighbourhood is all those potheads care for. The surface is still open for pre-emption though I think the timber is reserved. The principals of the Co. are Yankees so whatever enterprise they enter into their trade is certain to keep clear of us Britishers.

In 1886 Sir John A. Macdonald drove the last spike in the E&N.[29]

Dunsmuir quieted fears about the negative effect of the land grant by buying Baynes Sound coal properties and opening the Union Mine in

---

[28] Carwithen to Blaksley, 1 March 1881, Carwithen Correspondence; see also Manson, "Sketches," p. 4; British Columbia *Sessional Papers* (1881), p. 518.

[29] Petition in British Columbia *Sessional Papers* (1883), p. 199; Carwithen to Blaksley, 2 December 1885, Carwithen Correspondence; see also Bowen, *The Dunsmuirs of Nanaimo*, p. 28; Reksten, *The Dunsmuir Saga*, pp. 55-68, 92; *From Shetland to Vancouver Island*, pp. 221-27. For the Settlement Act see also *Land of Plenty*, pp. 387-88.

1888. Comox, as the only urban centre in the valley, stood to benefit, and it was not inconceivable that the E&N Railway would reach Comox Landing itself.[30]

Subdivison, speculation, and townsite surveys were a natural response to Dunsmuir's appearance on the Comox stage. The town lots nearest the wharf went first. In the 1870s Drabble had bought Lot 6, next door to Rodello's store, for use as his office; he also bought Lot 15 on View Street, located on the site of the parking lot of the Comox mall. Teddy Rollings, the Lincolnshire shoemaker, had bought Lot 13, on the corner of View and Wharf, and McPhee owned a lot on Wharf Street immediately above Rodello. Others in business were Scotsman William Dingwall, who became an M.L.A., and American-born Adoph Mayer, whose main store was in Nanaimo. By 1885, Englishman George Howe, a butcher, had bought three lots; Holmes's partner Arthur Bullock had bought a single lot; and George McDonald bought the Elk Hotel after Rodello's death. "There are three or four stores and a butcher shop down at the wharf now," Carwithen told Blaksley in May 1885. In the next few years Robb extended his townsite westward to the limits of his property. In November 1889, at the end of View Street (now the corner of Comox Avene and Anderton), Drabble took his bearings from "West Gable of McDonald's House," "West Gable of Millet's House," "South Gable of Hall," "Gable of Swans Store," and "NE corner of Carters Barn."[31]

This was no longer the wilderness setting of the 1860s, but a landscape cleared of trees and dotted with houses and stores.

In the 1880s the whole peninsula from Comox back to Little River was pre-empted. Behind the townsite and around the waterfront, Alexander Grant (carpenter), George McDonald, Teddy Rollings, Henry Huxham, Matthew Lyttle, Joe McPhee, Dan Stewart (farmer), King and Casey, Tom Beckensell (farmer and constable), and John Hawkins (farmer) claimed pre-emptions between 1884 and 1889. These settlers established family farms and residences and held them for their value. In the next decade much of the land on the residential fringes of Comox was subdivided into town lots and medium-sized suburban lots.

These people tired of sending their children three miles to the Mission school, and they were concerned about the dangerous condition of the Long Bridge. They had the minimum fifteen children necessary, so in 1886 they persuaded the government to build them a school of their own. George McDonald donated the school lot on

---

[30] See c. 1905 map in Isenor, *Land of Plenty*, p. 255.

[31] Envs. 102, 121, 144; Isenor, *Land of Plenty*, p. 139; Carwithen to Blaksley, 10 May 1885, Carwithen Correspondence.

Anderton Road in Comox, Drabble surveyed it, and Alexander Grant built the school.[32]

Indeed the whole town of Comox spread westward in the 1880s. Robb's western neighbour, Alex Brown, had pre-empted lots 1 and 2 (161 acres) in the 1860s, and later sold them to Patrick Murphy, who in turn disposed of half to the Roman Catholic Church and the rest to Comox shopkeepers and merchants. Over the winter of 1885-86 Murphy hired Drabble to survey eight acres for Rodello (half of which Rodello later sold to Samuel Creech, a carpenter-turned Government Agent), as well as lots for George Howe, McPhee, and Holmes. Drabble also surveyed a large section for Mary Ellen McTucker of the Sisters of St. Ann and ten acres for Bishop Charles Seghers.[33]

In 1876 Rodello had built a small Roman Catholic chapel on his land near Comox wharf, and over the next decade at least two large Catholic families arrived, the Millers and the Andertons, both from Lancashire. The Roman Catholics of Comox built St. John's Church, Comox, on the land given by Murphy to Bishop Seghers; it was blessed by him in May 1886.[34]

Drabble was more than a surveyor. He also acted as a real estate agent, selling Murphy's land for a commission fee. "Murphys Land between Howe & Rodello," he wrote in his field notes in January 1887; "wants $600 and will pay me 5 per cent commission." Later, in 1887, Murphy sold his main waterfront section to Walter Bentley, a well-off Civil Engineer new to Comox. Between 1889 and 1893 Rodello, Creech, and McPhee subdivided their property into town lots known as "Joe Town" after Rodello. Robb's streets and street names were extended westward to include these new subdivisions.[35]

In June 1889 Drabble completed the subdivision of Rodello's lots, and later in the year those of Creech and McPhee, who started to sell them almost immediately. Among the buyers were Captain James Dillon Curtis, R.N., and James Archibald (Archie) Pritchard. Curtis, a keen naturalist and watercolourist, bought two lots; Pritchard, born at Wakefield in the Gatineau area of Quebec, came to British Columbia aged nineteen in 1872, split cedar shakes on what became the townsite

[32] Isenor, "For our Children, pp. 6-7; Rosemary Lowry, "Comox School, and Early Teachers," in Isenor, "The Comox Valley;" Department of Land and Works, Public Works, Contracts and Specifications, 1872-1896; env. 113.

[33] Envs. 47, 88, 121, Drabble Papers.

[34] L. J. Starace, "The Catholic Mission of Comox, B.C.," in The British Columbia Orphans' Friend Historical Number (Victoria: [Roman Catholic Archdiocese of Victoria; The Press Publishing Company], 1913), pp. 35-39; From Shetland to Vancouver Island, p. 201; Isenor, Land of Plenty, pp. 141-42; on the "Catholic Church lot" see env. 125.

[35] Envs. 11, 88; Harmston Diary, 26 September, 18 October 1887.

of Vancouver, logged at Oyster Harbour (Ladysmith), and moved to Comox in about 1882. He bought a lot from McPhee on what is now Comox Avenue for his wife Maggie Cameron and family.[36]

Drabble also secured a piece of Murphy's land for himself. In about 1885 he bought a four-acre lot, situated to the north of Joe Town, up what became Anderton Road, and next to a similar residential lot bought by Holmes. He built a cottage there, and over the next ten years improved the house and grounds, adding gates and fences, a woodshed with twelve-foot upright cedar posts, a cottage for his Chinese help, and an orchard and garden.[37]

As a civil servant Drabble had an important role in the community. He was a Government Agent from the mid-1870s until about 1890, and managed federal and provincial elections at Comox in these years. In 1871 he chaired a nomination meeting and served as Returning Officer in the first provincial election. He was Collector of Votes, and announced election results from the top floor of Rodello's "courthouse:" Holmes recalled that "Drabble more than once proclaimed the election from the balcony above." Elections in Comox were marked by lively debate and over-consumption of alcohol: in the 1878 election a supporter composed a poem in favour of D. W. Gordon, M.L.A., a member of the Walkem cabinet. It went as follows:

> All hail the power of Walkem's name;
> let miners prostrate fall;
> bring forth the whiskey in a tub,
> and crown him lord of all.[38]

Drabble's main role in Comox, however, was magistrate, a position that brought him into conflict with James Robb. In 1883 Drabble asked the government to appoint a third magistrate at Comox because "we are at the present moment divided in opinion upon a case which came before us to day, consequently the decision of the Court had to remain in abeyance." Drabble recommended William Machin, an old settler

---

[36] Envs. 79, 106; Drabble, [Plan of subdivision at west end of Comox Townsite, Section 1, Creech's land]; "Subdivision Plan of Part of Section 1. Being the Portion Colored Red. Comox District;" "Plan of McPhee's Subdivision of Lot 1 . . . Comox District;" John Pritchard, interview with Imbert Orchard, 6 April 1965, Imbert Orchard/C.B.C. Collection, BCARS; personal communication, Allan Pritchard, March 1995.

[37] Envs. 62, 88, 91, Drabble Papers.

[38] Victoria *Standard* 30 October 1871, p. 1; Drabble to Provincial Secretary, 18 March and 26 June 1874, British Columbia, Provincial Secretary, Correspondence Inward, 1871-1892; Holmes, "Reminiscences;" *From Shetland to Vancouver Island*, pp. 144-45, 148-49. On early politics see also Isenor, *Land of Plenty*, pp. 139, 445-50; McDonald, "Second Prize Article," Union *Weekly News*, 28 September 1897, p. 1 and Julian Brooks, "Joseph Hunter: Forgotten Builder of British Columbia," *British Columbia Historical News* 28:2 (Spring 1995), pp. 27-31.

and man of "strict integrity," but he was not appointed, and Drabble and Robb continued to disagree on points of law until Thomas Piercy was appointed. In May 1884 Drabble visited Comox Lake, where he observed a Native hunter killing elk. Again he and Robb disagreed. He asked the Provincial Secretary "if it was not the intention of the Government to punish Indians as well as Whites for killing Deer for their Skins alone:"

> A few days ago an Indian killed 5 Elk in this Distict and left the Carcases in the bush & brought in the Skins only. I wished to punish the Indian according to the "Game Act" & Mr. Robb differed in his opinion from me & refused to act in the matter.

The Provincial Secretary agreed that the individual should have been charged.[39]

Drabble became senior member of the Comox bench in about 1885 when Robb resigned. He found his services increasingly in demand as the population grew and the valley filled in with settlers. His pay, however, remained minimal, and his discontent boiled over in 1887, when he asked the Provincial Secretary for "a small rent for the office I erected, which is the only building that can be had here for Government use." "The building cost me a considerable sum," he continued, "and I think you will only consider it as justice to myself that I should receive some remuneration for it." The Executive Council decided that Drabble was not entitled to compensation, and he replied as follows:

> I cannot afford to use it any longer for the same purpose & have resolved to let it for a Store. When you consider that I have supplied all Stationary &c used in the administration of justice for the past twelve years and never received one cent remuneration and that the sum I received from the Government annually by commission does not amount to 50 cents per day it is easy to see I would be doing myself an injustice if I did not try and derive some little income from it, therefore I have notified my colleagues that it cannot be used by them any more and that they must provide themselves with accommodation for holding Court as I could not afford it & moreover that I did not intend taking any further part in the administration of Justice and from this time, shall decline to take part as it is a disadvantage and has been for a long time past.[40]

Drabble did not make good his threat to resign his legal work, and he was as busy as ever for another ten years.

In 1887 Drabble's old life in England caught up with him. He had continued to spend much time with *Silistria* shipmates and their fami-

---

39 Robb and Drabble to Provincial Secretary, 1 August 1883 and 21 May 1884, Provincial Secretary, Correspondence Inward, 1871-1892; Pidcock Diary, 16 May 1884.

40 Drabble to Provincial Secretary, 30 June and 18 August 1887, Provincial Secretary, Correspondence Inward, 1871-1892.

lies. Sam Cliffe had married Mary Harmston's daughter Florence and produced a large family. Drabble kept in touch with his mother Eliza, who sent him money occasionally. Born in about 1813, Eliza Drabble lived at least until 1885, as we know from Mary Harmston. In her diary of 1884 and 1885, Harmston noted that she had written to "Mrs Drabbles" or "Mrs Drabble," so communication was maintained between the old world and the new—alas now lost.[41]

After Sam Cliffe leased the Lorne Hotel in 1883 Drabble spent much of his time there, boarded there briefly, and regarded it as a second home. A couple of oblique references suggest that he occasionally holed up at the Lorne. "Fine," Mary Harmston wrote in her hotel diary on 17 October 1887, "Drabble here on the gas." The *Silistria* passengers remained a tightly knit group into the 1880s, as she recorded a few days before the twenty-fifth anniversary of their arrival:

> 10 November 1887. "Henry up who came out with us to this country."
>
> 11 November 1887. "Very stormy. Nixon Henry Drabble & Sam having a great talk about old times."

News of an inheritance came soon afterwards. "Drabble gone to Victoria," Harmston wrote on 2 December 1887; "he has had a lot of money left him by an uncle Mr. Ward he says he is going to England in six weeks." Drabble's inheritance seems to have made a sensation in Comox and indeed on Vancouver Island as a whole. It even gave Carwithen the opportunity to mention Drabble's name for once without condescension: he told Blaksley that "Old Drabble has just received news of a legacy of $100,000 or 20,000 pounds; reports vary, so he intends returning home shortly." The Victoria *Colonist* ran a story about the inheritance entitled "A Lucky Man:"

> Drabble, the government agent at Comox, has just received information that, through the death of an aunt in England, he has become the possesssor of £20,000. He leaves at once for England to claim his inheritance. Mr. Drabble will probably have no difficulty in agreeing with the old proverb that "It's as well to be born lucky as rich." We congratulate him on his good fortune.[42]

Just before leaving for England he made a note in one of his field books that read: "TL address. Druggist—160 Earles Court Road Kensington London SW."[43] This was his son Tom Lambe Drabble, whose address Drabble or Mary Harmston may have obtained from Eliza

[41] Harmston Diary, 9 April 1884, 24 September 1885.

[42] Carwithen to Blaksley, 8 December 1887, Carwithen Correspondence; *Colonist*, 20 November 1887, p. 4; see also Rodello to Crease, 17 November 1887, Crease Collection.

[43] Env. 91, Drabble Papers.

Drabble, or from Tom himself if he was on speaking terms with his father. It is this note that allowed Drabble's descendents to be traced in 1994. Drabble's children were in their mid- to late-twenties when Drabble returned to England in 1888: Tom was a chemist, trained at the Royal Botanical Gardens, Kew, and Lylie had recently married Weightman Bemrose, also a chemist.

Details of Drabble's spring 1888 visit to England are completely lacking on both sides of the Atlantic. Presumably he visited Tom, but there is no solid evidence that he did so; he may also have visited his daughters, but they may not have wanted to see him. All that is known for sure is that he did not inherit £20,000. His aunt Ann Ward (his mother's sister) left a personal estate of only £1,176, and she left it not to Drabble but to her husband John Ward, a farmer of Orgreave in the County of York. Drabble is not mentioned in the will at all. Perhaps the news of the inheritance was a hoax.[44]

&

Both Robb and Rodello, the founders of Comox, died in December 1889 within a few days of each other. "Rain," Harmston wrote in her diary on 16 December; "Mr. Robb buried. Just back when Rodello died about four o'clock had brought him down to the Lorne Hotel at dinner time." His old partner Drabble acted as Rodello's executor, while Sam Cliffe auctioned his belongings. Captain Curtis and his son James bought most of Rodello's furniture and household effects; Drabble bought Rodello's pony for $41 and his feather bed for $5.50.

Comox, then, was a lively and self-contained community in the 1880s—and remains so today. Even so, the valley's centre of gravity began to shift westward to the new mining settlements. Dunsmuir opened the Union mine in the spring of 1888, and McPhee hired Drabble to lay out the town of Courtenay later that year. Holmes summarized the effect of Dunsmuir's arrival on the village of Comox: "The opening of the Union Mines and the nucleus of the town of Courtenay had commenced, and Comox dwindled."[45] Comox peaked in the late 1880s and early 1890s; it never got the railway, and never got a sawmill or any real industry; but the inhabitants may have been grateful for this. Comox remains what it was a hundred years ago: the choice residental district of the valley, with a stunning panoramic view of the Beauforts and the harbour. Industry, when it arrived, would locate elsewhere, and Reginald Pidcock's sawmill on the Courtenay River led the way.

---

44 Marriage certificate of Weightman Bemrose and Eliza Burnby Drabble, 22 June 1882, GRO; probate will of Ann Ward, 15 May 1888, Principal Probate Registry, Somerset House, London; Clare McMillan to the author, 13 August 1994.
45 Holmes, "Reminiscences."

CHAPTER 12

Reginald's Sawmill

Tsolum's shrinking tide leaves bare
Beach and snag and sunken log.

FROM *June Days*, by Eric Duncan[1]

UNTIL the mid-1870s Comox settlers obtained their sawn
lumber from Victoria, from Sayward's sawmill at Shawnigan Creek, or
from Moody's mill on Burrard Inlet. As a trader, in 1873 and 1874,
Drabble had arranged such shipments with Captain Clarke of the
Douglas. In about 1877, however, Reginald Pidcock completed his
sawmill on the bank of the Courtenay River, providing a local source of
lumber and starting a chain-reaction of events that led, indirectly, to the
founding of the town of Courtenay eleven years later.

Sawn lumber was desirable, but not absolutely necessary, for house
construction. The settlers' first habitations had been log houses of
varying degrees of simplicity. The Australian miners, unaware of North
American methods of log house building, had contrived some remarkably primitive dwellings. Irishman James Clarke, for example, lived in a
log hut sunk to the roof in a hillside; Shetlander William Duncan's
house of 1862 was made of alder sticks chinked with moss and mud, and
with a thatch of fern held down by small logs. A Comox Valley settler's
first habitation was usually a simple one-room log and shake cabin.
Reginald Carwithen built such a cabin in 1862, as did George Curtis in
the late 1880s at his pre-emption at Bates Beach, near Cape Lazo. New
Brunswicker Henry Grieve, by contrast, built his first cabin from hand-
hewn square timber.[2]

Houses improved in quality as settlers accumulated a little experience—and some cash from selling farm produce. In 1865, for example, William Duncan, lately joined by his brother Oliver, replaced his
primitive dwelling with a "decent habitation" modelled after the Shet-

---

[1] Duncan, *The Rich Fisherman*, p. 74.

[2] Duncan, "Comox District Fifty Years Ago;" *From Shetland to Vancouver Island*, p. 73;
Anfield, "Pioneer Woman Remains Remarkably Young at 94," *CVFP*, 18 April 1956. On
early Comox logging see also Isenor, *Land of Plenty*, pp. 171-77.

lands cottage where he grew up, but instead of stone and mortar he used spruce and fir. He hired Gideon Halcrow, a wandering Shetland carpenter formerly with the Hudson's Bay Company, to build the house, as Eric Duncan recalled:

> This new Comox cottage had fir sills hewn straight on two sides; round trimmed fir poles for studding, joists and rafters; and was weather boarded on the outside with split spruce boards and roofed with spruce shingles. It was lined inside and floored with six-inch tongue and groove lumber brought up from Victoria.[3]

There was still need for local lumber, and this was supplied by Drabble's friend Reginald Pidcock, the "young, well-educated Englishman" who had, in 1863, pre-empted 170 acres (Section 17) on the east bank of the Tsolum. In 1870 he sold this farm to the Anglican Church, and moved across the river to what is now Courtenay. Just north of Courtenay the Tsolum and Puntledge rivers join, and for the last mile of their journey their combined waters are known as the Courtenay River. In October 1870, on the west bank of this short but major river, Pidcock pre-empted 160 acres of forest (Section 61) in what the settlers called New Siberia. The dense forest here stopped snow from melting and threw winter shadows across the river. This was the edge of the "wilderness profound" contemplated by Duncan from his sunny farm on the opposite bank. Pidcock's land contained a single, small, natural clearing near the modern Condensory Bridge, where he built a log cabin for his wife and small children. He hired his old hunting partner George Drabble to survey his new pre-emption.[4]

Pidcock pre-empted this piece of wilderness with the express purpose of starting a sawmill. In this one gesture he left the rural, agrarian life of the valley for an industrial life in the surrounding forest. Duncan recalled the beginnings of the mill:

> In one of his hunting excursions there he had come across a small creek, tributary to the Puntledge, and conceived the idea of bringing it down to the high bank of the Courtenay to run a saw-mill by overshot power. He ran a line where he wanted it, and the other settlers, tired of erecting log and shake buildings, turned out in force and dug the long ditch for him.[5]

At first, Pidcock had a partner in this enterprise: 1862 argonaut Harry Guillod, who in 1871 moved from the Port Alberni area to Comox, where he became Willemar's missionary catechist. Pidcock and Guillod,

---

[3] *From Shetland to Vancouver Island*, p. 74.

[4] Duncan, "Every English County Represented Among Comox Pioneers," *Vancouver Province*, March 1927; *Rural Rhymes*, pp. 17-18; "Early Days and Early Settlers;" *Comox Argus*, 30 March 1955, p. 1.

[5] *From Shetland to Vancouver Island*, p. 181.

in the 1874 Comox Voter's List, are both identified as mill owners. The mill site was on the Courtenay River across from the mouth of Green's Slough; it was "jammed into the bush on the river bank" near the foot of present 8th Street.[6]

In principle Pidcock's sawmill was identical to Drabble's grist mill on Portuguese Creek, where the dammed and diverted waters of Finley Creek provided power. In 1873 Pidcock obtained permission to divert water from Mill Creek, and he built a ditch or aquaduct two miles long which carried the water to the Mill Pond, where the Safeway store is now. (See map 8.) A wooden flume took the water down to the mill at a sufficient velocity to turn the water wheel. The settlers volunteered their time and labour, glad at the prospect of a local supply of lumber; by June 1875 the mill ditch had been dug, and within a year the mill dam and sawmill had been erected.[7]

In August 1877 Pidcock received the Crown Grant to his preemption and finished his mill at about the same time. When Duncan arrived the sawmill had just been built, and Pidcock himself stated that he started sawing in 1877-78. The mill was powered by a turbine water wheel of forty-five horsepower.[8]

Pidcock obtained his first timber from his own land, taking Red Fir (i.e., Douglas Fir, so-named on account of its orangy tinge) from the present site of the Courtenay Museum on Cliffe Avenue. He logged with oxen to start, and cut timber on the Tsolum which he floated to the mill and kept in a boom on the river bank. "He had plenty of logs handy to the mill;" Duncan wrote; "that quarter of the town now called 'The Orchard,' held a splendid stand of clean red fir." At first he furnished only rough lumber, but in 1878 his friends in London sent him a planing-machine by way of Cape Horn, and then he could supply every requirement of the valley.[9]

---

6   Smith, "Harry Guillod's Journal," p. 192; Newman, "The Reverend Jules Xavier Willemar;" "List of Persons Claiming to Vote," 26 June 1874; the mill buildings are shown on Plan 480, Comox District, SGB; Duncan, "Every English County Represented."

7   Pidcock to CCL&W, 4 February 1873, British Columbia, Lands and Works Department, Correspondence Inward, 1872-1918; Pidcock to CCL&W, 18 June 1873, in British Columbia, Department of Lands and Works, Vancouver Island Pre-emptions; *Comox Argus*, 30 March 1955; Carroll, *Wild Roses and Rail Fences*, pp. 106-09; *Comox Free Press*, 4 October 1951; British Columbia, Department of Public Works, contracts, specifications, 1862-1909; Isenor, *Land of Plenty*, pp. 71, 77.

8   Comox Land Registers, p. 32; Duncan, "Every English County Represented;" British Columbia, Attorney General, [Bench Books, 1864-1964], [Civil Court, Comox, 1886]; R. T. Williams, *The British Columbia Directory for the Years 1882-83. . . .* (Victoria: R. T. Williams, 1882), p. 186.

9   "Settlers Soon Made Loggers," *Nanaimo Free Press*, undated newspaper clipping, Buckham Collection; *From Shetland to Vancouver Island*, p. 181.

After building the mill Pidcock employed local men to work at the mill, in the woods, and on the river. He hired the sons and nephews of the original British settlers as well as the recent arrivals from Eastern Canada. In 1882 and 1883, for example, he employed Joe Fitzgerald, Willie Harmston and William Duncan (Jr.) from the settler group, and Archibald Pritchard and Joe Grieve from the Canadian group. He established a logging camp on his property on the Courtenay River, probably just north of the Courtenay River bridge.[10]

Until the early years of the twentieth century the Courtenay Townsite with criss-crossed with corduroy skid-roads left by oxen logging. "We didn't know it then," Leila Carroll recalled of her arrival in 1902; "but we were following the route oxen had plodded many times before. It was the remains of an old skid road over which logs were drawn to the sawmill on the river bank."[11]

Pidcock's venture coincided with the arrival of the first Comox loggers like John Berkeley and King and Casey, who supplied timber in booms to big southern mills, namely Sayward's mill in Victoria and Andrew Haslam's in Nanaimo. Berkeley established the first logging camp in the Comox area in the 1870s; he operated with oxen under contract to Sayward. In 1879 the three logging camps in the Comox region were those of John Berkeley, J. Lewis, and J. M. Walker. They paid their Chinese cooks a dollar a day, but rates for "white" workers were higher: Sam Piercy, from New Brunswick, got his first work in Comox logging by hand for $2 a day and dinner.[12]

King and Casey were the main loggers. Both came to the valley in about 1880, and both married into local families: Michael King, from Michigan, married Mary Cowie, daughter of Alexander and Sarah Cowie, Ontarians who had settled at Fanny Bay in 1884; Nova Scotian Lewis Casey married Jennie Creech, daughter of Englishman Samuel Creech of Comox.[13] Casey was boss of the partnership. In the 1880s King and Casey logged up the Tsolum in the Headquarters region, drove millions of feet of lumber down the river to their booms in the harbour, and sold their logs to Haslam. This operation had mixed success, logger Hugh Stewart recalled, some of the timber "being too

[10] Mildred Haas, "The Fitzgeralds," in Isenor, "The Comox Valley;" Carroll, *Wild Roses and Rail Fences*, p. 31; Pidcock, Diary 1 January 1883–2 June 1884.

[11] Carroll, *Wild Roses and Rail Fences*, pp. 31, 66.

[12] Hugh Stewart, letter to editor of *The Comox Argus*, 31 March 1921; Rodello to Provincial Secretary, 3 September 1879, Provincial Secretary, Correspondence Inward, 1871–1892; Anfield, "Pioneer Woman," *CVFP*, 18 April 1956; for "Mr. Walker's" 1891 activities see env. 69, Drabble Papers.

[13] Mitchell, *Diamond in the Rough*, pp. 80-83; British Columbia, Attorney General, Inquests, 1865-1937 (Rodello's fire inquest, 1881). See also Isenor, *Land of Plenty*, p. 140 and Fred Walker's Account Book, 1884-1886, env. 82, Drabble Papers.

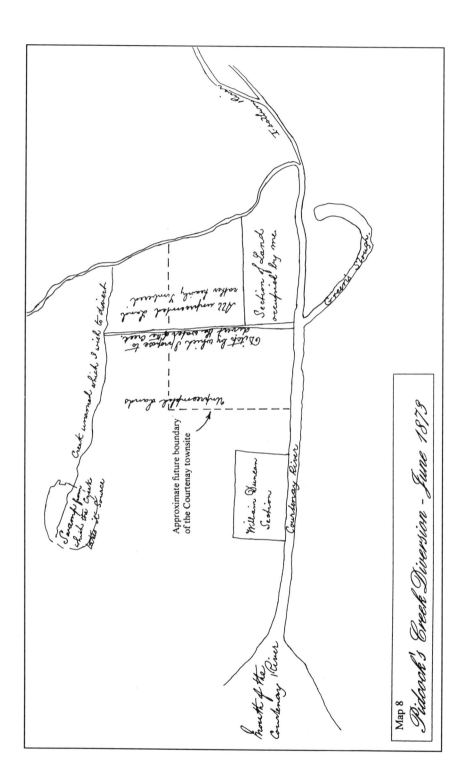

Approximate future boundary
of the Courtenay townsite

Map 8
Piteock's Creek Diversion – June 1873

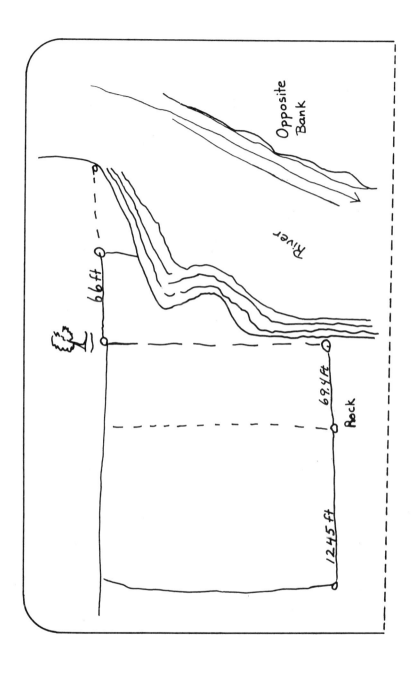

Sketch of boundaries of Urquhart's (previously Pidcock's) mill property,
Courtenay River, September 1889.

large and heavy for river driving." In 1884 Drabble himself spent a week surveying a timber claim on the upper Tsolum for John Hendry and David McNair of Royal City Planing Mills of New Westminster and Nanaimo. Henry Croft and William Angus of Chemainus also had timber interests on the Tsolum. King and Casey may well have logged under contract to these southern lumbermen.[14]

In the 1880s four logging camps opened at Union Bay on Baynes Sound, at least one of them run by New Brunswicker Thomas Piercy. Every two weeks, Isabella Piercy recalled, loggers came to Rodello's Elk Hotel to celebrate. "The bachelors used to have their jugs filled on the boat and every two or three miles on the way back they'd take a little drink, and half way home they'd curl up under a tree and sleep it off." Settlers needed a good local supply of split cedar shingles, and these were supplied in the 1880s and 1890s by the McFarlane and Graham families of Denman Island, Maritimers who were known for their efforts as "the Woodpeckers."[15]

At first, these loggers used teams of oxen to drag the logs to the water; oxen were so prevalent that there was no work for a blacksmith in 1878 when twenty-four year-old Robert Grant arrived in the valley. He opened a shop at the Comox wharf, but found insufficient business to remain, and moved to Nanaimo. Oxen, unlike horses, did not require hand-forged metal shoes, and the few horses then in Comox went mostly barefoot, there being no gravelled roads. Horses later replaced oxen in the woods.[16]

Logging was a risky business with a high injury and mortality rate. Mary Harmston recorded in her diary when Pidcock broke a rib or hurt himself in the mill. In December 1880 Bob Jones, the young son of Welsh settler Abraham Jones, was drowned while retrieving logs from the Tsolum. Sixty years later Mary Harmston's grandson Lou Cliffe recalled that Jones had been drowned in the Tsolum when he was sacking the river for logs, that is, "picking up stray logs that had got lodged on the banks, the early-day equivalent to 'cherry-picking' on the logging railway of today. He was working for King and Casey and his body was never found."[17]

---

[14] "Settlers Soon Made Loggers," *Nanaimo Free Press*, undated newspaper clipping in Buckham Collection; Hugh Stewart, letter to editor of *The Comox Argus*, 31 March 1921; [Rene Harding] "History of Lumbering in the Comox Valley," *Comox Argus*, 9 February 1955, p. 10; envs. 117, 123, 125.

[15] Anfield, "Pioneer Woman," *CVFP*, 18 April 1956; env. 92; *From Shetland to Vancouver Island*, p. 119.

[16] Duncan, "Spring in Comox Valley," *The Daily Province* [1935], Duncan, Newspaper Cuttings and Scrapbook.

[17] Harmston Diary, 8-11 December 1880, 18 May 1881, 2 November 1882; *Comox Argus*, 11 April 1940.

Pidcock's was a communal sawmill. Settlers had helped dig the aquaduct and build the flume, and were only too glad to convert their forested wilderness to lumber. They carted their timber to the mill or rafted it down the river. "Settlers could build their homes more cheaply," historian Leila Carroll wrote, "since they could draw their own logs to the mill and also help to saw them, as at first extra help there was welcome." In 1877 the Presbyterians built their first church from logs taken from the beaches, sawn into rough lumber by Pidcock, and hand-planed by the members of the kirk.[18]

Drabble was a close friend of Pidcock and often stopped at the mill for social visits; likewise Pidcock visited Drabble at the Landing. They were hunting companions, and both were Justices until Pidcock re-signed in the mid-1870s. In 1875 Drabble supervised the construction of the Courtenay River bridge (briefly known as the Mill Bridge or Pidcock's Bridge); settlers living on the farming side of the river and at Comox could now collect lumber directly from the mill. One person not happy with the new bridge was Alice Pidcock who, Duncan remembered, wanted to put a gate on it "to keep stray cattle from coming across at night and disturbing them with their bells."[19]

Drabble's many dealings with Pidcock survive in a scattered form in his survey field books. In 1880, he sold him a tin of dogfish oil for greasing the corduroy on his skid roads, or perhaps as machinery oil. Drabble appears in his diaries; for example on Saturday, 27 January 1883 Pidcock noted that: "Drabble came soon after dinner and stayed all night," and the next day, "Rained and snowed heavily with wind till 11 am. Then cleared up & was fine the rest of the day. None of us got to church. Drabble went about 4 p.m."[20]

A barter system prevailed in early Comox, and it applied to Pidcock's lumber business as well as to the farming economy. The mere presence of locally sawn lumber was not enough to introduce a cash economy to the district; what was needed was a large employer with a regular cash payroll earned from the sale of bulk primary resources to urban or industrial consumers. Robert Dunsmuir was better at this than Pidcock. Duncan recalled that the new mill lowered lumber prices but had no effect on the barter system:

> And lumber became cheap in Comox then,—$10 for rough and $15 for dressed, and many a fine log was yanked out of the Orchard by oxen. Slabs and edgings were free for the taking and the owner used to tell with enjoyment how one rancher, who had come for a load of edgings to make a

---

[18] Carroll, *Wild Roses and Rail Fences*, p. 107.

[19] Duncan, "Every English County Represented." For "Pidcock's Bridge" see env. 121, Drabble Papers.

[20] Env. 141; Pidcock Diary, 27-28 January 1883.

chicken fence, and had been forestalled by a neighbour, remarked:—"Why, Pidcock, you make very poor edgings now-a-days." But money was scarce— 25 cents and 30 cents was a top price both for eggs and butter, and sometimes there was no sale at all for the latter. Beef and pork were from 5 to 7 cents on foot, and potatoes were often fed to stock. "Well," remarked the sawmill man one day as he lugged in a big sack of spare-ribs, "if we can't get money for lumber, we can always get something to eat."[21]

This abundance of food was welcome in the growing Pidcock household. In March 1881 Alice Pidcock had borne five children and was expecting a sixth. "Pid has been doing pretty well this last summer in the lumber business;" Carwithen wrote; "it is certainly a great accommodation for all hands but his Mrs. keeps up the family supply also with five chicks and another expected."[22]

Pidcock's 1882-83 diaries convey a vivid sense of his life and work at the mill. He tended to his flume and dam, sawed and planed ("ground") lumber for farmers and settlers, and agreed with Pritchard to cut logs on the Comox Lake Road and convey them by oxen to the mill. He drafted a petition to D. W. Gordon, asking for the removal of snags and other debris from the river, and he dealt with many early settlers:

19 January 1883. "Heatherington and Sam Piercy came for lumber."

1 February 1883. "Prichard came & after dinner went with him to look at the timber on the Lake road."

5 February 1883. "Prichard came and we made an agreement about his coming to haul logs."

5 March 1883. "Hooper came to work at about 10 o'clock, & Fitzpatrick came with him to get some lumber and rafted it down. Got the road skidded as far as the hill. Joe Fitzgerald chopping most of the day."

21 March 1883. "Sawed all day but didn't do much. Piercy brought two bales hay & took a load of lumber for the new logging camp. Finley came."

16 May 1883. "Mathewson came with Stewart for lumber and had great trouble to get his horses to start with the load."

16 July 1883. "Halliday came down in the morning & told us they had been burnt out in the morning & he came for more lumber."[23]

By 1884 Pidcock was doing well at his mill. "He has succeeded with his sawmill splendidly," Carwithen remarked, "only for the babies there would be no stoppage."[24]

---

[21] Duncan, "Early Days and Early Settlers."

[22] Carwithen to Blaksley, 1 March 1881, Carwithen Correspondence.

[23] Pidcock Diary, 1882-83.

[24] Carwithen to Blaksley, 24 February 1884, Carwithen Correspondence.

A lawsuit provides another view of early logging at Comox. "Reginald Heber Pidcock vs. Lewis Casey" was heard in Comox in April 1886 before Judge Henry Crease with George Drabble acting as Court Registrar. After an initial and indecisive hearing the case was adjourned and resumed in Nanaimo in June.

Pidcock held that Casey owed him $230 for saw logs obtained illegally by him and sold in the way of trade. In September 1884 King and Casey had been logging about seven miles up the Tsolum. They and their gang had felled perhaps 750 or 1,000 trees (a million feet of lumber), limbed them, tapered their ends for skidding, and dragged them out with oxen to the Tsolum in anticipation of a fall freshet, which would allow them to send them down to their boom on the tide flats. They planned to sell their logs to Nanaimo lumberman Andrew Haslam.

The first freshet arrived on 6 September 1884, and King and Casey started sending logs down the river. Meanwhile, Pidcock was preparing for a winter of activity. He had bought his last sawlogs just two days before, and he had a full boom in front of his mill containing about seventy-five logs (75,000 feet). About a week earlier John Grant had delivered a load of Red Pine, and before that, Archibald Pritchard had sold Pidcock 26,000 feet of valuable White Pine (that is, Western White Pine, a rare tree favoured in boat-building and fine carpentry; Red Pine or Douglas Fir was known for its solid lumber favoured in house construction). Pidcock sold the White Pine to Victoria manufacturers Muirhead & Mann—makers of domestic and church furnishings such as doors, sashes, pulpits, and pews.

On 6 September, Pidcock was sawing lumber when Casey sent his logs down the engorged Tsolum in the first freshet. His logs struck Pidcock's boom with such velocity that they destroyed it, sending his logs down the river and into Comox Harbour. About 100,000 feet of Casey's million feet escaped from his main boom at the harbour, but the Comox Indians retrieved most of the logs, and they and Casey's men gathered all logs regardless of origin and stored them in the boom on the mud flats. Neither Pidcock nor Casey marked their logs in any way and they were virtually indistinguishable.

The next morning, with the log drive still in progress, Casey went to Pidcock, apologized, and promised to return the missing logs, but the current was too strong to take them up the river. He told Pidcock to "catch some logs as they came down the river" to compensate, but instead Pidcock and his associate Alex Urquhart took four boom sticks (extra-long and thin logs that framed a boom) down the river and helped themselves to thirty-five Douglas Fir logs from Casey's boom.

The next morning, however, Casey ordered King not to allow Urquhart to take them back to the mill.

Pidcock waited for Casey to return his logs, and finally he took him to court for 12,000 feet of White Pine (valued at $12.50 per thousand feet), and 20,000 feet of Douglas Fir (worth $4 per thousand feet) for a total of $230.

In his defence, Casey stated that Pidcock's logs had broken away because Pidcock's boom was secured insufficiently. He thought the damage had been done by "by a big Tree coming down the Courtenay River." He argued that Pidcock was in the habit of helping himself to his stray logs and that "Pidcock always took my logs instead of his own." "I seen Pidcock take my logs twice," his brother James Casey stated. Judge Crease, however, decided in Pidcock's favour, and Casey had to pay $230, plus legal costs, to Pidcock.[25]

Pidcock's annoyance at Casey's destruction of his boom and theft of his logs came at a time of deepening financial crisis. He had overextended himself in the early 1880s. Indeed in 1886, when he took Casey to court, he no longer owned the mill. He had sold it to meet debts incurred in building the steamer *Daisy*. He had planned to build this ship as early as March 1881, when Carwithen voiced his concerns at the expense of the undertaking. "There is to be a new steamer built by Pidcock that will run up into C. Green's slough;" Carwithen wrote, "at least that is what Pid has in contemplation now. It would be just the desideratum for us, though I fear it would be a risky undertaking for him."[26]

Pidcock, Duncan recalled, wanted to make the Courtenay River the business centre of the valley instead of Comox Landing, and the *Daisy* would carry mail and freight and a few passengers up to the bridge. Farmers and loggers on the Tsolum constituted potential customers. Green's Slough (now Courtenay Slough) was then, as now, a safe anchorage, and Pidcock believed that the settlers were too dependent on the Comox wharf for their supplies, postage, and communication. "Pidcock has six in family and is now building a steamer," Carwithen wrote in February 1884; "I scarcely think it will be a paying investment but he seems to have great hopes."[27]

Financial reality gradually overtook these great hopes, and to help pay for the steamer, Pidcock sold the mill and ten acres of riverfront

---

[25] See British Columbia, County Court (Comox), Originals, 1886, 1896, Civil case files; British Columbia, Attorney General, [Bench Books, 1864-1964], [Civil Court, Comox, 1886].

[26] Carwithen to Blaksley, 1 March 1881, Carwithen Correspondence.

[27] *From Shetland to Vancouver Island*, p. 182; Carwithen to Blaksley, 24 February 1884, Carwithen Correspondence.

land to Harry and John Urquhart in January 1885. Within a few months he regretted the sale because he still hadn't paid for *Daisy* and had lost the revenue generated by the mill. Carwithen wrote in May 1885 that Pidcock was "interested in a small steamer he had built recently. I believe he now wishes he had kept the mill." In December of the same year he repeated that "Pidcock is in a bad way, having swapped his sawmill and all he has in attempting to build a small steamer."[28]

Pidcock had ordered the boat's engine from England, where his brothers were supposed to pay for it. Instead, it arrived in Victoria "C.O.D." Pidcock could not pay for it. He was in a tight fix. He owed money for a brand new steam engine. He owed money for supplies to McPhee. "The undertaking was beyond his means," Duncan recalled; "and when the steamer was built she fell into the hands of Victoria men who had advanced him money, and who used her as a tug, *The Daisy*, at Chemainus." Finding himself land rich and cash poor, Pidcock took in McPhee as part owner of his land and sold him the northern part of his 160 acres. At an opportune moment (perhaps with the help of Harry Guillod, since 1881 an Indian Agent) Pidcock was offered the Kwawkiulth Indian Agency by D. W. Gordon, and he moved to Fort Rupert in November 1886. Things had gone from bad to worse for Pidcock. The little steamer undid his life and work so effectively that he had to leave Comox altogther. It would not be last time on the coast of British Columbia that the dream of a boat had upset carefully laid plans.[29]

The loggers of Comox continued their litigious ways after Pidcock sold the mill. In April 1886 Drabble heard the case Urquhart Brothers vs. Archibald Pritchard in the Comox courtroom: the previous May, Pritchard and his partner Adam Bruce had agreed to provide a load of White Pine to the Urquhart brothers. They were to deliver the logs for 12$ per thousand to the river bank in front of the mill, or for $12.50 right to the mill. They also agreed to exchange an ox shed, cart-wheels, and other items for a quantity of lumber. Both sides carried through with the agreement, but Pritchard refused to hand over the shed and cart-wheels to the Urquharts owing to the poor quality of the lumber they received. "We refused to pay for it or return it," Pritchard said, "It was old lumber when we took it from the Mill." Drabble decided that Pritchard had not carried through with the agreement and ordered

[28] Duncan, "Early Days and Early Settlers;" *From Shetland to Vancouver Island*, p. 182; Carwithen to Blaksley, 10 May and 2 December 1885, Carwithen Correspondence.

[29] Isenor, *Land of Plenty*, p. 172; *From Shetland to Vancouver Island*, p. 182; Duncan, "Early Days and Early Settlers;" on the sale to McPhee see also Carwithen to Blaksley, 19 December 1890, Carwithen Correspondence; Harmston Diary, 26 November 1886.

him to pay Urquhart Brothers $9.25. The Urquharts subsequently installed a steam sawmill and logged off the entire Comox townsite and much land around.[30]

Logging continued to be a hazardous business. In February 1885 John Urquhart was drowned during a freshet on the river, and his body washed up on Denman Island. Two years later Bob Cliffe was drowned on his way up to King and Casey's Camp. He slipped while getting off the logging scow onto the steamboat.[31]

King and Casey continued to log on the Tsolum until about 1888, and kept on sending logs down the river. For two weeks in February 1886 they tried to tow away an enormous log boom that was wedged on the mud flats in Comox Harbour, and finally the steamships *Dunsmuir* and *Etta White* succeeded in dislodging the massive boom. The next year, in November 1887, Eric Duncan wrote a poem about the plight of salmon having to dodge logs sent by lumbermen down the Tsolum.[32]

But already King and Casey were looking for greener pastures. Technology limited their endeavours to rivers and the coastline. This was the era of logging with oxen and horses, of chopping down every tree laboriously with an axe. Steam donkey engines and logging railways had not yet been introduced, and the interior sections of the island would not be touched for thirty or forty years. So King and Casey had to do their business on the sea and on the river, and in 1887 they began their move to Quadra Island and Campbell River, where they hired Drabble to survey their timber limits.

Meanwhile, down Baynes Sound, others were looking for coal.

[30] British Columbia, County Court (Comox), Originals, 1886, 1896; *From Shetland to Vancouver Island*, p. 182. For Drabble's Urquhart surveys see envs. 47, 140, 144.

[31] Harmston Diary, 1-24 February 1885, 16 April 1887.

[32] Harmston Diary, February 1886; Duncan, *Rural Rhymes*, p. 37.

CHAPTER 13

Robert Dunsmuir's Last Adventure

There are now two whisky houses at the wharf, also a new store or two, so unless something turns up besides farming some of them will have to breakfast on clams pretty often.
—Reginald Carwithen to Harry Blaksley, 29 August 1880[1]

*I*N the 1870s and 1880s industrial activity started up on Baynes Sound just south of Comox—activity that Drabble, in his various capacities, could survey, regulate, or adjudicate. Coal had been found in the valley by Robert Brown and his fellow-explorers in 1864, and with further discoveries on the Beaufort slopes of Baynes Sound, the local economy promised to diversify away from an agrarian footing and at the same time give Comox farmers a nearby market for their produce. An 1883 immigration guide to British Columbia urged settlers to appreciate the benefits of living in a mineral country. Mines, the tract explained, provided direct employment and created "local markets which otherwise might not exist for generations."[2] But successful mining claims were the exception not the rule, and Comox farmers had to wait for magnate Robert Dunsmuir to provide them with a secure local market.

Three mining companies set up operations on the eastern slopes of the Beaufort Mountains: the Baynes Sound, Perseverance, and Union Coal companies. Their owners—miners, merchants, and capitalists from Nanaimo and Victoria—sold their entire holdings to Dunsmuir in the 1880s when insufficient capital resources and a depressed market prevented them from operating the mines at a profit. Drabble was involved with these mines as a surveyor and magistrate. (See map 9.)

The first of the mines—and the most distant from Comox—was the Baynes Sound Coal Company. In about 1863 coal had been found on the Tsable River, which empties into the narrow passage between Den-

---

[1] Carwithen to Blaksley, 29 August 1880, Carwithen Correspondence.

[2] *Province of British Columbia, Canada: Its Climate and Resources, with Information for Emigrants* (Victoria: R. Wolfenden, 1883), p. 82. I owe this reference to Ruth Sandwell.

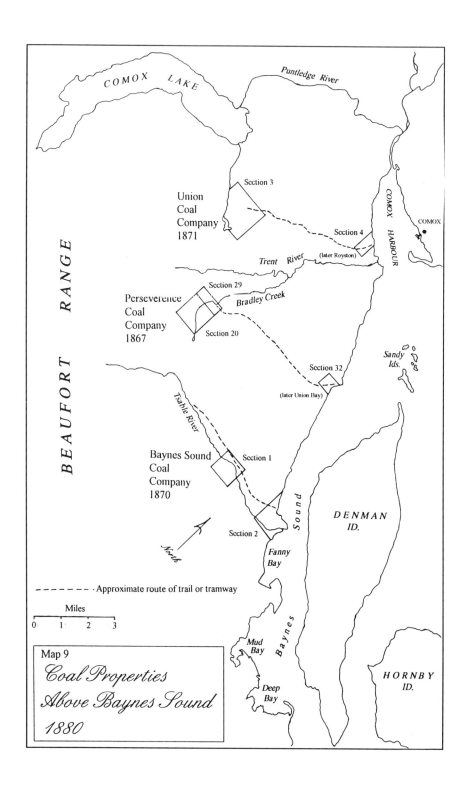

COMOX LAKE

Puntledge River

Section 3

Union
Coal
Company
1871

Section 4

COMOX HARBOUR

COMOX

(later Royston)

Trent River

Section 29

Bradley Creek

Perseverence
Coal
Company
1867

Section 20

Section 32

Sandy
Ids.

(later Union Bay)

BEAUFORT RANGE

Table River

Baynes Sound
Coal
Company
1870

Section 1

Section 2

Sound

DENMAN
ID.

North

Fanny
Bay

- - - - - - Approximate route of trail or tramway

Miles

0   1   2   3

Mud
Bay

Baynes

HORNBY
ID.

Deep
Bay

Map 9
*Coal Properties
Above Baynes Sound
1880*

man and Vancouver islands known as Baynes Sound. A group of Victoria capitalists started trading shares a few years later, and in 1869 they hired John Trutch of Victoria to survey their claim. A year later they incorporated the Baynes Sound Coal Mining Company, and leased or bought over 5,000 acres, including coal land in the interior and a shipping point on the sound. Among the syndicate were Hudson's Bay Company officer Joseph McKay (who had explored the Comox Valley in 1852 and opened the Hudson's Bay Company's mines at Nanaimo in the same year); Roderick Finlayson, a mayor of Victoria and another old fur trader; and David Lenvenu, a Victoria grain merchant. Their stated object was "coal mining on Vancouver Island, boring for and making coal oil, the erection of smelting works and sawmills, and trading generally on lands held by the Company." The reference to coal oil is significant: in the 1850s a Nova Scotian, Abraham Gesner, had found a way of distilling oil from coal hydrocarbons, and by the 1860s coal oil had become a standard domestic lighting fuel in Canada.[3]

By 1873 the Baynes Sound syndicate had opened a trail from Fanny Bay to the coal mine on the Tsable River. They built a wharf at Fanny Bay—some ten miles from Comox—and in 1875-76 opened a three-mile narrow-gauge railway from there to the mine. The first exports of coal were made in 1876. The people of Comox expected a population increase to result, and they were not disappointed: in 1876 fifty-five men were employed at the mine. This sudden influx brought miners from Fanny Bay in search of liquor with troubling results for the magistrates Drabble and Robb, who persuaded the government to build a new jail at Comox.[4]

The Baynes Sound mine did not only attract the "unscrupulous characters" regretted by Drabble and Robb. It also, Eric Duncan recalled, "drew a number of eastern Canadians to Denman Island as a handy location to raise produce for sale to the miners." Among them were the large McFarlane, Piercy, and Graham familes, all from New Brunswick, most of whom went into logging. Though heavily-timbered, the island contained sections of soil of good quality, and "quite a number of

[3] Philip Hankin, "Return of the Lands Preempted . . . in different Districts of Vancouver Island during the year 1870," Herald Street; Torrance to CCL&W, 21 November 1882, British Columbia, Department of Lands and Works, Correspondence Inward, 1871-1883; "Baynes Sound Coal Mine," Buckham Collection; *The Canadian Encyclopedia*, Volume 2, p. 740. On these early mines see also Isenor, *Land of Plenty*, pp. 252-59, 283-88.

[4] Richardson, "Report on the Coal Fields of the East Coast of Vancouver Island," pp. 77-81 and "Report on the Coal-Fields of Vancouver and Queen Charlotte Islands," pp. 32-65; Buckham, "Summary History—Coal Discoveries—Comox District," Buckham Collection (hereafter "Summary History);" Cole and Lockner, *To the Charlottes*, p. 197, n. 433; Willemar, "St. Andrew's, Comox," p. 29.

settlers" arrived on Denman in 1876. These were the first European residents of Denman, which had been struck hard fifteen years earlier in the great smallpox epidemic.[5]

In 1875 the local M.L.A. wrote that a sudden cessation of demand for Pacific coals at San Francisco had meant that there could be no extensive shipment of coal that year, and two years later a coal depression in San Francisco caused the Baynes Sound mine to close altogether, throwing everyone out of work except for Michael Watt, a Scottish caretaker who lived on Denman across from the mine. The provincial government dropped its plans to build a wagon road from Comox, and when George Dawson of the Geological Survey of Canada visited in October 1878 he found mining operations suspended. He took a photograph of the Fanny Bay wharf, and he noted that the miners had "got into some trouble with faults &c."[6]

Dawson was particularly intrigued by the shell midden exposed at Fanny Bay. Then, as now, middens are often revealed during construction on the sheltered coastline of the Gulf of Georgia. To archaeologists their complex stratigraphic sequences reveal hearths, post-moulds, and house platforms. Dawson wrote that:

> Where the rail way to the mine follows parallel to the shore a cutting has been made in the face of a narrow flat between it & the beach. Here for several hundred yards a great thickness of Indian shell heaps has been exposed. From 12 to 15 feet seen in some of excavations, without bottom being shown. Clams, oysters, (small), mussels, sea-eggs &c. form alternating layers or are mixed together. Some layers Calcined, & many burnt stones scattered through the mass. Appears as though village must have been here, but very long ago, as forest trees several hundred years old grow on the upper layers.[7]

With the closure of the mine in 1877 the workers departed, leaving only a few pre-emptors clinging to the Vancouver Island and Denman shorelines. The company had spent over $100,000 on the mining properties, transport, bridges, wharf, train, and labour. In March 1881 only three of the Denman Island settlers remained; Carwithen wrote that they had arrived "at the time the Baines Sound mine was started unfortunately for them it turned out worthless."[8]

---

[5] *From Shetland to Vancouver Island*, pp. 118-19; Courtenay *Weekly News*, 1 February 1893.

[6] Ash to CCL&W, 11 and 13 July 1875, in British Columbia, Department of Lands and Works, Correspondence Inward, 1871-1883; Buckham, "Summary History;" Cole and Lockner, *To the Charlottes*, pp. 87, 90.

[7] Cole and Lockner, *To the Charlottes*, p. 90.

[8] Heisterman to CCL&W, 11 Feb 1879, British Columbia, Department of Lands and Works, Correspondence Inward, 1871-1883; Carwithen to Blaksley, 1 March 1881, Carwithen Correspondence.

The second of the mines was the Perseverance Coal Mining Company, formed in 1867 by ten Victoria and Comox merchants, including druggist and pamphleteer A. J. Langley, politician and Deep Bay landowner Dr. John Ash, Comox merchants and whiskey traders Jack Hart and John Holder, and miner Henry Bradley.[9]

Their mine, known as the Perseverance Claim or the Beaufort Coal Mine, was located on Bradley Creek, a tributary of the Trent River. By 1873 they had built a trail to the mine, and in 1875 they bought a 160-acre lot at Union Bay just south of Langley Point (then also known as "Jack Hart's Point"), near the mouth of Hart Creek, and hired Drabble to survey a townsite within this lot. They planned to use Union Bay as their shipping point. Though some work took place at the mine throughout the 1870s, there is no record that coal was ever exported, and in the 1880s a 700-foot shipping wharf languished at Union Bay.[10]

In 1882 and 1883 the Perseverance shareholders hired Drabble to do a complete survey of their mining and townsite properties and to survey a trail and railway level to the mines, perhaps as a prelude to opening the mine. In November 1882 Drabble surveyed the company's 1,000-acre Bradley Creek mining property, and in December he moved down to Baynes Sound to the 160-acre "Perseverance Townsite"—now the town of Union Bay.[11]

A working memo has survived in Drabble's 1882 field book. While engaged in these Persverance surveys he ordered goods and supplies from Comox. He needed a pair of "No. 5 Boots" with brass toes from Teddy Rollings, the Comox shoemaker. "Dont send Sullivans Boots," he added, with reference to Irishman Dan Sullivan, a farmer who had settled on Baynes Sound in 1876, and he continued: "McPhee 5 lb Sack Salt. Fish Hooks Trout Line. Canoe on Sunday for Boring Rods."[12]

A year later Drabble returned to Baynes Sound to survey a trail and railway level to Bradley Creek and Trent River. From October until December he hired John Bruce of Comox, John Howe of Hornby, and fisherman Peter Berry of Denman at $2.50 a day, and an Indian named Gladstone for a day for $1.75, probably for canoe hire. They started at

9 "Nelson Survey," Buckham Collection.

10 Richardson, "Report on the Coal Fields of the East Coast of Vancouver Island," pp. 77-81; map after page 64 in Richardson, "Report on the Coal-Fields of Vancouver and Queen Charlotte Islands;" Beaven to Drabble, 18 December 1882, in "Nelson Survey," Buckham Collection; Buckham, "Summary History;" env. 144, Drabble Papers.

11 Gore to Drabble, 11 December 1882, in "Nelson Survey" file, Buckham Collection; Drabble field notebook, 5 June–29 October 1877 and November 1882, Buckham Collection; Glover-Geidt, *The Friendly Port*, p. 2.

12 Env. 72, Drabble Papers; Drabble field notebook, 5 June–29 October 1877 and November 1882, Buckham Collection.

the end of September 1883 at the southeast corner of the company's beach claim, crossed Thomas Piercy's skid road, and spent a week surveying up the hillside from the high water mark. Drabble noted creeks named Fall, Camp, Lake, Grindstone, Corduroy, Prospect, Boulder, and Deep, and he kept a list of "aneuroid readings" showing elevations. On 7 October, he and his men reached the cabin at Bradley Creek, six and a half miles above the Baynes Sound. From there they surveyed along the bed of Bradley Creek, where Drabble noted that the creek ran right over the coal; he also identified "Drabble's seam" and "Drabble's Falls" on Bradley Creek. Drabble Falls, about twenty feet high, were 2,480 feet above sea level.[13]

Within a few years both the Baynes Sound and Perseverance mines would be bought out by Robert Dunsmuir, who also acquired the third—and ultimately the most productive of the mines—the Union Coal Company. In 1870 Sam Harris of Nanaimo had discovered coal on Coal Creek, which flows into Comox Lake. Among the original shareholders forming the Union Coal Company in 1871 were Adam Horne, Captain Clarke of the *Douglas*, Sam Cliffe, the ubiquitous David Lenvenu, and seven members of the Allan, Hamilton, and Hoggan families, all Nanaimo miners. The mine was named in honour of the union of British Columbia and Canada in 1871.[14]

This company applied for 1,000 acres of coal lands east and south of modern Cumberland, and for a coal-shipping point seven miles away on Comox Harbour. They moved quickly. In the summer of 1871 they cut and cleared four miles of the tramway. In 1873 Cliffe and his associates completed the Union Mine Road from the mine to what is now Royston, and in December 1873 Chief Commissioner of Lands and Works Robert Beaven instructed Drabble to lay out the coal company's claim at what became Cumberland.[15]

By July 1874, the mine owners had spent $10,000 in prospecting the seams and building the tramway, but all for nothing. After this initial work and layout, work on the mine stopped, due to the high cost of opening a mine, tramway, and shipping facility in the wilderness. In the late 1870s the mine seems to disappear from sight. The knowledge, however, that valuable deposits of coal lay at their doorstep gave the

---

13 Envs. 92, 144, Drabble Papers; Drabble field notebooks, September–October 1883 and 11-13 October 1883, Buckham Collection.

14 Courtenay *Weekly News*, 18 January 1893; Buckham, "Summary History."

15 *The Daily Standard*, 27 October 1873, p. 3; Buckham, "Summary History"; Richardson, "Report on the Coal-Fields of Vancouver and Queen Charlotte Islands"; Buckham, "Royston's Ancient Story," in Isenor, "The Comox Valley"; Hugh Stewart, letter to editor of *The Comox Argus*, 31 March 1921; Beaven to Drabble, 15 December 1873, Canadian Collieries file, CDMA.

Comox settlers hope that one day the mines might provide them with a local market. Dora Crawford, the schoolteacher's daughter, wrote later that the knowledge of rich coal deposits "encouraged the farmers to stick to their farms and improve them."[16]

༺༻

Many in the valley admired the empire Robert Dunsmuir had created since his arrival on Vancouver Island in 1851 as a penniless miner employed by the Hudson's Bay Company. He saved his money, lived frugally, and spoke frugally. "A capitalist is a man who lives on less than he earns," he once said. He also had an uncanny ability to find coal: in 1871 he opened his Wellington mine near Departure Bay, and by the end of the decade he was making huge profits. The three Comox-area mining companies failed while his company was wildly successful, and Dunsmuir (like a successful "Monopoly" competitor) bought in succession the Baynes Sound (July 1881), Union (March 1884), and Perseverance (January 1888) mines. He bought them one share at a time by offering the investors good prices. Most were probably relieved to get some return for their unprofitable outlay.[17]

Dunsmuir's Wellington mine profits allowed him to diversify his activities to include Vancouver Island railways as well as coal mines. He obtained his controversial land grant in 1884, completed the Esquimalt and Nanaimo Railway two years later, and extended the line from Esquimalt to Victoria in 1888.

Dunsmuir's arrival caused a boom in the Comox region after 1884. Speculators moved into Baynes Sound soon after he bought the Union Mine. J. B. Holmes secured a 160-acre pre-emption next to the Perseverance townsite, where he made a clearing and built a house to prove his claim. Judge Crease bought Rodello's farm on Denman Island, right across from the Baynes Sound and Perseverance holdings, where he planned to open a hotel. Both men hired Drabble to survey their lots. Banker Alfred Green of Victoria, Adam Horne of Nanaimo, and Victoria merchant Morris Moss suddenly appear in the 1880s tax assessment rolls in Baynes Sound and Denman Island. These men must have suspected that Dunsmuir would open one or all of his mines, and extend his railway to service them.[18]

---

[16] Buckham, "Summary History"; Richardson, "Report on the Coal Fields of Nanaimo, Comox, Cowichen [sic], Burrard Inlet and Sooke," pp. 162-68; Courtenay *Weekly News*, 18 January 1893; Crawford, "First Prize Article."

[17] Bowen, *The Dunsmuirs of Nanaimo*, p. 21; Reksten, *The Dunsmuir Saga*, pp. 47, 94; Buckham, "Summary History."

[18] Env. 147, Drabble Papers; 1888 Assessment, Comox District; Crease–Rodello Correspondence, Crease Papers.

After gaining control of all three mines in 1888, Dunsmuir acted quickly. He selected the richest of the mines and the best shipping facility for immediate use. Union was the richest mine and the Perseverance Company's townsite at Langley (Jack Hart's) Point was the best shipping point, so he bought the marginal Perseverance holdings for the sake of the Langley Point area, which he renamed Union Bay. Historian Alexander Buckham recorded in 1960 that "there is a local story up here, for which I have no proof, that Dunsmuir originally wanted to ship from Comox, and offered James Robb a high price for his land, which Robb refused."[19] If true, Dunsmuir would have approached Robb between his purchase of Union mines in 1884 and his purchase of the Perseverance Mine with its excellent shipping point at what became Union Bay in 1888.

On 15 February 1888, Dunsmuir announced that he would open the Union mine. "NEW COAL MINES!" shouted the *Nanaimo Free Press.* "THE UNION AND PERSEVERANCE SEAMS OF COAL AT COMOX!" "TO BE OPENED AT ONCE!" And the paper contined:

> We understand that it is the intention of Messrs. R. Dunsmuir & Sons, the proprietors of the far-famed Wellington mines, to at once open up the coal seams on their Union and Perseverance Properties on Baynes Sound, Comox. This move is caused by the increased demand for coal and the intention of this enterprising firm to meet that demand as speedily as possible.

> Mr. John Dick, who has been prospecting at Wellington for Messrs. Dunsmuir & Sons, will at once transfer his labours to this new tract of coal land recently acquired by the present proprietors.

> In a few weeks' time the surveyors will be sent up to survey for the road, loading wharves, etc., as it is the intention to ship coal at Jack Hart's Point at the earliest possible moment, and as soon as possible to bring the output up to 1000 tons per day.[20]

Comox Valley settlers greeted the news with jubilation; the *Nanaimo Free Press* recorded that the people of Comox were "greatly excited" by the news: "The settlers felt quite jubilant and the price of farms are [*sic*] said to have gone up 100 per cent at a single bound. Some showed their joy by having a 'jolly time' all night." Until this time, settlers were trapped in their old pattern of shipping produce by steamer in the care of travelling trader John Wilson. "Old Wilson is worth about as much as anyone on the coast, and still keeps on the boat," Carwithen had commented in 1884; "he swindles awfully, but we can't help ourselves,

---

[19] Buckham, "Summary History."

[20] *Nanaimo Free Press*, 15 February 1888.

and must grin, and wait for a home market."[21] Dunsmuir gave the settlers that home market.

Within weeks of taking control of all three coal properties Dunsmuir sent a party to inspect the Union mine. Mary Harmston, in her invaluable Lorne Hotel diary, recorded the arrival of Dunsmuir, his heavy mining machinery, and his Chinese workers—the corollaries of industrial progress in nineteenth century British Columbia. From her upstairs vantage point she made the following entries:

> 1 March 1888. "J. Dick up with a lot of Chinamen to work on Coal road."
>
> 3 April 1888. "The Pilot has brought up 135 Chinamen."
>
> 7 April 1888. "Stormy. The Yousemite brought up the Coalmines owners they sleep aboard & go over in the morning. Horses are engaged for them to ride up to the mine."
>
> 8 April 1888. "Fine. Mrs Cliffe Mrs Ingle & I were aboard the Boat were introduced to Mr Dunsmuir by Cap Rudlin we had quite a little chat with Dunsmuir before we left the Boat left between 4 & 5."
>
> 19 April 1888. "A lot more Chinamen to mine."
>
> 18 October 1888. "The Alexander is bringing Railroad irons for Coalmine."
>
> 3 November 1888. "A large Steam Boat to Union with Machinery for the Mine."
>
> 2 January 1889. "All except Mrs Cliffe & twins accross to see the Railroad & Locomotive & have a ride."

The great nineteenth century industrial revolution had arrived in Comox at last. Dunsmuir set about building a modern coal mine at Union and establishing a company town to service the mine and house the miners and their families. Many hoped he would extend his railway from Nanaimo. Farmers were elated at the prospect of a market, landowners expected a windfall, and a spirit of optimism prevailed. The opening of Union mines ended a quarter century of isolation for the farmers of Comox and caused a great influx of people and capital to the valley—as Shetlander William Duncan noted in his diary entry in September 1889:

> This is the fifth anniversary of my arrival in Comox and I have been thinking what a difference there is commercially in Comox from what it was five years ago. Then almost everybody knew everybody . . . now we meet many strangers. We have in our district a coal mine employing a large number of white men and a larger number of Chinese. A large wharf is in the course of construction, also a bridge across Gartley's [Trent] River. R. Dunsmuir, the

---

[21] *Nanaimo Free Press*, 18 February 1888; Carwithen to Blaksley, 24 February 1884, Carwithen Correspondence.

president of the Island Railway is the owner of the coal mine and much of the prosperity and future prospects of Comox are due to his wealth and enterprise.[22]

An admiration for Dunsmuir was tempered with concern at his policy of hiring Chinese, who were paid by mine managers half what "white" workers received. It was little wonder, Eric Duncan observed, that "mine-owners, lumbermen, and farmers endeavouring to clear land avail themselves as far as possible of the services of the heathen." Dunsmuir's white miners, who had managed to prevent the hiring of Chinese miners at Wellington, were outraged when Dunsmuir hired them at Union in 1888.[23]

His venture at Union would be Dunsmuir's last. He died suddenly in April 1889 at the age of sixty-three, much lamented by the progress-minded in the valley, who admired him for his support of capital and his example of what the frugal settler could achieve. A week after his death J. B. Holmes wrote to Joseph Hunter—Dunsmuir employee and Comox M.L.A.—that news of his death had reached Comox belatedly, "& only for want of communication & knowledge many in Comox would have availed themselves of the opportunity of paying their last respects to one so worthy."[24]

Dunsmuir's instant town of Union was situated 500 feet above sea level near Comox Lake. Named Union from its inception in 1888, its name was changed to Cumberland in 1898. "Work was at once commenced," an early historian wrote, "and pushed forward with vigor, and in June 1889 the first shipment of coal was made."[25] Dunsmuir transferred tradesmen, engineers, shippers, and managers from his established Wellington and Departure Bay operations. Union was an industrial outgrowth of Nanaimo and Wellington, though a few merchants and tradesmen moved up from Comox as well.

Conditions were primitive. Minnie McIntyre, who arrived at Union Camp in the summer of 1888 from Departure Bay, recalled many years later that Union consisted of nothing but "a number of rough shacks thrown up on the side of a hill near the new workings." Her own shack contained no furniture and no beds; it was bare, and she, her engineer husband, and four children slept on a shack floor for a week before

[22] William Duncan Diary, 13 September 1889.

[23] Duncan, "Vancouver Island," p. 368; Alan Grove and Ross Lambertson, "Pawns of the Powerful: The Politics of Litigation in the Union Colliery Case," *BC Studies* 103 (Fall 1994), pp. 3-31.

[24] Holmes to Hunter 18 April 1889, in Joseph Hunter, Correspondence Outward.

[25] Cumberland *Weekly News*, 8 March 1898; Courtenay *Weekly News*, 18 January 1893.

their own cabin was finished. "There was no regular water supply," she recalled, "all water coming from a swamp below the diggings and the shacks. It was no wonder that many of the men went down with a form of malaria." After two months she and her husband decided that this was "no place for a woman with four children," and Minnie and her children went back to Departure Bay. On their return in February 1889 they found that many more shacks had gone up, wells had been dug, and a school was being built.[26]

Lumber was needed immediately, and Dunsmuir bought a brand-new mill and leased it to Wellington lumbermen Robert Grant (one-time Comox blacksmith) and Lewis Mounce. Dunsmuir, Duncan wrote, admired Grant's "pushful aggressiveness," and sent him ahead to Union to furnish lumber for the dwellings and mines. The mill was operational by February 1889 at the latest. "Their saw-mill supplied all the coal-mine timbers," Duncan continued, "and built both the old and new towns of Cumberland." A number of other businesses opened and talented tradesmen arrived, like Nova Scotian carpenter John Carthew, former proprietor of the Elk Hotel.[27]

The first requirement was a road from the bay to the mine, and this was provided early in 1888 by Chinese miners, who completed a "coal road" five and a half miles up from Royston. Up this rough road the labourers dragged the makings of a mine and the ingredients to make it work. By February 1889 Dunsmuir had spent nearly half a million dollars on labour, the road, railway, wharves, mine, shafts, and sawmill; 450 men were then employed. The railway from Union reached Baynes Sound south of Royston and followed the coast to the 1,690-foot shipping wharf at Union Bay. The deck of the wharf was a full thirty feet above the high tide mark. Alongside was a freight wharf 1,100 feet in length. Moving stock of a hundred coal cars and four engines drew the coal between the mine and the port. Coal was loaded onto steam and sailing ships from all over the world.[28]

Union Bay serviced the mine's shipping and processing requirements. In January 1893 the editor of the Courtenay newspaper wrote that the projected coke ovens at Union wharf would cause a flourishing village to appear, and a few years later James Dunsmuir built coal

[26] *Comox Argus*, 11 April 1940.

[27] Isenor, *Land of Plenty*, p. 177; Courtenay *Weekly News*, 18 January 1893; Duncan, "Spring in Comox Valley," *The Daily Province* [1935], Newspaper Cuttings and Scrapbook; Harmston Diary, 5 February 1889; "Settlers Soon Made Loggers," *Nanaimo Free Press*, undated clipping in Buckham Collection; *From Shetland to Vancouver Island*, p. 227; H. Cartwright, "James Arthur Carthew," in Isenor, "The Comox Valley."

[28] *The British Columbia Monthly and Mining Review* 1:2 (February 1889), p. 15.

bunkers and coke ovens at Union Bay. The Perseverance Townsite laid out at Union Bay ten years earlier by George Drabble became an active little community.[29]

In 1893 two slopes were open at Union yielding coal in such abundance that the Dunsmuirs abandoned plans to open the neighbouring Perseverance Mine, though a trail linked the two mines. By 1897 the mine turned out from 700 tons to 1,000 tons a day of the best steam coal, and employed six hundred men (whites, Chinese, and Japanese) earning from $2.50 to $5 a day, making for a very large monthly payroll. By 1897 Union had about 3,000 inhabitants.[30]

The mines were a godsend to the farmers of the Comox Valley. Union furnished them with a ready market for their produce and increased the value of their farms. A close connection grew between the two settlements. "The first great event in the history of the Valley was the opening of the Cumberland mines in 1888," the quotable Eric Duncan reflected; "This furnished a home market and brought producer and consumer together." The centre of trade and commerce began to shift from Comox to Union, and "the coal mines brought cash into the Valley and set the farmers on their feet." The opening of the Union Mine also benefited Comox itself. Outside communication increased to a weekly boat, the *City of Nanaimo* replaced the *Robert Dunsmuir*, and later the *Joan* was put in service.[31]

Comox Valley farmers had a difficult time getting their produce to Union. At first they had to go along the coast to Royston, and then follow the company's road inland to the mines. Minnie McIntyre and her family took this route in the summer of 1888 after landing at Royston, and many years later she described her awful trip to a reporter:

> The only communication then between Union and the beach was from Royston, a very rough wagon road forming the means of communication. There was no dock and passengers had to be taken to shore on a scow. From Royston it was a rough passage, too, for the young mother and her four small children. For a seat there was a mattress and they rode on a Chinaman's cart. The cart bumped over the road from one stump to another. At one time a wheel went through a bridge and it was some time before the journey could be resumed. The road ran like a tunnel through the forest.[32]

29 Courtenay *Weekly News*, 11 January 1893; 18 January 1893; Tarbell, "Third Prize Article;" *The Weekly News*, 13 April 1897.
30 Lou Cliffe in *Comox Argus*, 11 April 1940; *The Weekly News*, 13 April 1897; Courtenay *Weekly News*, 18 January 1893; Crawford, "First Prize Article."
31 Crawford, "First Prize Article"; Duncan, "Early Days and Early Settlers"; [Duncan, Draft Description and History of the Comox Valley]; Holmes, "Reminiscences."
32 *Comox Argus*, 11 April 1940.

Similar stories survive from Comox farmers who delivered produce to Union before the completion of the Union Road (now the Cumberland Road) in 1890. Eric Duncan recalled that:

> The trail was the roughest imaginable, and for long stretches the wagon-wheels rarely touched earth, but hopped from stone to root and from root to stone, and woe to any spring vehicle! Many a day I walked ahead of the wagon, throwing out stones; and eggs had to be solidly packed in straw to stand the racket. Yet it was a home market, and we were no longer compelled to ship our produce merely for what it could fetch after paying the heavy freight to Nanaimo and Victoria.

Despite the ardours of the road, Duncan welcomed the opportunity to abandon the old barter economy of the valley. He or his brother William made weekly trips to sell farm produce, "and worked up quite a business, there being a regular monthly pay-roll—a new thing for Comox District." He sold onions and other vegetables from his half-acre garden at Sandwick, and of course he sold his coveted potatoes. On one occasion he carted a ton of potatoes up through the trails to Union for Robert Grant, who bought them for his sawmill workers. "Money may be scarce in the valley," Grant remarked, "but there is lots of it here," and he counted out twenty one-dollar bills. Other local commodities sent to Union included fresh salmon, delivered by Harry McQuillan's Courtenay teamsters.[33]

The old Comox farmers did not make the best accountants. "Some good farmers were very dense in these matters," Duncan wrote; "One man went around Cumberland a whole day offering his own eggs at 30 cents, or three dozen for $1.00, and wondered why the people limited their purchases to two dozen." Union also provided a market for Comox butter, which previously had spoiled before it reached Nanaimo or Victoria.[34]

Several farming families took their produce to Union. Stan Rennison told me that William Matthewson, his grandfather, made two trips a day to Union by horse and buggy: "There were no fridges back then." In one year Alex and Margaret Urquhart made 17,000 pounds of butter and sold it all for cash. William Beach made weekly trips in his horse and democrat to Union with butter and other produce, while for nine years Sam and Isabella Piercy took milk there.[35] Valley farmers shipped milk

---

[33] *From Shetland to Vancouver Island*, pp. 156, 195, 218; Edith McNish, "Livery Stables in the Comox Valley," in Isenor, "The Comox Valley."

[34] Duncan, "Spring in the Comox Valley," *The Daily Province* [1935], Newspaper Cuttings and Scrapbook.

[35] Interview with Stan Rennison, 1 June 1994; Forbes, *Wild Roses*, pp. 127-29; Mildred Haas, "William Beech," in Isenor, "The Comox Valley;" Anfield, "Pioneer Woman," *CVFP*, 18 April 1956.

and other dairy products under the care of teamster Jack Fraser and his brother Thomas, who started the "Milk Brigade." In March 1893 Union teamster William Davidson wrote a song celebrating their feat that appeared in the *Weekly News*, which went in part:

MILK BRIGADE

About six miles from Courtenay
    High up upon a hill
There is a camp called Union
    Where miners dig for coal,—

A great conglomeration
    From China and Japan
Belgium, Sweden, Scotland and
    The Nova Scotian man.

The miners live in cabins
    Which are not of the best,
And if the one is useless
    It's no more than the rest.

They like both milk and honey,
    Of cash they're not afraid;
So Thomas and Jack Fraser
    Commenced the milk brigade.

Chorus:
O, 'tis the same old story,
    You'll hear it everywhere,
How Mathewson and Crawford
    Are dealing on the square;
But Harrigan, the farmer,
    His fame forever made
When he hung up the harrow
    And joined the milk brigade.[36]

Minnie McIntyre recalled the strong social connections that formed between the two communities:

Very friendly relations existed between the two little communities. The farmers had a steady line of customers they called on week by week and when what is known in the history of Union as "The Shut-Down" came and the miners were left without money and without resources for six months, the farmers plodded their way to Cumberland just the same and kept their friends and customers supplied with eggs and butter and vegetables although they knew they might have to wait for an indefinite period for their money.[37]

---

[36] Courtenay *Weekly News*, 24 March 1893.

[37] *Comox Argus*, 11 April 1940.

Chinese miners on their days off came down to the valley in search of chickens, geese, and pigs. Barbara Marriott recalls that her father William Duncan sold chickens and pigs to them. Once, William came along to find his father Robert Duncan—who had just arrived and still spoke broad Shetland—trying to do business with a Chinese who spoke very little English. The two men had made no progress. On another occasion William Duncan took some pigs to Cumberland to sell to the Chinese, but one of them got loose and fell down a well, creating pandemonium until rescued.[38]

Some settlers had never seen Chinese people before the mines opened. One boy—Lou Cliffe—ran in fear when six Chinese miners appeared in Comox, but most relations were cordial. Leila Carroll recalled that the Chinese would come jogging down into Courtenay "in single file of eight or ten, with a loose knee-bending jogging pace, each carrying across his shoulder a long bamboo pole with a wicker basket hanging from each end." They went around bargaining for chickens and geese, which they put into their wicker baskets; on the way back their baskets sagged with the extra weight.[39]

The farmers, then, took full advantage of the market offered by the new coal mines. At the turn of the century Eric Duncan observed that "Between the collieries and the lumbering operations, the farmers find an ample market for all the food-stuffs they can raise, and there are large importations besides."[40] Gone were the days when farmers had to ship their produce to Nanaimo and Victoria through the agency of Captain Clarke, George Drabble, or John Wilson, and when their butter turned rancid before it could be sold.

The opening of the Union Mine early in 1888 led directly to the founding of Courtenay in September of the same year, when Pidcock and McPhee hired Drabble to survey a townsite near the confluence of the Courtenay and Puntledge rivers. Thus Robert Dunsmuir wheeled a kind of Trojan Horse of progress into the valley, and from his initial decision to open the mines at Union came the urbanization of the lower valley

[38] Interview with Barbara Marriott, 19 December 1994.
[39] *Comox Argus*, 11 April 1940; Carroll, *Wild Roses and Rail Fences*, pp. 73-74.
[40] Duncan, "Vancouver Island," p. 368.

CHAPTER 14

Joe McPhee and
the March of Improvement

> *There are lots of strangers moving around and I suppose*
> *when the Railroad is completed to Nanaimo, and then to*
> *here, there will be no privacy in the bush.*
>   —Reginald Carwithen to Harry Blaksley, 10 May 1885[1]

NEWS that Robert Dunsmuir had bought the Union Mine in March 1884 promoted the Comox Valley. While there was no guarantee that Dunsmuir would open the mine, his presence on the doorstep had a certain anticipatory effect. Settlers felt that land so close to the coal mine was bound to become valuable. Moreover, as Carwithen suggested, there was every reason to believe that sooner or later Dunsmuir would extend his Esquimalt and Nanaimo Railway to the valley. Settlers had only to look to the example of Burrard Inlet, where the promise of a transcontinental rail terminus created a frenzy of speculation that even a catastrophic fire could not halt: "Vancouver very nearly destroyed by Fire and several lives lost May 13th 1886," Mary Harmston noted in her diary.[2]

The four years between Dunsmuir's purchase of the mine and its opening in 1888 saw the tentative beginnings of urban development at what became Courtenay. Dunsmuir's arrival drew activity and capital west of the Courtenay River, where Drabble surveyed pre-emptions for twenty-five settlers in the mid to late 1880s. By 1886 these settlers and speculators had pre-empted all the land to within two miles of Union. Others had pre-empted all the land from Courtenay River to the mouth of the Trent River, where the Union Coal Company's tramway reached the sea. Little of this region was good for farming: the timber was dense, the ground was swampy, and trails and roads were absent. Settlers had previously shown little interest in it. Some of the shoreline pre-emptors were genuine settlers, but others were established merchants at Comox

---

[1] Carwithen to Blaksley, 10 May 1885, Carwithen Correspondence.
[2] Harmston Diary, 15 May 1886.

or farmers who, having proved their previous claims and obtained their Crown grants, staked new claims. There was nothing stopping them from pre-empting again.

In one of Drabble's notebooks is a sketch map dating from April 1886 showing nine pre-emption claims extending westward from the Courtenay River. They belonged to Reginald Pidcock, John Berkeley, Joe Rodello, William Duncan, John Holmes, James Bowler, Isaac Davis, Reginald St. Clair Sinclair, and James Prestige—the original owners of land at Courtenay.[3]

Pidcock's land was in the best location of all. Though generally regarded by his contemporaries as having conceived the idea of the town of Courtenay, Pidcock did not stay around for long enough to see it come into existence owing to his financial crisis of 1885-86. He transferred his remaining title in Section 61 to his wife Alice, perhaps because he was bankrupt. Alice then entered into a partnership with McPhee on her husband's behalf.[4]

Though doing a good business at Comox as a merchant, McPhee found himself holding a choice piece of land when Dunsmuir came to the valley. Pidcock had started to log the magnificent stand of Douglas Fir on Section 61, so that the sunlight now found its way onto this centrally located slope next to Courtenay River. Dunsmuir announced in February 1888 that he would open the Union Mine, and five months later McPhee and Pidcock decided to establish a townsite on their stump-covered land.

Pidcock and McPhee were an odd couple: Pidcock, a privileged clergyman's son, idealist, and dreamer; McPhee, a hard-nosed self-made man. Fortunately Pidcock kept a diary, in which he recorded the very origins of Courtenay on Saturday, 11 August 1888:

> Went down to the Bay & had a talk with McPhee about the land at the Bridge. As he was going up to the Coal mine I drove up with him to the Bridge. It certainly does seem the most central place in the settlement.[5]

What made it central was its crossroad location between Union Mine, Comox, and the valley. It lay directly across the bridge, over which all traffic crossed, and it was adjacent to the Urquharts' mill and to the deep, slow, and navigable waters of the Courtenay River. "Went up to McPhee's," Pidcock wrote two days later, "and settled with him about the land." Pidcock's son recalled many years later that his father and

---

[3] Env. 87; Reginald St. Clair Sinclair, "Certificate of Pre-emption Record," Buckham Collection; Courtenay *Weekly News*, 11 January 1893.

[4] Env. 136, Drabble Papers. On early Courtenay see also Isenor, *Land of Plenty*, pp. 212-26.

[5] Pidcock Diary, 11 August 1888.

McPhee on this occasion had talked until two in the morning about founding the Courtenay townsite.[6]

With Pidcock back at Fort Rupert, McPhee wasted little time. In September and October 1888 he hired Drabble to survey ten acres of the land he held jointly with Pidcock. McPhee and Pidcock agreed to name the townsite "Courtenay" after the river, and Drabble first used the name in November 1888. His four-week survey of the townsite was the real beginning of the settlement: he and three unnamed assistants surveyed the ten acres into town lots. Drabble set up a camp near the bridge and worked steadily for a month, taking only Sundays off and one day when it rained too heavily to work. In the back of his survey book he made a list of milk, butter, and potatoes bought from the farms across the Courtenay River. He bought the milk by the pint, jug, and pail, and butter by the roll; and he bought "60 lbs Potatoes Duncan. 1 Bucket for Davis."[7]

In this survey, Drabble extended the 1864 Comox Valley survey orientation into the new urban street plan. Valley lots had not been laid out according to the cardinal points of the compass in the standard north-south or east-west axis, like almost everywhere else in colonial Vancouver Island. William Ralph had intentionally abandoned the north-south alignment to give all settlers access to the Tsolum River, and he had extended this peculiar alignment to George Ford's and Robert Scott's pre-emptions, Sections 41 and 42, on the west bank of the Courtenay. Pidcock's Section 61 had been tied into the same survey, and Drabble applied the same axis to the Courtenay townsite. Though formed thirty-five years apart, the Comox Valley farms and the City of Courtenay are, therefore, permanently united in their irregular survey orientation.

Having laid out the core of the Courtenay townsite, Drabble then moved into the woods to survey the cluster of pre-emptions between the Courtenay River and Union Mine. Some of these lots were speculative appendages to Dunsmuir's opening of the Union mine. So numerous were these pre-emptions that they occupied Drabble from October 1888 to March 1889—his longest sustained survey of a single area. He charged about $15 for each survey. When he had finished he had surveyed most of the present city of Courtenay and its southern and western suburbs. Drabble was so busy that in the spring and summer of 1889 he hired F. W. Cook to survey pre-emptions in the valley, Qualicum, and elsewhere.[8]

[6] *Comox Argus* 15 July 1953. See also *Land of Plenty*, p. 214.

[7] Courtenay *Weekly News*, 11 January 1893; Duncan, "Early Days and Early Settlers;" envs. 67, 136. See also James Morley Curtis Diary, 15 September 1888.

[8] Envs. 67, 80, 110, 112, 137, Drabble Papers; William Duncan Diary, 31 January 1889.

All these pre-emptors—even established merchants like McPhee and Rodello with no intention of living on their land—had to satisfy the authorities (in this case, Drabble) that they had cleared some land and spent a certain amount on improving their claims. Accordingly, Drabble noted their improvements: McPhee had a "chopping" (that is, a clearing)—a necessary condition to the pre-emption process; William Duncan had part of his land under crop; Thomas Rosborough had made a 400×500 foot clearing; Isaac Davis had made a clearing; Thomas Graham's claim included a grass meadow.

Meanwhile, back at the townsite, Joe McPhee had been confirmed in his hope that some sort of business would result from the opening of the Union mine. Union was at first a closed town where all the land and houses were owned by the Dunsmuirs and rented to miners and merchants. Robert Dunsmuir's paternalist policies prohibited private sales of land in his company town, and to McPhee's advantage several enterprising miners moved down to Courtenay to buy houses for their families. Some of the miners wanted their houses and gardens, Eric Duncan recalled, and the nearest location for this was the bank of the Courtenay River.[9]

By September 1889, McPhee had sold two lots to Evan Thomas, two to Leonard Davis, two to Dr. Percy Scharschmidt, one to Thomas Piercy, and four to John J. Grant. McPhee took possession of several lots on the river bank for his store. Eric Duncan recalled that some houses went up along Union Street (5th Street), "whose owners made a precarious living by road work." In 1889 or 1890, John Grant built the large and commodious Riverside Hotel, situated on the finest part of McPhee's townsite, a block from the river. "It was a bold undertaking then," a resident noted in 1893, "but time has shown its wisdom." Courtenay's first streets were named, from the river east, Drabble, Victoria, Alice, Union, Walter—renamed, alas, in the 1940s, 2nd, 3rd, 4th, 5th, 6th. Other original streets and avenues—Courtenay, Clarence, George, Lake, and Wallace—have also been capriciously renamed.[10]

The future of the town looked very promising. In October 1889 a meeting was held to get Courtenay incorporated, and the next month McPhee showed his confidence by moving there from Comox. "McPhee & Family have left the Bay & gone to live at Courtenay," Mary Harmston noted with a touch of concern. This was a place with potential, as Carwithen reported in December 1890. "There is also a store and many other buildings. It is thought the Railway Depot may be just over

9 Duncan, "Early Days and Early Settlers;" *From Shetland to Vancouver Island*, pp. 182-83.
10 Env. 140; Duncan, "Early Days and Early Settlers;" Courtenay *Weekly News*, 11 January 1893.

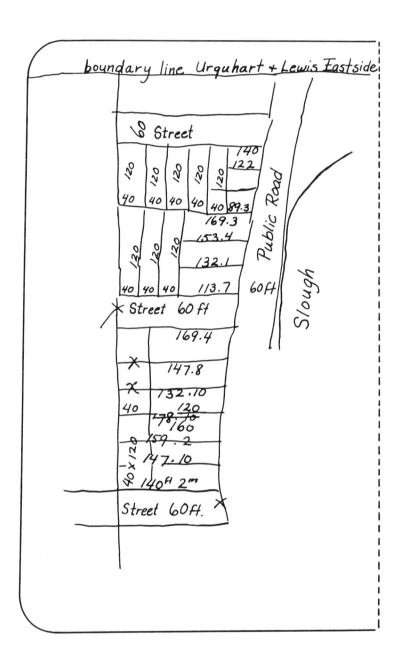

Part of William Lewis' subdivision,
east side of Courtenay River, March 1892.

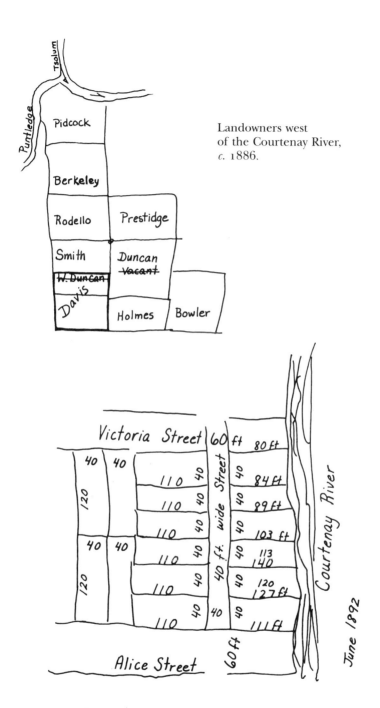

Landowners west
of the Courtenay River,
c. 1886.

Part of Courtenay subdivision for Alice Pidcock, June 1892.
(Victoria Street is now 3rd Street; Alice Street is 4th Street.)

the south side as there is a flourishing coal mine 6 miles back." "Pidcock still owns 100 acres there."[11]

Courtenay's existence owed much to Dunsmuir's mine, and in the spring of 1890 a rough wagon road was completed to Union. The contract went to logger Joe Fitzgerald and farmers William Harrigan and Joseph Knox. Harrigan was a settler in the Minto Valley, just east of Union. "Labour is cheap just now," Government Agent Walter Bentley wrote; "Harrigan has oxen but I understand the other party has not and that makes a great difference, besides the fact that Harrigan lives close up the road." Bentley, a civil engineer, blazed the line of the road. In June 1891, Joe McPhee and Robert Graham received a very large ($5,000) contract to upgrade this road. Within a few years of the mine's opening, trails and roads connected Union with Courtenay, Comox, Union Bay, and Royston.[12]

Courtenay also got its own school: in July 1891 Drabble surveyed a school lot on Isabel Street adjoining the Urquharts' west boundary. Encouraged by McPhee's success, landowners on both sides of the Courtenay River subdivided their land into townlots in 1891 and 1892. In about July 1891 Harry Guillod hired Drabble to lay out seventy-six town lots on part of his Section 69. The boom continued into 1892. Rumours that the railway would be extended brought a promise of prosperity, as Fred Nunns of Campbell River noted. "They say land is booming in Comox owing to the railroad going to be extended," he wrote in his diary of January 1892. A few months later he had dinner with McPhee. "Courtenay is booming," he wrote.[13]

In February 1892 McPhee prepared a statement of building lots sold in the Courtenay Townsite since Drabble's survey of September 1888. McPhee had sold thirty-four lots, ranging in price from $40 to $100, for a total of $1,945, all of them in the Courtenay townsite he held jointly with Alice Pidcock:

John J. Grant	4	lots
Evan Rowland Thomas	1	"
Thomas Piercy	2	"
Maurice McArdle	1	"
Adam McKelvey	4	"
Thomas Graham	1	"
John McDonald	1	"

[11] Harmston Diary, 5 October 1889, 11 November 1890, 4 February 1891; Carwithen to Blaksley, 19 December 1890, Carwithen Correspondence; Courtenay *Weekly News*, 11 January 1893.

[12] British Columbia, Department of Public Works, Contracts, specifications, 1862-1909.

[13] Envs. 48, 69; Drabble's survey of plan 480, Comox District, SGB; Nunns Diary, 31 January and 23 April 1892. For railway rumours see Victoria *Colonist*, 17 June 1892.

John Berkeley	3	"
Mrs. Joyce	1	"
Joseph McPhee	5	"
Alice Pidcock	1	"
Percy Fremlin Scharschmidt	1	"
Bruno Mellado	4	"
Kenneth Grant	1	"
J. Wilson	2	"
William Gleason	2	"

McPhee noted that he had spent $200 on Drabble's survey, $125 for grading Union Street, and $80 on clearing land. Total profits after expenses were $1,354, of which half was due to Alice Pidcock. Around this time McPhee himself moved his main general and hardware store from Comox Landing to the foot of Union Street and the Courtenay River Bridge.[14]

By June 1892 a few more people had bought town lots from McPhee: Hawthornthwaite & Co., Lind, George Roe, and blacksmith George Leighton. In the same month Drabble made a note of his survey charges. He charged per town lot, and the denser the forest the higher his price:

Prices
$3.50 Heavy Timber (small area).
$2.40 Acre Lots Moderately heavy.
$1.50 Lots in heavy Timber.
$1.25 Open Timber Land.[15]

Meanwhile, across the river, similar urban developments were underway on the Duncan and Lewis farms. Courtenay, in the 1890s, included three quite distinct commercial areas: Courtenay townsite proper, William Lewis's townsite across the river, and the Duncan Brothers' store and post office at Sandwick.

Sandwick appeared soon after Courtenay. A few months after Drabble completed his September 1888 survey for McPhee, the younger generation of Duncan brothers—William, Eric, and Robert—opened a store. "The store and the dwelling place in connection with it has been finished (the outside work) and we are now carrying on business under the name of Duncan Brothers," William Duncan noted in his diary on 1 January 1889. In the same year, Eric Duncan established a post office at what was then known as The Mission or Mission Corner. The name, however, was changed to Sandwick after the Duncans' home parish in

---

[14] Harry Pidcock Papers; Duncan, "Early Days and Early Settlers."
[15] Env. 48. On Leighton see Duncan, "Spring in Comox Valley," *The Daily Province* [1935], Newspaper Cuttings and Scrapbook.

the Shetlands because there was already a place called Mission in British Columbia. Serviced by a weekly mail from Comox Landing, Sandwick or Duncans Corner post office was manned for many years by Eric Duncan. "Eric was a tall young man with legs a little longer than the ordinary plan," Leila Carroll recalled; "and it was natural for him to take long strides and easy to hoist the mail onto his back and stride off with it to the Bay when the Steamer came in on Thursday every fortnight."[16]

In 1889 William Lewis hired Drabble to survey part of his land into town lots. "Lewis's townsite" was located at the head of Green's Slough, around the junction of the roads from the Courtenay River bridge, Sandwick, and Comox Landing. This land (Section 14) had been pre-empted by Charles Green in 1862, but in 1881 Green had sold it to Welshman Lewis, who had arrived in the valley about ten years earlier and had worked for Green. Lewis and his wife Margaret went into Jersey cattle, delivering butter and milk to Union when the mines opened. "Mrs Lewis a/c for Butter & Milk," Drabble wrote during his April 1889 survey, "31 Pints Milk 5 Rolls Butter. G.F.D. a/c 30 Pints Milk 6 Rolls Butter."[17]

On Lewis's property a small village grew up that for a time challenged McPhee and Pidcock's urban venture across the river. In September 1891 John McKenzie leased a lot from Lewis where he built a blacksmith shop. The site is now occupied by the British Car Centre. At about the same time Robert Grant, in partnership with Lewis, built the Courtenay Hotel (at the corner of Comox Road and the Island Highway) to compete with the recently built Riverside Hotel on McPhee's townsite.[18]

Indeed, a little village sprang up on the north side of the Courtenay River which included the Courtenay Hotel, two blacksmith shops, a dentist's office, barber shop, Masonic Hall, and McQuillan's bustling livery stable, which provided the only public transport between Courtenay and Comox. (A few years later Drabble noted that McQuillan had two lumber wagons, an express wagon, two buggies, a stage wagon, and eight horses). In 1893 the Comox Agricultural and Industrial Association was formed—a reincarnation of the old Comox Agricultural Society of 1873. The new title reflected the valley's new industrial character: the valley now possessed a mine, sawmill, and the hope of a railway. After holding its first fair on the Duncan brothers' field, the agricultural

[16] William Duncan Diary, 1 January 1889; *From Shetland to Vancouver Island*, pp. 173-75; Carwithen to Blaksley, 19 December 1890, Carwithen Correspondence; Carroll, *Wild Roses and Rail Fences*, pp. 85-86.

[17] *From Shetland to Vancouver Island*, p. 169; Courtenay *Weekly News*, 14 June 1893; Mrs. Rees Rogers, "William Lewis," in Isenor, "The Comox Valley;" env. 79.

[18] Env. 74; Duncan, "Early Days and Early Settlers."

association leased a three-acre parcel of Lewis's land in what is now Lewis Park.[19]

Drabble had plenty of work in 1892 with rumours of the impending arrival of the railway. Helped by one of the Radford brothers and Robert Swan of Denman, he spent three weeks in March surveying for Lewis near the Courtenay River bridge. For ten days in late May and early June, Alice Pidcock hired Drabble to survey a new batch of lots on the Courtenay townsite, next to the Courtenay River. The survey included Judson, Alice, and Victoria streets. At the end of the month he and his men went back across the river to lay out more lots for Lewis, mainly in the Slough area.[20]

Meanwhile, in November 1892, Mr. Whitney, "an elderly American," started the *Courtenay Weekly News*. The *Free Press* of Nanaimo remarked that it was a "newsy little paper, and apparently is looked upon as quite a welcome arrival among our northern friends." Whitney was a staunch booster of the local economy. Later in the decade he supported James Dunsmuir in his successful election to the legislature, and Dunsmuir rewarded him by keeping the paper running with $1,200 of his office cash. Whitney was a Dunsmuir supporter from the moment he arrived in Courtenay.[21]

A typical late-nineteenth-century urban booster, Whitney aimed to tug the Comox Valley into the age of progress, and he found a fairly sympathetic audience, at least in Courtenay and Union. His views were shared by McPhee, who in December 1892 took out a large advertisement in Whitney's paper:

COURTENAY LOTS

I have some splendid lots for sale, both business and residential.

Now is the time to buy to advantage before the Canada Western Railway reaches here.

With the advent of the railway, in addition to the other conceded advantages of the place, prices must rule very high.

The town is located in the midst of the largest agricultural settlement on Vancouver Island. It is within six miles of Union Mines affording the farmers of the valley the very best home market, and is situated on the only highway leading from the settlement to the mines. The lumber interests of this section are most extensive, and are an important factor in our progress.

[19] Courtenay *Weekly News*, 11 January and 4 October 1893; Mrs. Rees Rogers, "William Lewis," in Isenor, "The Comox Valley;" envs. 74, 143.

[20] Envs. 48, 69, 143, Drabble Papers.

[21] *Nanaimo Free Press*, 13 November 1892; G. W. Clinton to Canadian Collieries, 1 January 1911, vertical file "Comox—Newspapers," BCARS.

The per cent of improvement of this town during the present year is greater than any other place the Coast can boast of, and the march of improvement is steadily onward.

The prosperity of the town has for its foundations, therefore are large mineral, agricultural, and timber resources. It may also be added that no section furnishes a better field for the sportsman. Fish and game are always abundant and our hotels of the best.

For particulars address:

Joseph McPhee
Courtenay B.C.[22]

McPhee's advertisement was really a manifesto for the continued urbanization of Courtenay, and in a sense for the Comox Valley in the twentieth century. Such language had been unknown in the 1860s and 1870s when farming had dominated the valley economy. Bridging both eras was George Drabble, whose services continued to be very much in demand. "Geo. F. Drabble of the Bay was up here last Friday surveying for J. McPhee," Whitney wrote in December 1892. "Judge Drabble was up here surveying the Wilson Addition to the Courtenay townsite," he wrote the following autumn.[23]

Whitney also agitated for a post office at Courtenay, even though one already existed a mile away. Postmaster Eric Duncan of Sandwick suggested a compromise: that a new office should be built at the Agricultural Hall on Lewis's property but, as Duncan recalled, "Courtenay refused to cross the bridge east, and the farmers balked at going west," so in June 1893 a post office opened at Courtenay after much agitation by Whitney. To his annoyance, he was appointed postmaster.[24]

Whitney also appointed himself Courtenay's main booster. "The business establishments, at present," he wrote in January 1893, "are a saw mill, soda water works, bakery, general store, drug store, two splendid hotels, real estate office, newspaper, blacksmith shop, two liveries, club rooms, etc." In addition to his self-confident bombast, Whitney had a go-ahead streak that might have shocked the casual old British settlers of 1862. In June 1893 he editorialized that Courtenay needed useful amenities like a wharf and roads more than it needed a railway:

In a new country like ours the cities will take care of themselves if only the country is developed. All the energies of the government should, therefore, be exerted in developing the natural resources of the country.

22 Courtenay Weekly News, 1 December 1892.
23 Ibid., 15 December 1892; 2 August 1893.
24 Courtenay Weekly News, 5 July 1893; Duncan, From Shetland to Vancouver Island, p. 183.

It follows that government expenditure must be of a practical character, and made with a view to development. Works of beauty, grandeur and art may well await a later period. This is the utilitarian period with us.[25]

Whitney complained that the Victoria and Vancouver papers ignored the Comox District. "The press looks constantly to the east," he barked in July 1893. Moreover, the press favoured stories from the Kootenays, where there was then an important hardrock mining boom in progress. One newspaper had written that the Comox District had 260 inhabitants, an innocent error that caused Whitney to explode:

> Two hundred and sixty settlers! In addition to the largest and most flourishing farming settlement on the island, it has three important villages, one of which has three-fourths of a thousand inhabitants alone. It is self-sustaining, getting its support from the soil, woods and coal, and not like Victoria living off tourists, illegal seal poaching, and opium smuggling; nor like Vancouver fattening as a go-between on what sticks to her hands of other people's property.[26]

In the absence of a railway, "Courtenayites" settled for improvements to their roads and communications. The Courtenay-Nanaimo telegraph line opened in 1893. Whitney was especially anxious about the road to Comox which, because of its shelter and wharf, continued to receive the only steamer service in the valley.

Whitney had great faith in the valley's abundant and varied natural resources. In October 1893 he thought that the valley would flourish despite the "general depression" in British Columbia, but in May 1894 times were still dull, and Whitney moved his paper up to Union; they got duller still when James Dunsmuir put his Union town lots on the market in 1895. Dunsmuir changed the name to Cumberland in 1898 to avoid confusion with the coal port of Union Bay. The newly opened town, Duncan wrote, stopped all further sale of lots to miners at Courtenay, and both Holmes and McPhee built stores at Union, and "poor Courtenay came to a dead stop" in the mid-1890s recession—not to recover until the building of the Co-operative creamery in 1901 and the very belated arrival of the E&N in 1912. Indeed, Courtenay did not finally overtake Comox as the business centre of the Comox Valley until after 1918.[27]

The opening of Cumberland to private ownership made Courtenay less attractive to the miners, who preferred not to travel six miles to their place of work. McPhee, Pidcock, Lewis, Guillod, and others had

---

[25] Courtenay *Weekly News*, 11 January 1893; 14 June 1893.

[26] *Ibid.*, 5 July 1893.

[27] Courtenay *Weekly News*, 11 October 1893; Duncan, "Early Days and Early Settlers;" *From Shetland to Vancouver Island*, pp. 92, 183-84.

flooded the market with townlots hoping for a quick and substantial return. But much of the townsite remained deserted in 1900, covered with stumps and a jungle of deciduous bush. Between the stumps grew wildflowers, roses, and daisies; wild blackberries grew on Lake Trail Road, and in the undrained parts grew skunk cabbage. Union, by contrast, was the thriving local centre and market for valley produce.[28]

McPhee, however, held fast. When his lots stopped selling in the 1890s he decided he might as well put his land to use, so he planted an orchard of 1,000 trees on ten acres of land at the west end of his townsite, adjacent to the Puntledge River. He planted Russets, Kings, Northern Spy, and Gravensteins; he planted apples that would ripen early and those that would ripen late, and he planted cherry trees. Today, McPhee's trees are still productive—though gnarled with age— and the residential end of Courtenay above the Puntledge is still known as "The Orchard."[29]

Despite Cumberland's ascendance, Courtenay and Comox continued to be patronised by most people from the surrounding farming districts—districts that attracted new settlers in the last decades of the nineteenth century.

---

28 Carroll, *Wild Roses and Rail Fences*, pp. 16-17; 75-79.

29 Haas and McPhee, "Joseph McPhee," in Isenor, "The Comox Valley;" Carroll, *Wild Roses and Rail Fences*, pp. 20, 27; interviews with Barbara Marriott and Bruce McPhee, 19 December 1994; interview with Bob McPhee, September 1995.

CHAPTER 15

Maritimers, Midwives, and Lawsuits

*It rains every day, real Sywash weather, I am swinging the
broken stick every day threshing for pigs.*
—Reginald Carwithen, Comox, 2 December 1885[1]

THE towns of Union and Courtenay brought new settlers
and a new prosperity to the Comox Valley in the late 1880s and early
1890s. No longer dependent on distant markets in Nanaimo and Victoria, the established farmers brought more land into production while
their families grew up. The large valley farms contained enough land
for the owners to increase the portion under cultivation or pasture, and
farmers often had grown-up children to help in this expansion. Some
families showed an astonishing rate of fecundity—something that had
been lacking in the first years of settlement. Farmers were also a quarrel-
some bunch, and Judge Drabble was called on to settle disputes over
fences, livestock, and property. Cooperation, litigation, racism, fertility,
productivity, and humour characterized the social history of the Comox
Valley in the last twenty years of the nineteenth century.

Settlers from the Maritime provinces discovered the valley in the
1870s and 1880s. Members of a handful of families arrived, staked
claims around the valley edges and, as they saved money, bought up old
and productive farms in the valley bottom, while others went straight
into logging. The 1862 settlers—many of them veterans of the gold
rushes—were with a few exceptions single men. In the 1870s several
extended families arrived from Nova Scotia and New Brunswick, and
with the completion of the Canadian Pacific Railway to the west coast in
1886, more settlers arrived from Britain, Ontario, and the Maritimes.
The later immigrants, unlike those of 1862, tended to be married with
children, and for this reason most of today's old settler families date
their arrival to the 1870s and 1880s rather than earlier.

The first Nova Scotian to settle in the Comox district was Samuel
Crawford, who came with his family in 1870. He was followed by Joe
McPhee two years later. The next Maritimers to arrive were Matthew

---

[1] Carwithen to Blaksley, 2 December 1885, Carwithen Correspondence.

Piercy and George Grieve from New Brunswick; they came in 1874 with their grown-up children and extended families, and Nova Scotians Lewis Casey and Robert Cessford came at about the same time. They were followed shortly after by William Matthewson and George Grant McDonald and their families, also from Nova Scotia. One member of the Piercy family, Harry—born in 1857 in Harvey Station, New Brunswick—worked his way across the Rockies with a C.P.R. survey in 1878.[2] The others reached the Pacific via the United States.

These families from the Maritimes had an enormous influence. Crawford was the schoolteacher for most of the 1870s; McPhee a builder, merchant, and co-founder of Courtenay; the Piercy, Grieve, and Matthewson families were among the leading farmers and loggers, and George McDonald took over the Elk Hotel from John Carthew—another Nova Scotian. The Piercys and Grieves married one another, and most of the older non-Native families of Comox are related to them. Indeed, so great was their influence that some later commentators even assumed that the valley was first settled by Maritimers, but it was this mistake that moved Eric Duncan to begin his memoirs in the 1920s.[3]

These families swelled the number of young adults and children in the valley and put a strain on the valley's rudimentary school and churches. Anglican Bishop George Hills wrote in 1877 that the settlers were "mostly of the working class, but respectable. Recently about forty came from New Brunswick, all Presbyterians." The 1881 census reveals no less than sixteen Grieves and twenty-six Piercys in the valley, most of them under the age of twenty. These two families still contribute a column of entries in the Comox Valley phone book. Eric Duncan recalled that Matthew and Agnes Piercy and George and Jane Grieve had come as children from Northumberland, and all retained the Northumberland "burr" in their speech.[4]

The Maritimers were sound and seasoned farmers and embraced, as well, the hard work of Drabble's government road parties. Piercy bought part of John Wilson's farm, and George Grieve settled in the woods west of McKelvey. "He was said to have cleared two bush farms in New Brunswick," Duncan recalled, "and he certainly looked the ideal hard-bitten woodsman. He now faced heavier timber, but with the help of his sons he soon made a wide clearing, and in ten years they had a

2 Duncan, "Early Days and Early Settlers;" *From Shetland to Vancouver Island*, p. 215; Mildred Haas, "Harry Piercy," in Isenor, "The Comox Valley."

3 Duncan, "Early Days and Early Settlers."

4 Hills is quoted in Willemar, "St. Andrew's, Comox," p. 22; *From Shetland to Vancouver Island*, p. 215. See also Mildred Haas, "The Henry Grieves and Sam Piercys," Isenor, "The Comox Valley."

good place." Grieve then moved to Musters' old farm on the Upper Prairie where, in the 1880s, he and his sons owned and operated the first steam threshing machine in the valley. Grieve designed some parts of the machine, and "built the patterns from wood for the bearings and shafts of the threshing machine and sent them to Victoria to be moulded in iron." It was no longer necessary to thresh grain manually or with a horse-drawn treadmill. In autumn, Duncan recalled, "the well-known whistle was heard as it made its rounds, danced after by successive generations of boys."[5]

In 1877 these Maritimers built a Presbyterian Church for themselves. Since 1864 the only Protestant church in the valley had been the log-built Anglican St. Andrews at Sandwick, where the valley's Presbyterian Scots had worshipped in the absence of their own church. Indeed, Anglican minister Jules Willemar hoped that the Maritimers would simply join the Anglican church as the earlier Presbyterians had done. "I am very much pleased with the new comers," Willemar wrote in January 1875, "and I believe that, though they are Presbyterians, they will attend church very regularly." This ecumenical harmony ended in 1877 when a Presbyterian minister arrived, as Bishop Hills noted: "Previously the Church of England for many years had been the only means of grace, and all came to church. Now the Presbyterians have built a church, and most of those brought up in the kirk have naturally joined. Some have remained with the Church, having learnt to appreciate our system and Liturgy." One who divided his allegiance was Eric Duncan, who for many years attended both churches.[6]

All the newcomers had a hand in the construction of the 1877 church, named St. Andrews (like the Anglican church) after the great missionary. Matthew Piercy and Samuel Crawford donated land on their common hilltop; George Grieve and Alex Grant designed the church, and Grieve built and plastered it, using ground clam shells for plaster. Jane Grieve painted it. Church members made shingles at home during their spare time, and bees were called to raise the frame and get it shingled.[7]

Not all new immigration was from the Maritimes. The Scots and Irish immigrants of 1862 wrote home and advertised the good land and

[5] *From Shetland to Vancouver Island*, pp. 197-98, 215; Audrey Menzies, "George Grieve," in Isenor, "The Comox Valley;" Carroll, *Wild Roses and Rail Fences*, p. 45; Duncan, "Late Spring in the Comox Valley," *The Daily Province* [1933], Newspaper Cuttings and Scrapbook.

[6] Willemar, "St. Andrew's, Comox," (1876), pp. 22, 29; *From Shetland to Vancouver Island*, pp. 214-15.

[7] See 1957 history of Sandwick United Church, Buckham Collection; Carroll, *Wild Roses and Rail Fences*, p. 141; *From Shetland to Vancouver Island*, pp. 215-20.

economic opportunities. A couple of Shetland families, prominent on the coast ever since, came in the 1870s and 1880s. William Duncan was followed by a crowd of relations including Eric Duncan, Michael Manson, and the Mouat Family. Adam McKelvey and his son Stafford, from County Derry, attracted at least fourteen Ulster Protestants in the 1880s. Though disgraced in legal circles, McKelvey was a successful farmer on the west bank of the Tsolum River, owner of three properties. The story of his opulence, Eric Duncan wrote, "brought out a whole crowd of young Ulsterman to the district. There were three McQuillans, three Gilmours, two Crocketts, two Surgenors, two Steeles, a Johnson and a Morrison. Some of them stayed and some went elsewhere, but they were all good workers." Most of these men were labourers, but Harry McQuillan hired at least one Crockett as a driver at his Courtenay livery stable.[8]

Most early settlers had been English. Vancouver Island had been a British colony until 1871, and before the 1886 completion of the Canadian Pacific Railway there had been no easy way to reach British Columbia from elsewhere in Canada. Whereas ships sailed direct from British ports to Victoria, Canadian immigrants had to make their way with difficulty across the mosquito-ridden Isthmus of Panama, around Cape Horn, or across the United States. The new continental railway promoted direct immigration to British Columbia from Britain almost as effectively as from Canada.

The valley attracted English urban immigrants, for example William Anderton, a carpenter from Lancashire and a Roman Catholic. In the 1870s he had emigrated with his family to Ontario, but as "times were tough" in Toronto he crossed the border and soon found himself in Denver, Colorado. Here he witnessed a lynching, which so disturbed him that he continued to San Francisco and then to the Comox Valley, which had been recommended to him by a man he had met in Toronto. He arrived in Comox in 1881, aged forty-five, and soon sent back for his wife and seven or eight children.[9]

Anderton pre-empted Section 84, consisting of 160 acres of wilderness about three miles from the Comox townsite where he and his grown-up son John built a house in about 1882. His daughter Mary Downey later wrote a memoir, "A Settler in the Early Eighties," in which she recalled that the Andertons found themselves "ranching in the backwoods and blissfully ignorant of all that meant." They were as

---

[8] *From Shetland to Vancouver Island*, p. 105. See also Mildred Haas, "Adam McKelvie," [*sic*] in Isenor, "The Comox Valley."

[9] Ben Hughes interview with Leo Anderton, 26 April 1956, p. 1, CDMA; Mrs. P. Downey [Mary Anderton], "A Settler in the Early Eighties," in Isenor, "The Comox Valley."

"green as our surroundings, scarcely knowing whether to feed cows on hay and turnips, or on roast goose and plum pudding." And she continued:

> A never-failing spring had been located, so this was to be the heart of our home in the western wilds. On one hand were great stretches of alder swamp, which were not so hard to clear, but we must have enough higher land for a building site. As I stood on the spot chosen and viewed the serried ranks of giant firs growling defiance, I confess to feeling somewhat appalled, child as I was.
>
> A former settler had squatted here for a short time and had cleared about an acre in the swamp, and built a small log cabin. But this would scarcely accommodate a family of nine or ten even in pioneer days.
>
> Father sent to the mill on Courtenay River an order for lumber, set big brother clearing a road to the nearest highway, over a mile away, and set himself to work on the big trees with an auger.
>
> In three months we had cleared about an acre except for the huge hot low stumps. There was no T.N.T. stumping powder then, nor even Giant powder and the process of burning these stumps out was a slow one indeed. We had also built the house, a mere shell, and bought three cows with their calves. . . .[10]

In 1885 Drabble, as Commissioner of Lands and Works for Comox District, extended the road out to Anderton's Place (Anderton Road), and William Anderton asked Drabble—now in his private capacity as surveyor—to record the improvements required to secure title to the pre-emption. These he recorded in a June 1885 field book:

ANDERTON'S IMPROVEMENTS.

1	Two Story House Framed 16×28 $100
1	Works & Wood Shed two story 22×16 $50
85½	chs picket fence $20
	Cow Shed 24×16 log $20
3	acres Cultivated & cleared $150
6	acres cutting & cultivating $300
2	acres around house clearing & cultivating $120
1000	rails picketing & erecting $40
	Log fencing $60
40	chains brush fencing $30

[Total]: $895 Corrected $840[11]

Drabble surveyed the lot in November 1887. The land contained a creek, a prairie, a "Salmon Berry Bottom," a swamp of alder, salmon-

---

10 Downey, "A Settler in the Early Eighties," in Isenor, "The Comox Valley."

11 Envs. 121, 122, Drabble Papers.

berry, and skunk cabbage, as well as a great deal of timber—cedar, spruce, balsam, Douglas Fir, and hemlock. He recorded a log fence around the clearing, a picket fence around the garden, and a chicken house. Anderton received title to the land in April 1888.[12]

Other English immigrants to the Comox-Point Holmes region in the 1880s included William Hawksby, Jack Hawkins, and Walter Gage from Somerset—later the valley's photographer. Some urban immigrants were scared away by the prospect of clearing the dense forest. In 1887 Herbert and Richard Church, sons of a classicist at University College, London, crossed Canada on the newly-completed Canadian Pacific Railway and arrived in Comox in search of a farm. "Very likely we were too easily deterred from trying to clear a farm," Herbert recalled, "but we had been very much attracted by the vast grass-covered prairies through which we had passed when coming from eastern Canada. I have in later years revisited some of the scenes of our prospecting trip and found perfectly level farms where we then could see nothing but virgin forest and a prospect of apparently endless labour." The Church brothers ranched in the Alberta foothills and later in the Chilcotin.[13]

The best source for the rural history of the Comox Valley in the late nineteenth century is Eric Duncan—farmer, poet, and historian. Long after Drabble left his farm to concentrate on his diverse jobs at Comox Landing, Duncan remained at home on his valley farm, cultivating an ascetic lifestyle and ignoring the commercial opportunities around him. Of course, with some of the best land in the valley he could afford to do this—though he found the time to speculate in a large suburban lot in Courtenay. Recording details of crops and animals, the weather, and the seasons came naturally to Duncan. He wrote, for example, that the year 1887 stood apart as "the year of extremes":

> The previous winter had been average, with moderate snow, and the spring was a good working one, but late and frosty, with snow low down on the mountains. May brought tree-crashing southeasters, with torrents of rain, swamping green grain in the fields. Then the sky cleared and the sun came back scorchingly and ruled like a tyrant through June, July and August, insatiably draining all moisture, and the crops were very poor.[14]

---

[12] George Drabble, "Field Notes of land Surveyed for Wm. Anderton Nov. 24th 1887," SGB.

[13] H. E. Church, *An Emigrant in the Canadian Northwest* (London: Methuen, 1929), pp. 13-14; see also Patrick A. Dunae, *Gentlemen Emigrants: From the British Public Schools to the Canadian Frontier* (Vancouver: Douglas & McIntyre, 1981), pp. 92-98.

[14] Duncan, "The Autumn in Comox Valley," *The Daily Province*, [1934], in Newspaper Cuttings and Scrapbook. For Duncan's resolute potato-based diet see Isenor, *Land of Plenty*, p. 129.

Principal crops changed over the years as markets came and went. Potatoes remained the staple kitchen crop. For general use every farmer had a "truck wagon"—the nineteenth century predecessor of the pick-up truck. Every wagon was drawn by a horse, and every horse needed winter feed. Even today, resting forlornly in driveways and front lawns beside the Island Highway are hay and truck wagons converted into ornamental flower gardens. Hundreds of others have been sacrificed for the sake of their wheels, which decorate gates and fences as mementos of a productive rural era.

Drabble's grist mill had belonged to a specific point in the history of the valley, a time when the valley was isolated from markets, and when a dependence on American imports encouraged attempts at self-sufficiency. However, with the completion of the Canadian Pacific Railway, farmers gave up trying to grind their own wheat, and instead imported flour from Manitoba which—while not home-made—was both patriotic and high-quality. What grain they grew was fed to cattle. Dairying became the principal industry in the valley in the 1890s, with markets at Union, Courtenay, Comox, and elsewhere. Every farmhand had to be a good milker, Duncan noted, and the favourite cattle, in their order, were the dairy short-horns—Jerseys, Holsteins, and Ayrshires.[15]

A good supply of hay was vital to these farms in the era before the internal combustion engine. Horses, cattle, and oxen needed feed, and every farmer devoted a portion of his land to hay crops. In 1897 Whitney of the *Weekly News*—that urban booster—ridiculed Mr. Woodruff of the Burdette Ranch for piling his wet hay on stumps hoping it would dry faster:

> He reasoned thus: The nearer the fire the hotter; the sun is a ball of fire, therefore the nearer the sun I get my wet hay, the sooner it will dry. The ranch was dotted with tall black stumps, and upon the top of each he placed a cock of hay. That was the condition of things when our informant left. It is said there is a considerable excitement in the valley. Some farmers had dug, pulled or blown out their stumps, not knowing they were their best friends.[16]

There were, of course, problems for the farmers. In the 1880s and 1890s cougars continued to come down from the mountains in search of livestock, and every farmer kept a rifle handy in case one of the big cats appeared. "McKelvey shot a whacking old panther on one of his pigs a short time since," Carwithen wrote in 1882. In 1887 Drabble sent bounty vouchers to Victoria for the scalps of three cougars, and over the next ten years the bounty rose from $5 to $15. "Some enterprising

---

[15] Duncan, "Vancouver Island," p. 367.
[16] *The Weekly News*, 6 July 1897.

farmer will be starting a panther ranch yet," Whitney remarked in 1896.[17]

Labour was a source of concern for most farmers. Skilled farm labour was scarce and expensive owing to easy access to land and to the high wages available in the industrial cities and work camps of the coast. "Good hired men are scarce on the farms," Duncan wrote in 1903, "and readily get five pounds a month [$25], with board and lodging all the year round, and six or seven pounds [$30–$35] if employed during the three months of haying and harvest." In April 1895, Drabble interfered on behalf of Dominick Larue, a farm labourer, who had not been paid by his employer Charles Bridges. He made the following note:

> Dominick Larue worked for C. Bridges from March 18th 1895 and quit April 17th 1895 $26 per month—[Bridges] agreed to pay on Saturday the 27th. Now says he will not pay for 6 months or perhaps never. Larue is owed $26.50.
>
> Cr. Tobacco $1.25.
>   1 Shaving mug .75.
>   Washing .30 = $2.30
>
> Owed $24.20. Summons for May 2nd at 2 o'clock.[18]

Native people remained a source of seasonal labour into the late nineteenth century. Since 1862 they had been hired for a good many tasks: land clearing and general farm labour, digging potatoes, working on the roads, taking settlers to and from Nanaimo by canoe. Their wages were a good deal less than those paid to "Whites," which generally ran at $1.50 to $2.00 a day. Indians cleared land for twenty-five cents a day in the 1880s: "Pay was 25 cents a day and a day was ten hours or longer," Agnes Edwards told an interviewer; "Some of the settlers felt the workers should bring their own food at this wage while others, and those more popular with the Indians, provided meals for their workmen." They got much better rates at the Fraser River canneries and hop fields, where a ten-hour day paid $1.25. In the same decade Comox Indians collected stray logs for King and Casey and piled lumber on rafts at Pidcock's mill for delivery to Tsolum River settlers. During renovations to the Lorne Hotel in 1988 a scrap of paper dated 4 May 1890 was found behind one of the walls. It was addressed to logger J. M. Walker by farmer John Coates. "Dear Sir," it reads, "If you want any more

---

[17] Carwithen to Blaksley, 23 May 1882, Carwithen Correspondence; Drabble to Provincial Secretary, 23 June and 4 August 1887, Provincial Secretary, Correspondence Inward, 1871-1892; Union *Weekly News*, 28 January 1896.

[18] Duncan, "Vancouver Island," p. 367; env. 74, Drabble Papers.

salmons for your camp I will send you some by Siwashes. Yours Truly, JAC."[19]

Native women worked as domestic help; Mary Harmston hired "Clootchmen" (grotesquely abbreviated to "Clootch" and "Clutch") to dig potatoes, and later to do cleaning work at the Lorne Hotel in the 1880s.[20] Harmston noted this in her hotel diary:

25 August 1886. "Fine. Clutch washing."
20 December 1886. "Clutch washing."

Increasingly, Native people were replaced in the domestic sphere by Chinese workers, whose employment was very controversial. The first references to Chinese at Comox date from 1875, when—to the settlers' outrage—Victoria contractors Baker and Nicholson hired eighteen "Chinamen" on the Flat Road. In 1879 only four Chinese lived in the district: three were logging camp cooks earning $30 a month, and the fourth was Willemar's household servant. In 1883 Pidcock hired two Chinese: one at his mill and one at his house for $25 a month.[21]

In January 1885, Land and Works Department officials stipulated that Chinese were not to be employed in any capacity in the construction of the Denman Island wharf. Drabble met with a similar response later that year from his neighbour Charles Stewart when he built a "China House" for his domestic servant on Anderton Road. "Memo," he wrote, "On Sunday Sep 27th 1885 Charles Stewart said that if any Chinaman lived in my house he would break the windows."[22] So contentious an issue was the hiring of Chinese that in the spring of 1886 Anthony Stenhouse referred to the "Chinese question" in his Comox election broadsheet:

The presence of the Mongolian on the Pacific coast, once a necessary evil, is now a nuisance unatoned, and the despair of an expiring ministry. In justice to the genuine settler, I shall protest against the employment of these aliens on public works in our own or any other district.[23]

Maitland was elected.

---

[19] Ede Anfield, "Radfords Here Before Roads or Bridges Came," *CVFP*, 7 March 1956. On Native labour see also Isenor, *Land of Plenty*, pp. 73, 132.

[20] Isabelle Stubbs, "Indian History Recounted by Matriarch," *CVFP*, 30 October 1952; Pidcock Diary, 19 April 1883; note found in wall of Lorne Hotel, Comox, 1988.

[21] Env. 97; Rodello to Provincial Secretary, 3 September 1879, Provincial Secretary, Correspondence Inward, 1871-1892; Pidcock Diary, 12 September, 22 December 1883.

[22] British Columbia, Department of Public Works, Contracts, specifications, 1862-1909; env. 62.

[23] A. Maitland Stenhouse, "To the Free and Independent Electors of the District of Comox," 1 March 1886, Vertical file, BCARS.

Dunsmuir, of course, hired a good many Chinese at Union, where a sizeable Chinatown appeared. Drabble, in common with the conservative establishment, did not hesitate to buy the products of Chinese merchants, hire Chinese workers, and support them in the legal system. In 1896 he bought cloth from Chun Wo Tong at Union, and in the same year, as Justice of the Peace, he jotted down the details of the case of "You Chinaman" who worked for farmer James Clarke:

> You Chinaman Worked for James Clarke of Comox Cutting Hay in June hired for 30$ per month with board—Worked 10 days & 1 bottle of Whisky bought by this Chinaman at Grants. Clarke to pay but has not done so— Board was bad that caused this man to leave Clarkes employ—owed $12.50 due. Asked Clarke for money & he refused to pay—Chinaman said he Could not work on the food provided Breakfast 4 crackers & Tea. Dinner Potatoes & Corn beef chopped up & fried. Supper 2 pieces Bread & Tea.[24]

An interdependence of farming and logging began in the 1870s when Pidcock hired settlers at his sawmill. Other farmers cut trees on their own pre-emptions and floated them to the mill or sold them to King and Casey. Increasingly, farmers relied for cash on seasonal logging work. Even today as you drive around the valley you will see small farms

Plan for gate at Drabble's house, Comox, and memo about
Charles Stewart and Chinese, 27 September 1885.

---

[24] Envs. 68, 77, 105, Drabble Papers.

of five or ten acres—remnants of the original holdings—with brand-new logging trucks parked in their narrow gravel driveways. In 1897 Duncan noted that although the arable area of Vancouver Island was limited, it possessed other resources which employed far more labour than farming, of which logging was primary. "Settlers without capital often work part of the year in the camps."[25]

Established farmers prospered and brought up large families in this rural landscape with its dual employment in the farms and forest. Farmers, Leila Carroll wrote, "brought their visions of farms and well tilled fields, big barns, comfortable houses with roomy kitchens where a whole family could congregate daily and thus help turn a house into a home." Some early settlers produced great numbers of children in the 1870s and 1880s—children they put to work in the fields. Two such couples were Reginald and Margaret Carwithen and William and Anna Beach. In 1885 Carwithen reflected that he had not been to Victoria in eleven years. "It takes me all my time to attend to stock and fences," he told Blaksley; "already the children are of great use, and then again they take another turn in generally smashing things." Two years later he repeated that: "We have six now, the three eldest are of great help already so the farm may stand a chance of being properly cultivated some day."[26]

Anna Beach had eight children. Her husband William, a settler of 1862, impressed his friend Eric Duncan with his large working family:

> Beach had none of the modern fear of large families. "Children are wealth," he told the writer more than forty years ago, and just as soon as ever they were able he set them to work on the land, and thenceforward did little himself but supervise. Year after year he could be seen seated at his verandah, pipe in mouth, watching his boys and girls busy in the fields below. They married early and cleared out; but as fast as the older ones went, younger ones took their place, and even grandchildren came back under the yoke.[27]

Another couple, Eliza and William Parkin, had seventeen children. The daughter of Nanaimo midwife Lavinia Malpass, Eliza married William Parkin in 1866 and moved to Dove Creek in 1885, where they bought the Thomas farm after Mrs. Thomas was killed by a cow. By the 1890s the Parkins and their sons owned over 600 acres of farm-land on the Dove Creek Road, and when Eliza Parkin died in 1935 at the age of 87, she was survived by ten sons, two daughters, thirty-nine

[25] Crawford, "First Prize Article;" Duncan, "Vancouver Island," pp. 367-68.
[26] Carroll, *Wild Roses and Rail Fences*, p. i; Carwithen to Blaksley, 10 May 1885 and 8 December 1887, Carwithen Correspondence.
[27] Forbes, *Wild Roses*, pp. 130-31; *From Shetland to Vancouver Island*, pp. 107-08.

grandchildren, forty-one great-grandchildren, and two great-great-grandchildren.[28]

Bishop Hills noted in 1885 that there were about 100 children in the settlement. Anglican minister Jules Willemar married eighteen couples and baptised 129 babies between 1871 and 1893. Almost all of the babies were delivered by midwives, two of whom were Mary Harmston and Isabella Robb, Englishwomen who came to the valley in 1863. In her diaries Harmston refers to confined women as being ill or sick. "There were no doctors;" Eric Duncan recalled, "victims of accident—fortunately few—were taken sixty miles by canoe to Nanaimo; and women did the best they could, helping one another." Nanaimo midwife Lavinia Malpass would not accept payment for her services, but occasionally a salmon, roast of venison, eggs, or a chicken would be found on her front doorstep. Isabella Robb—"a healthy, hearty, happy woman" with a background in nursing, would travel many miles in all kinds of weather to help the sick or attend to women expecting babies.[29]

Mary Harmston supplied only brief descriptions of her work. One entry relates to Mary Willemar, who gave birth on 29 June 1881 after a long labour: "Fine. Mr. Willemar came to Murphys for me his wife was ill she was not confined till Wednesday morning June 29th—half past three I was there untill July 14th." These midwives found their work restricted with the arrival in the 1890s of Harrison Millard, the valley's first permanent resident doctor, who would race around on his horse delivering babies.[30]

Historian Leila Carroll praised the cooperative nature of the settlement. "They not only passed money around," she wrote, "they passed themselves around, answering calls to sit up with the sick or the deceased, or responding to calls to 'bees'—shingling bees, barnraising bees; the ladies did the same for quilting bees."[31]

Not all relations between the settlers were amicable and cooperative. Difficulties existed and petty disputes were common. The only recollection of Drabble's judicial character comes from Eric Duncan, who remarked that he was "rather cynical, and in the frequent disputes over fences, cattle and pigs, it was said that he would always decide in favour of the party who gave him the best dinner." If anything, Drabble tended to side with the plaintiffs; that is, with those seeking recourse to the legal

28 Rhoda Beck, "Parkin Reunion," 1 August 1980; Margaret Biscoe, "Mrs. William Parkin" and Lilian Hunden, "The Parkin Family," in Isenor, "The Comox Valley."

29 Isenor, *Land of Plenty*, p. 71; Courtenay *Weekly News*, 8 November 1893, p. 1; *From Shetland to Vancouver Island*, p. 137; Lugrin, *The Pioneer Women of Vancouver Island*, p. 159; Beck, "Parkin Reunion," p. 3.

30 Harmston Diary, 27 June 1881; Carroll, *Wild Roses and Rail Fences*, pp. 97-99.

31 Carroll, *Wild Roses and Rail Fences*, p. 86.

system, but this was the case elsewhere. Drabble, Robb, and later magistrates settled most disputes out of court. For example, in 1884 Robb sent to Victoria a Return of Convictions heard by him and Drabble in the preceeding two years. He noted that "There have been some other cases before the court of so trivial a nature as to be dismissed. In all cases, as between neighbours, the Justices have nearly always succeeded in persuading the parties to settle matters out of court." Such persuasion may have taken place—as Duncan suggested—over dinner, or in some other informal setting.[32]

In 1886 a flurry of farming cases came to court, cases that open windows into the early rural settlement. Drabble was by then senior member of the bench, Robb having retired. Merchant Arthur Bullock took farmer Charles Bridges to court over of a barrel of flour. William Beach was acquitted of stealing a barrel of sugar from John Coates, and Alex Urquhart took his neighbour William Lewis to court for "Dogs Chasing Cattle."

In July 1886, Lewis took three men to court: Charles Bridges, James Rees, and William Halliday. Three years earlier Bridges had failed to meet an agreement to reap ten acres of Lewis's oats. Drabble ordered Bridges to pay $6.25. Lewis took Rees to court for money owed since 1883, when he had "served" Rees's cows with his Jersey bull, mown fourteen acres of his grass, and hired an Indian for three days during "Hay time." Drabble ordered Rees to pay Lewis $21. Finally, Lewis took Halliday to court for non-payment of "Cow Served by Bull" in June 1883. Halliday was then aged sixteen: "I hereby give Notice that I intend to defend the above case on the grounds of being under Age," he pleaded. Drabble ignored this and ordered him to pay Lewis $13. This young offender was William May Halliday, who later abandoned farming to become Kwakiutl Indian Agent and author of *Potlatch and Totem*.

In October 1886 Richard Creech prosecuted William Parkin for losses sustained when two of Parkin's horses attacked his horses, causing them to bolt and break a harness. One of Parkin's horses, a stallion, was "entire," that is, uncastrated. Drabble decided in Creech's favour and awarded him $11. Two days after Christmas another case arose concerning horses: Mary Harmston noted that "Willie Robb & his man Lumb had a fight Willie got his head cut." Drabble decided that Robb was in the wrong: "he was beating the Mare which caused the quarrel."[33]

[32] Duncan, Notes from Sandwick Store Cashbook; Robb to Provincial Secretary, 8 October 1884, Provincial Secretary, Correspondence Inward, 1871-1892.

[33] British Columbia, County Court (Comox), originals 1886, 1896; Drabble, "Returns of Convictions Comox District," in Drabble to Provincial Secretary, 24 March 1887, British Columbia, Provincial Secretary, Correspondence Inward, 1872-1924; Harmston Diary, 3 June, 27–28 December 1886.

Cases heard by Drabble ranged widely. George Bates related the story of two brothers who wound up in court regularly for fighting. One day in court, one of them suddenly picked up a large map of British Columbia attached to a heavy wooden roller and knocked his brother out the window.[34] Some cases never made it to court, and records of others survive only as scribbles in Drabble's notebooks, or laconic entries in Harmston's diary:

> 2 May 1882. "Metheson [Matthewson] came up in the evening about some Siwash dog he had shot & been summoned for."

> 22 April 1890. "Great excitement one Siwash it is supposed has killed another under the influence of Liquor the Justices are hearing them (11 PM)."

> 31 May 1890. "Two coulered men & two Siwashes in the jail for being drunk."

> 19 August 1890. "A trial of some Belgians who had been quarreling."

> 17 November 1890. "A law cause between McKelvey & the Dimond Drill men about a Cat & Dog Mc Won it was decided in his favour."

> 21 November 1891. "A man brought from one of the Logging camps with a bad cut face a man had jumped on his face with calks in his boots."[35]

In 1894 Judge Drabble heard the case of C. H. Williams, who took Thomas Provis to court for assault and battery. These men leased a farm in partnership, and one day while ploughing Provis struck and kicked his horse. Williams witnessed this and interfered, saying "it did no good to kick the horse," and a fight ensued. Drabble fined Provis $20 for assaulting Williams, and a week later Provis and Williams dissolved their partnership.[36]

ஒ

The early settlers brought notions of class to the valley along with their alternately cooperative and acrimonious social habits. The first settlers had represented a microcosm of British society, with literate and illiterate, wealthy and poor, alike pre-empting the fertile valley land over the winter of 1862-63. Perhaps half were illiterate or barely literate (judging from their signatures on land records), penniless, and completely dependent on their own manual labour. As a result, a great gap separated them from the privileged, educated, settlers. Bishop Hills' description of the Maritime settlers as generally "working class, but

---

[34] G. R. Bates, "Clokwasa's Old Comox Tales," *CVFP*, 9 April 1958.

[35] Harmston Diary, 1882-92.

[36] Courtenay *Weekly News*, 11 July 1894; 18 July 1894.

respectable"—while perhaps accurate—could only have been made by an Englishman. Pidcock's grandaughter told me, with some incredulity on her part, that "the English class system was hard at work in the valley." This gap appeared in several other rural districts in British Columbia, though few of the despised "Remittance Men" stayed in the valley in early years. Eric Duncan, who grew up in a stone house with a dirt floor in the Shetlands, wrote that "this is no country for 'gun-and-rod farmers'; it has long been strewn with the wrecks of that class, because temptation is strong, and men of means find plenty of sport. A self-dependent man must foreswear all that."[37]

Some of the educated English continued to receive money from their families in England (certainly Pidcock, Musters, and Drabble), and they tended to receive choice government jobs like Government Agent, Justice of the Peace, and Indian Agent. These jobs required much more than basic literacy, and Drabble and Pidcock spoke the same language and came from the same background as government officials in Victoria. The educated English contributed a white collar, middle-class immigrant group which ran local government offices and performed most professional funtions. Their income allowed them to maintain their privileged position in the New World; income from land rent and sales of wheat, which had sustained the English gentry and ultimately the whole class system, did not pertain in Comox.

Sooner or later, however, they or their descendents would have to adapt like everyone else to the local economy; they would have to make a living from local sources of wealth as loggers, miners, farmers, fishermen, traders, and shopkeepers. In a sense, their lives would be more difficult if they tried to retain professional status: they would need money to do so, and would have to leave the valley for training. For the "respectable working class," education offered a chance of escape from the valley, while for descendents of the educated English it became a respectable refuge that allowed the retention of professional status.

In the 1880s this valley community was bursting at the seams, and Drabble surveyed new roads into the surrounding wilderness.

---

[37] Interview with Ruth Barnett, 23 December 1994; Duncan, "Vancouver Island," pp. 366-67.

CHAPTER 16

Up the Colonization Road

For to my mind, however beautiful a view may be, it requires the presence of man to make it complete, but perhaps this is because I have lived so much in the wilderness, and therefore know the value of civilization, though, to be sure, it drives away the game.

FROM *King Solomon's Mines*, by H. Rider Haggard[1]

*I*N February 1884 the government passed a comprehensive piece of legislation called "An Act to amend and consolidate the Laws affecting Crown Lands in British Columbia." The act created the position of "Assistant Commissioner of Lands and Works" to administer the land laws in each district. These assistants were usually drawn from the ranks of stipendary magistrates. In the spring of 1885, Drabble was appointed Assistant Commissioner of Lands and Works for Comox District, a position that gave him the superintendence of road construction for a second critical time in the valley's history.[2]

This act stipulated that Crown land could be bought outright for $2.50 an acre in minimum sections of 160 acres or, as earlier, pre-empted through a lengthy process of occupation and improvement. Every step in the pre-emption process now required, in this bureaucratic late Victorian era, the completion of a form signed by an Assistant Commissioner or Justice of the Peace. Qualifications were generous within the narrow criteria of eligibility: "Any person being the head of a family, a widow, or single man over the age of eighteen years, upon his making a declaration of his intention to become a British subject," was entitled to pre-empt 160 acres on the coast—320 acres in the interior —of Crown land that was not already an Indian settlement. Additional allotments for wives and children were no longer permitted. While

---

[1] H. Rider Haggard, *King Solomon's Mines* (London: 1885; New York: Dover Publications, reprint, 1951), p. 259.

[2] *Statutes of the Province of British Columbia* (Victoria: 1884), pp. 71-97; Drabble to Provincial Secretary, 26 June 1885, Provincial Secretary, Correspondence Inward, 1871-1892.

protecting existing Native rights to their reserves, the act did not extend to "any of the aborigines of this continent." Those wanting to become British subjects had to complete Form 1, a Declaration of Intention, which required a formal renunciation of "allegiance and fidelity to all and any foreign prince, potentate, state, and sovereignty whatsoever"— a step that Americans, for instance, did not undertake lightly.

The settler was to place, at each corner of his claim, a post at least four feet tall and four inches square. On each post he had to attach a notice reading, say, "Horace Smith's land, N.W. Post." He also had to complete a sketch plan of the land. Once he had done these things, he was free to complete Form 2—a declaration that he had staked his land properly, that it was not an Indian settlement or otherwise occupied, and that he was not acting in collusion with anyone else, but wanted the land "honestly on my own behalf for settlement and occupation." The act also stipulated that all pre-emptions were to be of a square or rectangular shape, measuring forty by forty chains or eighty by twenty chains, and that all lines must run true north, south, east, and west. Irregular shapes were permitted only when lakes, rivers, the coastline or other natural boundaries intruded themselves on this orderly and economical subdivision of the wilderness.

Successful compliance with these conditions, and payment of $2, enabled the applicant to complete Form 3, or Certificate of Pre-emption Record, which enabled the land to be recorded officially in his name. He then had thirty days to occupy the land in question; if he did not, the Assistant Commissioner had the power to cancel the record altogther, take possession of all improvements for the Crown, and record the land for someone else. The act defined "occupation" as "a continuous bona fide personal residence by the pre-emptor, his agent, or family . . . but Indians or Chinamen shall not be considered agents."

Next, the pre-emptor had the land surveyed at his own expense by a qualified surveyor (in this case, wearing another hat, Drabble) who sent the field notes and a sketch map to the Lands and Works Department. The government then advertised the pre-emption for sixty days in the *British Columbia Gazette* in case anyone else had prior rights to it. After the survey and the *Gazette* notice, Drabble (as Land Commissioner) then completed Form 4, Certificate of Improvement, in which he declared that the pre-emptor had occupied the claim continuously and had made permanent improvements to the value of $2.50 per acre. Drabble and two other Justices of the Peace or commissioners then filled in Form 5, a joint declaration that the pre-emptor had made the necessary improvements. The pre-emptor was then free to pay a dollar an acre for his land in four instalments over a five-year period. When he had done so, he was entitled to receive his Crown Grant, for which he had to fill in Form 6.

Several things are notable about this act and Drabble's role in its implementation. It was aimed specifically at turning unsurveyed wild land into productive agricultural land peopled by British subjects. Chinese and Native Indians were excluded. Non-British settlers could not pre-empt land until they formally renounced their allegiance to their country. This occurred, for example, in 1886-87 when two Americans and two Swedes—David Jones, Michael Fitzgerald, Eric Olaf "Peter" Lindberg, and John Holmes—were naturalized before Judge Crease at Comox.[3] The act was intended primarily to benefit male British subjects who were also "the head of a family." Only widowed women could embark on the pre-emption process. Unmarried or single women of any age or ethnicity were excluded.

Also notable is the extent of Drabble's private and public involvement with the pre-emption process. He surveyed claims, kept track of vacant Crown land for intending settlers, matched incoming settlers' requirements with the available land, inspected and approved settlers' improvements, guided settlers (frequently illiterate) through the pre-emption process, drew maps for the land office, corresponded on points of procedure, signed every conceivable form and document (often in triplicate) required by settlers and the land office, surveyed roads to new areas of settlement and finally, as Magistrate, listened to squabbles between settlers he had put on the land in the first place.

Hundreds of Drabble's maps and surveys, in rough draft and final copy, have survived at the Campbell River Museum and Archives and at the Surveyor General's Branch in Victoria. Surviving settlers' diaries also record his activities. "Paid G. F. Drabble $5.00 for surveying my claim," William Duncan wrote in May 1887. Drabble made sure that pre-emptors occupied their land through personal residence and cultivation, and punished them when they did not—as when in 1886 Adam McKelvey fraudulently obtained a Certificate of Improvement for Section 74, Comox District. Drabble fought for extensions of settlers' instalment payments, urging, for example, that the "Govt will consider the disadvantages under which they have to labour . . . Cessford is in Esquimalt at the Tannery." He gave settlers equal access to sources of fresh water when it was in limited supply.[4]

3 British Columbia, County Court (Comox), Originals, 1886, 1896.

4 William Duncan Diary, 19 May 1887; William Calhoun to CCL&W, 20 November 1872, Lands and Works Department, Correspondence Inward, 1872-1918; British Columbia, Attorney General, Documents, 1857-1966; Rodello [Drabble] to Provincial Secretary, 5 July 1876, Provincial Secretary, Correspondence Inward, 1871-1892; interview with Rene Harding, 8 January 1994.

The whole of the pre-emption process appears in Drabble's field notes. He often referred to "choppings"—an early, and accurate, term for "clearing." Most settlers pre-empted part of the dense forest, part of which they first chopped down for house, garden, and livestock enclosure. Trees were chopped by axe (or burned with hot coals deposited by auger) to produce a stump-filled chopping. The fallen trees were then burned; there was no point in selling the timber unless the chopping happened to be on a river or on the ocean. Millions of board feet of timber were simply burned before donkey engines made it possible to yard large logs from the woods. "Hot," Mary Harmston noted in her Lorne Hotel diary on 27 July 1889. "Fires all over. People setting fire to their Choppings."

Drabble's late field books are a rich resource for rural and material history. He determined the value of settlers' capital expenditures so that they could calculate their Certificates of Improvement. Dan Sullivan on Baynes Sound, Henry Grieve of Comox, and William Grove of Deep Bay were three of his customers:

> 4 April 1884. "June 8 1876 Dan Sullivan located on his claim in Baynes Sound. 1 house $65. 5 Acres under Timothy 50$ $250. Fencing 1500 Rails $52. 5 Acres of Chopping $200. 1884 50 Acres sown with Timothy $30. [Total]: $595.

> 6 July 1885. "H. Grieve's Imps. House 26×14 $200 Barn framed 45×30 Sheds around $300. Wood Shed & Dairy $50. 50 Acres of Wood land cleared and under Cultivation $2500. Fencing &c 50$. [Total]: $3250."

> 13 January 1887. "Grove's Imps Jany 13/87. 5 Acres Chopped: 110. 4 acres ditto: 50. 2 acres ditto & Cleared & burnt part Cultivated & fenced: 100. 1 House 48×18 ft: 200. 1 Chicken House 18×10: 30. 1 Chicken House 12×12 & water closet: 20. [Total]: $510."[5]

These settlers found themselves with 160 acres of land, of which they cultivated at first only five or ten acres—usually a rich pocket of valley land, or if they were lucky a shoreline stretch with a clear and fertile Indian midden. The rich unbroken prairie encountered by the 1862 settlers was a thing of the past.

Drabble's 1885 appointment as Assistant Commissioner for Comox District entailed the responsibilty for road superintendence. He once again surveyed new roads and awarded contracts for repairs to existing ones. His previous appointment (1872-78) had coincided with the construction of the Comox wharf, Courtenay River bridge, and Long Bridge; between 1885 and 1887 he surveyed and supervised the construction of the Colonization Road from the Upper Prairie to Oyster

---

[5] Envs. 72, 88, 121, Drabble Papers.

Bay—now the central section of the Island Highway between Courtenay and Campbell River.

Since the early 1860s settlers had known that an Indian trail extended up the Comox Valley towards Campbell River. Indians at Salmon River told Richard Mayne, an early naval visitor, that they could reach Comox in a day and a half by this trail.[6] From Comox Harbour the Tsolum extended about fifteen miles inland, and the coastal lowland continued for another fifteen miles through the watersheds of Black Creek and Oyster River to Campbell River. The land in this region was inferior to that of the lower Comox Valley, but some of it was cultivable, and in the 1880s it became increasingly desirable as valley land was taken up and Union provided a local market. Indeed, agricultural settlement could not grow in any other direction from Comox: the Beaufort Range rose abruptly to the west and south of the valley, and the Gulf of Georgia dominated the other sides. The northern coastal lowland offered the greatest hope for continued settlement.

The Colonization Road originated in the 1870s as an inland extension of the Upper Prairie Road. In April 1872 a group of settlers had urged the government to extend the road up the valley in order to open a new region for settlement. Several people, they wrote, "have been looking for land on which to settle, and have been well pleased with the land further inland a mile or two, but have left again, because they had no road to come out. We hope that this road will be extended to these prairies so that no more persons will be disappointed and the Country settled up."[7] In the summer of 1872 William Hassard extended a trail five miles into the Upper Prairie, and thereafter the road was gradually extended. In the process its name changed from Section C to the Upper Prairie Road to the Colonization Road to the Island Highway—though Upper Prairie Road still applied to the part nearest Courtenay.

The need for a good road into the upper valley increased in the 1880s. By this date most of the waterfront land at Comox, Kye Bay, and Point Holmes had been pre-empted or occupied. Dunsmuir's growing interest in coal properties in the region had led to the rapid settlement of the region south of the Courtenay River and the lowland strip along Baynes Sound.

In October 1885 Drabble surveyed and blazed the line of what he called the Colonization Road from William Beach's western boundary for four miles up the valley. (See map 10.) The contractor was to cut

---

[6] Richard Mayne quoted in Isenor, *Land of Plenty*, p. 17.

[7] Coleman et al. to Pearse, 11 April 1872, British Columbia, Department of Lands and Works, Correspondence Inward, 1871-1872.

down hillocks, remove stumps, lay corduroy, and "make a Road way 10 ft wide having a uniform grade without sudden pitches or rises." At the end of the month he called for tenders on the project and received nine, ranging in price from $50 to $140 per mile. He selected the lowest offer, that of John J. Grant.[8]

Drabble's selection of the name Colonization Road is significant. The term was popular in early nineteenth century Ontario, where Colonization Roads were built by the government or by private colonization companies. They extended into the wilderness in perfectly straight lines, and their object was to make land available to settlers as quickly and cheaply as possible. Without such roads settlement would have stopped, and distant farmers would have been unable to market their produce.[9]

Part of Drabble's job as commissioner involved hiring a good solid wagon to cart around rocks and soil. He hoped to rent one in 1886, as Comox merchant J. B. Holmes noted in his letters to Hirst Brothers, his Nanaimo suppliers:

29 June 1886. "Send up the Horse & Cart as soon as possible. Let the horse be a *good* one if suitable. Drabble govt agent here tells me that he will frequently want to hire it at $2 1/2 per day which will be quite an item."

26 August 1886. "The cart—I am sorry you sent it, it is really little or no use for the purpose I want it, no one can lift heavy loads on it."[10]

In April 1886 Drabble, after inspecting Grant's work, reported to the Surveyor General that the new road had been completed for four miles past William Beach's claim. The road, if extended, would "pass through very fair land and would also be a convenience to some Settlers living in Oyster Bay near Shelter Point who have at present to travel by Canoe to Comox which is dangerous & inconvenient in Winter time." A little political pressure may have been exerted by the new Comox M.L.A., Anthony Stenhouse, who in his March 1886 platform promised to build "a solid thoroughfare uniting Comox to the great chain of settlements which are bound in due time to push their prosperous way from here to the extreme north." In the fall of 1886 the government authorized Drabble to extend the Colonization Road, and for three weeks in October and November he and his crew surveyed past Black Creek and toward Oyster River. He made a note that he needed "3 Grubbers

[8] Env. 123; British Columbia, Department of Public Works, Contracts, specifications, 1862-1909.

[9] Don W. Thomson, *Men and Meridians. The History of Surveying and Mapping in Canada* Vol. 1 (Ottawa: Queen's Printer, 1966), pp. 239-42.

[10] Holmes to Hirst Brothers, 29 June, 26 August 1886, Planta Collection, NCA.

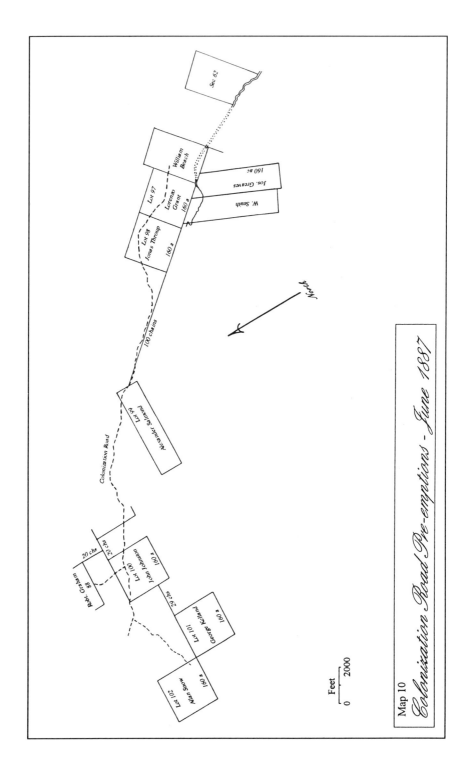

North

Feet
0   2000

Map 10
Colonization Road Pre-emptions - June 1887

Sec. 62

William
Beach

Lot 97
Lorenzo
Grant
160 a

Jos. Greaves
160 ac

W. Smith

Lot 98
Jonas Throup
160 a

100 chains

Lot 99
Alexander Silberad

Colonization Road

20 chs   20 chs

R.H. Graham
88

Lot 100
John Johnston
160 a

Lot 101
George Kellam
160 a

20 chs

Lot 102
Allan Scott
160 a

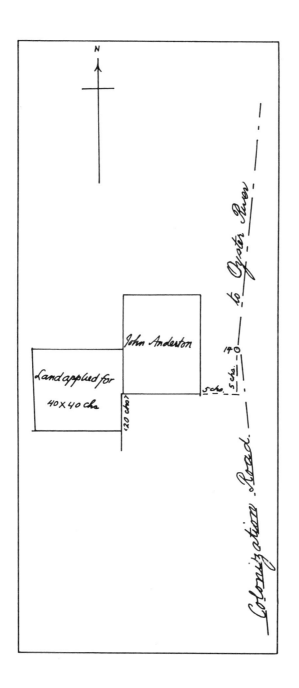

Map for Land Office, Victoria, accompanying William Joseph Miller's
Certificate of Pre-emption Record, March 1887.

4 Shovels 2 axes" for roadwork, and he recorded the days he spent "Packing & Cutting," "Cutting & chaining," "Chaining & packing," "Clearing & Cutting," and "Picking."[11]

Drabble then returned to Comox and drew up contracts for the extension of the Colonization Road to a point near Oyster River. He accepted the bids of John Anderton and George Kelland to build the road ten feet wide and construct an eighty-three foot bridge over Black Creek. In December he wrote to the Surveyor General as follows:

> In accordance with your instructions to me with regard to cutting more Roads with a view to opening up the Country I have to say that I surveyed a line of nearly 7 miles towards Oyster River from the end of the former Road. . . .
>
> Whenever the Road is cut the entire distance to Oyster River it will enable the Settlers living in the neighbourhood of Cape Mudge to ride to Comox instead of having to travel by Canoe and suffer much hardship in blowing weather.[12]

By January 1887 the Colonization Road had been completed as far as Oyster Bay. One young settler, Eustace Smith of Black Creek, recalled that the trail cut by Judge Drabble led "into the wilds of the upper valley beyond Black Creek. It suggested adventure."[13]

The Colonization Road, like the town of Courtenay, was also inspired in part by Dunsmuir's opening of the Union mine. Settlers could now venture north in search of land with the knowledge that a local market existed for their produce. Roads and bridges were essential to the settlement of this heavily forested region. The land was fair. "The first pioneers of Black Creek," wrote historian Walter Philippsen, "found ideal places for their homesteads in the large swamps of this area. These swamps were not boggy, as their name might imply, but were merely tracts of damp, grass-covered land, which had been used for years by the Indians as hunting-places for deer and elk." In the late 1880s new settlers arrived in the valley in search of land. Most of them were from Britain and Ontario, and most had reached British Columbia on the new continental railway. M.L.A. Stenhouse, in his 1886 election campaign, commented that "A wave of immigration in its normal course has

[11] British Columbia, Department of Public Works, Contracts, specifications, 1862-1909; Stenhouse, "To the Free and Independent Electors of the District of Comox;" envs. 88, 123.

[12] For a sketch of "Black Creek Bridge" see env. 88; Drabble to Surveyor General, 17 December 1886, in British Columbia, Department of Public Works, Contracts, specifications, 1862-1909.

[13] McKelvie, "The 'S' Sign," p. 47.

broken over our district," resulting from the progress and completion of the Canadian Pacific Railway and persuasive immigration booklets.[14]

After laying out the road and supervising its construction, Drabble returned between 1887 and 1889 in his private capacity to survey pre-emptions for George Kelland, Allan Snow, John Johnston, Lorenzo Grant, John Throup, Alexander Salmond, Robert Graham, Horace Smith, John Honeyman and John Baird, John Anderton, and William May Halliday—the first settlers in the Merville-Black Creek area.

Settlers sometimes asked Drabble to survey their land years after they staked it, so the date of survey does not always reflect date of occupation. In 1892 he surveyed lots for James Graham and a great patchwork of pre-emptions at what is now Merville: William C. Smith, Alexander Ledingham, Edward Phillips, Lawrence Manson, H. R. McIntyre, Frank Cunliffe, Thomas Scott, and Robert Creech. His surveys showed "Smith's clearing," "Ledinghams Clearing," "Phillips Clearing," indicating that these settlers' industry was genuine. The early assessment rolls identify most as "labourers," with the exception of Anderton and Cunliffe, who were carpenters; Salmond, who had been an officer in the British Army; Horace Smith, a gentleman; and Honeyman, a Cambridge-educated architect.

The Colonization Road supported several families. Eric Duncan, still anxious to show that the valley had been settled by British not Maritime immigrants, recalled that the first pre-emptors on the Colonization Road came from England and Scotland:

> In 1889 I got married, and about this time several new men entered the Valley, and the settlement stretched up through the woods to Black Creek and beyond. The chief of these were Sergeant Major Salmond from Kincardineshire, who had been with Roberts in Afghanistan, Horace Smith from Derbyshire, John Blackburn from Lancashire, George Kelland from Devonshire, and John Johnston from Perthshire.

These men objected to going eight or nine miles to Comox Landing for their letters, and in the 1890s a post office was established near the start of the Colonization Road. It was called "Grantham" after John Grant, who leased a farm there from D. W. Gordon.[15]

One settler on the road was Alexander "Sandy" Ledingham, a native of Ontario. Ledingham came to Comox without means in the summer of 1885 and—Eric Duncan recalled—"took hold of 140 acres of bush land in the upper valley, sheltering under a huge capsized tree root till

14 Walter Philippsen, "Black Creek," in Isenor, "The Comox Valley;" Stenhouse, "To the Free and Independent Electors."

15 *From Shetland to Vancouver Island*, p. 173. For the general trend of valley settlement see McKelvie, "The 'S' Sign," pp. 26-7.

he gathered enough material to build a shack." He ran the engine at Grant and Mounce's Union sawmill for a time, and with the cash he bought some cattle for his farm. "Of a strong mechanical turn, many of his tools and implements were home-made, and he was an expert saw-filer and tree-pruner. He was always ready to help those who needed it, not only with useful hints and suggestions, but also with hard labour." [16]

Another settler, Alexander Salmond, lived eight miles from Courtenay on the Colonization Road at what is now Merville. Born in 1846 in Scotland, Major Salmond and his wife Emma came to Canada in 1886, crossing the country with their infant son on the C.P.R. Drabble, in his June 1887 survey of Salmond's land, noted "Swamp full of Willow & Course Grass," "Enter Skunk Cabbage & Swamp." Salmond, like the others, subdued only a small part of his 160 wilderness acres, and in 1893 editor Whitney described a drive up the Colonization Road to visit the Salmonds:

> Except for the open space made here in the heart of the forest by patient and intelligent industry, all was wild and primeval. To go to a neighbour's was to pass through the woods. Not far off were the mountains. The Gulf lay to the right about three miles through the giant cedars and tall firs. All around the little opening, the dense forest! Near the margin of the garden and meadow were the tracks of the black bear, and other wild beasts. Here the panther sometimes faced the conquering rifle, and the forest yielded its game and the not far off stream its fish in as prodigal abundance as the garden its vegetation. [17]

Later the Salmond farm was subdivided into three parts, one of which was bought by Stan Hodgins—husband of Merville historian Reta Hodgins and father of novelist Jack Hodgins, who grew up here. [18]

A third Colonization Road settler was eighteen year-old Horace Smith, who arrived in 1886 on one of the first C.P.R. trains to reach the west coast. The eldest son of a cheese manufacturer in Ashbourne, Derbyshire, Smith had answered an advertisement in the British outdoor magazine *The Field* placed by George Dillon Curtis, a newly qualified architect. Both were keen sportsmen. Horace had briefly been at Oxford University. The two young men reached the west coast shortly after the great Vancouver fire of 1886, and finding nothing there but blackened stumps, crossed the Gulf of Georgia in time to look for land up the Colonization Road.

[16] *From Shetland to Vancouver Island*, pp. 229-30.

[17] Env. 135; Reta Blakely Hodgins, ed., *Merville and its Early Settlers 1919-1985* (Campbell River: Kask Graphics, 1985), p. 161; Courtenay *Weekly News*, 12 July 1893; Del Hall, *Island Gold: A History of Cougar Hunting on Vancouver Island* (Victoria: Cougar Press, 1990), p. 39.

[18] Hodgins, *Merville*, pp. 96, 161.

George Curtis claimed lot 128 at Bates Beach, to the east of the road, where he built a cabin. Horace Smith got a pre-emption at Black Creek in an unorthodox way. One day he was down at the Comox wharf where he met a settler named William or Bill "Whiskey" Jones, who was much the worse for wear after spending all his money on drink at the Elk Hotel. For five gold sovereigns Jones sold Smith his right to the "Black Creek Ranch" at the 4 Mile post of the Colonization Road.[19]

Both men sent enthusiastic letters back to England, and both were soon joined by their families: George by his father Captain James Curtis, R.N., and by his brother James. Smith was joined in August 1887 by his mother Amelia and seven of his younger brothers and sisters. They left England in July on the *Sircassian* to Quebec, and took the C.P.R. transcontinental train to Vancouver, which by 1887 had been rebuilt after the fire. Their arrival in Comox was noted by the hotel chronicler Mary Harmston on Friday, 12 August 1887. "Fair," she wrote, alluding to the weather; "Horace Smiths Mother and family came." They were: Maud (aged sixteen), Mabel (eleven), Eustace (nine), Cecil (eight), Harvey (four), Hilda (three), and one year-old Neville. Horace Smith Sr. did not want to leave England, but he arrived a year later with more of the children after winding up the cheese business. Ida, the eldest Smith girl, never came out to Canada.[20]

Muriel Dann, the Smiths' grandaughter, told me that they worked hard at Black Creek building a house and clearing enough land to obtain a Certificate of Improvement, but the Smiths were "no farmers" and the land was of marginal quality. Fortunately Amelia, the backbone of the family, had inherited some money and was able to support the family in early days. Reginald Pidcock met her at the Willemars' in August 1888. "Found a Mrs Smith there a rather nice person or lady I should say, mother of a numerous family."[21] This was an auspicious beginning, considering that two Pidcock children would marry two Smith children.

The Black Creek farm must have been too small for Horace Smith Jr. because he rented Drabble's house in Comox. "S. Creech left House," Drabble wrote on 16 March 1889; "Smiths moved into House March 26th/89." "Horace Smith took possession of House 10$ per month to Oct 26th 7 months 70$."[22]

---

[19] On Smith and Curtis see Hodgins, *Merville*, p. 169; Comox Assessment Roll, 1887; Richard Mackie and Alexander Mackie, "Roughing it in the Colonies: an Englishman on Vancouver Island," *The Beaver* 70:2 (March 1990), pp. 6-13.

[20] Harmston Diary, 12 August 1887; notes from Smith family bible obtained from Muriel Dann, 14 April 1994.

[21] Pidcock Diary, 8 August 1888.

[22] Envs. 102, 106, Drabble Papers.

The many Smith children eventually had to be self-supporting. They adapted to their surroundings in the most appropriate ways. Horace became a log skidder at Urquharts' Mill, a cougar hunter, fishing and hunting guide, and lumberman. In about 1900 he turned over his dogs to his younger brother Cecil, who after trying his hand at farming became "Cougar Smith," the famous bounty hunter. Eustace trained as a surveyor and became the best-known timber cruiser on the coast; Neville went to McGill University and became a lawyer in Vancouver. Percy logged for King and Casey at Campbell River. The girls, limited in the choice of career, trained as teachers and nurses. The Smith children married into the professional English families in the valley: Horace married Maud Beadnell, a doctor's daughter from Denman Island; Cecil married Mary Pidcock; Ella married a Pidcock son. Percy married one of the McDonald girls of the Elk Hotel. George Curtis, meanwhile, worked for Drabble as chainman on his island surveys before joining his Black Creek neighbour in the firm Honeyman & Curtis, architects of Nelson and later of Vancouver.[23]

The Colonization Road extended only as far as Oyster River until 1890, when a trail was opened to Campbell River. On 12 October of that year Drabble, on his return from northern surveys, walked the length of the Colonization Road from north to south and noted the timetable:

> Left Oyster River 9.30.
> Black Creek Bridge 11.30.
> 4 Mile Post Smiths 12.20.
> Passed Salmonds 12.50.
> Arrived at Beach's 2.05.

He walked ten miles in four and a half hours.[24]

In addition to opening a new area for agricultural settlement, the Colonization Road also went straight through cougar habitat, and cougars preyed on livestock all the way to Black Creek and beyond. The road also opened a new region to hunters. Since the 1860s the prairies in the upper valley had been known as the Elk or Wapiti patches or prairies, but valley settlement gradually encroached on elk habitat until those ungulates retreated to the upper Black Creek area. At the same time the valley became something of a mecca for sportsmen; not for nothing Rodello had named his hotel the Elk. Carwithen kept his old hunting pal, Harry Blaksley, abreast of these changes in August 1880:

---

[23] On Percy Smith see Mitchell, *Diamond in the Rough*, p. 89; Hall, *Island Gold*, p. 39. On Honeyman and Curtis see Anthony A. Barrett and Rhodri Windsor Liscombe, *Francis Rattenbury and British Columbia: Architecture and Challenge in the Imperial Age* (Vancouver: UBC Press, 1983).

[24] Env. 14, Drabble Papers.

I would far sooner choose this bush where Wapiti abound. Some splendid heads have been fetched down lately. We have a moneyed sportsman named Captn. Vidler with wife, servants and dog-cart camping out; certainly a most enjoyable mode of living.[25]

In 1882 he wrote that the deer had been "very plentiful all winter though one was my total, they still come out on the prairie," but in December 1885 with the building of the Colonization Road this had changed. "The little prairies up the river are gone now," Carwithen lamented; "strangers are there. There is also a road 5 miles beyond the elk patches." Two years later, with King and Casey and Colonization Road settlers cutting and burning the forest, he complained to Blaksley about the loss of "his" elk patches — hunting grounds that he, Blaksley, Drabble, and Pidcock had brazenly usurped from the Comox Indians only twenty years before:

> The bush is being cut down in many places and fires destroyed a great deal of timber this summer and consequently deer are very scarce up around me; though not very far away many have been shot, and also Wapiti. Many sporting men now make this their headquarters in the fall. The two hotels encourage the loafers, but I don't see what right they have in our bush, eh![26]

Hunting was just as popular among the English immigrants of the 1880s as it had been among those of the 1860s. The Curtises, for example, were keen hunters, and George Curtis's sketch of his cabin at Bates Beach shows half a deer carcass hanging from the roof and several raccoon pelts. The diaries of Curtis and Nunns are full of references to hunting. These immigrants must have absorbed a huge amount of protein. Abuses occurred. Lou Cliffe remembered "a party of alleged sportsman, who went out to hunt at Black Creek. They got into a herd of elk and butchered eleven cows and calves as well as some bulls. Their bodies were allowed to rot." Most hunters were more ethical. John Fannin, curator of the Provincial Museum in Victoria, went into the head of Black Creek after elk at the end of October 1890. Sam Cliffe's Lorne Hotel letterhead advertised, in 1891, "Good Accommodation for Families and Hunting Parties," and Royal Navy officers went out for bears, elk, deer, and cougar up the Colonization Road, sometimes hiring Horace Smith as a guide.[27]

---

[25] Carwithen to Blaksley, 29 August 1880, Carwithen Correspondence.

[26] Carwithen to Blaksley, 23 May 1882, 2 December 1885, 8 December 1887, Carwithen Correspondence.

[27] *Comox Argus*, 11 April 1940; Nunns Diary, 30 October 1890; Edith McNish, "Livery Stables in the Comox Valley," in Isenor, "The Comox Valley;" *The Cumberland News*, 5 June 1901; 12 June 1901.

Within feet of every road and fence began Eric Duncan's "Wilderness Profound:" the dense, silent, unlit forest. A visitor to the Colonization Road noted the "intense loneliness of the place," which generated a feeling of "pleasure mixed with awe." Several settlers got lost in the wilderness, sometimes harmlessly and sometimes tragically. In December 1890, Drabble was staying with Campbell River settler Fred Nunns when, Nunns wrote in his diary, "A man named McDaniels came in midday. He belongs to a party trapping and got lost and found his way out to beach." In the same year Nunns himself got lost on a deer-hunting excursion and spent half a day getting back to his house. "Forgot compass and got astray," he commented. In his surveys Drabble noted places where the bush was really thick: in August 1891, when surveying Robert Mountain's claim near Little River, he noted a "Dense growth of Willow Alder & Scrub brush," "Thick Brush," and "Devil's Puzzle."[28]

Newcomers seemed especially vulnerable. One of them was Eric Duncan's father Robert. "My father was fifty-three when he left Shetland in 1883," Eric Duncan stated, "and it was a great and undesirable change for a man who had never previously seen a tree; in fact he was like an old tree transplanted, he never could adapt himself to his new surroundings. He even got lost in a half-acre wood lot in one of the fields, and I had to hunt him out of it when he did not turn up for dinner."[29]

Four early settlers got very lost: two of their bodies were recovered and two were never found. They were Charles Belas, Annie Fitzgerald, Jack Rowe, and George Grieve. Belas, a settler west of Courtenay River, was lost while hunting deer in November 1888. A search party was organized. William Duncan spent five days looking for him. Indians found his body in the river on 29 December.[30] Mary Harmston recorded the events in her diary:

> 8 November 1888. "Fine. Mr. Belas went out hunting yesterday had not returned at dark tonight party have been out looking for him more are going tomorrow."
>
> 9 November. "Rain. A.M. fine. Twenty or more men been hunting for Belus he is not found yet."
>
> 10 November. "Stormy. Mr. Belus not found several wild stories but what is true is not known."

[28] Milligan, "Fourth Prize Article;" Nunns Diary, 27 September and 1 December 1890; env. 90.

[29] *From Shetland to Vancouver Island*, p. 179.

[30] William Duncan Diary, 29 December 1889.

11 November. "Dull. Men still out Hunting for Belas not found."

12 November. "Fine. Still hunting for Belas."

13 November. "Fine. Have heard nothing of Belas today."

17 November. "Belus not heard of."

30 December. "The remains of Belus found in the River yesterday."

5 February 1889. "Mrs. Belus had a Sale."

A few years later, Belas's neighbour Jack Rowe went astray in the woods behind Cumberland and was never found.[31]

Scots-born Annie Fitzgerald, mother of Joe Fitzgerald the timber cruiser, got lost while berry picking in the summer of 1892 near the Colonization Road. The *Courtenay Weekly News* reported the discovery of her remains three years later:

> She was quite aged and nearly blind and had gone out blackberrying. She was last seen alive between 4 and 5 o'clock on the day she was lost, on the road between Harry Grieve's and Joe Grieve's, by one of Mr. Beech's boys. Alarmed at her not returning search parties were organized and the woods scoured in all directions. The search was kept up for two or three days but without result. All sorts of surmises found adherents, but not the slightest clue could be obtained.
>
> Some time after a large haystack was removed to satisfy some who thought it might reveal a mystery. A little over a year ago an attempt was made to organize another search party, but it resulted in no great effort, as it was deemed useless.
>
> The mystery remained unsolved until last Sunday morning when young Johnny Beech, son of William Beech of Grantham, while out hunting, accidentally stumbled upon her remains, near the road above described. A fire had burnt over the place and nothing was left but a ghastly pile of blackened bones, her shoes still in form and recognizable, and her pail in which she was gathering her berries.[32]

The final incident occurred in May 1909, when eighty-two year old George Grieve—who had built the first threshing machine in the valley—started out "one fine day" to visit his married daughter. His granddaughter Audrey Menzies told me that his daughter-in-law hung a pair of heavy grey underwear over the warming oven, saying "He'll be cold when he comes in." He never reached his destination. Hundreds

---

[31] For Roe or Rowe see identification on Lorne Hotel group photograph, Comox 1888 or 1889, CDMA 141.

[32] Union *Weekly News*, 3 December 1895. See also Carroll, *Wild Roses and Rail Fences*, p. 33; Mildred Haas, "The Fitzgeralds," in Isenor, "The Comox Valley;" Anderson to Hussey, 5 December 1895, British Columbia, Provincial Police Force, Correspondence In-ward, 1891-1910.

of people and a bloodhound could not find him. "Everybody knew him, and he was hunted for months, both by concerted bands and singly, and rewards were offered, but all in vain," Eric Duncan recalled. What was strange was that Grieve, an old setter from New Brunswick, was quite used to the bush. "Little that was new to him could any one tell the wiry old woodsman about the woods, yet he walked into them one day . . . and was never seen or heard of more."[33]

[33] *From Shetland to Vancouver Island,* p. 199; "Early Days and Early Settlers;" Interview with Audrey Menzies, 12 April 1994; Audrey Menzies, "George Grieve," in Isenor, "The Comox Valley."

CHAPTER 17

Across the Gulf

> And went a day and a night
> until, becalmed,
> sails wet and slack,
> we lay off a third island,
> which was the same one
> in a different place.

FROM *The Emissaries*, by Robin Skelton[1]

THE 1880s and 1890s witnessed a great increase in interest in the northern Gulf of Georgia region. By 1888 Dunsmuir had obtained a massive land grant, completed the Esquimalt and Nanimo Railway, and embarked on a new coal mine. There was every possibility that he would extend the railway to Comox. Accessible shoreline timber stocks in the southern part of the Gulf were depleted, and south coast lumbermen obtained massive timber leases in the north which provided them with fodder for their sawmills. Cannery owners began to exploit the salmon runs of the central coast. Logging, fishing, and mining interests required land, and their managers and workers staked claims. Fewer settlers wanted land for strictly agricultural purposes. The best land in the river valleys around the Gulf basin had already been pre-empted, and the remaining land was too rocky, too swampy, or too densely forested for large-scale farming. Drabble's favourite adjective for the agricultural quality of the land he surveyed in the Gulf was "worthless." An 1860s Comox farmer, he knew good land when he saw it.

Regardless of the reasons that people wanted land—and regardless of the agricultural theory that lay behind the pre-emption laws—all settlers had to conform to the minimum agricultural requirements of the 1884 Land Act, for without doing so they could not obtain their Certificates of Improvement. Settlers used the pre-emption law to get the land they wanted, and ultimately they contributed to the local

---

[1] Skelton, *Landmarks*, p. 29.

economy in a number of ways unrelated to farming. In practice, few settlers did more than clear an acre or two for garden and livestock— enough for a subsistence life supplemented by the riches of the intertidal zone.

Geologist George Dawson had discerned the general character of settlement in the Gulf of Georgia in May 1878 when he sailed to Nanaimo through the "beautiful little islands" of the southern Gulf. The islands, he noted, were forested, "with occasional little patches of prairie & grass-grown points":

> There is, however, with all very little soil on these islands & few of them are suited for anything but the maintenance of a few sheep or Cattle. Here & there a settlers house may be seen on some spot of good land, also an occasional little establishment for the trying of Dog-fish & many a little Shanty & potato patch of the Indians, whose canoe may be Seen with a little bag like sail shooting before the wind from one island to another.[2]

The settlers of the 1880s and 1890s had the same two basic priorities as Native people: shelter and fresh water. They selected their pre-emptions on rivers or creeks, or on land with a fresh-water spring. In the absence of roads they chose land in protected bays and at the mouths of navigable rivers. The pre-emption act did not allow settlers to claim land occupied by Native people, but several claims contained abandoned "Indian Houses" that Drabble faithfully marked in his field notes. Such sites possessed fresh water and the level, well-drained land characteristic of village sites. Settlers also found advantages in pre-empting land near Indian reserves: Native people offered work and trade. Michael Manson, for example, established a trading post at his Cortes Island pre-emption in 1882 and did a profitable business there for fifteen years.[3]

As a private surveyor Drabble was busiest between 1887 and 1892— the peak years of the Dunsmuir boom. In December 1890 he was a founding member of the Association of Provincial Land Surveyors of British Columbia. In a typical year he made three or four surveying trips into the Gulf. The rest of the time he was at home in Comox—surveying in the valley or up the Colonization Road, holding court and investigating cases, laying out townsite subdivisions, and corresponding with the government on land and legal affairs.

Drabble's surveying territory extended far beyond the Colonization Road to include the coastline and islands on both sides of the Gulf— from Lund and Texada islands in the east to Nanoose and Qualicum in

---

[2] Cole and Lockner, *To the Charlottes*, p. 14.

[3] Manson, "Sketches;" Walbran, *British Columbia Coast Names*, p. 317.

the south and Quadra Island and Quatsino Sound in the north. He was the only surveyor north of Nanaimo, and when people needed his services they asked him to visit when he was next in their neighbourhood. He had many advantages over surveyors in Nanaimo and Victoria: he lived locally and knew the region, he was trustworthy and efficient, knew instantly what land had been alienated and what was still Crown land, and kept the land records at Comox.

For a typical Gulf survey, Drabble rented a canoe at Comox for fifty or seventy-five cents a day. He hired both Indian and "White" assistants on his surveys; he paid them $1.50 and between $2 and $2.50 a day respectively. His Native workers from Comox included Frank, "Indian Tom," and "Indian Dick," and among his many settler assistants were George Curtis, Alfred Radford, and Robert Swan. Most pre-emptions took two to three days to survey, and his overall charge in the 1880s was $5 a day.

His assistants tended to be young unmarried men in need of cash for starting their own farms. He treated them, in a sense, like protégés or

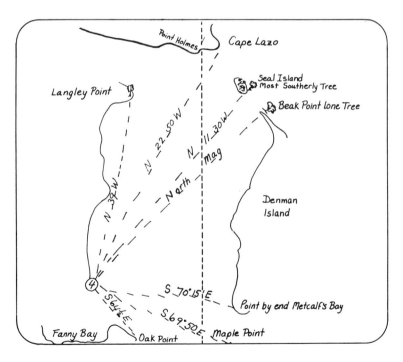

Bearings from Alexander Garven's pre-emption,
Baynes Sound, April 1884.

even sons. He set them up in the kind of land they wanted. One of them was architect George Curtis, who had arrived in Comox with Horace Smith in 1886. Curtis's son told me that his father was Drabble's chainman, and that surveying for him was a "bread and butter stop-gap measure." Drabble hired Curtis to survey around Comox in 1892, and in May of that year he employed him at his office.[4]

Drabble assigned permanent section or lot numbers to all the land he surveyed, and he obliterated Native cultural, spiritual, or economic sites beneath a cartographic grid of squares, rectangles, and straight lines. By 1900 the official map of the northern Gulf was a mass of lines, lots, leases, licences, and numbers assigned by surveyors for settlers and businessmen intent on extracting wealth from the land. Between them, or on their edges, were tiny lots marked "I.R." for Indian Reserve—ridiculously small allotments awarded to First Nations people by self-interested or greedy colonial authorities. Most Indian Reserves, shamefully, were smaller than the average pre-emption.

His surveys took him south to Baynes Sound, where in 1884 he surveyed adjacent pre-emptions for Alex Garven and Dan Sullivan near the Perseverance mining claim. Both men located on their land in June 1876 in connection with the arrival of the Baynes Sound Coal Company. In 1886, on J. B. Holmes's pre-emption south of the Perseverance claim, Drabble recorded a skid road, "Piercy Ox Shed," "Piercy's Rollway," "Shed Road," and "Piercys Cook House," showing that the New Brunswick logger Thomas Piercy had been active in the region.[5]

He surveyed the first pre-emptions on Denman and Hornby islands in the 1870s and also laid out the first roads there. When editor Whitney visited Hornby in 1892 he found settlers working hard at transforming a few acres of their forest and swamp into farmland: for example, of 304 acres pre-empted in 1879, William Heatherbell had "rescued from the forest" forty or fifty acres; Tom Williams had cleared twenty of 153 acres pre-empted in 1884; William Sutton had a large clearing on his 120 acres; John Howe "a large opening" in his 160-acre pre-emption. Two farmers were luckier and possessed good natural open pasture: D.L Herbert of England owned Henry Maude's old property of 1,050 acres with thirty acres cleared and "any amount" of pasture and George Ford had about 1,000 acres, of which 200 were in shape for use, besides much pasture.[6]

---

4 Env. 101; Mackie and Mackie, "Roughing it in the Colonies."

5 Envs. 72, 92, Drabble Papers.

6 Courtenay *Weekly News*, 8 February 1893; Murray, *Homesteads and Snug Harbours*, pp. 172-75.

Across Baynes Sound from Denman, Drabble surveyed a lot at Fanny Bay for Alex Urquhart, who sold out to Ontarian Alex Cowie in the mid-1880s. Cowie in turn brought out many relations, and Drabble laid out the Fanny Bay and Deep Bay pre-emptions of the extended Cowie family. At Deep Bay, he surveyed for John Ash and for John Murdock and Nanaimo hotel-keeper John Jenkins. He recorded a "Deserted Indian House" on a small cove on the waterfront, and nearby an ox shed left behind by New Brunswick logger John Graham. At Deep Bay and Mud Bay he surveyed lots for J. Shaw, Ezra Cook, James Rosewall, and William Grove, and at Qualicum he laid out the claims of Nanaimo miners S. B. and Archibald Hamilton.[7]

His government work took Drabble further down the Gulf. "Oil Stove tobacco butter coffee Plates & Kettles Frying pan," he wrote in a memo before leaving Comox in September 1887 on a survey of the proposed Qualicum-Baynes Sound trail. He finished the survey on the last day of October, and then he drew up the specifications for "Qualicum Trail commencing North of Niles." He referred here to Philip Niles, "labourer." The Qualicum Road of Drabble's day is now the Island Highway between Qualicum Bay and Deep Bay, and a highway bridge still crosses Nile Creek.[8]

In February and March 1885 Drabble worked at Nanoose for John Enos, Frank Bilboa, and James Hamilton. Bilboa's claim, he wrote, was

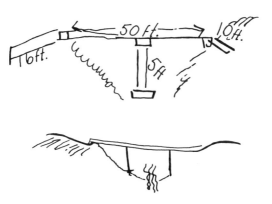

"Qualicum Train north of Niles," October 1887.
Sketches of bridges needed on Comox-Qualicum trail.

[7] Ens. 44, 61, 78, 91, 101, 109, 114, Drabble Papers.

[8] Ibid., env. 91

"situate on the Sea Shore a little south east of Schooner Cove." His survey for Enos showed a house, orchard, stable, barn, garden, fence, hayfield, and boat house. He took bearings from one of the Ballenas Islands and drew a curious sketch of man in a canoe in Schooner Cove beneath the Vancouver Island mountains.[9]

In June 1889 Drabble moved out into the Gulf to survey Sangster Island for English-born mining entrepreneur Morris Moss of Victoria. He took bearings from the Nanaimo Lighthouse, Mt. Arrowsmith and the "Gable end of Hirsts farm house Englishman River." In October, he left Comox on another survey for Moss. He spent a night at John Piket's on Denman and another at James Rosewall's at Deep Bay, and surveyed an unnamed island near Norris Rock, Hornby Island, for David Hoggan —Glaswegian, miner, and speculator, and for Moss he surveyed an

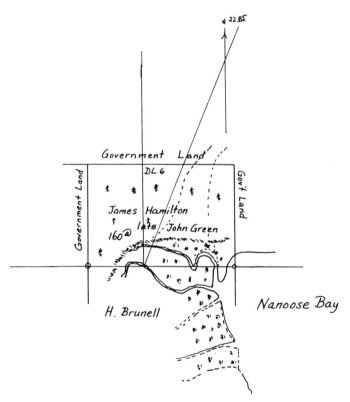

Survey of James Hamilton's pre-emption claim,
Nanoose Bay, 7 February 1885.

---

[9] Joseph Enos Diary, 14 January–6 February 1885, BCARS; envs. 44, 84, 85, 86.

Man in canoe, probably at Schooner Cove, Gulf of Georgia, sketched by Drabble at conclusion of Survey for Frank Bilbooa, Nanoose Bay, February 1885.

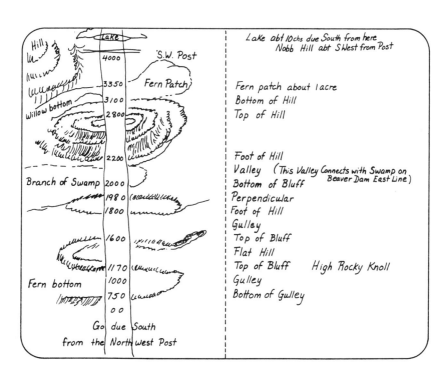

Part of Survey for John Enos, Nanoose Bay, March 1885.

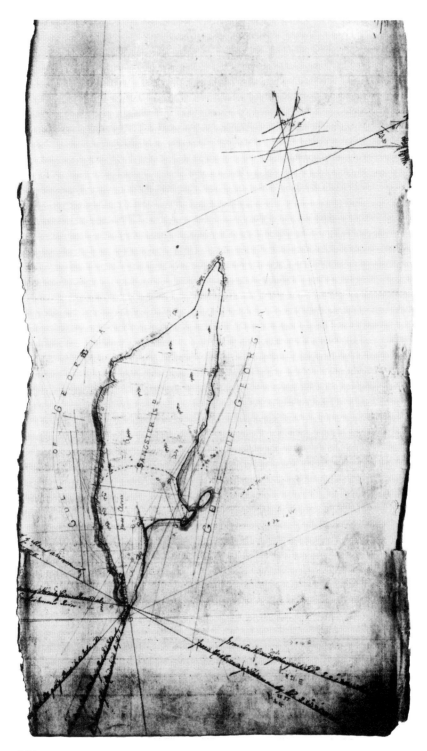

254

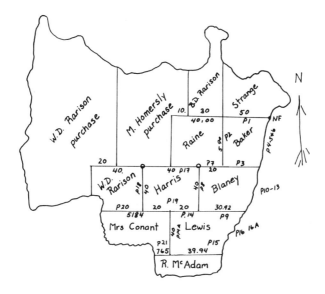

Drabble's survey of pre-emption and purchases
on Hernando Island, Gulf of Georgia, June 1894.

island in Tucker Bay on Lasqueti Island across from William Jeffries'
house. Jeffries had deserted his ship in the early 1860s and explored the
Gulf of Georgia in a large, sail-equipped canoe.[10]

Rich mining properties existed throughout the Gulf, and in the
Drabble Papers are notes of an 1874 survey at Gillies Bay, Texada Island.
"Magnetic needle no use on account of iron," Drabble wrote. Utah
Mines worked an open pit mine here for fifteen or twenty years. In 1878
Drabble returned to Texada to survey a marble quarry at Blubber Bay
for Captain Henry Sturt of Nanaimo on behalf of the Texada Marble
Company, but at the end of his rough notes he wrote: "I think the whole
affair is a bilk"—a swindle.[11]

In 1891 Drabble visited three locations on the far side of the Gulf:
Hernando Island, Savary Island, and Lund. Before his June trip to
Hernando—south of Cortes—he made a note to buy "1 Tin Mustard 1
Tin pepper 1 Tin Coffee 5 lbs Rice 1 Sack Oatmeal Peaches Canned
Meat 2 lbs Currants Candied Peel." He visited the claims of C. N. Baker,
William Blaney, William Harris, Richard Lewis, and Ellen Conant at the
south end of the island. He took bearings from "the most easterly visible
Tree on Cape Lazo" and from the then-unnamed "peak of remarkable

[10] Envs. 66, 109; Walbran, *British Columbia Coast Names*, pp. 343-44; Murray, *Homesteads and Snug Harbours*, p. 134; Elda Copley Mason, *Lasqueti Island: History & Memory* (Victoria: Morriss Printing, c. 1991), pp. 4-5.

[11] Envs. 34, 93, 128; Murray, *Homesteads and Snug Harbours*, pp. 151-53.

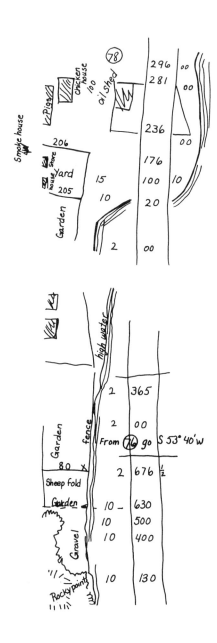

Part of survey of John Green's land,
Savary Island, July 1891.

Rough sketch of pre-emption claims at Lund,
September 1891.

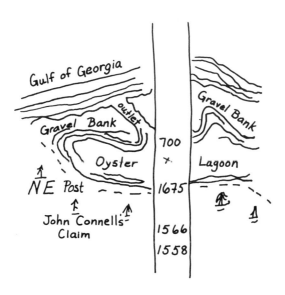

Part of survey of lagoon at Oyster Bay, Vancouver Island,
July 1890. John Connell's pre-emption.

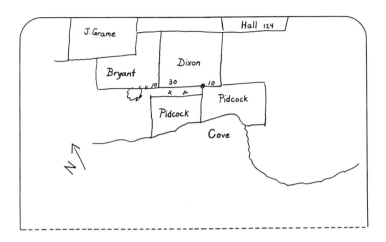

Pre-emptions at Quathiaski Cove,
Quadra Island, September 1885.

Cone shaped Mountain over NE point of Hernando Isld" (known, since the 1930s, as Mt. Dalgleish). These claims were densely forested and unsuited for farming: Baker's survey included thick timber, a deep water swamp, and a small garden patch near False Passage where he grew potatoes and corn. Blaney's claim contained "poor soil," Lewis's contained "Sandy Soil thinly timbered," and Harris's a "Side Hill dense growth of Sallal." At the end of the survey he noted that Blaney of the Hastings Saw Mill Company wanted to pre-empt a quarter section of land on Mink Island in Desolation Sound.[12]

Drabble, in July 1891, worked on Savary Island for settler and trader John Green. Born in England, "Jack" Green had farmed at Nanoose until the 1880s when he crossed the Gulf to Savary. Drabble was not impressed with Savary's ubiquitous sand and dubious agricultural value. He did a swift traverse of the entire island, setting up seventy-seven survey stations on the beach. He catalogued "Worthless Sand," "Sand bluffs 100 ft.," and crossed the island in the middle where he noted "Sand Knolls & bottoms covered with Sallal and stunted red Fir & small bull pines, worthless for farming land." He sketched Green's oil shed, chicken house, pig shed, store, yard, garden, fence, and sheep fold, all on the western shore of Savary.[13]

Two years later, Green's rustic life came to a sudden end. "On Savary Island lived an old man by the name of John Green," explained the *Colonist* in 1894, "Several hundred acres of land used to pasture a flock

---

[12] Envs. 36, 45, 69, Drabble Papers.

[13] *Ibid.*, envs. 36, 69.

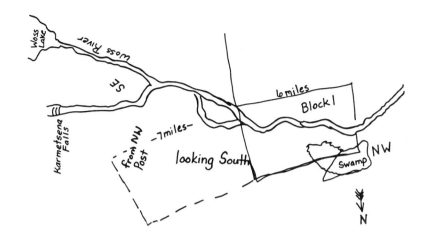

Block 1 and 2, Nimpkish River northeast of Woss Lake, July 1884.

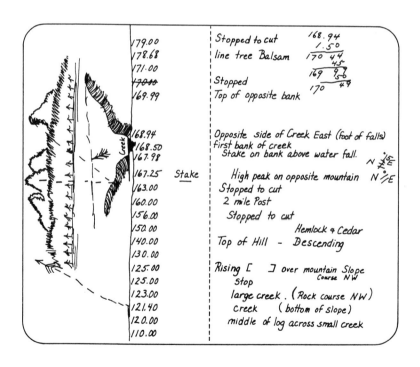

Part of Block 1, Nimpkish River, 30 July 1884.

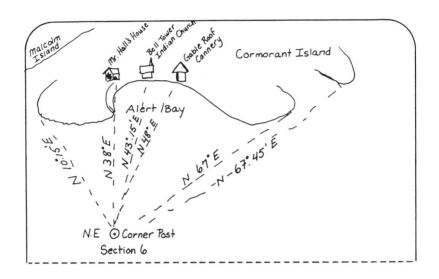

Bearings taken from Section 6, Broughton Strait,
to Cormorant Island and Alert Bay, October 1884.
Part of survey at mouth of Nimpkish River
for the Alert Bay Cannery Company (S. A. Spenser).

"Pass through mountains looking north from Karmetsena Falls,"
21 August 1884.

of sheep, and a small store stocked with goods for Indian trade, furnished him with a means of livelihood. Many years ago Green lost money by the failure of a bank, and from that time never trusted to anything but his own strong box." Rumours of his secret cache spread through the Gulf, and in November 1892 he was visited by Hugh Lynn, the shiftless son of a respectable Royal Engineer. For years Lynn had canoed and rowed the inside waters between Seymour Inlet and New Westminster. He killed Green for his money and crossed the Gulf to Little River, north of Comox, leaving a trail of evidence which led to his capture. After a widely publicized trial he was hanged for murder in August 1894.[14]

Early in September 1891 Drabble left Comox in a sloop for the settlement of Lund, founded two years earlier by Charles Thulin, a twenty-six year old Swede. Son of a farmer, Thulin reached Winnipeg via the United States in 1886 and found work with the C.P.R. He came to Burrard Inlet in the same year and helped build the line between Port Moody and Vancouver. He hand-logged on the mainland coast, and in 1889 he pre-empted land at a sheltered little bay which he named Lund after the ancient Swedish university town. Soon he was joined by his Swedish fiancée and by his younger brother Frederick. Drabble spent the whole of September 1891 surveying pre-emption claims at Lund for the Thulin brothers, Albert Hansen, Charles Nelson, Alfred Swanson, and William Thomas. Charles Thulin's claim included a cabin, wharf, "chicken Kraal," and "2 Indian Houses;" his brother's claim included an alder bottom, potato patches, stores, a root house, a pig pen, and an "Indian House" surrounded by a potato patch. Swanson's claim contained what Drabble called "worthless broken Country."[15]

The Colonization Road led to Campbell River and beyond. Its completion brought a small rush of settlers to the river and creek mouths between Oyster Bay and Campbell River. In 1887 Drabble surveyed the claims of William Tree, James Knight, and Joseph Stewart at Shelter Point, all of whom had met the minimum agricultural requirements — partly chopped forests, partially drained swamps, log houses, small barns, chicken houses. North of Oyster River at "Kukashon" or "Koohushon" Point he found James McIvor, John Connell, and logger David Anderson. McIvor had been shipwrecked at the mouth of the

---

[14] Victoria *Daily Colonist*, 24 August 1894; Ian Kennedy, *Sunny Sandy Savary. A History of Savary Island 1792-1992* (Vancouver: Kennell Publishing, 1992), pp. 38-52; Courtenay *Weekly News*, 8 November 1893; British Columbia, Attorney General, Correspondence, 1872-1937; Anderson to Hussey, 23 and 30 November 1893, British Columbia, Provincial Police Force, Correspondence Inward, 1891-1910; Frederick Hussey Scrapbook, 1887-1901.

[15] Env. 51; Mitchell, *Diamond in the Rough*, pp. 98-100.

Oyster River, and liked the location so much that he built a cabin and staked a claim. He cleared seven acres next to the river. In July 1890 Drabble took a bearing from Mt. Dalgleish—"Remarkable Cone Shaped Mountain across Gulf in Coast Range." Connell's claim at the "Oyster Pond" is now Salmon Point Resort; Anderson's pre-emption between McIvor and Connell is now the University of British Columbia's farm on the Island Highway. In 1891 Drabble surveyed the Willow Point pre-emption of logger Andy Galarno, across from Cape Mudge on the shore of Discovery Passage.[16]

Early in 1889 the few settlers beyond Oyster Bay petitioned the government to complete the final sixteen miles of the Colonization Road to Campbell River. This road was built by John Berkeley and his crew in December 1890, and the Oyster River bridge was finished the following year.[17]

With the road open to Campbell River, Drabble was asked to survey there. He surveyed lots for William McKeon and Edward Barton Hill, and laid out a lot on the river for the Nunns brothers from Ireland— Jack, Fred, and Lawrence—of whom only thirty-year old Fred stayed permanently. Fred's letters from Wonderfontein, Groot Marico, South Africa, back to his family in Dublin show his agricultural ambitions. "Jack and I are off to British Columbia via Australia," he wrote in 1887; "Jack's and my plan about going to Columbia is to start farming and if we do any good get the rest of you to join us." Level delta land surrounded the river mouth, but rock, swamp, and forest dominated, and Campbell River was known from the beginning not for its farms but for its salmon and timber.[18]

Drabble appointed Fred Nunns a Special Constable and later recommended him for the position of Justice of the Peace. In return, Nunns kept track of legal and other matters in his diary:

26 November 1890. Wednesday. "Heard a steamer whistling in afternoon."

27 November 1890. Thursday. "Blowing. Drabble is over at the Cove. He sent word over for Jack Quocksusta to come over for him but it was blowing too hard."

28 November 1890. Friday. "Jack went over to Cove to fetch Drabble but returned without him but is to take his things over for him tomorrow."

---

16 Envs. 31, 41, 53, 55, 56, 62, 68, 139, Drabble Papers; Mildred Haas, "One Kind Deed of the Loved Piercys," in Isenor, "The Comox Valley."

17 Fred Nunns to Ernest Nunns, 31 March 1889, in Nunns Correspondence; Fred Nunns Diary, 23 July 1890; *From Shetland to Vancouver Island*, pp. 177-78.

18 Envs. 10, 11; Fred Nunns to unidentified, n.d., *c.* 1887; Nunns to Ernest Nunns, 2 March 1887, Nunns Miscellaneous Correspondence; D. E. Isenor, E. G. Stephens, D. E. Watson, eds., *Edge of Discovery A History of the Campbell River District* (Campbell River: Ptarmigan Press, 1989).

29 November 1890. Saturday. "Drabble came over midday. Good news. Dunsmuir won't sell any more lands and the Island Railroad is to be connected in spring."

∾

14 January 1891. "Tom Quacksusta came and told me his father had been stabbed by another Siwash in a drunken row. Sent him over to Drabble who is still at Bob Hall's."

16 January 1891. "Jack Quacksusta came back. He says Tom and George went over to Comox with Drabble to bring up Anderson the policeman. Also says the man who stabbed Quacksusta has given him 2 large canoes and some blankets to stay proceedings."

21 January 1891. "Anderson the policeman from Comox has been up and taken down the man that stabbed Capt. John."

30 January 1891. "The man who stabbed Capt. John was fined $22 but Capt. John had to return canoe and blankets so I expect he is sorry he had him arrested."

In the 1890s Campbell River attracted settlers like Englishman John Peacey from the Comox Valley. He bought Hill's ranch in 1892 for $1,500, and he and his family cleared seven or eight acres and sold their produce to passing ships. They left after a few years of torment by cougars and bears, which terrorized their livestock despite all precautions.[19]

Campbell River also achieved early fame for its salmon. "The Salmon fishing is excellent," Nunns wrote; "Salmon have been caught, hand trolling, up to 80 lbs. while 50 lbs. are every day occurence." One Campbell River fishing fanatic was Irish baronet Sir Richard Musgrave, who in September 1890 was taken up to Salmon River by Sam Cliffe. A year later Musgrave married Robert Dunsmuir's daughter Jessie, but to the end of his days, Terry Reksten writes, "he would recall as the proudest moment of his life the autumn afernoon on Vancouver Island's Salmon River when he had landed a 70-pound salmon, 'the biggest salmon ever killed with a rod and line.'"[20]

For most of his northern surveys Drabble walked up the Colonization Road to Fred Nunns' place and took a canoe to Quadra Island; sometimes he took a steamer from Comox right to Cape Mudge or Quathiaski Cove. As elsewhere, he hired Native assistants; in August 1882, for example, he hired Thomas and Nimnin to survey Gowlland and Drew Harbours for $1.50 a day. In later years he hired employees of the

---

[19] Fred Nunns Diary, 4, 22 April 1892; Mitchell, *Diamond in the Rough*, p. 90; Hunter to Peacey, 16 October 1893, in Joseph Hunter, Correspondence Outward, August 1893–November 1900.

[20] Nunns, Miscellaneous Correspondence; Reksten, *The Dunsmuir Saga*, p. 129.

lumbermen who worked in the region in the 1880s and 1890s: Sayward of Victoria, Hendry of New Westminster, King and Casey of Comox, and others.[21]

Logging was the main reason for the settlement of Quadra Island — known until 1903 as Valdes Island. In 1890 there were two settlers at Campbell River (Nunns and Hill) and about fifteen on Quadra Island — including Captain Clarke, Thomas Earle, Reginald Pidcock, John Smith, Robert Hall, King and Casey, Cornelius Bowater, John Wilson, Thomas Leask, and Alfred and Walter Joyce. These settlers occupied most of the available land on Gowlland Harbour, Quathiaski Cove, Drew Harbour, Hyacinthe Bay, and along Sutil Channel. Drabble surveyed pre-emptions at Duncan Bay for H. B. Roycraft and John Kirkup, Lewis Casey, N. P. Snowdon, for the partnership of Tompkins, Grant, and McLeod, for Michael King, and one for himself and John Wilson.[22]

Most of these men were connected in some way with logging, though they also did just enough to prove their pre-emptions. In 1890 and 1891, for example, Drabble filed Certificates of Improvement for John Smith, Robert Hall, and Cornelius Bowater on Quadra. These show that the minimum improvement of $2.50 an acre (that is, $400 for a 160 acre pre-emption) was barely being met on this rocky and difficult island:

> John Smith, December 1890. "Log House 21 × 12 $ 50. 2 acres of land Cleared & seeded 60. 8 acres Slashed & part burnt 96. Fencing 300 Rods 58. Road Cutting — 1 month 60. Well digging 60. 58 chs draining 3 × 3 — 174. 24 chs [drains] 2 × 2½ 48. [Total]: $606."

> Robert Hall, December 1890. "1½ acre Cleared & seeded $120. 4½ acres Slashed 72. House 22 × 17 heavy Logs 150. Ditch — 10$. Cutting down Timber near House 50. [Total]: 400."

> Cornelius Bowater, c. 5 May 1891. "C. Bowaters Imps. House 22 × 17 hewed logs $120. 6 acres Slashed 72. 3 acres cleared [@] 50 [=] 150. Ditching 25. Timber cutting down near House. 20." [Total: $387].[23]

Many settlers kept chickens, which did not require rich soil for their sustenance and lived on household scraps, and Drabble recorded an egg recipe in one of his Quadra Island field books: "To preserve Eggs," he wrote; "½ peck Slaked lime. 5 Pails full of Water. 3 quarts of Salt.

---

[21] Env. 29; King's 1886 application in Nunns, Miscellaneous Correspondence, 1888; Mitchell, *Diamond in the Rough*, p. 79; Nunns Diary, 23 June 1890, 12 March 1892.

[22] Walbran, *British Columbia Coast Names*, p. 407; Nunns, Miscellaneous Correspondence, CRMA; for Drabble's Quadra and Duncan Bay surveys see envs. 1, 4, 5, 7, 8, 9, 10, 24, 29, 30, 31, 32, 35, and 140; for his maps and pre-emption certificates see envs. 2, 12, 15, 16, 17, 19, 20, 21, and 22, Drabble Papers.

[23] Envs. 7, 21, 68, Drabble Papers.

Stir and only use the liquid without sediment. Place in earthenware Jars not full with Eggs least they may be left uncovered with liquid & Spoil."[24]

Drabble, as Justice of the Peace, figured in cases involving the very settlers and loggers whose pre-emptions he had surveyed. In June 1893 an American fugitive named Jack Myers or Meares, travelling under the name Ben Kennedy, murdered logger John O'Connor on Read Island, near Quadra. Kennedy, who was rumoured to have worked with the Jesse James gang, was captured the next month at a cabin on Ramsay Arm. He was taken to Comox, where Drabble held a preliminary examination before sending him on to a superior court at New Westminster. In November he was sentenced to life in prison for the murder of O'Connor.[25]

Another notorious incident occurred in October 1894, when John Smith of Quadra murdered Christian Benson of Read Island for paying inappropriate attention to his wife. Benson was last seen alive on Read Island on 9 October; his body was found three weeks later floating in his half-submerged rowboat. Smith, it turned out, had clubbed Benson to death. He refused to let the police talk to his wife in private, but in June 1895, when he finally went to work in Dineen's logging camp on Quadra, the police interviewed Mrs. Smith. She confessed the whole story. "Smith acknowledged his guilt to his wife and threatened to kill her if she gave him away, and said he would not be taken alive by the police." The police arrested Smith in his bed at a Quadra shanty and took him to Comox, where Drabble committed him to the nearest court of competent jurisdiction. "The prisoner is an elderly man," wrote the *Free Press*, "probably 50 years of age." "Mrs Smith is fully 40 years old and is by no means good looking." Smith was tried in Vancouver in November 1895 for Benson's murder, but he was discharged by the jury. "Smith killed Benson in a fit of uncontrollable passion," editor Whitney observed, "aroused by the visual evidence of great wrong. He had no right to take the law into his own hands, but even a British Columbia jury will not convict a man who strikes down the villain who destoys the sanctity of his home."[26]

Drabble worked for wealthy capitalists even further afield than Quadra. In the summer and fall of 1884 he made the longest survey trip of his career. He and his assistants Phillip Goepel, Thomas Miller, and

---

24 *Ibid.*, env. 7.

25 British Columbia, Attorney General, Correspondence, 1872-1937; British Columbia, Attorney-General, Inquisitions, 1872-1937; British Columbia, Attorney General, Documents, 1857-1966; British Columbia, Provincial Police Force, Correspondence Inward, 1891-1910; Courtenay *Weekly News*, 19 July 1893, 16 August 1893, 15 November 1893; McKelvie, "The 'S' Sign," pp. 56-59; Hussey Scrapbook.

26 *The Weekly News*, 25 June and 26 November 1895; Nanaimo *Free Press*, 21 June 1895.

Skillen left Comox on 5 July and sailed to Johnstone Strait, facing strong headwinds all the way. A week later they reached Fort Rupert, where Drabble was welcomed by George Blenkinsop (1822-1904), apparently an old acquaintance. A Native of Cornwall, Blenkinsop was then Indian Agent at Fort Rupert, but he had been on the coast for forty years. He had lived at Victoria, where he gave his name to Blenkinsop Valley.[27]

At Alert Bay, Drabble and his party hired assistants Ko-mah-laglees, Kileoquits, and Charley, and canoed up the Nimpkish River to Nimpkish Lake. Beyond Nimpkish Lake the river was then known as the Ne-nahl gace River. Drabble called it a "Survey of Land on the 'Ne-nahl gace' River for Mr. Dupont & other Americans." He drew maps showing the location of Block 1, a proposed timber lease on the Nimpkish just west of Woss Lake, but after several weeks he abandoned his survey, "the Land and Timber being worthless." Block 2, in the Woss River area, was not much better: "Land worthless & Timber principally Hemlock." On 17 September he made his way back down to Broughton Strait via the Ne-nahl gace River, passing "Blenkinsops Camp," Kisnogyawlah Falls, and Karmetsina Falls.[28]

At the mouth of the Nimpkish, in October 1884, he worked for S. A. Spenser of the Alert Bay Cannery Company. Here Spenser claimed the old village site of the Nimpkish River Indians, who a few years before had moved to Alert Bay. Drabble began his survey at a deserted house on the left bank of Nimpkish near a "disused Indian Village." He noted an Indian carved post and an "Old Mound formerly built upon, no inhabited Houses." He took bearings to Alert Bay, where he noted "Mr. Halls House, Bell Tower, Indian Church, Gable Roof, Cannery." Drabble returned to Comox on 15 October 1884, having been away for three and a half months.[29]

In the spring of 1890 Drabble embarked on a second ambitious northern survey, this time of mineral properties on the west coast of Vancouver Island for Nanaimo businessmen John Bryden and W. A. Lindsay. Bryden—who had married Elizabeth, another of Dunsmuir's many daughters—was manager of Dunsmuir's mine at Wellington. Drabble and George Curtis left Nanaimo on the steamer *Skidegate*, reached Fort Rupert on 17 May 1890, and arrived at Winter Harbour

---

[27] Richard Mackie, "George Blenkinsop," in Cook, *Dictionary of Canadian Biography* Vol. 12, pp. 87-89.

[28] Env. 28, book 1; env. 27, books 1, 2, 3, and 4; Walbran, *British Columbia Coast Names,* pp. 276-77, 357; on Goepel see Carwithen to Blaksley, 24 February 1884, Carwithen Correspondence.

[29] Env. 28, book 2, pp. 1-13; Cole and Lockner, *To the Charlottes,* p. 17.

two weeks later, having been windbound at Cape Sutil and San Josef. At Winter Harbour they met Ah witte, Chief of the Quatsino. They surveyed five small islands in Koprino Harbour and a small island "opposite Koprino Indian Houses" for Bryden and Lindsay.

Their five-week expedition nearly behind them, Drabble and Curtis forsook the wretched trip back around Cape Scott, taking instead the overland trail to Fort Rupert. "Left Koprino at 5 am," Drabble wrote; "Arrived at end of Fort Rupert Trail 2 pm packeting Transit about 2 miles ahead and hid under newly chopped Balsam & went back to Camp." On 21 June 1890 he and Curtis caught the steamer *Mystery* for Alert Bay, where they waited for a few days in the rain for the southbound steamer *Boscowitz*. "Wednesday 25," Drabble wrote, "At Alert Bay. Left 2 Books 2 parcels papers 1 Leather Bag with Mr. Blenkinsop." Curtis was a good draftsman and artist, and amused himself on this journey by producing watercolours and sketches of Alert Bay and of the Indian village and old Hudson's Bay Company buildings at Fort Rupert.[30]

Drabble's surveys, then, took him to many obscure parts of the Gulf of Georgia and northern Vancouver Island—places that he considered "worthless" for agricultural purposes, but which were in demand for their other natural wealth, especially their lumber and minerals. In the end he always returned to Comox—the protected little village under the Beauforts where he spent the last difficult decade of his life.

30 Reksten, *The Dunsmuir Saga*, pp. 39, 50; envs. 6, 19, 23; Mackie and Mackie, "Roughing it in the Colonies."

CHAPTER 18

The Rising Tide

Nothing would pry him
loose; no rock
could chip the lip
of the thick shell,
and the tide was rising.

FROM *Last Song,* by Robin Skelton[1]

THE 1890s began on a very positive note. The C.P.R. brought
new immigrants. The industrial era arrived in the valley with the opening of the Union mine. Valley farmers now had a market and the
promise of a railway, and Drabble was busier than ever with his judicial
work and his surveying. The recession that arrived with such force in
1893 and 1894 had a great effect on Drabble. Surveying, his bread and
butter work, suddenly dried up, and Drabble—overextended financially—had to sell his main Comox property. Two men brought lawsuits
against him for improprieties in his land transactions. Both suits were
dismissed, but they brought Drabble's name into disrepute, and he
never recovered financially.

Court, even in the recession, was the best entertainment in town.
During the long wet winters it "helped very materially to relieve the
monotony," as editor Whitney put it. Comox's new courthouse, built
in 1891, was open to the public to the satisfaction of people like
Mary Harmston, who attended religiously and observed Drabble, senior
member of the Comox bench, defend God, Queen, Country, Empire,
and Property against all challengers. In 1893, for example, he gave "two
disorderly Siwashes" "a most severe lecture in regard to the duties that
all British subjects were bound to uphold in carrying out justice." He
heard the case of three seamen from the *J. D. Peters* who had refused to
do their duty: he sent one of the men to prison for a month and the
others for three months. His judgements seem harsh. In what became
known as the "Gilbert-Bean Case" he jailed a man for a month for

---

[1] Skelton, *Landmarks,* p. 48.

stealing a can of beans. Robert Gilbert, commonly known as the painter, was a cook at the Riverside Hotel in Courtenay. Constable Anderson arrested him in Comox with stolen beans and potatoes in his possession and Drabble sent him to jail in Nanaimo for thirty days. The *Colonist* of Victoria and the Nanaimo *Free Press* found this sentence too severe, but Whitney of the *Weekly News* sprang to Drabble's defence:

> The fellow had stolen a lunch of which no complaint was made. He had furthermore proved himself a general sneak thief, pilfering little things for months, for which he should long ago have been sent up. After a while patience ceases to be a virtue, and the can of beans was the last straw that turned the scales. Let it be known also that Mr. Sam Cliff is not an ordinary boarding-house keeper but a first class landlord and proprietor of a first class hotel. The fellow was captured by Officer Anderson with the stolen goods upon him and with a record black as Hades. Queer case for sympathy.[2]

At the busy Comox courthouse—the only one on the north Gulf—Drabble heard cases from Cortes, Quadra, and Campbell River referred to him by justices Manson, Nunns, and Pidcock. He issued a search warrant when a Quadra fisherman named C. Jurgenson had his nets stolen. He fined John Jordan, a settler at Salmon River, $50 for supplying liquor to Indian Mary. In 1894, he and Anderson investigated a case of theft on Camp Island near Cortes. "I wish to call your attention to the fact that Mr. Drabble, who under took the trip cheerfully, had to leave his work to go and has not had a penny for his trouble," Anderson told his boss.[3]

Comox grew so rapidly in the late 1880s that the Anglicans decided to build their own church; St. Andrews at Sandwick was three miles away. Drabble, along with Holmes and others, consituted the building committee for St. Peters, Comox, built between 1890 and 1892. In the spring of 1890 Willie Robb donated the site (lot 39 on Comox townsite). Carpenter Sam Creech got the contract to build the church; Nathaniel Lambert and Horace Smith hauled the lumber from the wharf to the building site. Muirhead and Mann of Victoria supplied the doors, windows, and other specialized church furnishings, and others provided labour and material. Drabble surveyed the lot in March 1891, and construction began a few months later. The church was completed in July 1892, but overbudget, so Drabble paid off the debt by arranging

---

[2] Courtenay *Weekly News*, 22 March 1893; 5 April 1893; 12 April 1893; 3 May and 15 November 1893.

[3] Anderson to Hussey, 1 September 1892 and 1 February 1893, British Columbia, Provincial Police Force, Correspondence Inward, 1891-1910; Courtenay *Weekly News*, 25 April 1894, p. 1.

a fund-raising Rag Ball at the Knights of Pythias Hall, Comox, in May 1894.[4]

This church occupied a prominent spot on what was then Drabble Street, now Church Street. Viewed from the end of the wharf the Comox townsite took on the appearance of a proper village, with white-painted wooden spires silhouetted against the dark forest behind.

Gradually Drabble adopted a more sedentary life, restricting himself to his legal work, to his additions to the Comox and Courtenay townsites, and to a few local surveys. He continued to work from his office near the wharf, though it was nearly demolished in 1893 when Willie Robb's runaway horse team and buggy crashed through the gate. His last big project was the Dyke Road. The "rickety wheezy" old Long Bridge, built on spindly pilings by Baker and Nicholson in 1875, had little life left in it after nearly twenty years of hard use, floods, and winter storms. "Some day it will collapse like Ford's theatre at Washington," Whitney wrote in July 1893; "There will be a few first class funerals, and after that in due course of time we shall have another bridge. People shouldn't be too impatient." And in August:

> The long bridge is gradually growing weaker, and requires constant repairs in spots to prevent disaster. Notwithstanding this patchwork, the time cannot be distant when there will be a collapse. It is not uncommon to see a team passing over with some one more cautious than the rest walking some distance in the rear.[5]

Despite extensive repairs, the Long Bridge remained a threat until replaced in 1895 by a permanent earthen embankment known as the Dyke, which still carries the main road between Comox and Courtenay. In July 1894 Drabble surveyed the site and lumberman Robert Grant constructed a model. Drabble, Whitney wrote on 18 July, had started the survey; "It is understood that the superintending of the dyke will be awarded to him. It will be an appointment fit to be made." The contract, worth nearly $5,000, was awarded to Robert Grant, Robert Graham, and Hugh Stewart with the aid of local farmers William Matthewson, Thomas Cairns, and Byron Crawford. Work started in mid-September 1894 and was completed about a year later. The dyke was twenty feet wide on the top with two flood-gates or culverts for the outlet of water from the north side of the dyke. These culverts, each equipped with a water-tight swing door, were designed to let the Tsolum's annual flood waters out. Scotsman Thomas Cairns—formerly one of Dunsmuir's

---

[4] Most records of church construction are in envs. 8, 50, 69, and 114; Harmston Diary, 31 July 1890, 8 and 23 July 1891; Courtenay *Weekly News*, 18 April 1894; 16 May 1894. See also Isenor, *Land of Plenty*, p. 145.

[5] Courtenay *Weekly News*, 5 April 1893; 2 August 1893; 26 July 1893; 9 August 1893.

managers at Wellington—contributed his knowledge of the obscure art of puddling, as Mildred Haas recalled:

> One day Cairns happened to be watching some of the workers and remarked, "You must puddle it, puddle it, man," he finally told them what he meant, so Cairns was given the job of completing the dyke. Workers were soon put to work gathering cedar boughs, wool was brought in from the Tolmie Farm in Victoria. The cedar boughs, wool and earth were all tramped and puddled together, making the dyke a success. At last the water was held back.[6]

The nature of local industry meant that some social problems did not go away. Logging and mining contributed to an ongoing gender imbalance; Whitney in September 1894 ran a jocular story about the urgent need for 100 "wives" for all the bachelors of the district. Population growth and urbanization, on the other hand, created sudden breaks from precedent. The "wilderness profound" of the 1860s was under assault as roads, telegraph lines, town lots, suburban lots, tramways, speculators, and real estate agents arrived—many of them employing Drabble. The wildlife of the Comox District inevitably suffered. The earliest settlers had regarded the valley as a sportsman's Eden, stocked with limitless game. As late as 1893 Whitney could claim that the Comox Valley was the "place for the poor man. He can with a little effort get all the game and fish he may desire for his own use." But as the valley filled in, concerns were expressed about market hunters, who sold deer, elk, and wildfowl to the butcher shops of Union and Courtenay. This practice was condemned by many of the older settlers, who hunted frugally for their own table. "There are many people," wrote Anderson in 1891, "who shoot a quantity of game and make a practice of selling them, either to the steamers plying here, or hawking them about the mines and other places."[7]

"The game season is nearly out," wrote a correspondent in the upper valley in December 1892, "but as its observance has not been overly strict it may not make much difference." Drabble presided over a case concerning the shooting of willow grouse out of season, and in March 1893 a valley resident named only "Argus" (guardian) wrote to the paper asking "Why this slaughter?" of birds:

---

[6] Courtenay *Weekly News*, 13 September 1893; 11 July 1894; 18 July 1894; 25 July 1894; 12 September 1894; 19 September 1894; envs. 74, 144; British Columbia, Department of Public Works, Contracts, specifications, 1862-1909; British Columbia, Department of Lands and Works, List of Public Works and names of those submitting tenders; Comox Dyke specifications, Herald Street Collection; *From Shetland to Vancouver Island*, p. 117; Mildred Haas, "Thomas Cairns," in Isenor, "The Comox Valley."

[7] Courtenay *Weekly News*, 12 September 1894; 15 March 1893; Anderson to Hussey, 17 September 1891, British Columbia, Provincial Police Force, Correspondence Inward, 1891-1910.

Pot-shots, wing-shots, snap shots, any shots so long as something is killed or wounded. It cannot be that they want the birds to eat, for two men could not eat one tenth of the birds killed. For sale? Perish the thought! Here in Comox, any man of Anglo-Saxon colour, who shoots game for sale, is considered as being only one step above a seller of Indian whiskey. Perhaps they may be making a "World's Fair Record;" Who knows? I cannot but think that these slaughterers will never cry enough until the last feather of game bird, the last foot of game beast, the last fin of game fish is wiped off the face of the earth.[8]

Drabble suffered during the bust that followed the boom of the early 1890s. In 1894 he owned a house and three cottages as rental properties; he owned two townlots in the Comox townsite and about nineteen acres on the Anderton Road worth $3,900. Money he had earned as a surveyor he had put back into real estate. He had plenty of work; he was a landlord, magistrate, respected member of the community and a popular figure in town, as Whitney hinted in June 1894: "G. F. Drabble is contemplating getting up an excursion and pic-nic, which will include some of the most novel features of modern times."[9] At this time Drabble was urged to write the history of the settlement, but always refused, though he did supply Whitney with his recollections of early days.[10]

Then came the crisis of the recession, which originated as a financial crisis in the United States and spread to Canada late in 1893. Whitney hoped that the diverse resource base of the valley could help it withstand the recession, as he wrote in the fall of 1893:

> The farmers have had good crops, the mines are being vigorously worked, and the logging camps have done a fair business. We feel, in money matters, the influence of the general outside depression, but there are no unemployed, unless it be strangers who have lately come in large numbers to the mines. Therefore let us be contented and remain in our district ark until the waters of depression have elsewhere subsided.[11]

---

[8] Courtenay *Weekly News*, 28 December 1892; 22 March 1893; *The Weekly News*, 29 September 1896.

[9] British Columbia, Surveyor of Taxes, Assessment Rolls, Comox Assessment District; Courtenay *Weekly News*, 15 June 1894.

[10] Duncan, "Early Days and Early Settlers." See the following articles in the *Weekly News*: "Comox District," 28 December 1892 and 4 January 1893; "Early Settlers," 11 January 1893; "Courtenay," 11 January 1893; "Union Mines," 18 January 1893; "Early Times," 9 August 1893; "The Mission," 8 November 1893; "A Correction," 22 November 1893; "A Comox Story," 23 March 1897; and the five historical articles by Dora Crawford, Flora McDonald, Ellen Tarbell, Rose Milligan, and Mary Milligan published between 21 September and 2 November 1897.

[11] Courtenay *Weekly News*, 11 October 1893. On the recession see Ormsby, *British Columbia*, pp. 312-13.

The recession years would not be a picnic for Drabble. He did fewer surveys in 1893 than in any of the previous ten years, and his properties still required much expensive work. Early in 1894 he applied for the position of Stipendary (salaried) Magistate at Union. "There is a rumour that Mr G. F. Drabble will be appointed Stipendary Magistrate," Whitney wrote; "We hope it is true. He would make a most excellent one." Drabble reminded Frederick Hussey of the Provincial Police that he had "acted in the capacity of Justice of the Peace here and have sacrificed a great deal of my time for little or no remuneration for the past 20 years." A month later, in December 1894, when he heard a rumour that Union storekeeper James Abrams would receive the appointment, Drabble wrote again to Hussey. "However much Mr. Abrams may be entitled to the appointment, in return for any political pull as he calls it upon the Government, an old Servant should not be ignored & I have every confidence that you will do your best for me." Drabble's letter-writing campaign had no effect, and Abrams got the job.[12]

Meanwhile, rather unwisely, he disagreed with Abrams on a very contentious subject: the granting of liquor licences. In December 1894 Dickson & Company of Union applied for a retail liquor licence. Abrams, as presiding Magistrate, heard the case along with most of the justices from Union, Courtenay, and Comox—Drabble, John McKenzie, A. McKnight, William Walker, Thomas Cairns, and Robert Grant. Opinions were divided, but the overall decision was to reject the application. In February 1895 the justices met again, five of whom dissented, while Drabble and McKenzie broke rank and issued a licence to Dickson & Company of Union. Their action provoked a storm of protest from the temperance forces and the other justices. Finally, in the summer, Judge Harrison of Nanaimo ruled that Drabble and McKenzie had been wrong: "The full bench had apparently gone into the matter and had declined to grant the license upon grounds which they thought to be sufficient. The minority had no right to overrule their action."[13]

Around this time, Drabble ran into financial difficulties that resulted in the laying of a serious criminal charge against him. The case originated in November 1894 when settler Richard Walsh and Union hotelkeeper Billy Davidson asked Drabble if a certain piece of land in the E&N land grant were available. Drabble wrote to Leonard Solly, the Victoria-based Land Commissioner for the E&N. "Will you be good

---

[12] Courtenay *Weekly News*, 6 June 1894; Drabble to Hussey, 28 November and 20 December 1894, British Columbia Provincial Police, Correspondence Inward, 1891-1912.

[13] Courtenay *Weekly News*, 18 December 1894; 5 February 1895; 12 February 1895; 2 July 1895; 27 August 1895.

enough to inform me if the block of land lying between lots 94 and 126 . . . is for sale and if so at what price. A person has requested me to make the enquiry for him." Solly replied that the land—lot 233 between Union and Courtenay—was for sale at $3.25 an acre. Drabble then showed the letter from Solly to Davidson and Walsh; Walsh gave him $130, and Drabble gave him a receipt.

Davidson told Sam Creech, Government Agent at Comox, that he and Walsh had bought a piece of land from the E&N through Drabble. Creech replied that he was "very foolish; that Mr. Drabble had no right to sell the land as he was not agent for the Co." Davidson and Walsh asked Drabble several times for the official receipt from the E&N; he told them he had left it at his office. They tracked him down at Curtis's cabin, and Drabble gave them $10 to cover their expenses. He told them that he had given the money to a friend to pay to the E&N, but this friend had neglected to pay it. Later, Walsh testified that Drabble "would not tell us who the friend was he sent the money by; Mr. Drabble said he would make it all right; Mr. Drabble kept promising to pay the money back to me but he never did it when we went to see him."

In August 1895 they wrote to Solly stating that they thought "some crooked work" was being done. They asked if Drabble was authorized to act as the company's agent, and if Solly had received the money. Solly replied that Drabble had no authority to do business for the E&N, and that "Any person employing Mr. Drabble to transact business on their behalf with this office does so on their own responsibility."[14]

Drabble, clearly, was broke; he applied for the magistrate's job at Union, and his behaviour grew decidedly eccentric. In March 1895 he leased the Westwood farm at Point Holmes where, Whitney reported, he "will devote part of his time to philosophy and agriculture." In September he put all his land at Comox up for sale, presumably in a desperate effort to come up with the $130 for Walsh:

VALUABLE PROPERTY FOR SALE AT COMOX BAY.

The undersigned will sell the following described property on easy terms, viz:

LOT 6 In the townsite of Comox, delightfully situated near the wharf having a frontage on the south to Comox Bay, and on the north to Front street, opposite the K. of P. Hall, with 5 roomed cottage, hard finish, with every convenience for a family.

LOT 15 Also in the townsite of Comox, fronting on View Street, with a two storey house, hard finished, five rooms, commanding a fine view of the Bay and Gulf.

---

14 Regina vs. Drabble, British Columbia, Attorney-General, Correspondence.

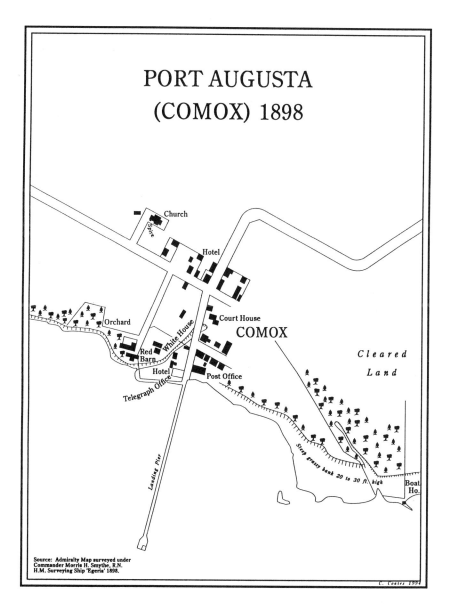

PORT AUGUSTA
(COMOX) 1898

Church

Spire

Hotel

Orchard

Court House

COMOX

White House

Red Barn

Hotel

Post Office

Telegraph Office

Cleared Land

Landing Pier

Steep grassy bank 20 to 30 ft. high

Boat Ho.

Source: Admiralty Map surveyed under
Commander Morris H. Smythe, R.N.
H.M. Surveying Ship 'Egeria' 1898.

C. Coates 1994

Port Augusta (Comox), 1898,
from an Admiralty survey conducted by H.M.S. *Egeria.*

Also part of section 1, containing 18½ acres, well fenced, having a frontage of about twelve hundred feet to the public road, with a nearly completed five room cottage and five stall stable with hay loft over and carriage shed adjoining, with excellent garden stocked with fruit trees, well fenced and never failing spring of water, and every convenience, making it one of the most desirable residences in the district.

Also on same property a cottage, containing three rooms with stable, and orchard of about one acre. This property would be sold in smaller lots, if desired, the whole of which is delightfully situated.

Apply to G. F. Drabble.[15]

Davidson and Walsh grew tired of waiting. They rejected Drabble's written promise of mid-October to pay them the money within a month, and informed the Attorney General, who opened an investigation. In November 1895 Judge Abrams heard depositions in the case "Regina v. Drabble" at Union. The Crown charged that Drabble "unlawfully and by false pretenses obtained from Richard Walsh the sum of one hundred and thirty dollars, with intent to defraud," and that Drabble, "presenting himself as the Agent of the said Co. did unlawfully appropriate to his own use the said sum One hundred and thirty dollars."

Abrams took depositions from Davidson and Walsh, who were cross-examined by Drabble and his attorney C. H. Beevor-Potts. They had spent nine hundred dollars buying the land and improving it, and had employed four men and a team of oxen. Under cross-examination by Drabble, Walsh admitted that he could not remember the wording of the receipt from Drabble, which he had lost. He also admitted that Drabble's receipt had not read "E. & N. Ry. Co. per G. F. Drabble," as Davidson had recalled, nor did he recollect that Drabble had formally represented himself as E&N agent. Walsh admitted that he had promised not to prosecute if Drabble paid the money, and stated that he had "also heard of Mr. Drabble doing wrong to another person."

The examination complete, the depositions and documents were sent to Victoria, and the case resumed in Union in December 1895. The news was not good. Drabble was arrested and charged with theft. "Prominent Citizen Arrested," Whitney announced:

Last Wednesday, Mr. George F. Drabble was up before James Abrams, S. M., A. McKnight, J.P. and W. B. Walker, J.P., on the charge preferred by Richard Walsh of misappropriating funds collected for the E. & N. Railway Co'y for which it is claimed he was not agent. He was bound over, on own recognizance in $500 and the bond of R. Grant in same sum to appear at the spring assizes to answer any indictment that may be presented. C. H. Beevor-Potts appeared for the defendant. Mr.

---

15 *The Weekly News*, 19 March 1895; 3 September 1895.

Drabble is an old citizen and has been a very useful one to the district, and public opinion should be suspended until his defence is heard in court.[16]

The case was heard at the Nanaimo spring assizes in May 1896, but was dismissed as "Not a true Bill" at the preliminary hearing. "No Bill" meant that the Crown had insufficient evidence to proceed with the proposed charges, perhaps because there was no firm evidence that Drabble had ever called himself the E&N's agent. By this time Drabble had paid Walsh the $130.[17]

Drabble's troubles were not over. A few months later he got into difficulty regarding his Anderton Road land. In May, two weeks after the trial, he negotated to sell his property to Miss Spencer of Nob Hill for $3,250. Then in November, lumberman J. B. Giddings of Union claimed that Drabble had sold him the property but had refused to leave. Lawyer Louis Eckstein of Union wrote that Giddings owned the land while Drabble remained in possession. "The defendant wrongfully neglects and refuses to give up possession to the plaintiff." "Some enquiries have been made about Mr. G. F. Drabble," wrote the *Weekly News* on 1 December 1896, "but we understand he is on Denman Island, and forgot to notify the public before going over to attend to a little job of surveying." For unknown reasons, Giddings wholly withdrew his action against Drabble only two weeks after instituting it.[18]

His own encounters with the legal system did not prevent Drabble from maintaining his work as Justice of the Peace, and he held court until 1898. Cases he heard in his twilight years resembled earlier ones. In February 1896 a Comox Native woman named Mrs. Garge was arrested in Union for drunkeness. After an investigation, Robert Saunders, an employee of the Riverside Hotel in Courtenay, was arrested for selling whiskey to "Long Tom," who had sold it to four Lekwiltok Indians. Anderson arrested the Lekwiltok at "the Indian encampment at Kigh Bay," put them in chains and took them to Comox, where Drabble fined them a total of $69 for selling whiskey to Mrs. Garge.[19]

---

[16] *The Weekly News*, 10 December 1895.

[17] Nanaimo Fall Assizes 1895, British Columbia, Supreme Court, Assize Record Book, 1895-1907; "Supreme Court of British Columbia Nanaimo Spring Assize 5th May 1896," British Columbia, Supreme Court (Nanaimo), Registrar's Assizes Record Book, 1888-1912; *The Weekly News*, 12 May 1896.

[18] Env. 77; Giddings vs. Drabble, 30 November 1896, British Columbia, County Court (Comox), Originals, 1886, 1896; British Colummbia, Plaint and Procedure Book from Comox (Union), January 1896–June 1898; British Columbia, County Court, Nanaimo, Plaint and Procedure Books, 1876-1881; 1885-195; *The Weekly News*, 1 December 1896.

[19] *The Weekly News*, 11 February 1896; 17 November 1896.

After Rodello's death in 1889 Drabble became something of an unofficial Indian Agent at Comox. Agent William Lomas, Drabble's old shipmate from the *Silistria*, was based far away in Duncan, but when in Comox he consulted Drabble on Indian matters. According to William Duncan, Drabble had a salutory effect on local habits as long as he was a Justice of the Peace, but in 1898 Drabble had a dispute with Union — possibly with his nemesis Abrams. In September 1898 Duncan complained to the police that the "Comox indians" were being supplied abundantly with liquor, and that on 9 September "four of them were drunk at Courtenay in broad day light and one to such an extent that he was scarcely able to stand up. They (the indians) have become aware that Mr. Drabble has ceased in the mean time to act as J.P. through some difficulty with Union and they seem to take advantage of it."[20]

In 1898, after twenty-seven years, Drabble retired as a Justice of the Peace. Despite his recovery, Drabble's age and health were against him, and his range of occupations contracted as the valley urbanized and younger, qualified professionals arrived, and gradually he confined himself to the village that he had helped build — a village that, to the surprise of the inhabitants, entered the Imperial orbit in the 1890s with the arrival of Britain's Royal Navy.

Comox, despite the growth of Union and Courtenay, still possessed the paramount advantage of the wharf, which gave access to visiting naval vessels. Royal Navy vessels had visited Comox periodically since 1862 to the satisfaction of local merchants and settlers. "A Gun Boat the Acorn it is to stay till Monday," Harmston wrote on 9 April 1890, "The officers & men are around a good deal."[21] In 1895 Comox — quiet corner of a vast Empire — became the bastion for a *fin-de-siècle* display of British imperialism when the Royal Navy built a new firing station and rifle range there.

Previously, the Royal Navy had used Coburg Spit in Esquimalt Harbour for practice, but the range of modern rifles exceeded the Esquimalt facility, and in 1895 the navy applied to use the government reserve at Goose Spit. At the end of the spit, right where the navy wanted to place its firing station, was a Comox Indian reserve containing a graveyard. Rear-Admiral H. F. Stephenson, Commander-in-Chief at Esquimalt, blithely assumed that the reserve might be "transferred without difficulty," and he was almost right. Indian Agent Lomas was summoned, and he reported in January 1896 that:

[20] Lomas Diary, 3 March 1898; Duncan to Hussey, 15 September 1898, British Columbia, Provincial Police, Correspondence Inward, 1891-1910.

[21] Harmston Diary, 9 April 1890. On the Royal Navy at Comox see also Isenor, *Land of Plenty*, pp. 136, 348-50.

The piece of Indian Reserve on the Goose Spit at Comox was and I believe is used as an Indian graveyard there are many graves and poles there. The Indians might however be induced to surrender the same, but according to the Indian custom here [Duncan], and I believe at Comox also, only a few old men are allowed to attend to or remove the bodies or rather bones of the deceased and these are always paid well for the work, so that a certain amount of money would have to be distributed in the shape of a potlatch on the reburial of these bones—that is to make the Indians feel that the white people respect the Graveyards of their people.

In April 1896 Lomas met with Chief Deaf Jim to arrange for the surrender of the Goose Spit reserve to the Royal Navy.[22]

Indian title safely out of the way, the navy constructed a 1,000-yard firing range. In 1897 a "Wimbledon Target" arrived from England, consisting of a wooden frame with canvas and paper targets; the bullets sped harmlessly into the Gulf. The navy also built a wharf and other facilities and hired Horace Smith as caretaker during the four months annually when no ship was at Comox. Thousands of British sailors practised their shooting on the spit before 1906 when the Royal Navy handed the facility over to the Canadian Navy.[23]

Summers at Comox became "a long session in gunfire," but Comox-ians endured them for patriotic, social, and economic reasons. The ships offered a market for local producers of vegetables, meat, and bread; the sailors patronized the hotels, and the officers hunted locally. Naval officers brought five-pound tins from the Spice Islands (Malaysia) as presents, one of them—an apple pie spice containing cinammon, nutmeg, and cloves—remained in use in the Radford family for many years.[24]

Farmers rushed to take advantage of the captive market. Settler and photographer Walter Gage, a recent arival from Somerset, started a strawberry bed at Nob Hill, where in one year, Drabble noted, he obtained 490 pounds of strawberries from one-twentieth of an acre before the third week of June. "Nob Hill is becoming famous for fruit," Whitney observed in April 1893; "It turns out the earliest potatoes, strawberries, and other berries. It's the place for a picnic too, and blackberries! Whew! You should see the crowds going out that way. There will be lots of jam regardless of the price of sugar."[25]

---

[22] Lomas Diary, 30 April 1896.

[23] "Miscellaneous Correspondence Relating to Comox Rifle Range," "Great Britain, Admiralty, Originals, 1848-1898;" *The Weekly News*, 13 April 1897; Naval Historical Section, Ottawa, "Comox Harbour and the Navy," in Isenor, "The Comox Valley"; G. R. Bates, "Story of the Spit," *CDFP*, 28 November 1959; see also Walbran, *British Columbia Coast Names*, p. 260.

[24] Holmes, "Reminiscences;" Interview with Phyllis Currie, 14 May 1994.

[25] Env. 132; Courtenay *Weekly News*, 9 August 1893.

Margaret Matthewson, who farmed on the flats, used to stay up all night baking bread from 200 lb sacks of flour. Holmes himself in 1896 got the contract to supply H.M.S. *Satellite* with meat, and a couple of years later rancher Herbert Church supplied foodstuffs from his thirty-acre farm situated only 500 yards from the wharf. Church recalled his strategy:

> As the naval ships stationed at Esquimalt used to come to Comox regularly to do their firing at the range on Comox spit, I grew a large garden and sold the vegetables to the ships; also butter, cream, and eggs. The place was situated just right for this business, as the ships usually anchored only about 400 yards out, and I could load all my produce into a row-boat and deliver it in a few minutes. They paid good prices, and always in cash.[26]

The Navy and Army Illustrated reported that "Jack Tar" played cricket and soccer, and that sailors had also taken up the new craze for biking. "The men find acquaintances in the neighbouring ranches with whom they can talk about the 'old country.'" Weary of their confinement aboard ship, in 1897 the officers of H.M.S. *Imperieuse* held a walking race from the Elk Hotel to the Courtenay Hotel, an inter-universty match between Mr. Card, a Cambridge graduate, Dr. Philip (Aberdeen), and Rev. C. E. Panter (Oxford). Card won in a time of just over forty minutes. Others patronised McQuillan's stage service between the wharf and Courtenay. As many as twenty sailors at a time piled into a stage, and others chartered McQuillan's buggies for hunting and camping trips. Some of the sailors, homesick for the countryside, took solace in brushing horses and washing buggies for McQuillan.[27]

The officers patronized the Elk, and the sailors the Lorne, with the inevitable consequences. In January 1897 Judge Drabble heard the case of A. S. Hall, a seaman on *Imperieuse*: "Saturday morning one of the marines or sailors was arrested and brought before Mr. Drabble, J.P., for disturbing the peace and was let off with a lecture, but was again arrested about 3 p.m., for burglarizing Mr. Millet's house. He will probably go up."[28] When *Imperieuse* left Comox in February 1899 the chaplain, Rev. Panter, held service in St. Peters Anglican and the ship's choir sang at St. Johns Catholic church:

---

[26] Margaret Biscoe, "Mrs. Mathewson," in Isenor, "The Comox Valley"; *The Weekly News*, 3 March 1896, 15 November 1898; Church, *An Emigrant in the Canadian Northwest*, pp. 52, 60-61.

[27] *The Navy and Army Illustrated*, 8 October 1898, quoted in Naval Historical Section, Ottawa, "Comox Harbour and the Navy," in Isenor, "The Comox Valley"; Crawford, "First Prize Article"; *The Weekly News*, 19 January 1897; McNish, "Livery Stables in the Comox Valley," in Isenor, "The Comox Valley"; *Cumberland News*, 5 June 1901; Carroll, *Wild Roses and Rail Fences*, pp. 103, 105.

[28] *The Weekly News*, 12 January 1897.

A large number paid farewell visits to the Imperieuse Sunday afternoon. The ship sailed Monday morning, and will probably never return to this coast as she leaves shortly for England.

Our loyal fellow citizen, Mr. Cliffe of the Lorne, hoisted the Union Jack in farewell as the Imperieuse steamed majestically out of the harbour Monday.[29]

By the late 1890s the Royal Navy was part of the fabric of Comox. Marriages took place between naval officers and local women. "The people of the Bay are putting on Imperial airs," noted the Union newspaper in 1897. The new ironclads of the high Victorian, *Pax Britannica* era somehow complemented the old agricultural settlement, as these newspaper reports suggest:

[July 1896]: The haying at the Bay is all over, and harvesting will soon begin. Up the valley the grass has nearly been cut. Her Majesty's Gunboat Icarus came in on Saturday and will go from here to Behring Sea. H.M.S. Satellite is expected in a day or two.

[June 1899]: Comox never presented a more beautiful scene than on last Tuesday—the anniversary of Her Most Gracious Majesty's coronation. The green sea of fields, fringed with the darker border of trees, stretched down to the glancing waters below on which floated a contingent of the British monarchs of the brine. On shore, those loyal citizens, Geo. McDonald, Cliffe and Lucas, waved Union Jacks and Canadian flags to the breeze. The Amphion and Virago were decked from stem to stern with flags and signals of every hue, while from the main top mast of the former floated proudly the Royal Ensign.[30]

෴

Drabble retired from the legal profession in 1898. Out of his financial crisis of 1895-96 he maintained, for a time, both his five-roomed cottage and office near the wharf and his house on View Street, though he had to sell his Anderton Road estate to Giddings.

Until nearly his death he pursued his passion for surveying. He was involved with the subdivision of the old valley farms, such as Thomas Finley's in 1898. In the spring of 1899 he surveyed for a new Courtenay River Bridge (the 5th Street Bridge), to replace the one built in 1875. "Mr. G. F. Drabble surveyed Courtenay River," the *Cumberland News* noted in August 1899; "From this survey plans and specifications will be made for the new bridge. It is greatly needed." And on 15 September: "The Courtenay Bridge is receiving temporary repairs at long last and and now we can cross it for the next few weeks without making our wills (if we have anything to will) before doing so." Fall freshets washed away

29 *The Cumberland News*, 28 February 1899.
30 *The Weekly News*, 12 January 1897; 28 July 1896; 24 June 1899.

the temporary supports under the bridge, in November tenders were called, and the new bridge was under construction in February 1900. Drabble conducted his last survey in January 1901, for J. J. R. Miller at the site of the King Coho Resort.[31]

In the last few years of his life, Drabble was apparently a cantankerous, misanthropic old man. Stories were told in the mid-twentieth century by men and women who had been children in the 1890s and whose memories reflect their age perhaps as much as reality. The Anderton children recalled the sour old man in a frock coat whose dog Queenie bit them, and rumours swirled about Drabble's mysterious relationship with "Drabble's Mary." Smoke often indicates the presence

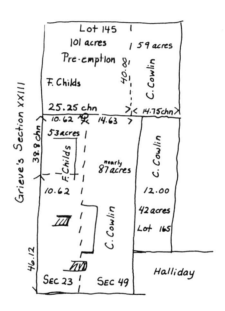

Drabble's subdivision of Thomas Finley's Farm,
Comox Valley, 28 April 1898.

[31] Envs. 73, 118; *The Cumberland News*, 12 August 1899, 15 September 1899, 11 November 1899.

of fire, and Anderson, in his 1901 obituary, wrote that Drabble was once "reputed fairly well off, but in later years misfortune overtook him and he died a poor man." It would seem that Drabble experienced an unknown financial crisis in the last year or two of life, the details of which are unknown. In 1899 he sold both his remaining properties, and in 1900 he owned nothing.[32]

Drabble's health was failing. In February 1900 the *Cumberland News* stated "with great pleasure that Mr. Drabble is improving," but the paper did not mention the nature of the illness. In the spring of 1901 Drabble checked into the Cumberland hospital for the last time. A unidentified merchant somewhere in the valley made the following sale: "G. F. Drabble. April 1901. To 2 pr. Drawers $1.50 2 vests $1.50 2 pr Socks 50c $3.50." These clothes may have been for his hospital stay.[33]

He died on 10 September 1901 at the Cumberland Hospital of "Softening of the brain & convulsions 6 months." He was sixty-eight. Court Administrator Henry Collis wrote he had made a "diligent and careful search in all places where the said deceased usually kept his papers" without finding a will. The total value of his personal effects did not exceed $50. He must have disposed of all his remaining property in the six months before his death.[34]

His old friend Teddy Rollings died in 1899; Adam Horne and Reginald Pidcock died just months before him. Queen Victoria, whose reign his own life neatly encompassed, had died in January 1901. His friends Joe McPhee, J. B. Holmes, and Jules Willemar lived on and on. Willemar died in 1932 aged ninety-two and McPhee in 1946 aged ninety-eight. Eric Duncan died aged eighty-five in 1944, having taken upon himself the mantle of Comox Valley historian that Drabble had refused to wear.

[32] Wagner, "George Drabble," pp. 4-5; British Columbia, Surveyor of Taxes, Assessment Rolls, Comox Assessment District, 1888-1942; *The Cumberland News*, 18 September 1901.

[33] *The Cumberland News* 10 February 1900; Reksten, *The Dunsmuir Saga*, p. 168; [Comox or Courtenay Account Book, unidentified merchant, *c.* 1901-04], CDMA.

[34] British Columbia, County Court (Cumberland), Probate Files, 1901-1917.

Conclusion

It is possible to feel
That this profusion of life
In this north-west
Corner of the world
Might shake free the traces
In something less than an age.

FROM *North West Coast*, by Peter Huston[1]

THE colonial settlers of the 1860s had little else in mind than farming. There was a reason for this: the colony contained few of the industries or institutions that immigrants had known, and they embraced farming for its security and familiarity. The pre-emption laws were intended to get colonists onto the land and allow them to make something of it. At the same time, there were some very unfamiliar, un-European, things about the Comox Valley, namely the resident Native people and the vast and ultimately compelling unexploited potential of the surrounding wilderness. Settlers valued the Comox Indians for their cheap provisions and inexpensive labour. The combination of new land and Native labour was effective, and farming dominated the valley economy until 1888.

In the 1880s loggers and miners entered the region. Dunsmuir's Union mines and King and Casey's logging camps provided farmers with markets and seasonal work and stimulated agricultural production. The arrival of the Royal Navy at Comox provided another local market. By 1890 the valley was known equally for its farms, coal, and timber; the best farmland had been pre-empted, but the best coal and timber lands awaited exploitation. This would be the project, in part, of the Comox Logging Company in the twentieth century.

Eric Duncan's *From Shetland to Vancouver Island* reflects the character of the early settlers: modest, anecdotal, and grounded. The nineteenth century colonists referred to the Comox Valley as the Settlement, and

---

[1] Lander, *To an Inland Sea*, p. 16.

the surrounding region as the District. They called themselves settlers rather than "pioneers," a name that entered the Comox vocabulary only in the early twentieth century. Moreover, they talked not about a "frontier" but about the wilderness that began at the edge of the farming settlement. The quiet simplicity of their life and work was reflected in the words settler and wilderness, which are without a trace of individualist bravado or frontierist self-glorification.

The resources of the valley and District attracted capital as the century drew to a close. Dunsmuir spent half a million dollars in the first year of his operations at Union. Industries required people to run them, and people required urban facilities. The townsites of Comox, Union, and Courtenay were established by Robb, Dunsmuir, and McPhee in response to the urban needs of workers in different industries. Government officials, professionals, tradesmen, and others provided essential services.

Drabble figured in every stage in the history of the valley in the nineteenth century. He participated in the transition from a farming to a diverse local economy. He sold his farm in 1875 to capitalize on his own professional skills and the wider commercial opportunities available in the northern Gulf. As a surveyor he welcomed the trinity of settler, business, and government capital: he surveyed farms for individual pre-emptors, properties for mining, logging, and fishing companies, and laid out courthouses, jails, schools, bridges, and roads on behalf of the government. The project initiated by Drabble is an ongoing one. As a Government Agent and Magistrate he participated in the great expansion of government institutions on the late nineteenth century. It is curious to find Judge Drabble settling disputes between farmers who were put on the land in the first place by Surveyor Drabble.

New industries meant new opportunities for settlers and a wider range of occupations for subsequent generations. A farmer's son might stay on the farm, but more likely he would work in the woods, in the mines, or possibly in an urban occupation like retailing. When he married, his parents might let him build a house on their land, which would be home base during his seasonal rounds of work. The old pre-emptions were split up in this way. His wife usually came from a farm somewhere else in the District. Farming, generally, was a summer occupation and logging a winter pursuit. Settlers worked in the woods in the winter to earn cash to establish and sustain their farms. With time, more people identified themselves as loggers than as farmers or settlers. People could afford to have children in such a climate; family names that have nearly died out in England continue to flourish here.

The Native people of Comox were marginalized. In the 1860s they were placed on small reserves and were denied legal access to the resources of Crown land. They were dispossessed and alienated from their own land. They were not permitted to pre-empt land; they were not considered "settlers." Projects initiated by Drabble—roads, mining railways and tramways, bridges, and pre-emptions—led to the destruction of Native and archaeological sites. This destruction continues today. But the early settlers might be surprised at the survival of Native culture. They expected Indians to die away, especially in the smallpox era, and they did their best to rename the landscape in their own fickle way. Take, for example, an irate editorial by Whitney in 1893:

> The lake near Union Mines is properly called Union Lake, and the river flowing from it the Courtenay River. Don't let us follow the Indian fashion of calling every bend and turn in the river by a different name.[2]

Whitney's warning fell on deaf ears. His coveted name Union has almost disappeared from the map. Union Lake is still called Comox Lake and the river flowing from it is still called Puntledge River. The Courtenay River stubbornly refuses to adopt the name of either of its sources, the Tsolum or the Puntledge, let alone extend itself all the way inland to Comox Lake. Maybe "Indian fashion" prevails after all.

The settlers adapted to this land—and changed as they did so. They remained, of course, English from London or Lincolnshire, or Scots from the Shetlands or Fife, or Canadians from Nova Scotia or New Brunswick, but they and their children became something else again. After 1862 the valley was no longer a Native place, and after the arrival of the Maritimers in the 1870s it was no longer a British colonial place. Many spoke the Chinook jargon, but they were not Indians, any more than Indians who spoke Chinook were Englishmen. The Smith family of Black Creek, for example, had been in the cheese business in Derbyshire, but the Canadian Smiths produced no cheese-makers. Among their children were a timber cruiser, a logger, a hunting guide, a cougar hunter and game warden, a lawyer, and a nurse. Second-generation occupations such as these were determined in part by family traditions and money, but mainly by the nature of local economic opportunites, which were based directly on wilderness elements that could be exploited for profit: the forest (logging and timber cruising) and wildlife (guiding and cougar hunting). The result was something both familiar and strange: Lou Cliffe called himself a "second-growth Englishman," an organic metaphor that conjures up the old and the new.

Characters who appear most clearly are those who wrote diaries, letters, or reminiscences. Reginald Pidcock was almost boyish: full of

---

[2] Courtenay *Weekly News*, 7 June 1893.

reckless energy, fascinated with water wheels and steam engines. He trusted equally to providence and family money to see him through, and when those failed the local M.P. got him the Indian Agency at Fort Rupert. Carwithen stayed on his 1862 farm, where he brought up a large family of children. He complained that his young children grew helpful as they got older, but they took their turn "generally smashing things up." He ran unsuccessfully for political office, and grew cynical before his early death from pleurisy in 1893. Mary Harmston, Drabble's shipmate of 1862, knew a good deal about the people in the valley; her later life was a rotation of visits to her son Willie's farm and to the Lorne Hotel, home of her daughter Florence Cliffe. She ranged the valley bringing babies into the world and calling on her friends. Her diary holds many clues to the social history of the valley. Her son-in-law Sam Cliffe was a jovial, good-natured story-teller. He travelled the Gulf collecting signatures for a liquor licence while Florence split her own firewood back at the Lorne. Joe McPhee comes across as a driven man with the makings of a tycoon, a model of probity—farseeing, a self-made man in the tradition of Samuel Smiles. Holmes, another merchant, remembered his charivari and other events with nostalgia and humour. Eric Duncan watched in his observant way, wrote poems about what he saw, recorded his impressions in his recollections, and found solace in his deep faith.

Some early settlers and visitors, unable to find the words to describe the people and society of the Comox Valley, resorted to analogies taken from the rich Victorian literary canon. Robert Brown in 1864 found several "Micawber" types in the valley—an allusion to a character in Charles Dickens' *Great Expectations*. Eric Duncan found that Drabble looked much like Anthony Trollope, and J. B. Holmes, who arrived in 1884, wrote that only Dickens could have described early Comox characters like George Drabble and Sam Cliffe.

A writer of fiction might make more of Drabble than a mere historian and biographer. Like many more eminent Victorians, his public life was very public, and his private life was very private, and questions remain unanswered. Much about him is shadowy or unknown. Where was he educated? Was he a blackguard, a cad, who cared little for his wife and children? Did he decide to emigrate while feeling in "good humour" at a farewell party on the *Silistria*, as Sarah Butler asserted? Did he maintain contact with his children after Louisa Drabble died in 1863? Why did he report that he inherited £20,000 when he had inherited a good deal less? Who was his Native wife or partner: was she Julia from Clayous, or was she Drabble's Mary, and did he really live with her in the green-stained cottage on Anderton Road? Did he help bring up his son Johnny Drabble, alias Tlagoglas? What became of the money given him by Walsh and Davidson? Fifty years ago, certain people could have answered these questions, but Drabble's friends and children are all gone, and the surviving records are not of a very intimate nature.

His wife's death must have hit him very hard, and his father-in-law's refusal to let his children join him in Comox must have distressed him. His inner world was anguished. He pursued his self-interest enough to get together with Drabble's Mary, but the nature of their relationship is vague. They had a child, but no evidence exists that they were married. His private life may have been in shambles and unsatisfactory, but he participated in public life with vigour, if sometimes poor judgement. The gap between his sad private life and his extroverted public life reflected his character and experience. His public persona was one of respectability, conservative rectitude, and Imperial bluster, but these qualities were adopted even by Victorians whose private lives were more conventional and happier than Drabble's. What he possessed with certainty—and even his detractors admitted this—was a high professional ability. Though without legal training, he learned the details of civil law so that he could render the most precise judgements as a magistrate. His surveys, according to Gordon Wagner, were of a high standard, and his roads and bridges lasted for years.

In the 1890s he suffered from the disgrace of the Walsh-Davidson land scandal. His posthumous reputation continued to deteriorate, due mainly to Eric Duncan's pointed reference to his drinking problem, which was repeated and embroidered upon by later writers. Paralleling this treatment has been Drabble's civic neglect: both Comox and Courtenay once had a Drabble Street, named not by Drabble with an eye to posterity, but by James Robb and Joe McPhee in return for his help and expertise. Drabble Street in Courtenay was renamed First Street in 1945 by the City of Courtenay in a fit of utilitarian simplification. The name, however, was recycled in the form of "Drabble Place,"— now an unmarked strip of asphalt sixty feet wide and a hundred and ten feet long separating the rowdy Arbutus Hotel from its parking lot.

In Comox, Drabble Street was renamed Church Street in 1948 for no good reason at all. One informant told me that Comox village council simply "didn't like the name." There is, indeed, a church on the street—but many streets contain churches, and not all are named Church Street. Local historians objected when they heard of the change, and in 1958—British Columbia's centennial year—the Comox Valley Historical Society passed a resolution asking that Drabble's name be restored. "In recognition of his years of service," Alex Buckham and Rupert Williams wrote, "it is but right and proper that his memory should be perpetuated, and we ask that the name of this worthy pioneer be applied, at the earliest opportunity, to one of the streets

288

which may be established in future in the Village of Comox."[3] The resolution was ignored, and Drabble remains unnamed on the Comox street plan.

Despite the premature removal of his name from the streets of the towns he laid out, Drabble has not gone entirely without recognition. Drabble Lakes in Strathcona Park commemorate him, and between the wars Norman Stewart, a local mountaineer and surveyor, named a mountain after him on Forbidden Plateau. Visible from most of the Comox Valley, Mt. Drabble is 4,442 feet high. Previously Mt. Drabble was known as Mt. Lytton after Edward Bulwer Lytton (1803-73), English statesman and novelist known for his historical romances and for his opening line, "It was a dark and stormy night." Lord Lytton had been Queen Victoria's Secretary of State for the Colonies during the gold rush era. Stewart and his naming committee contacted Lytton's descendents in England and asked them if they would mind the name change. They graciously acquiesced (while perhaps perplexed at the need), and overnight Mt. Lytton became Mt. Drabble.[4]

Drabble might have smiled at the irony that he, a somewhat disreputable colonist of 1862, had usurped the name of a powerful man whose decisions influenced colonial history the world over.

---

[3] Buckham and Williams to Comox Village Clerk, 6 February 1958, Buckham Collection.
[4] Interview with Ruth Masters, 10 March 1994.

Bibliography

Abbreviations used.

BCARS   British Columbia Archives and Record Service
BCSP   British Columbia Sessional Papers
CDMA   Courtenay District Museum and Archives
CRMA   Campbell River Museum and Archives
CVFP   Comox Valley Free Press
DCB   *Dictionary of Canadian Biography*
GRO   General Record Office, London
NCA   Nanaimo Community Archives
PRO   Public Record Office, London
SGB   Surveyor General Branch, Victoria

1. UNPUBLISHED SOURCES

Anderton, Leo. Interview with Ben Hughes, 26 April 1956, CDMA.

Barnett, Ruth (née Sterritt). Interview with Richard Mackie, 23 December 1994.

Barraclough, William. "Selected Items on the Life of Adam Grant Horne: 'Nanaimo's Trader Horne,'" August 1962, CDMA.

Bates, Captain G. R. "Narrative." 1956. CDMA.

Beck, Rhoda. "Parkin Reunion," 3 August 1980. Private Collection.

Beley, Joan (née Drabble). Interview with Richard Mackie, March 1994.

Biscoe, Margaret B. "Reginald Terry Carwithen and Harry Blaksley. Comox Valley. 1862-1893," [c. 1942], in "Pioneers Comox Valley" file, CDMA.

British Columbia. Attorney General. [Correspondence]. BCARS GR 419.

———. Attorney General. Correspondence, 1872-1937. BCARS GR 429.

———. Attorney General. Correspondence Inward, 1883-1888. BCARS GR 996.

———. Attorney General. Court Records Guide. BCARS.

———. Attorney General. [Bench Books, 1864-1964], [Civil Court, Comox, 1886]. BCARS GR 1727.

———. Attorney General. Documents 1857-1966. BCARS GR 419.

———. Attorney General. Inquests, 1865-1937. BCARS.

———. Attorney-General. Inquisitions, 1872-1937. BCARS GR 1327.

———. Attorney General. Miscellaneous material, 1864-1879. BCARS GR 1459.

———. Attorney General. Record Book for the Nanaimo Coroner's Office, 1866-1905. BCARS GR 2935.

———. Attorney General. Register of Justices of the Peace and dates of Commission, 1872-1875. BCARS GR 1805.

———. Colonial Correspondence. Originals, c. 1858-1871. BCARS.

———. County Court (Comox). Originals, 1886, 1896. Civil case files. BCARS GR 1947.

———. County Court (Cumberland). Plaint and Procedure Book from

Comox (Union), 1896-1898. BCARS GR 2870.

———. County Court. Nanaimo. Plaint and Procedure Books, 1876-1881; 1885-1950. BCARS GR 2129.

———. Department of Lands. Certificates of Improvement 1871-1887. BCARS GR 211.

———. Department of Lands. Originals, 1860-1912 [Papers concerning the Esquimalt and Nanaimo Railway Belt]. BCARS GR 1404.

———. Department of Lands. Preemption Records and Registers, 1859-1971. BCARS GR 112.

———. Department of Lands and Works. Correspondence Inward, 1871-1872. BCARS GR 1039.

———. Lands and Works Department. Correspondence Inward, 1872-1918. BCARS GR 1440.

———. Department of Lands and Works. Correspondence Inward, 1871-1883. BCARS GR 868.

———. Department of Lands and Works. Vancouver Island Preemptions, 1861-1885. BCARS GR 766.

———. Department of Lands and Works. Correspondence Inward from William Duncan, 1864, 1868, 1879, 1871. BCARS.

———. Department of Lands and Works. BCARS GR 1069 (Herald Street Collection).

———. Department of Lands and Works. List of Public Works and names of those submitting tenders. . . . 1888-1898. BCARS GR 832.

———. Department of Lands and Works. Preemption Records for Comox District, 1885-1887. BCARS GR 2311.

———. Department of Land and Works. Public Works, Contracts and Specifications, 1872-1896. BCARS GR 80.

———. Department of Lands and Works. Public Works. Contracts, specifications, etc., 1862-1909. BCARS GR 87.

———. Department of Lands. Originals, 1862-1933. Comox Land District, Vancouver Island. Land registers, Sections 1-113 and lots 1-251. BCARS GR 2627.

———. Lands Branch. Correspondence Inward, 1872-1918. BCARS GR 1440.

———. Lieutenant-Governor. Correspondence. BCARS GR 443.

———. Nanaimo Magistrate's Office. Gaol Register, 1877-1884. NCA.

———. Provincial Police Force. Correspondence Inward, 1891-1910. BCARS GR 55.

———. Provincial Police. Private Correspondence, 1895-1910. BCARS GR 66.

———. Provincial Secretary. Correspondence Inward, 1871-1892. BCARS GR 526.

———. Provincial Secretary. Correspondence Inward, 1892-1917. BCARS GR 1330.

———. Provincial Secretary. Correspondence Outward, 1873-1918. BCARS GR 540.

———. Provincial Secretary. Index to correspondence outward, 1895-1897. BCARS GR 538.

———. Provincial Secretary. Letters Inward: indexes and registers, 1872-1910. BCARS GR 524.

———. Provincial Secretary. Letters Inward to the Department of the Provincial Secretary, 1892-1917. BCARS GR 1330.

———. Provincial Secretary. Originals, 1867-1923 [Justices of the Peace oaths, etc]. BCARS GR 610.

———. Provincial Secretary. Records relating to Indian Affairs, 1876-1878. BCARS GR 494.

———. Provincial Secretary. Register of Letters Inward, 1881-82. BCARS GR 1494.

———. Supreme Court. Assize Record Book, 1895-1907 and Speedy Trials Record Book, 1895-1912. BCARS GR 2663.

———. Supreme Court (Nanaimo). Registrar's Assizes Record Book, 1888-1912. BCARS GR 2301.

———. Surveyor of Taxes. Assessment Rolls. Comox Assessment District, 1888-1942. BCARS GR 1999.

———. Surveyor of Taxes. Comox Assessment Rolls, 1897-1902, CDMA.

Brown, Robert. Collection, BCARS.

Buckham, Alexander Fraser. Collection, BCARS.

———. "Summary History—Coal Discoveries—Comox Coalfield," Buckham Collection, BCARS.

———. "Residents of Comox Provincial Constituency—1883," 13 January 1958, CDMA.

Butler, Sarah. "Reminiscences," BCARS.

Canada. [Census Branch]. 1891 Canadian Census for Comox, BCARS.

Carwithen, Reginald Terry. Correspondence to Harry Blaksley, 1880-1890, Private Collection.

Cliffe, Sam and Florence. Lorne Hotel Register, 1888-1895, Private Collection.

[Comox or Courtenay Account Book, unidentified merchant, c 1901-04], CDMA.

Crease, H. P. P. Collection. BCARS.

Currie, Phyllis (née Radford). Interview with Richard Mackie, 14 May 1994.

Curtis, James Morley. Diary, 15 September–16 December 1888. CDMA.

Dann, Muriel (née Smith). Interview with Richard Mackie, 14 April 1994.

Drabble, George Fawcett. Field Books, 1873-1901, Drabble Papers, CRMA.

———. Field Books, 1877, 1882, 1883, 1898, Buckham Collection, BCARS.

Duncan, William. Diary 1887-1889; 1891, CDMA.

Enos, Joseph. Diary, 6 January 1881–5 June 1892, BCARS.

Good, John Booth. "The Utmost Bounds of the West," BCARS.

Good Templars Lodge, Comox Branch. "Minutes of Bateman Lodge No. 83," IOGT, 1884-1892, Private Collection.

———. "Minute Book of Bateman Lodge IOGT," 1892-1895, Private Collection.

———. "The Bateman Journal," Volume 1, Nos. 1-10 (23 April 1887 to 31 December 1887) [William M. Halliday and William Duncan, eds], Private Collection.

Great Britain. Admiralty. Originals, 1848-1898. BCARS.

———. Colonial Office, Correspondence with Vancouver Island, 1865-67, (C.O. 305), microfilm copies at BCARS.

Harmston, Mary Florence. Diary, 19 March 1865–30 December 1866; 15 April 1880–22 April 1892, Private Collection.

———, William. Diary, 1 January–16 July 1866; 23 March–4 April 1868, Private Collection.

Harding, Rene. Interview with Richard Mackie, 8 January 1994.

Hawkins, Bob. Interview with Richard Mackie, 8 March 1994.

Hunter, Joseph. Correspondence Outward, 1878-1893, BCARS.

———. Correspondence Outward, 1893-1900, BCARS.

Hurford, Richard. "Old Ms. record book of land sales [preemptions] in the Comox District," 1941, CDMA.

Hussey, Frederick Hussey. Scrapbook, 1887-1901, BCARS.

Isenor, D. E., ed. "The Comox Valley. Its Pioneers. Parts 1-8," 1962, complete copy in Buckham Collection, BCARS.

Johnstone, Angus Rutherford. Papers, BCARS.

Lewis, W. R. "William Chaworth-Musters," 1995, Private Collection.

Lomas. , William Henry. Correspondence. Miscellaneous letters to and by W. H. Lomas, BCARS.

———. Correspondence of the Cowichan Indian Agency, 1866-1897, BCARS.

———. Daily Journal, 1896, BCARS.

———. Daily Journal, 1898, BCARS.

———. "Log of William Henry Lomas from Liverpool to Victoria on the Emigrant Ship 'Silistria' White Star Line," BCARS.

Lorne Hotel. Documents and Artifacts found in 1988 Renovations, Private Collection.

McDonald, Ranald. "Journal of the Vancouver Island Exploring Expedition," 7 June–22 October 1864, in Robert Brown Collection, BCARS.

McKelvie, B. A. "The 'S' Sign. A Biographical Sketch of Eustace Smith, Logger, Timber Cruiser and Forest Engineer," n.d., CDMA.

McPhee, Bruce. Interview with Richard Mackie, 19 December 1994.

Manson, Michael. Diary, 1 January 1895–7 January 1896, BCARS.

———. "Sketches from the life of Michael Manson," BCARS.

———. Papers, BCARS.

Manson's Store, Nanaimo. Ledgers 1885-1940, BCARS.

Marriott, Barbara (née Duncan). Interview with Richard Mackie, 14 April 1994.

Masters, Ruth. Interview with Richard Mackie, 10 March 1994.

Menzies, Audrey (née Grieve). Interview with Richard Mackie, 12 April 1994.

Newman, Bill. "The Reverend Jules Xavier Willemar," CDMA.

Nunns, Frederick Lloyd. Diary, [1888; 1890-1892], CRMA.

———. Miscellaneous Correspondence, c. 1884-1912, CRMA.

Pearse, Benjamin William Pearse. "Early Settlement of Vancouver Island," (1900), BCARS.

Pidcock, Harry. Papers, BCARS.

Pidcock, Reginald Heber. "Adventures in Vancouver Island. Being an Account of 6 years residence, and of hunting & fishing excursions with some Account of the Indians inhabiting the island," [1868], BCARS.

———. Diary, 4 March 1882–9 May 1882. Pidcock Family Papers, BCARS.

———. Diary 1 January 1883–2 June 1884. Pidcock Family Papers, BCARS.

———. Diary, 5 March 1888–25 December 1888. Pidcock Family Papers, BCARS.

Planta, Jacob Prhys. Collection, NCA.

Principal Probate Registry, Somerset House, London.

Pritchard, John. Interview with Imbert Orchard, 6 April 1965, Imbert Orchard/C.B.C. Collection, BCARS.

Rennison, Stan and Betty. Interview with Richard Mackie, 22 April 1994.

———. "William Coates Rennison," Private Collection.

Robinson, Edward W. "Log of Voyage from Liverpool to Victoria, Vancouver Island per Ship 'Silistria,' " BCARS.

Romaine, Beryl (née Atkinson). Interview with Richard Mackie, March 1994.

Sandwell, R. W. "Peasants on the Coast? A Problematique of Rural British Columbia," Paper Presented to the BC Studies Conference, October 1994.

Slemin, Chuck. "The Drabble Papers." Address Given to the Courtenay and District Historical Society, 19 November 1980, CDMA.

Smith, Eustace. "Eustace Smith—1950," [memoirs], CDMA.

Stenhouse, Anthony Maitland. "To the Free and Independent Electors of the District of Comox," [Election Notice], BCARS.

Talbot, Pat and Jack. Interview with Richard Mackie, 8 January 1994.

Vancouver Island. Colonial Secretary. Register of Correspondence Inward, 1864-1866, BCARS.

Vertical files of newspaper cuttings and miscellaneous material, BCARS.

Wagner, Gordon (ed). "Field Books of Comox Valley Surveys by George F. Drabble, Land Surveyor, 1870-1901," 1993, CDMA.

———. "George Drabble," ms. in possession of author.

———. Interviews with Richard Mackie, 8 March, 31 March, June 1994.

Whymper, Frederick. "Journal of the Vancouver Island Exploring Expedition," 7 June–18 October 1864, in Robert Brown Collection, BCARS.

2. PUBLISHED SOURCES

Akrigg, G. P. V., and Helen Akrigg, *1001 British Columbia Place Names* (Vancouver: Discovery Press, 1973).

Bailcy, Lloyd. *A Comox Harbour History* (Courtenay: Plateau Publishing, 1992).

Barman, Jean. *The West Beyond the West: A History of British Columbia* (Toronto: University of Toronto Press, 1991).

Barnett, Homer. *The Coast Salish of British Columbia* (Westport, Connecticut: Greenwood Press, 1955).

Baskerville, Peter, and Eric Sager. *1881 Canadian Census: Vancouver Island* (Victoria, B.C.: Public History Group, 1990).

Bate, Mark. "Reminiscences of Early Nanaimo," *Nanaimo Free Press*, 9 February–18 May 1907.

Belshaw, John Douglas. "Cradle to Grave: An Examination of Demographic Behaviour on two British Columbia Frontiers," *Journal of the Canadian Historical Association*, 5 (1994), pp. 41-62.

Boas, Franz. "Myths and Legends of the Catloltq of Vancouver Island," *The American Antiquarian* 10:4 (July 1888), pp. 201-11.

Bowen, Lynne. *The Dunsmuirs of Nanaimo* (Nanaimo: The Nanaimo Festival, 1989).

British Columbia. *British Columbia Gazette* (Victoria: Queen's Printer, 1873-75).

———. *The Laws of British Columbia* (Victoria: Government Printing Office, 1871).

The British Columbia Monthly and Mining Review 1:2 (February 1889), p. 15.

Brooks, Julian. "Joseph Hunter: Forgotten Builder of British Columbia," *British Columbia Historical News* 28:2 (Spring 1995), pp. 27-31.

Brown, Jonathan. *Steeped in Tradition. The Malting Industry in England since the Railway Age* (Reading: University of Reading, 1983).

Carroll, Leila. *Wild Roses and Rail Fences* (Courtenay: E. W. Bickle Ltd., 1975).

Church, H. E. *An Emigrant in the Canadian Northwest* (London: Methuen, 1929).

Clayton, Daniel. "Geographies of the Lower Skeena," *BC Studies* 94 (Summer 1992), pp. 29-59

Cole, Douglas. *Captured Heritage: The Scramble for North West Coast Artifacts* (Vancouver: Douglas & McIntyre, 1985).

———, and Ira Chaikin. *An Iron Hand Upon the People: the Law Against the*

Potlatch on the Northwest Coast (Vancouver: Douglas & McIntyre, 1990).

Corrigal, Margery. *The History of Hornby Island* (Courtenay: Comox District Free Press, 1969).

Crawford, Dora. "First Prize Article," Union *Weekly News*, 21 September 1897, p. 1.

Dunae, Patrick A. *Gentlemen Emigrants: From the British Public Schools to the Canadian Frontier* (Vancouver: Douglas & McIntyre, 1981).

Duncan, Eric. "Comox District Fifty Years Ago," Victoria *Times*, 24 March 1928.

———. "Early Days and Early Settlers in Comox Valley," *Comox Argus*, 17 and 24 March 1921.

———. *Fifty-seven Years in the Comox Valley* (Courtenay: Comox Argus Company, 1934) (reprinted 1967, 1979)

———. *From Shetland to Vancouver Island. Recollections of Seventy-Eight years* (Edinburgh: Oliver and Boyd, 1939) (first published 1934).

———. Newspaper Cuttings and Scrapbook, *c.* 1927-1936, Private Collection.

———. [Notes written in his Sandwick store cashbook, *c.* 1897-1903], quoted in "Shadowy Figures of the Past Live Again in Eric Duncan's cashbook," printed originaly in the *Argus*, n.d., reprinted in *Comox District Free Press*, 28 July 1967, p. 2.

———. *The Rich Fisherman and Other Tales* (London: The Century Press, 1910) (reprinted Toronto, 1932).

———. *Rural Rhymes and the Sheep Thief* (Toronto: William Briggs, 1896).

———. "The Tsolum River," *Gems of Poetry* 2:4 (New York: 14 June 1881), pp. 188-89.

———. "Vancouver Island from a Farmer's Standpoint," *Chambers's Journal* (June 1903), pp. 366-68.

Englebert, Renny. *This is Vancouver Island* (Victoria: Diggon-Hibben, 1948).

Feely, Jean, and Margery Corrigal, comps. *A History of "Tle-Tla-Tay" (Royston)* (Royston: Royston Centennial Committee, n.d., *c.* 1967).

Fisher, Robin. *Contact and Conflict: Indian-European Relations in British Columbia, 1774-1890* (Vancouver: University of British Columbia Press, 1977).

Forbes, Elizabeth. *Wild Roses at their Feet: Pioneer Women of Vancouver Island* (Vancouver: Evergreen Press, 1971).

[Forde, H. D]. *Courtenay: The Coming Railroad and Industrial Centre of Central Vancouver Island* (Victoria: British Columbia Investments, Ltd., *c.* 1912).

Galois, Robert. *Kwakwaka'wakw Settlements, 1775-1920: A Geographical Analysis and Gazetteer* (Vancouver: UBC Press, 1994).

Glover-Geidt, Janette. *The Friendly Port: A History of Union Bay, 1880-1960 (Campbell River: Kask Graphics Ltd., 1990).

Gough, Barry M. *Gunboat Frontier: British Maritime Authority and Northwest Coast Indians, 1846-90* (Vancouver: UBC Press, 1984).

Grove, Alan, and Ross Lambertson, "Pawns of the Powerful: The Politics of Litigation and the Union Colliery Case," *BC Studies* 103 (Autumn 1994), pp. 3-33.

Haggard, H. Rider. *King Solomon's Mines* (London: 1885; New York: Dover Publications, reprint, 1951).

———. *She* (London: 1887; reprinted New York: Dover Publications, 1951).

Hagen, Judy. *Comox Valley Memories. Reminiscences of Early Life in Central Vancouver Island* (Courtenay: Courtenay and District Museum and Historical Society, 1993).

Hall, Del. *Island Gold: A History of Cougar Hunting on Vancouver Island* (Victoria: Cougar Press, 1990).

Halliday, W. M. *Potlatch and Totem and the Recollections of an Indian Agent* (London and Toronto: J. M. Dent & Sons, 1935).

Harding, Rene. "Fallen Drabble Lived Alone with Queenie," *Comox District Free Press*, 28 October 1977, p. 7.

Harris, Cole. "Voices of Disaster: Smallpox around the Stait of Georgia in 1782," *Ethnohistory* 41:4 (Fall 1994), pp. 591-626.

Hayman, John, ed. *Robert Brown and the Vancouver Island Exploring Expedition* (Vancouver: University of British Columbia Press, 1989).

Hodgins, Reta Blakely, ed. *Merville and its Early Settlers 1919-1985* (Campbell River: Kask Graphics, 1985).

Holmes, J. B. "Reminiscences of an Old Timer," *Courtenay Free Press*, 20 December 1928.

Hughes, Ben. *History of the Comox Valley 1862 to 1945* (Nanaimo: Evergreen Press, c. 1962).

Ireland, Willard E. "Early Flour-mills in British Columbia. Part 1," *BCHQ* 5:2 (April 1941), 89-111.

Isbister, Winnifred A. *My Ain Folk. Denman Island 1875-1975* (Courtenay: E. W. Bickle Ltd., 1976).

Isenor, D. E., W. N. McInnis, E. G. Stephens, D. E. Watson, eds. *Land of Plenty A History of the Comox District* (Campbell River: Ptarmigan Press, 1987).

Isenor, D. E., Margaret McGill, Donna Watson, eds. *"For our Children:" A History of Comox Valley Schools [1870-1980]* (Courtenay: School Board District #71, [1980]).

Isenor, D. E., E. G. Stephens, D. E. Watson, eds. *Edge of Discovery A History of the Campbell River District* (Campbell River: Ptarmigan Press, 1989).

Jacobsen, Johan Adrian, *Alaskan Voyage 1881-1883. An Expedition to the Northwest Coast of America* (Chicago: University of Chicago Press, 1977).

Keddie, Grant. "The Victoria Smallpox Crisis of 1862," *Discovery, Friends of the Royal British Columbia Museum* 21:4 (1993): 6-7.

Kennedy, Dorothy I. D. and Randall T. Bouchard, "Northern Island Salish," in Wayne Suttles, ed., *Handbook of North American Indians* (Washington, D.C.: Smithsonian Insititution, 1990), pp. 441-52.

Kennedy, Ian. *Sunny Sandy Savary. A History of Savary Island 1792-1992* (Vancouver: Kennell Publishing, 1992).

Knight, Rolf. *Indians at Work: An Informal History of Native Indian Labour in British Columbia* (Vancouver: New Star Books, 1978).

Lander, Tim, ed. *To an Inland Sea: Poems for the Gulf of Georgia* (Nanaimo: Nanaimo Publishers' Co-operative, 1992).

Lavin, J. A. "British Columbia Government Employees in 1876: An Index," *The British Columbia Genealogist* 13:1 (March 1984), pp. 17-30.

———. "Comox Electors 1874-1894," *The British Columbia Genealogist* 13:3 (September 1984), pp. 76-98.

———. "Magistrates Appointed in the Colonies of Vancouver Island and British Columbia, and the Province, 1858-1883: an Index," *The British Columbia Genealogist* 13:2 (June 1984), pp. 38-46.

Lewis-Harrison, June. *The People of Gabriola: A History of our Pioneers* (Cloverdale, B.C.: D. W. Friesen, 1982),

Lowry, Malcolm. *October Ferry to Gabriola* (Harmondsworth, Middlesex, Penguin Books, 1979).

Lugrin, N. de Bertrand. *The Pioneer Women of Vancouver Island* (Victoria:

The Women's Canadian Club of Victoria, 1928).

Lunny, W. J. *A History of Saint Andrew's Comox District Church 1864-1964* (Courtenay, n.d.).

Lutz, John. "After the Fur Trade: The Aboriginal Labouring Class of British Columbia, 1849-1890," *Journal of the Canadian Historical Association* 3 (1992), pp. 69-95.

McDonald, Flora. "Second Prize Article," Union *Weekly News*, 28 September 1897, p. 1.

Mackie, Richard. "The Colonization of Vancouver Island, 1849-1858," *BC Studies* 96 (Winter 1992-93), pp. 3-40.

———. "George Blenkinsop," "Benjamin William Pearse," "William Parsons Sayward," in Ramsay Cook, ed., *DCB*, Volume 13 (Toronto: University of Toronto Press, 1994), pp. 87-89; 822-23; 926-27.

———. "Joseph William McKay" and "Joseph Despard Pemberton," in Frances G. Halpenny, ed., *DCB*, Volume 12 (Toronto: University of Toronto Press, 1990), pp. 641-43; 832-34.

———. *Hamilton Mack Laing: Hunter-Naturalist* (Victoria: Sono Nis Press, 1985).

———, and Alexander Mackie, "Roughing it in the Colonies: an Englishman on Vancouver Island," *The Beaver* 70:2 (March 1990), pp. 6-13.

MacLachlan, Donald F. *The Esquimalt & Nanaimo Railway. The Dunsmuir Years: 1884-1905* (Victoria: British Columbia Railway Historical Association, 1986).

Milligan, Mary. "Fifth Prize Article," Union *Weekly News*, 2 November 1897, p. 1.

Milligan, Rose Ann. "Fourth Prize Article," Union *Weekly News*, 19 October 1897, p. 1.

Mitchell, Helen. *Diamond in the Rough. The Campbell River Story*

(Aldergrove: Frontier Publishing Ltd., 1975).

Morton, James. *The Enterprising Mr. Moody, the Bumptious Captain Stamp. The Lives and Colourful Times of Vancouver's Lumber Pioneers* (Vancouver: J. J. Douglas, 1977).

Murray, Peter. *Homesteads and Snug Harbours: The Gulf Islands* (Victoria: Horsdal & Schubart, 1991).

Nicholls, Peggy. *From the Black Country to Nanaimo 1854* (2 Vols.) (Nanaimo: Nanaimo Historical Society, 1991 and 1992).

Norcross, E. Blanche and Doris Farmer Tonkin. *Frontiers of Vancouver Island* (Courtenay: Island Books, 1969).

Ormsby, Margaret. *British Columbia: A History* (Toronto: Macmillan of Canada, 1958).

Owen, H. B. "Comox," in *Twelfth Annual Report of the Columbia Mission for the Year 1870* (London: Rivingtons, 1871), pp. 26-28.

Pritchard, Allan. "Letters of a Victorian Naval Officer: Edmund Hope Verney in British Columbia, 1862-65," *BC Studies* 86 (Summer 1990), pp. 28-57

———. "The Shapes of History in British Columbia Writing," *BC Studies* 93 (Spring 1992), pp. 48-81.

Reksten, Terry. *The Dunsmuir Saga* (Vancouver: Douglas & McIntyre, 1991).

Reynolds, John. *Windmills and Waterwheels* (New York: Praeger Publishers, 1970).

Richardson, James. "Report on the Coal Fields of the East Coast of Vancouver Island, with a Map of their Distribution," in Geological Survey of Canada, *Reports of Explorations and Surveys 1871-72* (Montreal: Dawson Brothers, 1872), pp. 73-100.

———. "Report on the Coal Fields of Nanaimo, Comox, Cowichen [sic], Burrard Inlet and Sooke, British

Columbia," in Geological Survey of Canada, *Reports of Progress for 1876-77* (Montreal: "Published By Authority of Parliament," 1878), pp. 161-92.

———. "Report on the Coal-Fields of Vancouver and Queen Charlotte Islands, with a Map of the Distribution of the Former," in Geological Survey of Canada, *Reports of Explorations and Surveys 1872-73* (Montreal: Dawson Brothers, 1873), pp. 32-65.

Sager, Eric and Peter Baskerville. *1891 Canadian Census: Victoria, British Columbia* (Victoria, B.C.: Public History Group, *c.* 1991).

Sewid-Smith, Daisy. *Prosecution or Persecution* (Alert Bay: Nu-Yum-Balees Society, 1979).

Sharon, Margaret, ed. "Petitioners of Nanaimo & Comox Constituencies, 1884," *British Columbia Genealogist* 16:1 (1987), pp. 2-5.

Sinclair, Thomson Duncan. *From Shetland to British Columbia, Alaska and the United States. Being a Journal of Travels, with Narrative of Return Journey After Three Years' Exploration* (Lerwick, Scotland: Charles J. Duncan, 1911).

Skelton, Robin. *Landmarks* (Victoria: Sono Nis Press, 1979).

Smith, Dorothy Blakey, ed., "Harry Guillod's Journal of a Trip to Cariboo, 1862," *BCHQ,* 19:3 and 4 (July–October 1955), pp. 187-233.

Smith, Egerton. *A Guide to English Traditions and Public Life* (Oxford: Oxford University Press, 1953).

Spradley, James P., ed. *Guests Never Leave Hungry. The Autobiography of James Sewid, A Kwakiutl Indian* (New Haven and London: Yale University Press, 1969).

Starace, L. J. "The Catholic Mission of Comox, B.C.," in *The British Columbia Orphans' Friend Historical Number* (Victoria: [Roman Catholic Archdiocese of Victoria; The Press Publishing Company], 1913), pp. 35-39.

Stubbs, Dorothy I. *"All About Us." A History of the City of Courtenay* (Courtenay: *c.* 1965).

Tarbell, Ellen. "Third Prize Article," Union *Weekly News,* 5 October 1897, p. 1.

Thompson, F. M. L. *Chartered Surveyors: the Growth of a Profession* (London: Routledge and Kegan Paul, 1968).

Thomson, Don W. *Men and Meridians. The History of Surveying and Mapping in Canada* Vol. 1 (Ottawa: Queen's Printer, 1966).

Vancouver, George. *A Voyage of Discovery to the North Pacific Ocean, and Round the World* (London: G. G. and J. Robinson, 1798).

Vancouver Island. *A Collection of Public General Statutes of the Colony of Vancouver Island, Passed in the Years 1859, 1860, 1861, 1862, and 1863* (Victoria: British Colonist Office, 1866).

Walbran, John T. *British Columbia Coast Names* 1592-1906 (Vancouver: J. J. Douglas, 1977, first printed Ottawa, 1909).

Whittaker, John A. (comp). *Early Land Surveyors of British Columbia* (Victoria: Corporation of Land Surveyors of British Columbia, 1990).

Willemar, J. X. "Comox—St. Andrew's, in *Twentieth Annual Report of the Missions of the Church of England in British Columbia for the Year 1878* (London: Rivingtons, 1879), pp. 24-26.

———. "St. Andrew's, Comox," in *Seventeenth Annual Report of the Missions of the Church of England in British Columbia for the Year 1875* (London: Rivingtons, 1876), p. 29.

———. "St. Andrew's, Comox," in *Nineteenth Annual Report of the Missions of the Church of England in British Columbia for the Year 1877* (London: Rivingtons, 1878), pp. 22-23.

———, and H. Guillod. "Comox. St. Andrew's Mission," in *Thirteenth*

Annual Report of the Missions of the Church of England in British Columbia for the Year 1871 (London: Rivingtons, 1872), pp. 30-34.

Williams, R. T. *The British Columbia Directory for the years 1882-83 . . .* (Victoria: R. T. Williams, 1882).

Woodcock, George. *British Columbia, A History of the Province* (Vancouver, Douglas & McIntyre, 1990.)

3. MAPS

George Drabble, [Plan of subdivision at west end of Comox Townsite, Section 1, Creech's land], "deposited 25 June 1889," [Plan 241], SGB.

———. "Plan of McPhee's Subdivision of Lot 1. Colored thus. . . . Comox District," "deposited 16 March 1893," [Plan 503], SGB.

———. "Plan of the Townsite of Comox. Being Part of Sec. LVI," [1883], CDMA.

———. "Subdivision Plan of Part of Section 1. Being the Portion Colored Red. Comox District," "deposited 8 April 1890," [Plan 275], SGB.

Going, A. S. "Map Showing land in lieu of Alienated Lands in Esquimalt and Nanaimo Railway Belt," 17 February 1896, in British Columbia. Department of Lands. Originals, 1860-1912 [Papers concerning the Esquimalt and Nanaimo Railway Belt], BCARS, GR 1404.

Great Britain. Admiralty. "North America—West Coast. Vancouver Island. Port Augusta (Comox). Surveyed . . . under the direction of Morris H. Smyth, R.N. H.M. Surveying Ship 'Egeria' 1898," CDMA.

Ralph, William. [Plan of Ralph's 1864 Comox Survey], SGB.

Wagner, Gordon. "Plan of Ralph's 1864 Survey of the Comox Valley. Plotted by Gordon Wagner." Private Collection.

Index

Dupont, Mr., 266
Dyke Road, 114, 270-71

Earle, Thomas, 264
Eckstein, Louis, 277
Edwards, Agnes (née Curie), 50, 109, 118, 222
Elk, 60, 80, 81, 83-85, 171, 238, 242-43, 271
Elk Hotel, 18, 124, 157, 158, 159, 163, 164, 168, 180, 197, 216, 241, 242, 243, 280
Emily Harris (ship), 60, 77
Englishman River, 252
Enos, John, 53, 63, 251-52
Esquimalt & Nanaimo Land Grant, 166-67, 193, 273
Esquimalt & Nanaimo Railway 158, 167, 168, 193, 195, 202, 205, 208, 211, 213, 247, 263, 274, 276
Et-sat-sa, 149
Etta White (ship), 186
E-yees, 48
Ey-exen, 48

Fannin, John, 243
Fanny Bay, 106, 158, 177, 189-90, 251
Farquharson Farm, 73
Farming: agrarian ethos, 59, 68, 284-85; dairy farming and cattle, 40, 60-61, 69, 72, 73, 75, 90-91, 92, 102, 108, 109, 147, 157, 162, 181, 182, 199-200, 204, 210, 221, 227, 240, 280; vegetable and cereal crops, 69, 72, 73, 89, 91, 121-22, 162, 199, 221, 227; at Nanaimo, 58; poultry and eggs, 72, 75-76, 86, 162, 182, 199, 200, 201, 220, 264-65, 280; ignorance of farming, 61, 66; breaking the soil, 70-72; American competition, 76-77, 82, 89, 98, 221; pigs, 61, 70-71, 72-73, 75-76, 90-91, 92, 105, 109, 114, 145, 147, 201; farm implements, 73, 89, 92; fruit, 73, 214; co-operative creamery, 213; threshing machine, 89, 217; connection with logging, 224; strawberries, 279; and market provided by Royal Navy, 279-80; a summer occupation, 285; *See also* Potatoes, Horses, Oxen, Ploughs and ploughing, Grist Mill, Hay and haying, Labour, Choppings, Native labour, For markets, *see* Nanaimo, Victoria,

Union, Chemainus, Lumber Industry
Fawcett, Elizabeth, 26
Fawcett, Elizabeth (Eliza). *See* Eliza Drabble
Fawcett, George, 26
Fawcett, Thomas Lea, 153
Field's Sawmill, 90, 112
Finlayson, Roderick, 189
Finley, Thomas, 87, 182, 281
Finley Creek, 88, 89, 90, 176
Fitzgerald, Anne (Annie), 63, 245
Fitzgerald, John, 62, 63
Fitzgerald, Joseph (Joe), 63, 110, 177, 182, 208, 245
Fitzgerald, Michael, 232
Fitzpatrick, John, 127, 157, 182
Flat Road, 20, 111-15, 223
Fletcher, Charles, 65, 73
Forbidden Plateau, 289
Ford, George, 52, 62, 63, 67, 69, 107, 110, 204, 250
Fort Alexandria, 41
Fort Langley, 71
Fort Rupert, 39, 79, 146, 149, 185, 266-67
Fort Simpson, 46, 118
Forward (ship), 77, 148
Franklyn, Capt. William Hales, 58-59, 77, 78, 83, 92, 106, 146, 148-50
Fraser, Donald, 38, 44
Fraser, Jack, 200
Fraser, Thomas, 200
Fraser River gold rush, 38, 39, 40, 77
Fur trade, 117, 118, 121, 122-25, 162

Gabriola Island, 40
Gage, Walter, 220, 279
Galarno, Andy, 262
Garge, Mrs., 277
Gartley, George, 108, 110
Garven, Alex, 250
Giddings, J. B., 277, 281
Gilbert, Robert, 269
Gilmour family, 218
Gladstone (Indian), 191
Gleason, William, 209
Glover-Geidt, Janette, 19
Goepel, Phillip, 265
Goldsmid, Edward, 88, 145
Good, Rev. John Both, 79, 80
Goose Spit, Comox, 50, 278-79
Gordon, D. W., 105, 107, 157, 170, 182, 185, 239
Gordon, Elizabeth (née Robb), 157

305

Gough, Edwin, 39
Graham, James, 239
Graham, John, 251
Graham, Robert, 208, 239, 270
Graham, Thomas, 205, 208
Graham family, 180, 189
Grant, Alexander, 168, 169, 217
Grant, John J., 183, 205, 208, 224, 235, 239
Grant, Kenneth, 209
Grant, Lorenzo, 239
Grant, Robert, 20, 180, 197, 199, 210, 240, 270, 273
Grantham, 239, 245
Grappler (ship), 43
Greaves, Henry, 92, 107
Greaves, Road. *See* Anderton Road
Green, Alfred, 193
Green, Ashdown, 164
Green, Charles, 62, 63, 210
Green, John, 258
Green's Slough (Courtenay Slough), 20, 103, 107, 184, 210, 211
Grieve, George, 216-17, 245-46
Grieve, Henry (Harry), 174, 233, 245
Grieve, Isabella. *See* Isabella Piercy
Grieve, Jane, 216, 217
Grieve, Joe, 177, 245
GRIEVE FAMILY, 216
Grove, William, 233, 251
Guillod, Harry, 40, 66, 92, 175, 176, 185, 213
Gunderson, Salven ("Oliver"), 62, 66, 84, 87

Haas, Mildred, 17
Haggard, H. Rider, 21
Haida, 46
Halcrow, Gideon, 123, 174
Hall, Rev. Alfred James, 266
Hall, A. S., 280
Hall, Robert (Bob), 263, 264
Halliday, William, 165, 182
Halliday, William May, 54, 128, 227, 239
Ham-chit, 47
Hamilton, Archibald, 251
Hamilton, James, 251
Hamilton, S. B., 251
Hamilton family, 192
Hansen, Albert, 261
Harding, Rene, 17
Hare, Richard, 108
Hargreave, Henry, 68, 86, 87
Harmston, Florence. *See* Florence Cliffe
Harmston, Mary, 22, 45, 54, 56, 59, 63, 65, 83, 127, 157, 159, 164,
172, 173, 180, 195, 202, 205, 223, 226, 227, 233, 241, 244-45, 268, 278, 287
Harmston, William, 45, 56, 63, 65, 68, 75, 80, 83, 148
Harmston, William (Willie), 177, 287
Harney, Mr., 57
Harrigan, William, 88, 200, 208
Harris, Sam, 192
Harris, William, 255, 258
Harrison, Judge, 273
Harrup, Henry, 68, 78-79, 86
Hart, John ("Jack"), 77-78, 79, 117, 118, 122-23, 145, 191
Hart Creek, 191
Haslam, Andrew, 177, 183
Hassard, William, 105, 106, 234
Hastings Saw Mill Company, 258
Hawkins, Jack, 168, 220
Hawksby, William, 220
Hawthornthwaite & Co., 209
Hay and haying, 73, 86, 105, 221, 233, 281
Headquarters Road: *See* Lower Prairie Road
Heatherbell, William, 250
Hendry, John, 180, 264
Henry, Mr., 172
Herbert, D. L., 250
Hernando Island, 255, 258
Hetherington, John, 182
Hibben, Thomas Napier, 97
Hill, Edward Barton, 262, 263, 264
Hills, Bishop George, 94, 151, 216, 217, 226, 228
Hirst, J. J., 153, 164
Hirst, Thomas, 158, 162, 235
Hirst, William, 158, 162, 235
Hodgins family, 240
Hoggan, James, 252
Hoggan family, 192
Holder, John, 68, 78-79, 86, 87, 117, 145, 191
Holmes, Ellen, 159
Holmes, John, 232
Holmes, Joseph Burnard, 20, 123, 126, 154, 156, 158-59, 162-63, 169, 170, 173, 193, 196, 203, 213, 235, 250, 269, 280, 283, 287
Holmes, Nellie. *See* Nellie Stewart
Honeyman, John, 239
Honeyman & Curtis (firm), 242
Hooper, Charles, 110, 182
Hornby Island, 67, 149, 252

Horne, Adam Grant, 39, 40, 74, 93, 94, 105, 118, 121-23, 125, 192, 193, 250
Horne, Adam H., 123
Horne, Elizabeth, 123
Horne (Comox Indian), 78
Horses, 72, 73, 74, 84, 89, 102, 109, 112, 150-51, 180, 182, 186, 195, 199, 210, 221, 227; See also Transport
Howe, George, 113, 168, 169
Howe, John, 191, 250
Howse, A. R., ??????
Hudson's Bay Blankets, 73, 119, 125, 127, 162, 263
Hudson's Bay Company: 37, 46, 48, 51, 58, 94, 105, 114, 147, 162, 175; buckets, 71-72; store at Comox, 118-25, 158; and historical continuity, 123-24; See Adam Grant Horne
Hughes, Ben, 18
Humphreys, Thomas, 73
Hunter, Joseph, 196
Hunting, 80-81, 83-85, 91, 163, 175, 242-43, 244, 245, 271-72, 280; See also Wildlife, Deer, Elk, Cougar
Hussey, Frederick, 273
Huxton, Henry (Harry), 110, 168

Icarus (ship), 281
Immigrants. *See* Settlers
Imperieuse (ship), 280-81
"Indian Dick," 94, 249
"Indian Mary," 269
"Indian Tom," 249
Indians. *See* Native people
Ingle, Mrs., 195
Isbister, Winnifred, 19
Isenor, D. E., 19

Jackson, Robert, 122, 153
Jacobsen, Adrian, 51
Japanese workers, 198, 200
J. D. Peters (ship), 268
Jeffries, William, 255
Jenkins, John, 251
Jessop, John, 94
Jocelyn, Capt., 28, 31
Joan (ship), 198
"Joe Town," 169
Johnson, 218
Johnston, John, 239
Jones, Abraham, 180
Jones, Bob, 110, 180

Jones, David, 232
Jones, James (Jemmy"), 122
Jones, Thomas, 39
Jones, William ("Bill," "Whiskey,"), 241
Jordan, John, 269
Joseph, 127
Joyce, Alfred, 264
Joyce, Walter, 264
Joyce, Mrs., 209
Julia (Clayous), 127, 287
Jurgenson, C., 269
Justices of the Peace, 120, 145-54, 262, 269, 273; *See also* Administration of Justice

Kelland, George, 238, 239
Kendall, Capt., 77
Kennedy, Governor Arthur, 58
Kileoquits, 266
King, Alfred, 16
King, Mary (née Cowie), 177
King, Harold, 128
King, Michael, 159, 177, 264
King, Thomas, 128
King and Casey (firm), 168, 177, 180, 183-84, 186, 222, 224-25, 242, 243, 264, 284
Kirkup, John, 264
Klacklakia, 153
Knight, James, 261
Knights of Pythias Hall, Comox, 270, 274
Knox, Joseph, 208
Ko-mah-laglees, 266
Koprino Harbour, 267
Kuhushan Point, 261
Kus-kus-sum, 52
Kwakiutl. *See* Kwakwaka'wakw
Kwakwaka'wakw, 49, 125-26
Kye Bay, 234, 277

Labour, 95, 115, 122, 196, 197, 198, 200, 208, 218, 222, 239; at Nanaimo, 58; road workers, 105; on Flat Road, 112; agricultural labour, 105, 222; in logging camps, 177; *See also* Chinese labour, Native labour
Lake Road, 110-11, 182, 214
Lambert, Nathaniel, 269
Land laws. *See* Pre-emption laws
Langley, A. J., 191
Langley Point, 191, 194
Larue, Dominick, 222
Lasquiti Island, 255
Leask, Thomas, 264

Midwives. *See* Women
Milk. *See* Farming
Millard, Harrison, 226
Miller, J. J. R., 107, 169, 282
Miller, Thomas, 265
Millet, Edwin J., 168, 280
Milligan, Archibald, 84, 115
Mining Industry, 39, 45, 186-201, 255; *See also* Union Mine; Robert Dunsmuir, Baynes Sound Coal Company, Perseverance Coal Mining Company, Union Coal Company, Texada Marble Company, Wellington Mine
Mink Island, 258
Minto Valley, 208
Mitchell, George, 39-40, 42, 43, 62, 68, 70, 72, 75-76, 79
Mitchell, Helen, 19
Mitchell's Slough, 112
Mohun, Edward, 87
Moody, Sewell Prescott, 122, 174
Morley, Christopher, 68
Morrison, 218
Moss, Morris, 193, 252
Mouat family, 218
Mounce, Lewis, 197, 240
Mt. Arrowsmith, 252
Mt. Dalgleish, 258, 262
Mt. Drabble, xiii, 289
Mt. Lytton, 289
Mountain, Robert, 244
"Mowitch." *See* Deer
Mud Bay, 251
Muirhead and Mann, 183, 269
Munro, Malcolm, 102
Murdock, John, 251
Murphy, Patrick, 65, 73, 169, 170, 226
Murray, David, 126
Musgrave, Governor Anthony, 93
Musgrave, Jessie (née Dunsmuir), 263
Musgrave, Sir Richard, 263
Musters, Lucy, 64, 92
Musters, William Chaworth, 64, 72, 80, 83, 84, 86, 88, 91, 92, 95, 217, 229
Musters, William Musters, 64
Myers, Jack, 265
Myrmidon (ship), 108
Mystery (ship), 267

Nanaimo, 37, 38, 39, 40, 41, 42, 57-58, 78, 79, 118, 124, 151, 158, 168, 177, 183, 189, 196, 226, 235, 251, 266; market for Comox produce, 72-73, 75, 76, 77, 93, 123, 162, 199, 201; Nanaimo district includes Comox, 103, 105, 146, 151, 153; Jail, 152; Lighthouse, 252
Nanaimo Native people, 46, 58, 149
Nanoose, 41, 53, 63, 105, 251, 258
Nanoose Native people, 53
Native labour: as farm labourers for settlers, 53-54, 71-72, 148, 222, 227, 248; carry settlers on backs, 77; on Flat Road, 112; canoe hire, 121, 191, 222, 249; in lumber industry, 183, 222; at canneries and hop fields, 222; domestic labour, 223; replaced by Chinese, 223; supply provisions, 80; as surveying assistants, 97, 249, 263, 266
Native people: and smallpox epidemic, 38, 45-50, 286; population, 37, 50, 52; exploitation of roots and berries, 42, 70; warfare, 47, 48; fishing, 49, 52, 53, 54, 69, 109, 147, 148, 153; whiskey trade and consumption, 49, 146-48, 164, 228; cohabitation and marriage with settlers, 54, 67; and Hudson's Bay Company land, 118; trade and trade goods, 125, 162-63, 248; potlatches, 50, 54, 125, 162, 165, 279; deer and elk hunting, 52, 80, 171; and pre-emption laws, 52, 98, 230-32, 248, 250, 286; at Lund, 261; at Campbell River, 263; at Alert Bay, 266; at Nimpkish River, 266; at Quatsino, 267; *See also* Chinook, Native labour, Archaeological Sites, Lekwiltok, Nanaimo, Comox, Pentlatch, Haida, Tsimshian, Bella Bella, Sae-luth, Ey-exen, Kwakwaka'wakw, Weewiakay, Nanoose, Chilcotin, Fur trade
Neale, Mr., 87
Nelson, Charles, 261
Nicholson, Joseph, 111-13, 223, 270
Niles, Philip, 251
Nim-Nim, Joe, 49
Nimnin, 263
Nimpkish Lake, 266
Nimpkish River, 266
Nimskunitim, 153
Nixon, George, 172
Nob Hill (Comox), 277, 279
Nonmoncaas, 50
Norcross, Blanche, 53, 54

Settlers: as letter-writers, 22; from
England, 38, 39, 40, 42, 44, 62,
64-67, 218-20, 238-42; from
Ireland, 39, 44, 62, 63, 217-18,
262; from Scotland, 39, 44, 62,
217-18, 239, 240; from maritime
Provinces, 62, 174, 189, 200,
215-17, 228-29, 286; from Ontario
and Quebec, 62, 81, 218, 239-40;
"half-breed" children, 66; apathy,
61; transiency, 68, 83; cohabitation
and marriage with Native women,
67; pre-ponderance of male
settlers, 44, 66, 271; poverty, 61,
66, 73-74, 83; character of settlers,
66-68; families, fecundity, and
fertility, 66-68, 155, 215, 225-26;
Charivari, 159; primitive dwellings,
174; violence among, 67-68, 78-79,
155; style of dress, 73-74; marriage,
226; cooperative ventures, 176,
181, 226; notions of class, 228-29;
lost in the wilderness, 244-46; use
of terms "wilderness" and "settler,"
285; new occupational
opportunities, 285; adaptation to
new environment, 229, 242, 247,
285-86; as "second-growth
Englishmen," 286; resemblence to
Dickens' characters, 287; See also
Australian Miners, Pre-emptions,
"Twelve Apostles," Schools, Politics,
Stories, Bees, Women, Petitions,
Settlement Act, 167
Sewid or Seaweed, Chief, 126, 128
Shannon (ship), 40
Shaw, J., 251
Shelter Point, 235, 261
Shields, James, 126
Silistria (ship); 28, 29, 30, 40, 44, 45,
56, 57, 171-72, 287
Sinclair, Reginald St. Clair, 203
Sir James Douglas (ship), 76, 77, 93, 94,
121, 125, 174, 192
Sircassian (ship), 241
Sisters of St. Ann, 169
Siwash or Sywash Hill. See Comox Hill
Skid Roads, 125, 177, 180, 181, 182, 192
Skidegate (ship), 266
Skillen, Mr., 266
Smallpox. See Native people
Smith, Amelia, 241
Smith, Cecil, 241-42
Smith, Ella, 242
Smith, Eustace, 19, 84, 238, 241-42

Smith, Harvey, 241
Smith, Hilda, 241
Smith, Horace (elder) 239, 241
Smith, Horace (younger), 240-42, 243,
250, 269, 279
Smith, Ida, 241
Smith, John, 264, 265
Smith, Mrs. John, 265
Smith, Mabel, 241
Smith, Mary (née Pidcock), 242
Smith, Maud, 241
Smith, Maud (née Beadnell), 242
Smith, Neville, 241-42
Smith, Percy, 242
Smith, William, 56, 57
Smith, William C., 239
Smith family, 286
Snow, Allan, 239
Snowdon, N. P., 264
Solly, Leonard, 273-74
Somerville, James, 107
Sons of Temperance, 166
Spalding, Warner Reeve, 67, 103, 146,
149, 150, 151, 153
Spencer, Miss, 277
Spenser, S. A., 266
Sproat, Gilbert Malcolm, 98
"Steamer Day," 22, 158, 164, 210
Steele family, 218
Stenhouse, Anthony Maitland, 165,
223, 235, 238
Stephenson, H. F., 278
Stewart, Charles, 223
Stewart, Dan, 168
Stewart, Hugh, 177, 270
Stewart, Joseph, 261
Stewart, Nellie (née Holmes), 162
Stewart, Norman, 289
Stories: Bailey's bee story, 86; Muskes'
horse story, 84-85; hunting stories,
163
Sturt, Capt. Henry, 255
Sullivan, Dan, 191, 233, 250
Surgenor family, 218
Sutton, William, 250
Swan, Robert, 168, 211, 249
Swanson, Alfred, 261

Texada Island, 255
Texada Marble Company, 255
Thomas, Evan Rowland, 107, 205, 208,
225
Thomas, William, 261
Thomas, Mrs., 225
Thomas, 263

Errata

I am grateful to Robert Allen, Ruth Barnett, Dick Downey, Bill Lowry, Ruth Masters, Darrell McQuillan, and Eleanor Nordin for pointing out the following errors in the original text:

- The descendants of William Beach, who spelled his surname with an *a*, now spell their name "Beech."
- "Eliza's father" (p. 27, second paragraph) should read "Louisa's father."
- Charles Bridges was from Queen's County, Ireland. I should have clarified that, although Eric Duncan refers to Bridges as an "Ontario man" (p. 62), there were no Ontarians in early Comox.
- On map 5 (opposite p. 105), Reunion Road should be Bridges Road and Rabson's Road should be Section I, not Section H.
- Rosemary Lowry (p. 114): "née Anderton" should be "*née* Downey."
- On p. 123, "battens over the joists" should read "battens over the joints."
- "Comox townsite" (p. 186, second line) should read "Courtenay townsite."
- Bob McQuillan, not Harry McQuillan, owned the Courtenay livery stables (pp. 199, 218).
- The McKenzie blacksmith shop was across the road from the Courtenay Hotel, not on the site of the British Car Centre (p. 210).
- Eustace Smith, timber cruiser, did not train as a surveyor (p. 242).
- The caption "Qualicum Train" should read "Qualicum Trail" (p. 251).
- Ruth Barnett (p. 291): "née Sterritt" should be "*née* Pidcock."

Afterword

The Wilderness Profound was first published in October 1995. I am gratified that it sold well and that it attracted both popular and academic audiences. For this new printing in 2002, I am pleased to have the opportunity, first, to offer a new analysis of the book's themes; second, to present new information; and third, to correct mistakes in the original text (see Errata, opposite).[1]

Unlike many more eminent British Columbians of the nineteenth century, George Drabble did not leave behind personal diaries or letters. This fact made impossible an in-depth, personal biography. Instead, I had to reconstruct his career from government records at the British Columbia Archives, and the book that resulted was based largely on those records. In the end, the book's apparent weakness became its main strength. A necessary emphasis on Drabble's working life meant that what started as biography ended as regional history.

This book is about the imposition, in a few short decades, of a colonial regime in a Native world. It is about the extension of non-Native settlement and government institutions to the remote northern shores of the Gulf of Georgia; the introduction there of three lasting forms of colonial capital—settler, commercial, and government; and Drabble's role in all this.

Although the available sources determined the shape and content of this book, it was also illuminated by a decade of graduate study. It was not written in a vacuum, as one academic reviewer asserted; most of the topics and themes are germane to any study of nineteenth-century British Columbia, and my debt to contemporary British Columbian historians will be apparent from the bibliography. I was aware, for example, of Patricia Roy's 1982 call for a "thorough or systematic study of British Columbia in the Confederation era."[2] *The Wilderness Profound* contributes such a study on a local scale.

Some larger themes I bore in mind when I researched and wrote this book include the following:

• Adam Smith's assertion that the state must be involved directly in five aspects of a nation's economy: administration of justice, public works, public institutions, institutions of education, and defence.[3] Drabble helped put the first four in place on Vancouver Island.

• Karl Marx's analysis of the inexorable global extension of capital,[4] seen repeatedly here on a local scale, for example, in Drabble's remote surveys for timber, mineral, and cannery speculators and in the opening of Robert Dunsmuir's coal mine at Cumberland.

• Harold Innis's insistence that the "staple trades" (resource industries) have been the motors of Canadian economic growth for the last 400 years.[5] Locally, the single large industrial payroll at Cumberland stimulated urban growth, transport improvements, and agricultural production. Drabble's timber surveys promised the same potential.

• William Morris's concern that English factories were exporting cheap, mass-produced products to the whole world;[6] such products included the shards of transfer-print dinnerware shown on the front cover, shards I found on the beach at Baynes Sound.

• Thomas Hardy's rejection of cosmopolitan influences in favour of preserving and reconstructing local memories and histories— what he called "local knowledge."[7] Hardy's intense regionalism was an inspiration for *The Wilderness Profound.*

I was also influenced by the traditional methods of historical geography, especially the horizontal cross-section mapping technique, intended to illustrate change over time, which I used in the sequence of maps in the first eight chapters.[8]

The book's findings, therefore, apply to a larger stage than British Columbia or even Canada; they intersect with other colonial histories and with ideas pursued by historians and geographers of colonialism and empire. Daniel Clayton summarized these connections in a letter to me of March 1996:

> In our rush to write theoretically overloaded accounts of colonial encounters, we can easily forget that colonial realities were intricate and always multi-faceted. . . . Take Drabble: a man from a particular English class, with specific ideas about his past and colonial future, "going native" in the bush, working almost subterraneously as a colonial agent, helping to build the colonial state, harnessing the wilderness, building wooden and metaphorical bridges across creeks, and bringing one corner of Vancouver Island into spatial existence, so to speak. There must be hundreds of Drabbles in British Columbia, and thousands more like him throughout the British Empire, whose biographies are just as important as those of explorers, colonial governors, and naval captains. Ordinary people who turned Native territory into colonial space, who resettled the land.[9]

Brief biographies of two of these "hundreds of Drabbles in British Columbia"—John Clapperton (1835–1913) and Henry Edmonds (1837–1897)—have already been written.[10]

∽

Ever since *The Wilderness Profound* was published, I have kept a file of new material on George Drabble and his forty-year career on the Gulf of Georgia. Details of his life and work and of early Comox Valley history continue to reveal themselves.

Drabble's English career is still murky, though his great-granddaughter Sybil Carr found his elusive birthdate in a family Bible: 17 May 1833.[11] A novel by Thomas Hardy (1840–1928) provides glimpses of the work of bailiffs in rural England, where Drabble's father was a farm bailiff and Drabble worked in a land office. In *Desperate Remedies* (1871), Hardy wrote that the duties of a "land or building steward" included surveying, planning, and laying out estates; designing and erecting buildings; and making agricultural improvements.[12] In Nanaimo, where he was a bailiff in 1865, and in the Comox Valley, Drabble performed these functions and more.

Two important new sources for the early history of the Comox Valley came to light when I was researching *Island Timber: A Social History of the Comox Logging Company, Vancouver Island* (Sono Nis Press, 2000), a book that overlaps chronologically and thematically with *The Wilderness Profound* and is in a sense its sequel. The first new source is a diary kept occasionally between 1862 and the early 1870s by Drabble's friend Samuel Jackson Cliffe (1842–1908).[13] The second source comprises the reminiscences of Bob Piercy (1888–1958), a son of Comox settlers Matthew Piercy (1851–1909) and Mary Machin (1854–1941). Many of Bob Piercy's stories would have enriched this book; the following are two examples:

> In 1868 there was a big Indian war on the lower part of Machin place [Section 30]. There used to be many acres of blue berries there. . . . I remember when that was first ploughed the skulls were everywhere.
>
> *Bill Ross.* He was the district's first chicken farmer. He said he got more pleasure coming home to the chickens than a man did to his wife.[14]

Among the discoveries colleagues and I have made at the British Columbia Archives are the original plans for the Courtenay River Bridge (1874); plans for the "Comox Lock-up" (1875), which housed rowdy miners from the company town of Quadra on Baynes Sound; plans for a new courthouse at Comox (1891); and a painting by Victoria artist Josephine Crease entitled "Bridge in Comox Valley 1877," which shows the newly completed and controversial "Long Bridge" or "Long Trestle" over the mud flats in Comox Harbour.[15] One could scour the political, legal, and land records at the archives almost endlessly for references to Drabble.

New references have appeared to Drabble's surveys at Quathiaski Cove for Reginald Pidcock (1882), at Nimpkish River for S. A. Spenser (1884), and at Nanoose Bay for John Enos (1885).[16] The newspapers reveal details of Drabble's repairs to the Comox wharf (1888) and of a fire that destroyed his barn at Comox (1889), a barn he had rented to Horace Smith. According to the *Nanaimo Free Press*, "a young child built a fire alongside the barn, which quickly reached the barn. The child ran to the woods, and on returning said, 'I'll not do it again, I'm so sorry, put me under the pump!' Rather a severe kind of punishment."[17]

More light has also been shed on Drabble's sad final years, in the form of a confidential letter of January 1900 from Mary Bissett, editor of the *Cumberland News*, to the Attorney General:

> You may remember that when the govt made changes in the JPs of the province last year, one of the magistrates who failed to receive a new commission was Mr. G. F. Drabble of Comox. It was understood at the time that politics was the reason for his removal, i.e., some individuals (in Comox) who had more influence than he with the govt, and who had personal differences with him, had worked against Mr. Drabble. Whether this is correct, of course, I cannot say. However, though he never spoke on the subject, I am sure his dismissal weighed on his mind for he had held the commission upwards of twenty years and its cancellation he regarded as a reflection on his character. Putting all other considerations aside, no man in Comox has done so many kindnesses to his neighbours nor kept peace between them as Mr. Drabble. He has done many a good turn for all of us. The poor old man is dying now, and as one whom he has helped among others, I am writing to ask you to restore him his magistrate's commission. It may seem of no importance to a stranger, but it will give him a great deal of happiness and will, I feel certain, please the district generally.[18]

Drabble was reappointed in March 1900 and died in September 1901.

Posthumous developments: in the fall of 1936 an old brick block was renovated at the corner of Dunsmuir Avenue and Third Street in Cumberland. The *Comox Argus* reported that a dusty old ledger book had been found that listed the names of settlers and the land they took up in the Comox Valley in the first two years of colonial settlement, 1862–1863:

> It is written in a scholarly hand, just as plain and unblurred today as when it was penned nearly three quarters of a century ago. Although there is no name in the book, it is almost certainly the handwriting of that remarkable man of the early days, George Fawcett Drabble. . . . He was urged, Mr. William Duncan said, to write a history of the valley and it may well be that this was the beginning of it.[19]

This ledger is now in the Courtenay Museum.

Since 1995, I have made contact with Drabble's descendants in British Columbia and England. The Canadian family are all descended from Drabble's son John Drabble of Alert Bay. According to ethnographer Marius Barbeau, in about 1925 John Drabble (Kwawrhilanukumi) paid Mungo Martin $350 to carve "Raven-of-the-Sea" (*qwawis*), a pole featuring four figures: Raven- or Crow-of-the-Sea (*qwawis*), Sea Lion (*liken*), Grizzly Bear (*gylila*), and a man known as You-Speak-Through (*yeqandoq*) who, Barbeau notes, had "a protruding mouth shaped like a funnel." This is a reference to John Drabble's role as orator at Alert Bay. "A big feast was given by the owner at the time of its erection," states Barbeau. Raven-of-the-Sea was sold in 1947 to the Anthropology Museum at the University of British Columbia by John Drabble's wife Rachel Drabble (LaLahlewildzemkae).[20]

While John Drabble was commissioning Raven-of-the-Sea at Alert Bay, his English relative Richard Bemrose (son of George Drabble's daughter Lylie) was running his chemist shop on High Street, Dawley, Shropshire. Behind the counter in the 1930s were three schoolgirls: Richard Bemrose's niece Sybil Dunkey; her friend Lucilla Clayton, who later emigrated to Alberta; and their friend Edith Pargetter, who, under the pseudonym Ellis Peters, went on to write the successful "Brother Cadfael" stories set in twelfth-century Shropshire.[21]

The English and Canadian branches of the family, with their common ancestor and divergent histories, finally made contact in 1999 when two of Drabble's great-great-granddaughters met. Carole Donovan, Richard Bemrose's great-niece, visited Vancouver Island from her home in Spain; she met Alice Drabble's granddaughter Veronica King, born at Alert Bay in 1959.[22] I met Donovan as well.

It was two years earlier, however, that I first met a descendant of the Drabble family. I visited England and had the pleasure of lunching with Drabble's great-granddaughter Sybil Carr (née Dunkey) and her husband Tommy (Dr. Thomas Carr). I described the meeting in my diary entry for 30 September 1997:

> They live in a flat very near Putney Heath. Sybil took me up to the roof where we had a fine view of London in the sultry, smoggy autumn air. A well-thumbed copy of *The Wilderness Profound* lay upon the coffee table. We had tea, then sherry, then a hearty English lunch. . . . It turns out that Sybil inherited furniture from Crossburn House, Lincolnshire—the home of Drabble's wife Louisa Burnby. Three or four pieces, including a Georgian table, came from Crossburn House, and we ate from mid-Victorian cutlery and plates from the Burnby family. Indeed, Sybil still has the receipt for the purchase of the plates and table service. The receipt is dated 1857, the year of George and Louisa's wedding, and Sybil thinks they were a wedding present. *So I ate at a table from plates and cutlery that Drabble left behind in England in 1862!* Somehow I felt very fulfilled by this. . . . the day was important in terms of Drabble's memory. Some sort of laying to rest took place.

Now, 140 years later, the wounds caused by Drabble's abrupt departure seem to have healed.

RICHARD SOMERSET MACKIE
Cowichan Bay, British Columbia, January 2002

NOTES

1 This afterword has benefited immeasurably from archival material sent to me by Kathryn Bridge, Sybil Carr, Pete Dady, Chris Hanna, Brad Morrison, Allan Pritchard, Leona Taylor, and especially Jeanette Taylor. I also wish to acknowledge Diane Morriss, publisher of Sono Nis Press, and editor Dawn Loewen for their work on the afterword.

2 Patricia Roy, "British Columbia," in J. L. Granatstein and Paul Stevens, *A Reader's Guide to Canadian History 2: Confederation to the Present* (Toronto: University of Toronto Press, 1982), p. 164.

3 Adam Smith, *An Inquiry into the Nature and Causes of the Wealth of Nations*, Book V (Oxford: Clarendon Press, 1976).

4 Francis Wheen, *Karl Marx: A Life* (London: Fourth Estate, 1999).

5 For Innis's work see M. H. Watkins, "A Staple Theory of Economic Growth," in W. T. Esterbrook and M. H. Watkins, ed., *Approaches to Canadian Economic History* (Toronto: McClelland and Stewart, 1967), pp. 49–73. For a local elaboration of Innis's ideas, see Cole Harris, *The Resettlement of British Columbia: Essays on Colonialism and Geographical Change* (Vancouver: UBC Press, 1997), pp. 194–218.

6 William Morris, "How We Live and How We Might Live," in W. Morris, *News from Nowhere and Selected Writings and Designs* (Harmondsworth, Middlesex: Penguin, 1986), pp. 158–79.

7 Thomas Hardy, *The Woodlanders* (Harmondsworth, Middlesex: Penguin, 1998), p. 48. Hardy explains his preference for the local over the cosmopolitan in "General Preface to the Wessex Edition of 1912," reprinted in T. Hardy, *The Distracted Preacher and Other Tales* (Harmondsworth, Middlesex: Penguin, 1979), pp. 343–48.

8 H. C. Darby, ed., *Historical Geography of England before A.D. 1800* (Cambridge: Cambridge University Press, 1936).

9 Daniel Clayton to the author, 24 March 1996. See also Daniel W. Clayton, *Islands of Truth: The Imperial Fashioning of Vancouver Island* (Vancouver: UBC Press, 2000).

10 Patrick Dunae, "Jottings of a Gentleman," *British Columbia Historical News* 15:4 (1982), pp. 19–21; Robert A. J. McDonald, "Henry Valentine Edmonds," *Dictionary of Canadian Biography*, Volume XII (Toronto: University of Toronto Press, 1990), pp. 294–95.

11 Drabble family, "Family Register," copy sent by Sybil Carr, 3 December 1995.

12 Thomas Hardy, *Desperate Remedies: A Novel* (Harmondsworth, Middlesex: Penguin, 1998), pp. 102, 106.

13 Richard Mackie, "Two Colonial Diaries from the Comox Valley," Archives Association of British Columbia Newsletter (Winter 1998), pp. 9–10. Sam Cliffe's diary, which was preserved by his great-granddaughter Wilma McKenzie, is now at the Courtenay Museum.

14 Bob Piercy, [Reminiscences], n.d., Private Collection. This document was preserved by Audrey Menzies (née Grieve). Bob Piercy's lineage was provided by Donna Edwards, Roy Grieve, and Lola Sinclair.

15 "Specifications of the Courtenay River Bridge," n.d., (CM/B1633); "Comox Lock-up" [plan by James Mahood] (CM/BP-4); "Plan of Comox Court House, 1891 (CM/A2011), all in British Columbia Lands and Works Department, Plans and Map Microfiche collection, BCA; for the history of the town of Quadra, some twelve miles south of Comox, see Daryl Muralt, "Quadra—the Town That Almost Came to Be," *British Columbia Historical News* 20:2 (Spring 1987), pp. 21–22; Josephine Crease, "Bridge in Comox Valley 1877," PDP no. 14193, Paintings, Drawings, and Prints Division, BCA.

16 Rev. Robert James Roberts, "Log Book of Sloop *H. L. Tibbals*," [manuscript], BCA; Barbara Prael Siverts, comp., *A History of Nanoose Bay* (Parksville, B.C.: R.R. Desktop Publishing, 1999), p. 17.

17 *Nanaimo Free Press*, 27 June 1888 and 18 July 1889.

18 Mary Bissett to Hon A. Henderson, 24 January 1900, British Columbia, Attorney General, Correspondence Inward, 1899–1900 (GR 429).

19 *Comox Argus*, 14 January 1937. The paper noted that the old brick block had once been owned by a Mr. Willard, who took over Drabble's effects upon his death. This document appears in the bibliography under Richard Hurford as "Old Ms. Record book of land sales on the Comox District."

20 Marius Barbeau, *Totem Poles*, Volume 1 (Ottawa: National Museum of Man, 1950), pp. 682–85.

21 Lucilla Wilson (née Clayton) to the author, 16 March 1998.

22 Veronica King to the author, 22 June 1999. For Donovan's visit see Judy Hagen, "Pursuing a Paradox Past," *Comox Valley Echo*, 24 August 1999.